JESUS UNDER FIRE

Truth seekers
(189)

JESUS UNDER FIRE

MICHAEL J. WILKINS
J. P. MORELAND
GENERAL EDITORS

ZondervanPublishingHouse
Grand Rapids, Michigan

A Division of HarperCollins*Publishers*

Jesus Under Fire
Copyright © 1995 by Michael J. Wilkins, J. P. Moreland, Craig Blomberg, Darrell Bock, William Lane Craig, Craig A. Evans, Douglas Geivett, Gary Habermas, Scot McKnight, and Edwin Yamauchi

Requests for information should be addressed to:

▦ ZondervanPublishingHouse
Grand Rapids, Michigan 49530

Library of Congress Cataloging-in-Publication Data

Jesus under fire: modern scholarship reinvents the historical Jesus / edited by
    Michael J. Wilkins and J. P. Moreland.
        p.   cm.
    Includes bibliographical references and index.
    ISBN: 0-310-21139-5 (softcover)
    1. Jesus Christ—History of Doctrines.   2. Jesus Seminar.   3. Bible. N.T.
Gospels—Evidences, authority, etc.   I. Wilkins, Michael J.   II. Moreland,
James Porter, 1948–
BT198.J477   1994
232.9'08–dc20   94–42661
                                                                              CIP

Edited by Verlyn D. Verbrugge
Interior design by Joe Vriend

Printed in the United States of America

99 00 01 02 / ❖ DC/ 10 9 8 7 6

Contents

We dedicate this volume to that large host of intellectuals
from the resurrection of Jesus to the present who,
with intellectual vigor and passion of heart,
have dedicated their lives and thought
to the Jesus of the New Testament and the faith of the apostles,
once for all delivered to the saints.

PREFACE

Special thanks go to a number of people who have helped make this book possible. First, we are grateful to the fellow authors of this volume for the spirit and passion they brought to this project. When we initially contacted each about contributing to the book, they indicated that they were already overtaxed with research, writing, and teaching; yet they understood the significance of our endeavor and immediately agreed to be a part of our team and to make their chapter a priority.

Second, we are grateful to Roberta and Howard Ahmanson and the Fieldstead Foundation for a grant to Biola University that helped to make our editorial work possible. May God richly bless them and other Christians who use their resources to advance the kingdom of God.

We are also indebted to Zondervan Publishing House, specifically Stan Gundry, Ed van der Maas, and Verlyn Verbrugge, who streamlined the process in record time to get this book out into the hands of people who need to read it.

We also wish to thank our Dean, Dennis Dirks, along with the faculty and students at Talbot School of Theology, Biola University. Together they have provided support for the book and an intellectually and spiritually rich environment in which to work. Our energy for this project came from many of them.

Finally, we want to thank our wives and children. Their love for us and their joint commitment to the cause of Christ are our constant source of nourishment and strength.

Contributors

Craig L. Blomberg (Ph.D., University of Aberdeen), Associate Professor of New Testament, Denver Seminary.

Darrell L. Bock (Ph.D., University of Aberdeen), Professor of New Testament studies, Dallas Theological Seminary.

William Lane Craig (Ph.D., University of Birmingham, England; Th.D., University of Munich, Germany), Visiting Scholar, Emory University.

Craig A. Evans (Ph.D., Claremont Graduate School), Professor of biblical studies, Trinity Western University, Langley, British Columbia.

R. Douglas Geivett (Ph.D., University of Southern California), Associate Professor of philosophy, Talbot School of Theology, Biola University.

Gary Habermas (Ph.D., Michigan State University; D.D., Emmanuel College, Oxford), Distinguished Professor of apologetics and philosophy and Chairman of philosophy and theology, Liberty University.

Scot McKnight (Ph.D., University of Nottingham), Associate Professor of New Testament, Trinity Evangelical Divinity School.

J. P. Moreland (Ph.D., University of Southern California), Professor of philosophy, Talbot School of Theology, Biola University.

Michael J. Wilkins (Ph.D., Fuller Theological Seminary), Dean of the Faculty and Professor of New Testament language and literature, Talbot School of Theology, Biola University.

Edwin Yamauchi (Ph.D., Brandeis University), Professor of history, Miami University in Oxford, Ohio.

ABBREVIATIONS

ABRL	Anchor Bible Reference Library
AJT	*American Journal of Theology*
ANRW	*Aufstieg und Niedergang der römischen Welt*
BAR	*Biblical Archaeology Review*
BETL	Bibliotheca ephemeridum theologicarum lovaniensium
BA	*Biblical Archaeologist*
BJRL	*Bulletin of the John Rylands Library*
BBR	*Bulletin of Biblical Research*
BR	*Bible Review*
CBQ	*Catholic Biblical Quarterly*
CTQ	*Concordia Theological Quarterly*
CT	*Christianity Today*
EvQ	*Evangelical Quarterly*
HTKNT	Herders theologischer Kommentar zum neuen Testament
HTR	*Harvard Theological Review*
ISBE	*International Standard Bible Encyclopedia*
JBL	*Journal of Biblical Literature*
JETS	*Journal of the Evangelical Theological Society*
JHS	*Journal of Historical Studies*
JJS	*Journal of Jewish Studies*
JAOS	*Journal of the American Oriental Society*
JRH	*Journal of Roman History*
JRS	*Journal of Roman Studies*
JSNT	*Journal for the Study of the New Testament*
JSNTMS	Journal for the Study of the New Testament Monograph Series
JSOT	*Journal for the Study of the Old Testament*
LCL	Loeb Classical Library
NICNT	New International Commentary on the New Testament
NovT	*Novum Testamentum*
NTS	*New Testament Studies*
NTTS	New Testament Tools and Studies
SBT	Studies in Biblical Theology
SJT	*Scottish Journal of Theology*
TrinJ	*Trinity Journal*
TS	*Theological Studies*
TynBul	*Tyndale Bulletin*
TZ	*Theologische Zeitschrift*
WTJ	*Westminster Theological Journal*

INTRODUCTION:
THE FUROR SURROUNDING JESUS

MICHAEL J. WILKINS AND J. P. MORELAND

Jesus of Nazareth is under fire. Although he came on the scene of history nearly two thousand years ago, Jesus continues to be the object of devotion and controversy—much as he was when he first walked the landscape of Palestine. Many people today still acclaim him as Savior, as did his followers in the first century. And many others today still reject his claims and consider him a threat to the religious and political establishment, as did the religious and governmental leaders of Israel and Rome.

Jesus Under Fire

But Jesus is under fire in a different way now. Today some declare that Jesus never *said* most of what is recorded of him in the Bible. Some pronounce further that Jesus never *did* most of what the Bible records he did. They claim that Jesus of Nazareth was a far different figure than church history and the creeds have believed him to be. Therefore, if we are to be intelligent people, even intelligent *religious* people, we must not simplistically accept what the Bible records Jesus claimed for himself and what the early church claimed him to be. If we are to be truly modern in our religious quest, we must not simplistically hope that Jesus' actions as they are recorded in the Bible are factual, or that they have any relevance for us today. Jesus must be stripped of ancient myths that surrounded him as to what he said and did, so that the modern person can hear his true message. Jesus must be brought down to earth from the status to which the early church elevated him, so that we can understand who he was as he walked under Palestinian skies and comprehend what, if any, religious relevance he has for us today. To many today, the Jesus of Nazareth we find in the pages of the Bible is a fictitious creation of the early church, and he must be exposed for who he truly is if he is to have any value for people who face the twenty-first century.

Jesus of Nazareth and the Modern Worldview

At issue with this perspective on Jesus is whether the worldview reflected in the Bible is viable in the scientific age as an article of reasoned faith. The advent of historical reason in the modern era means that we are obligated to distinguish between factual and fictional accounts of the past. Just as scientific advances in medicine, astronomy, agriculture, and physics swept away old superstitions and

1

myths, so the application of scientific methods of investigation to Jesus of Nazareth is bound to sweep away archaic religious beliefs. The Christ of creed and dogma in the Middle Ages is thus said to be viable no longer for people who have witnessed the scientific revolution.

These salvos being fired at Jesus are certainly not new. They have been a staple of critical/liberal scholarly investigation and debate since the so-called Enlightenment brought new approaches to the study of Jesus. But Jesus is now under fire *in the public eye*. Scholars who have subjected Jesus to scrutiny in their private studies and disclosed their conclusions in closed academic circles are now waging their battle through the public media.

The Jesus Seminar

One group that has been at the forefront of this endeavor calls itself "The Jesus Seminar." Formed in 1985 to examine all the sayings attributed to Jesus in the New Testament and other early Christian documents, the Jesus Seminar has on the surface a simple academic purpose: "to assess the degree of scholarly consensus about the historical authenticity of each of the sayings of Jesus."[1] However, the Jesus Seminar has an agenda other than the academic one—an agenda for the people of the church. This group of scholars has decided "to update and then make the legacy of two hundred years of research and debate a matter of public record."[2] They want to liberate the people of the church from the "dark ages of theological tyranny" by liberating Jesus. As Robert Funk, cofounder of the Jesus Seminar states, "We want to liberate Jesus. The only Jesus most people know is the mythic one. They don't want the real Jesus, they want the one they can worship. The cultic Jesus."[3]

Hence, members of the Jesus Seminar are taking their show on the road, demanding attention for their scholarly work. Fellow cofounder John Dominic Crossan, professor of New Testament at DePaul University, states that there was an implicit deal: "You scholars can go off to the universities and write in the journals and say anything you want. Now," Crossan says, "scholars are coming out of the closet," demanding public attention for the way they think.[4] And Crossan is publicly heralding what he thinks: he denies the deity of Christ, declares that Jesus' pedigree—including his virgin birth in Bethlehem—is myth-making by the writers of the Gospels, and concludes that the stories of Jesus' death, burial, and resurrection were latter-day wishful thinking of the early church.[5]

Crucial Questions About Jesus

Regardless of one's reaction to these claims, we must try to understand what has led these scholars to such conclusions. Behind their claims are questions, the answers to which determine both their methods of investigation and the final picture of Jesus they draw. But the answers to these questions are not as clear-cut as they declare. Other scholars—from widely diverse theological and confessional perspectives—offer an alternative historical opinion: the biblical portrait is an accurate reflection of what Jesus did and said in history. The debate is now being carried out in both scholarly and popular publications because the issues have been raised in both venues. What are some of these central issues?

Can we know accurately anything about Jesus?

A central question raised in these discussions is this: Can we know accurately events of the first century? At issue here is what can be known accurately of what Jesus did and what he said. Many of the recent attacks on the historical Jesus stem from attempts to discover what really happened in history. This has produced an intriguing contradiction in methods and presuppositions among scholars who combine "modernism's" optimistic scientific quest with "postmodernism's" skepticism. On the one hand, these scholars attempt to be objective in their quest for the historical Jesus, establishing criteria that sift nonhistorical elements in the historical records from truthful ones. On the other hand, these scholars are influenced by postmodernism's declaration that objectivity is impossible: we all look through our own eyes, bringing our own perspectives and biases, so we can only make the best of what we see.

These idiosyncrasies of modern scholarship promote what Oxford New Testament scholar N. T. Wright dubs the "cultural imperialism of the Enlightenment," an attitude that assumes it is only in the last two hundred years that we have discovered what "history" is, "while writers in the ancient world were ignorant about these matters, freely making things up, weaving fantasy and legend together and calling it history."[6] When it comes to the Gospel records, critics like those in the Jesus Seminar contend that the evangelists were so influenced by the early church's portrait of Christ that the records of Jesus' life must be treated with skepticism.

Such skepticism is undue with regard to history in general and to the records of Jesus' life in particular. Standard historiography (the science of historical investigation) is applied to other ancient religious documents with profit (e.g., ancient mystery religions), and the same rules of validation of historical data should be applied to the biblical records. When mutually accepted standards of historiography are applied to ancient religious records, the Jesus of history fares well historically. Historian Edwin Yamauchi argues in chapter 8 that when we compare the records of religious figures of history—such as Zoroaster, Buddha, and Mohammed—we have better historical documentation for Jesus than for the founder of any other religion.[7]

Are the biblical records of Jesus' activities accurate?

The crucial question of what can be known of the Jesus of history leads to the related question of whether or not the biblical records of Jesus' activities are accurate. Many contemporary scholars assume that the biblical records are fictitious unless and until they can be proven truthful. Representatives of the Jesus Seminar state:

The gospels are now assumed to be narratives in which the memory of Jesus is embellished by mythic elements that express the church's faith in him, and by plausible fictions that enhance the telling of the gospel story for first-century listeners who knew about divine men and miracle workers first-hand.[8]

Hence, they adopt a "burden of proof" argument, demanding that supposedly historical elements in the Gospels must be demonstrated to be so. In other words, all of the activities ascribed to Jesus in the Gospels are assumed *not to be true* until proven otherwise.

This approach is largely supported by adopting a rigid distinction between the Jesus of history and the Christ of faith. The early church's faith in Christ so influenced the story of the historical Jesus, scholars claim, that when they retold it, all factuality was lost. As a result, the Gospel records cannot be considered factual accounts of historical events, but fanciful fictions of faithful followers.

However, other scholars of first-century religious figures are not so reticent to acknowledge the degree to which early Christian writers were intent to pass on an accurate portrait of the Jesus of history. Leading Jewish scholars, for example, declare that the New Testament portrait of Jesus was not controlled by exuberant faith, but rather was as faithful a passing on of historical data as we possess from the first-century Palestinian setting. Jewish scholars such as Geza Vermes and David Flusser declare that "we know more about Jesus than about almost any other first-century Jew."[9] Jewish scholar Jacob Neusner questions the scholarly agenda of the Jesus Seminar's reconstruction of the Jesus of history when he states that the Jesus Seminar is "either the greatest scholarly hoax since the Piltdown Man or the utter bankruptcy of New Testament studies—I hope the former."[10]

Is the supernatural possible in ancient and modern times?

A related question is: What are we to make of the biblical accounts of Jesus' performing supernatural deeds? The members of the Jesus Seminar are committed to a strict philosophical naturalism. Modern science and experience demonstrate that supernatural phenomena do not exist. Therefore, any record of supernatural events in the Gospels must be rejected as inauthentic. Recorded supernatural events are either mythic fictions created by the early church, or else they can now be accounted for by naturalistic explanations. This includes miraculous activity of healings, exorcisms, resurrection, prophecy, and inspiration of the biblical documents. Not only does philosophical naturalism automatically exclude large portions of the Gospel material, but it also has significant implications for related issues.

Take prophecy—predictions of the future found on the lips of Jesus in the Gospels—as an example. The Jesus Seminar suggests that any statements in the Gospels that reflect knowledge of events that occurred after Jesus' death (especially the destruction of the temple and Jerusalem, the Gentile and worldwide missionary outreach, and the persecution of apostles) could not possibly have originated with Jesus or with eyewitnesses. Whenever they detect "detailed knowledge of postmortem events in sayings and parables attributed to Jesus, they are inclined to the view that the formulation of such sayings took place after the fact."[11] Hence, they deny the possibility of Jesus' predicting the future. This leads to the conclusion that all the Gospels are late (at the least, post-A.D. 70, after the destruction of the temple and Jerusalem). This removes the Gospels from the possibility of having eyewitnesses as authors; and if none of the evangelists was an eyewitness, then the evangelists were not apostles. This in turn denies the reliability of the early Fathers' testimony concerning the apostolic authorship, dating, or destination of the Gospels.

The exclusion of supernatural elements from the record of Jesus of Nazareth's life and ministry begs the question. Such elements need to be examined for authenticity, not excluded simply on the basis of one's worldview. As Doug Geivett argues in chapter 7, if we have sufficient reasons for believing in God (e.g., from scientific or philosophical evidence and argument), then we must bring to our study of history a prior rationally justified acceptance of theism. In other words, we cannot exclude the possibility of miracles before we even investigate historical evidence; rather, the evidence itself must ultimately win the day. For example, when subjecting one supernatural element—the ability of Jesus to predict his crucifixion—to examination, the eminent Catholic New Testament scholar Raymond Brown emphasizes that "historicity, however, should be determined not by what we think possible or likely, but by the antiquity and reliability of the evidence. As we shall see, as far back as we can trace, Jesus was known and remembered as one who had extraordinary powers."[12]

These are some of the important issues that contribute to the furor surrounding Jesus of Nazareth. Some modern scholars, such as those of the Jesus Seminar, have taken the issues to extreme conclusions—denying the accuracy of the biblical portrait of Jesus found in the New Testament. Others have contended that the Jesus found in the Bible and declared in the creeds of the church is the true Jesus of history. What are we to make of these issues? We will explore them fully in the following chapters of this book. Before doing so, however, we turn to some important implications for the modern reader.

Why Does This Matter?

At this point you may be wondering if all of this really matters. What difference does it make if the arguments advanced by radical critics of the New Testament are correct? In the final analysis, isn't religion something you just have to take on faith, and isn't the point of religion that it helps you live your life well and cope with daily problems? In our opinion, the issues raised within the covers of this book matter a great deal. We are not overstating it when we say that these are life and death issues. The most important elements about any belief we may have about any topic are that the belief is really true and that we have good reasons for thinking it is true.

The Importance of Truth for Religious Belief

Consider first the question of truth. In medicine, we all know what a placebo is. It is an innocuous substance that doesn't really do anything to help an illness. But the patient's false belief that it works brings some mental relief. A placebo works because of the naive, misinformed, and false beliefs of the patient. Sadly, the placebo effect is not limited to medicine. Many people have worldview placebos—false, naive, misinformed beliefs that help them because they are living in a fantasy world of their own mental creation and not because the beliefs themselves are true. To see why this is sad, consider the fictitious story of Wonmug.

Wonmug was a hopelessly dumb physics student attending a large Western university. He failed all of his first semester classes, his math skills were around a fifth-grade level, and he had no aptitude for science. However, one day all the physics students and professors at his college decided to spoof Wonmug by making him erroneously think he was the best physics student at the university. When he asked a question in class, students and professors alike would marvel out loud at the profundity of the question. Graders gave him perfect scores on all his assignments when in reality he deserved an F. Eventually, Wonmug graduated and went on for his Ph.D. The professors at his university sent a letter to all the physicists in the world and included them in the spoof. Wonmug received his degree, took a prestigious chair of physics, regularly went to Europe to deliver papers at major science conferences, and was often featured in *Time* and *Newsweek*. Wonmug's life was pregnant with feelings of respect, accomplishment, expertise, and happiness. Unfortunately, he still knew absolutely no physics. Do you envy Wonmug? Would you wish such a life for your children? Of course not. Why? Because his sense of well-being was built on a false, misinformed worldview placebo.

Often, life is a struggle. We grow sick, lose our jobs, experience fragmented relationships with others, and eventually die. We want to know if there is anything real on which to base our lives. Is there really a God, and what is he actually like? What does God believe about the things that matter most? Is there any purpose to life and, if so, what is it? Why was I thrust into this world? Are values objective and real, or arbitrary and invented? Is there life after death? In what ways can I really count on God, and are there any true, effective ways to get close to him? When we ask these questions, we don't want answers that help us merely because we believe them. We want to be comforted because our answers to these questions are really true. For the wise person of virtue, a life well lived is based on the truth, not on a placebo.

The Importance of Reason for Religious Belief

But if truth really matters after all, then it follows that rationality also is crucial to a life well lived. Why? Because we have no other way available to us to put ourselves in the best position possible for making sure that among the things we really believe, we have the highest percentage of true beliefs and the lowest percentage of false ones. In the ordinary decisions of daily life, we try to base our beliefs and actions on the best evidence we can get. From sitting on a jury to buying a new house, we try to base our decisions on a careful assessment of all the relevant evidence we can get. If, for example, someone used blind faith and bought the first house he or she saw with a "for sale" sign in front of it, but made no effort to get information about the house and neighborhood, we would consider that person foolish. Why? Because when we use our reason and base decisions on the best assessment of the evidence we can make, we increase our chances that our decisions are based on true beliefs.

Now if this is the case for day-to-day issues, why should we suddenly abandon the importance of reason and evidence when it comes to religion? We should not! Any religious belief worthy of the name should be accepted because we take the belief to be true and do so by the best exercise of our mental faculties we can muster. Applied to Christianity, we want to know if Jesus was really like what the New Testament says he was like. Did he say the things attributed to him in the New Testament? Was he really the only begotten Son of God? Did he actually perform miracles and actually raise people from the dead in real space-time history? Are there good reasons for thinking any of these things is true?

If the answer to these questions is yes, then Jesus Christ has the right to require of us an unqualified allegiance to him. If the answer is no, then Christianity as a total worldview should not be believed or propagated. In our view, the claims of radical New Testament critics like the fellows of the Jesus Seminar are false and not reasonable to believe in light of the best evidence available. And in the pages to follow we are going to show you some of the reasons why we believe this way—hopefully, in a way accessible to the general reader.

Sources of Resistance

In spite of the points just made, you still may not be convinced about the importance of truth and reason for religious worldview commitments. There are at least two sources for such resistance that influence many modern people.

Irrational Faith and the Modern Worldview

The first one draws fuel from the mistaken, contemporary view of faith or belief. Many think that faith is a substitute for reason and that the important thing about a belief is that you believe it for yourself and are helped by accepting the belief. It really doesn't matter if the belief is true; all that matters is that you believe it. In other words, by their very nature, faith and religious beliefs are nothing more than relativistic, privatized placebos.

This view violates common sense and the spirit of Christianity. As philosopher Roger Trigg points out, common sense tells us that "any Commitment, it seems, depends on two distinct elements. It presupposes certain beliefs [to be true] and it also involves a personal dedication to the actions implied by them."[13] The very act of believing something means that you take the thing believed to be true. You may not be 100 percent certain that it is true, but if you believe something, you are saying that you are more convinced that it is true than that it is false. Put differently, a belief does not require complete certainty; it does, however, require that you are more than 50 percent certain about the belief. Otherwise, you would be in a state of suspended judgment and not really have the belief in question.

In addition to these common sense reflections about belief, it is important to say that throughout the history of the Christian Way, students of Scripture have held that faith is not opposed or indifferent to reason; rather, faith should have a rational basis. New Testament religion tells us to love God with the mind (Matt. 22:37), to have an answer in the form of good reasons for why we believe what we believe (1 Peter 3:15), to accept that God wishes to reason together with his creatures (Isa. 1:18), and to believe that human reason, though fallen, is still part of the image of God within us (Acts 17:27–28) and continues to be a gift we are to cultivate and exercise. Thus, the modern view of faith as something unrelated or even hostile to reason is a departure from traditional Christianity and not a genuine expression of it.

Philosophical Naturalism and the Modern Worldview

The second modern factor that has contributed to the widespread understanding that religious belief is private, practical, and relative, and need not be related to truth and reason is the widespread acceptance of philosophical naturalism as an expression of scientism. Philosophical naturalism is the idea that reality is exhausted by the spatio-temporal world of physical entities that we can investigate in the natural sciences. The natural causal fabric of physical reality within the boundaries of space and time is all there is, was, or ever will be. The supernatural doesn't exist except, perhaps, as a belief in people's minds. On this view, religious beliefs are simply ways of looking at things in our search for meaning and purpose; they are not ideas that correspond to a mind-independent reality.

Philosophical naturalism is an expression of an epistemology (i.e., a theory of knowledge and justified or warranted belief) known as scientism. Scientism is the view that the natural sciences are the very paradigm of truth and rationality. If something does not square with currently well-established beliefs, if it is not within the domain of entities appropriate for scientific investigation, or if it is not amenable to scientific methodology, then it is not true or rational. Everything outside of science is a matter of mere belief and subjective opinion, of which rational assessment is impossible. Applied to the question of the historical origins of Christianity, scientism implies that since we live in the modern scientific world where the sun is the center of the solar system, the wireless is available for our use, and the atom's power has been harnessed, we can no longer believe in a biblical worldview with its miracles, demons, and supernatural realities.

Obviously, it is impossible in the brief space of an introduction to critique adequately scientism and naturalism. Still, a few cursory remarks need to be expressed. (1) Scientism is simply false for three reasons. (a) It is self-refuting, i.e., it falsifies itself. Why? Scientism is itself a statement *of* philosophy *about* knowledge and science; it is not a statement *of* science itself. Moreover, it is a statement of philosophy that amounts to the claim that no statements outside scientific ones, *including scientism itself* (because it is a statement of philosophy), can be true or supported by rational considerations. (b) Science itself rests on a number of assumptions: the existence of a theory-independent external world, the orderly nature of the external world, the existence of truth and the reliability of our senses and rational faculties to gather truth about the world in a trustworthy manner, the laws of logic and the truths of mathematics, the adequacy of language (including mathematical language) to describe the external world, the uniformity of nature, and so on. Now, each one of these assumptions is philosophical in nature. The task of stating, criticizing, and defending the assumptions of science rests in the field of philosophy. Scientism fails to leave room for these philosophical tasks and, thus, shows itself to be a foe and not a friend of science. (c) There are many things we know in religion, ethics, logic, mathematics, history, art, literature, and so on that are simply not matters of science. For example, we all know that two is an even number, that Napoleon lived, that torturing babies for fun is wrong, that if A is larger than B and B is larger than C, then A is larger than C, and so on. None of these items of knowledge are scientific in nature, and scientism is falsified by their reality.

(2) Philosophical naturalism is false as well. For one thing, philosophical naturalism rules out the existence of a number of things that do, in fact, exist. And while we cannot defend their existence here, suffice it to say that, currently, a number of intellectuals have offered convincing arguments for the reality of universals and other abstract objects such as numbers, the laws of logic, values, the soul and its various mental states (including the first person point of view), other minds, libertarian or full-blown freedom of the will, and so on. None of these items can be classified as mere physical objects totally within the causal fabric of the natural spatio-temporal universe. In fact, it is not an exaggeration to say that there is not a single issue of importance to human beings that is solely a matter of scientific investigation or that can be satisfactorily treated by philosophical naturalists.

(3) Philosophical naturalism fails to explain adequately the fact that there are a number of arguments and pieces of evidence that make belief in God more reasonable than disbelief. Some of this evidence actually comes from science: the

fact that the universe had a beginning based on the Big Bang theory and the second law of thermodynamics, the existence of biological information in DNA that is closely analogous to intelligent language and that cannot arise from the accidental collisions of physical entities according to laws of nature, the reality of the mental and of free will according to a number of emerging psychological theories of the self, the delicate fine-tuning of the universe, and so on.[14]

Like it or not, a significant and growing number of scientists, historians of science, and philosophers of science see more scientific evidence now for a personal creator and designer than was available fifty years ago. In light of this evidence, it is false and naive to claim that modern science has made belief in the supernatural unreasonable. Such a view can be called ostrich naturalism—a position that requires its advocate to keep his or her head in the sand and not to acknowledge real advances in science. The plain truth is that science itself makes no statements about all of reality anyway, nor does science itself offer any support for philosophical naturalism. What does support philosophical naturalism are the ideological claims of naturalists themselves regarding what science ought to say *if we assume philosophical naturalism to begin with*.

In sum, it matters much that our religious beliefs are both true and reasonable. Moreover, there simply are no sufficient reasons for not believing in the supernatural, and there are in fact a number of good reasons (including but going beyond scientific ones) for believing in the supernatural. As we have said, space considerations do not permit us to defend this last claim here. But we will list some sources in the bibliography that adequately justify this claim. If you are an honest inquirer about the truth of religion, moral and intellectual integrity unite in placing a duty on you to read these works as a sincere seeker of the truth. It is well past time to rest content with the politically correct, unjustified assertions of scientism and philosophical naturalism. University libraries are filled with books that show the weaknesses of these views, and the fellows of the Jesus Seminar show virtually no indication that they have so much as interacted with the arguments they contain, much less have they refuted their claims.

Regarding Jesus of Nazareth, all of this means the following: Prior to investigating the historical evidence about his life, deeds, sayings, and significance, there is no good reason to bring to the evidence a prior commitment to naturalism. As later chapters will show, such a commitment is Procrustean in that it often forces the evidence of history to fit an unjustified antisupernatural bias. But when the evidence is evaluated on its own terms, and when such an evaluation is combined with the rigorous case for supernatural theism already available in the literature, then the claims of historic, orthodox Christianity can be reasonably judged to be true.

The Uniqueness of Jesus

The challenges being lodged against Jesus of Nazareth as we find him recorded in the Bible are consequential challenges indeed, with ramifications for Jesus' identity, his theological significance in history, and his religious value for modern society. The importance of these issues for modern people cannot be underestimated. If Jesus is who he claimed to be and who his followers declare him to be, then we are not dealing simply with academic questions. We are instead dealing with the most important questions of the modern person's daily life and eternal destiny. If he is not who the Bible declares him to be, then we are simply fooling ourselves if we hold to traditional beliefs.

Was Jesus God, the messianic Savior who came to earth to rescue his people, as he testified about himself and as his followers believed radically? Or was he an important religious figure, but one who was not, nor ever claimed to be, the divine Messiah?

Did Jesus perform a work on the cross that accomplished the means of salvation for humankind? Or was he a dedicated religious person who was actively involved in the social and spiritual world of his day, but who never performed or offered the unique and solitary means of salvation for the entire human race?

Is Jesus the only way to find salvation in this life or in the life to come, and is he a member of the triune God—Father, Son, and Holy Spirit—who is to be worshiped today? Or is he one among many ways by which a modern person can come to know and experience God, but who never accepted or advocated worship of himself as God in flesh?

The book has two overarching objectives. (1) We will address current teachings that undermine the biblical record of Jesus and his life and ministry (e.g., the Jesus Seminar). (2) We will present a rationally justified affirmation of the biblical teaching of the particular topics. Our main purpose is to help the church and the people of the broader community understand the issues currently being disseminated throughout popular culture, and to be able to counteract these ideas and respond to them intelligently and responsibly. This book combines the fruit of both New Testament scholars and philosophers/apologists. It both responds to current issues and provides biblical teaching, making its contribution unique.

The opening chapter by Craig Blomberg gives a direct response to the methodology of modern critical approaches to the study of Jesus' life and ministry. Blomberg pays special attention to the presuppositions and assumptions used by various critical scholars. He also presents beginning points for a study of the life of Jesus, including the question of the trustworthiness of the Gospel record. He surveys contemporary attacks on the reliability of the biblical text, including questions about the dating of the Gospels, the possibility of hymns and creeds in the New Testament letters, eyewitness accounts of Jesus' ministry, oral tradition, and archaeological support for the credibility of the biblical witness to Jesus.

Different positions on the critical issues raised by Blomberg generate different views of who Jesus really was. In chapter 2 Scot McKnight picks up the thread and addresses the latest wave of controversial books about Jesus. Modern authors are attempting to recast Jesus and to portray him differently, ranging from a cynic preacher to a magician to a peasant revolutionary. Each of these portrays a Jesus different from the orthodox Christian view. McKnight offers a critique of current studies and examines the more controversial portraits of Jesus. He also provides a positive statement of biblical Christology, based in part on Jesus' titles and self-disclosure statements, as well as the significance of the New Testament witness for contemporary Christians.

The current debate about Jesus does not focus merely on different pictures of who Jesus was. In fact, the argument about who Jesus was largely turns on an assessment of what Jesus actually said in his earthly ministry. The methodology of radical New Testament critics leads to several destructive conclusions. For example, members of the Jesus Seminar declare that only approximately 20 percent of the sayings attributed to Jesus in the Gospels were actually uttered by him. Chapter 3 by Darrell Bock critiques the presuppositions and methodology of the Seminar's analysis of the sayings of Jesus. He evaluates the various criteria of authenticity that have been offered by critical scholars and then presents a positive case for the authenticity of the New Testament sayings of Jesus.

Having looked at the debate about who Jesus was and what he said, the next important item to investigate is what Jesus actually did in his earthly ministry. In chapter 4 Craig Evans critiques the presuppositions and methodology of the Jesus Seminar's evaluation of the deeds of Jesus by examining certain crucial deeds of Jesus ascribed to him in the Gospel narratives. Evans goes on to present a positive case for the authenticity of the New Testament deeds of Jesus.

The first four chapters pay attention to the proper methods of approaching the Gospel accounts, in order to determine what we can actually claim to know about who Jesus was, what he said, and what he did. However, in the light of philosophical naturalism so widely embraced today, perhaps the most offensive part of the New Testament Jesus to modern sensibilities are miracles. Chapters 5 and 6 enter the discussion at this point and offer a spirited defense of the miraculous deeds of Jesus of Nazareth, including the grandest miracle of all—his bodily resurrection from the dead.

In chapter 5 Gary Habermas responds to a special criticism of the Gospel record of Jesus' life and ministry that has focused on his miraculous activities. He defends the historical reliability of the New Testament miracle stories, including healings, exorcisms, and nature miracles. His primary focus is on Jesus' miracles in their first-century social and cultural milieu, comparing them with other first-century miracle stories, magicians, rabbinic stories, and Hellenistic wonder-workers.

The heart of the Christian faith lies in the New Testament claim that Jesus rose from the dead. Each generation of Christians must address contemporary challenges to these claims. In chapter 6 William Lane Craig addresses both secular challenges to the resurrection and those within Christianity who are attempting to rethink its meaning. His article offers a rigorous, detailed historical defense of the truthfulness of the bodily resurrection of Jesus of Nazareth.

The credibility of miracles is one roadblock in the minds of many for accepting the orthodox view of Jesus. However, for many an equally sizable roadblock is the perceived injustice of the exclusive claims of salvation made by Jesus and his apostles and reaffirmed by the church for centuries. The issue of exclusivism and pluralism has never been more in the forefront of thought and discussion than at the present time. Following theologians such as John Hick, Christian leaders worldwide are rethinking, and in many quarters abandoning, these New Testament claims to the uniqueness of Jesus and Jesus' own self-claims to be the only way for salvation. This may be one of the most critical issues for the Christian church to address in the next decades.

With this in mind, Doug Geivett's chapter addresses pluralism in a stimulating and unique way. His approach is to emphasize the importance of a rational assessment of the truth claims of each religion irrespective of their cultural or emotional appeal. Geivett's main claim is that the evidence for the existence and nature of God provided by the natural world, in conjunction with an informed assessment of the human condition as we actually know it to be, provides the backdrop for assessing the religions of the world. Against the backdrop, says Geivett, the rational case for Christian theism can be judged as superior.

We will come full circle then. We begin by looking at various methodological issues at stake in understanding Jesus of Nazareth. In the light of these issues, chapters 2 through 6 present positive reasons for trusting the historical reliability of the New Testament accounts of who Jesus was, what he said, and what he did (including his miraculous deeds). Yet in the light of Geivett's argument about the importance of the case for Christianity in the marketplace of conflicting religious ideologies, it is more important than ever to be assured of the historical underpinnings of the orthodox understanding of Jesus as presented in this book.

One may well wonder what the historical evidence is for Jesus outside the Bible. Currently, a rise of best-selling books is rethinking the role and authority of the canonical Gospels in the light of extrabiblical data such as the Dead Sea Scrolls, Gnostic documents like the Gospel of *Thomas*, and hypothetical sources such as the document "Q." The final chapter by Edwin Yamauchi examines these studies in the light of the canonical biblical witness. What is the value of these extrabiblical sources? How should the modern Christian use such sources? What is the reliability of the New Testament witness to Christ? This chapter surveys extrabiblical and biblical evidence for the historical reality of Jesus of Nazareth and discusses contemporary questions about the reliability of the biblical text. It then provides lines of evidence supporting the reliability of the New Testament documents.

We hope that you will read the pages to follow with an open heart and mind.

The writing of this series of articles has been a difficult task because we have attempted to make available to a wide audience an examination of highly complex issues. On the one hand, we have written this book to be a popular treatment of the issues addressed in order to make them available to a wide readership. Given this objective, there have been times when we have had to treat important topics in a summary fashion. On the other hand, we have written this book to be a substantive response to technical issues in an intellectually responsible way. These two goals are difficult to accomplish jointly, and we have tried to keep them in balance in this volume. The authors of this volume are serious scholars deeply committed to the truthfulness and rationality of historic, biblical Christianity and the spiritual implications that follow from such a commitment. Thus we offer this work with the hope and prayer that it will be taken seriously by you, the reader, regardless of the religious orientation you bring to these pages.

Introduction: The Furor Surrounding Jesus

Notes

1. This purpose is expressed by Marcus Borg, a "Fellow" of the Jesus Seminar, in "The Jesus Seminar and the Church," in *Jesus in Contemporary Scholarship* (Valley Forge, Pa.: Trinity Press, 1994), 162.

2. Robert W. Funk, Roy W. Hoover, and the Jesus Seminar, *The Five Gospels: What Did Jesus Really Say?* (New York: Macmillan, 1993), 1.

3. Interview by Mary Rourke, "Cross Examination," *Los Angeles Times*, 24 February 1994, E1, E5.

4. Interview by Richard N. Ostling, "Jesus Christ, Plain and Simple," *Time*, 10 January 1994, 38.

5. Crossan develops these theses in full in *Jesus: A Revolutionary Biography* (San Francisco: Harper San Francisco, 1994) and *The Historical Jesus: The Life of a Mediterranean Jewish Peasant* (San Francisco: HarperSanFrancisco, 1991). For a brief overview by Crossan, see chs. 3 and 5 in *The Search for Jesus: Modern Scholarship Looks at the Gospels*, ed. Stephen Patterson et al. (Washington, D.C.: Biblical Archaeological Society, 1994).

6. N. T. Wright, *The New Testament and the People of God* (Minneapolis: Fortress, 1992), 84.

7. See ch. 8, below.

8. Funk, Hoover, and the Jesus Seminar, *The Five Gospels*, 5.

9. As Princeton Seminary Professor James H. Charlesworth reports in "The Foreground of Christian Origins and the Commencement of Jesus Research," in *Jesus' Jewishness: Exploring the Place of Jesus Within Early Judaism*, ed. James H. Charlesworth (New York: Crossroad, 1991), 81 and n.29. Charlesworth adds, "An exception to the statement, and the need for the adverb 'almost' in the sentence above, is the knowledge we have of Paul the Apostle. We know relatively very little about Honi, Hanina, Hillel, Shammai, Gamaliel, and Johanan ben Zakkai." Obviously, these are important observations in the light of the Jesus Seminar's reluctance to acknowledge the historical validity of Christian origins as recorded in the New Testament documents.

10. Ostling, "Jesus Christ, Plain and Simple," 39.

11. Funk, Hoover, and the Jesus Seminar, *The Five Gospels*, 25.

12. Raymond E. Brown, *An Introduction to New Testament Christology* (New York: Paulist Press, 1994), 25, n.24.

13. Roger Trigg, *Reason and Commitment* (Cambridge: Cambridge University Press, 1973), 44.

14. For more on this, see J. P. Moreland, ed., *The Creation Hypothesis* (Downers Grove, Ill.: InterVarsity Press, 1994); Philip Johnson, *Darwin on Trial*, 2d ed. (Downers Grove, Ill.: InterVarsity Press, 1993).

Chapter 1

WHERE DO WE START STUDYING JESUS?

CRAIG L. BLOMBERG

Craig L. Blomberg (Ph.D., University of Aberdeen) is Associate Professor of New Testament at Denver Seminary. He is the author of *The Historical Reliability of the Gospels*, *Interpreting the Parables*, *Matthew* in the New American Commentary series, and *1 Corinthians* in the NIV Application Commentary series.

Introduction

Jesus Christ has been the centerpiece of Western history for two thousand years. Yet while his followers have numbered in the millions, the movement he began has always had its critics. The most recent and best publicized of these, at least in North America, is a group of scholars known as the Jesus Seminar. Approximately twice a year for the last seven years, the Jesus Seminar has been making headlines in nationally syndicated news releases. This group of seventy-four scholars, claiming to represent a "consensus" of the modern critical perspective on the historical Jesus, has deliberately gone out of its way to disseminate the results of its deliberations to a wide audience.

The most detailed summary of its findings to date appears in a highly-touted volume, released at the end of 1993, entitled *The Five Gospels: What Did Jesus Really Say?* This unique book prints all of the passages found in the Gospels of Matthew, Mark, Luke, John and the apocryphal Gospel of *Thomas* and color-codes all the words in them attributed to Jesus. Red means "Jesus undoubtedly said this or something very like it." Pink means "Jesus probably said something like this." Gray implies "Jesus did not say this, but the ideas contained in it are close to his own." Finally, black means "Jesus did not say this; it represents the perspective or content of a later and/or different tradition."[1] In between the Gospel texts, Robert Funk, formerly professor of New Testament at the University of Montana and the mastermind behind the project, provides commentary on why the Seminar voted as it did in each case.

One reason *The Five Gospels* has received so much attention is because it colors less than 20 percent of all the sayings attributed to Jesus either red or pink, and well over half appear in black. In the entire Gospel of Mark, there is only one red-letter verse: "Give to Caesar what is Caesar's and to God what is God's" (Mark 12:17).[2] Only fifteen sayings (not counting parallels) are colored red in all of the Gospels put together, and they are all short, pithy "aphorisms" (unconventional proverb-like sayings) or parables (particularly the more "subversive" ones). Examples of the former include Jesus' commands to turn the other cheek (Matt. 5:39; Luke 6:29) and love your enemies (Matt. 5:44; Luke 6:27), and his blessing on the poor (Luke 6:20, *Thos.* 54). Examples of the latter include the parables of the good Samaritan (Luke 10:30–35), the shrewd manager (Luke 16:1–8a), and the vineyard laborers (Matt. 20:1–15). Seventy-five different sayings are colored pink, while at the other end of the color spectrum, several hundred appear in black, including virtually the entire Gospel of John and all of Jesus' claims about himself (e.g., "I am the way and the truth and the life"—John 14:6; "I and the Father are one"—10:30; and so on).[3]

What has led to such scholarly skepticism? Have there been some new finds in the Judean desert to cast doubts on traditional Christianity? No, not at all! For the most part, the Jesus Seminar does not reflect either responsible scholarship or critical consensus, and it is a pity that many in the media have allowed themselves to be deceived by its claims to the contrary. In many ways, *The Five Gospels* is an anomaly even among nonevangelical New Testament scholars and a throwback to nineteenth-century methods and conclusions (see the introduction to this book). Far more accepted and acceptable is a movement within contemporary research that has become known as the "third quest" for the historical Jesus (see below, pp. 25–28), though even this movement stops short of affirming historic orthodox Christian beliefs about Jesus.

How should thoughtful people respond? What are the objections that modern scholars have posed to accepting all of the Gospel record as historically trustworthy, and are those objections well founded? We maintain in this chapter that modern skepticism is unwarranted and that historic Christian confidence in the reliability of the Gospels remains defensible. The first section considers the problems raised by contemporary critics; then we will go on to provide reasons for believing in the trustworthiness of the texts.

Problems with the Jesus of the Gospels

As we have noted, two different trends may be discerned among current studies of the historical Jesus. Neither believes that all of the Gospels' data are historically accurate, but one is far more skeptical than the other. The smaller and more extreme position is represented by the Jesus Seminar and a handful of other works (see notes 15, 21–22 below); the larger and more middle-of-the-road position, by the so-called "third quest."

The Idiosyncrasies of the Jesus Seminar

Who are they?

Because *The Five Gospels* is the most widely publicized of recent discussions about the historical Jesus, and because work on a similar book on the *deeds* of Christ is also in progress, we must begin with the Jesus Seminar. Although this work repeatedly claims to reflect a consensus of modern scholars, this claim is simply false, even if one leaves all evangelical scholars to one side. Of the seventy-four "Fellows" of the Seminar, as they are called,[4] about fourteen of them are among the leading names in the field of historical Jesus scholarship today (e.g., John Dominic Crossan of DePaul University and Marcus Borg of Oregon State University). Roughly another twenty names are recognizable to New Testament scholars who keep abreast of their field, even if they are not as widely published. These, too, include several who have written important recent works on the ancient traditions about Jesus, particularly in various noncanonical gospels (e.g., Marvin Meyer of Chapman University and Karen King of Occidental College).

The remaining forty, or more than half of the entire Seminar, are relative unknowns. Most have published at best two or three journal articles, while several are recent Ph.D.'s whose dissertations were on some theme of the Gospels. For a full eighteen of the Fellows, a computer search of two comprehensive databases of published books and articles[5] turned up no entries relevant to the New Testament at all! Thirty-six of the group, almost half, have a degree from or currently teach at one of three schools—Harvard, Claremont, and Vanderbilt, universities with some of the most liberal departments of New Testament studies anywhere. Almost all are American; European scholarship is barely represented.

In short, the Jesus Seminar does not come anywhere close to reflecting an adequate cross-section of contemporary New Testament scholars.[6] These remarks are not meant to be taken in an *ad hominem* fashion, nor are they offered as a substitute for a detailed analysis and critique of the points they raise. Rather, they are meant as a response to the false but widespread perception that the ideas propagated by the Jesus Seminar represent the views of the majority of experts who are in a privileged position to know and disseminate the real facts to the public.

What's wrong with what they believe?

Not only are the individual Fellows not representative of scholarship at large, neither are their methods or their conclusions. We highlight six major areas in which few other reputable scholars (evangelical or otherwise) would follow the Seminar's leading, along with some of the reasons why this is so.

First, they establish far too restrictive principles for the forms *of speech Jesus could have used.* If an utterance is neither a parable nor an aphorism, they claim that Jesus did not speak it.[7] If a saying cannot be separated from its context so that it could have been preserved as an independent oral tradition, it cannot be colored red or pink.[8] In other words, Jesus never composed full-length sermons, and he never engaged in dialogue or controversy with others. He probably said something as he healed or exorcised people or worked other wondrous feats. But we have no way of knowing what that was, because such words are inseparable from their contexts, and the early church couldn't possibly have remembered a whole story about Jesus.[9]

These assertions, made repeatedly throughout *The Five Gospels*, are difficult to fathom. No other scholarship on Jesus, or on any other religious teacher for that matter, imposes such stringent restrictions. No sage in the history of the world is so limited in the forms of speech he or she could possibly have employed—not Buddha, not Confucius, not Mohammed, not even the modern avant-garde writers like Franz Kafka, with whom Jesus is often favorably compared in these circles.

Second, the Seminar is equally restrictive in the topics *that it permits Jesus to address.* Supposedly, Jesus never quoted Scripture or compared his teaching to that of the laws of Moses.[10] He never even hinted that he might consider himself some kind of Messiah,[11] though plenty of others in his day made messianic claims. He never called himself the Son of Man[12] (the most common title ascribed to him on the pages of the Gospels, even though this term is used differently in the Gospels than among most Jewish writers, and even though subsequent New Testament and later Christian writers hardly ever used it. He never predicted the future, never envisioned his coming crucifixion, and never spoke about God's judgment (a horrible concept unworthy of a great sage).[13]

Again, these assertions are groundless affirmations that the vast majority of scholars roundly reject. Even those who see no inkling of the supernatural in Jesus' life acknowledge that he set himself on a collision course with the authorities that many people could have predicted, that judgment was a major topic of conversation in the Jewish world of his day, that "Son of Man" is likely to be the *most* authentic of all of the titles for Christ in the Gospels, and that it would be natural for him to have seen himself as a special envoy of God in some sense.[14]

Third, and closely related to the previous two observations, the Seminar's Jesus simply is not sufficiently Jewish to be a historically credible figure. Instead, the Fellows envision a Jesus who resembles an itinerant Greco-Roman philosopher, a Cynic sage, or an Oriental guru—and an unusual kind: one who spoke only in short, cryptic utterances.[15] Any time his teaching finds partial parallels in the words of other Jewish teachers of antiquity, his words are dismissed as inauthentic and relegated to "the fund of common lore."[16] All of this, while the rest of the scholarly world is increasingly stressing the necessity of recovering Jesus the Jew, who engaged in debates about ritual cleanliness, Sabbath observance, and the application of Torah in the messianic age![17] Whatever else modern scholarship may disagree on, there is widespread consensus that Jesus must be read against the historical-cultural milieu of his world, a milieu that was above all Jewish. This the Jesus Seminar simply does not do.

Fourth, there is no convincing reason left in the Seminar's Jesus for his death—death as a criminal by crucifixion. How did a simple speaker of proverbs and parables ever alienate the Jewish and Roman authorities of his day to such an extent that he was executed in so gruesome a fashion? Again, there is almost unanimous agreement, including among the Seminar's Fellows, that Jesus died on the cross. But their exceedingly eccentric, somewhat pacifist Jesus, never once suspects that he might be angering others or endangering his life and does absolutely nothing to provoke such hostility. As John Meier, one of America's leading Jesus scholars, representing a moderate Roman Catholic perspective, observes wryly:

> A tweedy poetaster who spent his time spinning out parables and Japanese koans, a literary aesthete who toyed with 1st-century deconstructionism, or a bland Jesus who simply told people to look at the lilies of the field—such a Jesus would threaten no one, just as the university professors who create him threaten no one.[18]

Unfortunately, many people who have not studied much biblical scholarship do not realize that these professors pose no objective threat, and so they wrongly imagine that Christian faith has indeed been undermined.

Fifth, after ignoring Jesus' Jewish roots, the Seminar would have us believe that later Christians re-Judaized him. That is to say, Jesus was originally just a noteworthy teacher of wisdom, a "laconic sage" whose closest counterparts were to be found in the itinerant Cynics of the Greco-Roman world—wandering rebels notorious for flouting the conventions of society, living simply or even in poverty, and calling others to join them in radical freedom from the world. But a generation later, the wisdom traditions of the Gospels were overlaid with apocalyptic traditions—teachings attributed to Jesus about the destruction of the temple, the end of the world, and God's judgment.[19] This hypothesis, however, inverts the actual sequence of the development of early Christianity, which spread *from* the Jewish world *to* the Greco-Roman world. The older liberal consensus that the New Testament successively transformed Jesus from an apocalyptic Jewish preacher, who thought God would soon intervene to bring about the end of the world, into a Hellenistic divine man or god had its problems too, but at least it meshed with the direction of the spread of the gospel—from Jerusalem to Greece and Rome. This newer view would make sense only if Jesus had lived and taught somewhere outside of Palestine, and then left the second generation of Christianity to take his message to the Jewish world.

The inversion of wisdom and apocalyptic also presupposes a "revolutionary" rather than an "evolutionary" development of the gospel.[20] That is to say, it requires the assumption that someone, about a generation removed from the events in question, radically transformed the authentic information about Jesus that was circulating at that time, superimposed a body of material four times as large, fabricated almost entirely out of whole cloth, while the church suffered sufficient collective amnesia to accept the transformation as legitimate. Claremont University professor Burton Mack has written two major works that propose precisely this thesis, with Mark being the primary instigator of the distortion of the true picture of Jesus.[21] Unfortunately for his argument, there is no known parallel in the history of religion to such a radical transformation of a famous teacher or leader in so short a period of time, namely, during the lives of eyewitnesses of his or her life and work, and no identifiable stimulus among the followers of Jesus sufficient to create such a change.

The *sixth* and final way the Jesus Seminar is idiosyncratic within contemporary scholarship may be the most significant of all. One of the major reasons the Fellows believe that Jesus the sage preceded Jesus the apocalyptic prophet is because *they are convinced that the Gospel of* Thomas *contains numerous independent traditions about the historical Jesus that are at least as reliable, if not more so, than those found in the canonical Gospels.* They suggest a date for this document as early as A.D. 50–60, earlier than Matthew, Mark, Luke, or John.[22] And *Thomas*'s picture of Jesus is largely that of one who utters wise but cryptic teachings, never calls himself Son of Man, rarely introduces apocalyptic themes, and performs no mighty deeds (precisely because the document contains almost no narrative framework to link its 114 sayings of Jesus together). But which is more likely—that *Thomas* came first or last among the five Gospels? This question demands more detailed exploration.

What should we make of the Gospel of Thomas?

The Gospel of *Thomas* was discovered just after World War II at Nag Hammadi in Egypt among a collection of Gnostic writings. Gnosticism was an ancient Middle-Eastern religious philosophy with many variations, but unified at least in its commitment to a dualism between the material and immaterial worlds. The creation of the universe, in Gnostic mythologies, more often than not was the product of the rebellion of some "emanation" from the godhead. Matter, therefore, was inherently evil; only the world of the spirit was redeemable. Consequently, Gnostics looked forward to immortality of a disembodied soul, not the resurrection of the body. Salvation for them was accomplished by understanding secret or esoteric knowledge (in Greek, *gnosis*), which most of the world did not and could not know. Hence, the Gnostic libraries contained numerous documents that purported to be secret revelations of the risen Lord to this or that disciple, usually after Jesus' resurrection.

The Gospel of *Thomas* is no exception. Its opening line reads, "These are the secret sayings which the living Jesus spoke and which Didymos Judas Thomas wrote down."[23] Written in Coptic and dating to no earlier than A.D. 400, the Nag Hammadi version of this Gospel contains parallels to Greek fragments of an unknown document of late second-century vintage that were discovered about a hundred years ago. In other words, the document may have first been written as early as about A.D. 150, but *no actual evidence permits us to push that date a century* earlier as the Jesus Seminar does. Roughly one-third of the sayings in the Gospel of *Thomas* are clearly Gnostic in nature, between one-third and one-half are paralleled fairly closely in Matthew, Mark, Luke, or John, and the remaining sayings are not demonstrably unorthodox but could lend themselves to Gnostic interpretations. After the Coptic Gospel of *Thomas* was discovered and scholars had had time to analyze it in detail, a fair consensus emerged that it postdated the canonical Gospels and relied heavily on them for those passages that were paralleled there.[24] Four reasons proved particularly persuasive.

(1) Parallels emerged in *Thomas* to every one of the four Gospels and to every "layer" of the Gospel tradition—that is, to material common to all three Synoptic Gospels, information from "Q" (the conventional abbreviation for the hypothetical source—German *Quelle*—that probably accounts for material shared by Matthew and Luke), and traditions unique to each of the four Gospels. It seems unlikely that every Gospel and every Gospel source would independently use *Thomas* at an early date; rather, it is far more probable that *Thomas* knew and relied on the later fourfold Gospel collection.[25]

(2) Within *Thomas* itself, various series of sayings reflect how Jesus' original words underwent development in a gnosticizing direction. For example, Sayings 73–75 read:

> (73) Jesus said, "The harvest is great but the laborers are few. Beseech the lord, therefore, to send out laborers to the harvest." (74) He said, "O lord, there are many around the drinking trough, but there is nothing in the cistern. (75) Jesus said, "Many are standing at the door, but it is the solitary who will enter the bridal chamber."

The first of these texts closely resembles Matthew 9:37–38 and Luke 10:2. The second passage can be taken to make a similar point—Christ's followers should be recognizing, but are not, where true spiritual maturity would lead them; this saying has no canonical parallel. The final saying makes the same point a third way but uses two technical terms that recur in Gnostic literature for the true Gnostic (the solitary one) and his initiation into a "deeper life" (entering the bridal suite). It is easy to see how Jesus' original teaching was successively adapted, and not likely that any one of these sayings predates the version in Matthew and Luke.[26]

(3) Some sayings in *Thomas* seem to follow each other for no reason other than that is their sequence in the Synoptic Gospels. For example, Saying 65 gives a version of the parable of the wicked tenants (cf. Mark 12:1–8 pars.), which Saying 66 follows up with a version of Jesus' teaching about the "cornerstone" (cf. Mark 12:10–11). But without anything corresponding to Mark 12:9 to connect the two sayings, no one would guess they were related. It is more probable, therefore, that *Thomas* knew the Synoptics but omitted the connection (as this work does throughout in listing sayings in isolation from each other) than that Mark or someone else created a connected narrative out of two originally independent thoughts.[27]

(4) Many minor distinctives of the Coptic translation of the Gospel of *Thomas* parallel alterations of the Gospel tradition found in later second-through fourth-century documents, including Coptic translations of the canonical Gospels.[28] Others parallel developments of the canonical tradition in the late second-century harmony of the Gospels known as the Diatessaron, in literature attributed to the early church father Clement of Alexandria (ca. A.D. 200), and in sixth-century textual variants of the Gospel manuscripts. A good example is found in *Thomas*'s version of the parable of the dragnet, which has the fishermen keeping only one "fine, large fish" and throwing back into the sea all of the other smaller fish (*Thos.* 8). Not only does this reinterpretation of Jesus' original (Matt. 13:47–50) reflect Gnostic elitism, it also parallels Clement's later adaptation of this parable, in which a fisherman keeps one "choice" (lit., "elect") fish for himself out of all that he catches (*Strom.* 95.3).[29]

The cumulative effect of these and other arguments led Robert Grant and David Freedman, two of the past generation's leading New and Old Testament scholars respectively, to conclude already thirty years ago that *Thomas* was substantially later than and dependent on our four canonical Gospels. *Thomas's* lack of historical narrative and lack of apocalyptic reflects the Gnostic worldview, which cares nothing for God acting in *history* to redeem the world. The Gospel of *Thomas* is an important historical source—but for Gnosticism, not for Christianity. Or, more precisely,

> It is probably our most significant witness to the early perversion of Christianity by those who wanted to create Jesus in their own image. Thus it stands, like Lot's wife, as a new but permanently valuable witness to men's desire to make God's revelation serve them. Ultimately it testifies not to what Jesus said but to what men wished he had said.[30]

Several important recent studies concur.[31] Scholars in general are a little more open today to the idea of some traditions making their way into *Thomas* that were independent of the canonical Gospels (e.g., the otherwise unattested parables of the empty jar and the assassin [*Thos.* 97–98]), but few would date the entire document to the first century.[32] John Meier again reflects a more sober approach when he concludes, "Since I think that the Synoptic-like sayings of the *Gospel of Thomas* are in fact dependent on the Synoptic Gospels and that the other sayings stem from 2d-century Christian Gnosticism, the *Gospel of Thomas* will not be used in our quest as an independent source for the historical Jesus."[33] It should not be used in *anybody's* quest, except perhaps for a saying here or there.

All six of the above observations demonstrate the extreme idiosyncrasies of the Jesus Seminar and cast serious doubt on their claims to speak for a consensus of modern scholars. Attention needs to be devoted instead to a much more promising and substantial development in studying the historical Jesus, to which we now turn.

The Third Quest for the Historical Jesus

Where does it come from?

Quite different from the work of the Jesus Seminar and worthy of much more careful attention is a group of studies that has been dubbed the "third quest" for the historical Jesus.[34] The first quest included romantic, nineteenth-century lives of Christ, the simple Jewish teacher, which were decisively debunked by the famous missionary-musician-scholar, Albert Schweitzer, at the turn of the century.[35] The second quest began after World War II by followers of Rudolf Bultmann, dissatisfied with his well-known pronouncement that we could know little about Jesus beyond the mere fact that he lived.[36] A well-known representative of this school of thought from the University of Chicago, Norman Perrin, summarized in 1974 the following well-established facts about the life of Jesus: his baptism by John, the proclamation especially in parables of the present and future kingdom of God, a ministry of exorcism, his gathering of disciples across socio-economic boundaries, his sharing a common meal that celebrated their new relationship to God, his challenge to the Jewish teachers of his day, the arousal of opposition that led to his arrest, his trials by the Jewish authorities on a charge of blasphemy and by the Romans for sedition, and his crucifixion.[37] Even this collection of established facts was more generous than that of the Jesus Seminar today, but clearly this second quest still called the reliability of a sizable portion of the Gospels into question. In response to this the third quest has arisen.

What does it do?

The third quest of the historical Jesus began about fifteen years ago by scholars who realized that they had to place Jesus much more self-consciously into the Jewish world in which he lived and ministered. They sought to use historical criteria that were more defensible than those of the Jesus Seminar (or even the second quest), similar to criteria that other historians of antiquity were employing.

Intensive study of Jewish apocalyptic literature and thought has spawned a substantial optimism concerning how much of the first three Gospels reflect historically trustworthy material. Thus Ben Meyer, professor at McMaster University in Canada, sees the restoration of Israel as Jesus' dominant concern, symbolized by his choice of twelve apostles (corresponding to the twelve tribes of Israel). Contrary to what many skeptics have claimed, Jesus did intend to found the church and planned for a community of his followers to outlive him and implement his program for a renewed people of God.[38] E. P. Sanders, of Duke University, is more inclined to stress Jesus' threats of impending judgment on Israel, but he too stresses that Jesus foresaw a new age inaugurated by his death. Much of Jesus' teaching revolved around the scandalous claim that he could pronounce God's forgiveness on sinners even before they had demonstrated their contrition through repentance.[39]

James Charlesworth, of Princeton Seminary, observes the muted claims Jesus makes about himself throughout the Synoptics, especially in the parable of the wicked tenants (Mark 12:1–12 pars.)—claims that would have been more explicit had the later church been creating them. He therefore concludes that Jesus probably did believe himself to be the Son of God in the sense of Messiah and anticipated his role as suffering servant.[40] Geza Vermes, a leading Jewish scholar from Oxford, likens him to certain prominent, charismatic holy men in Israel at that time. Richard Horsley (University of Massachusetts at Boston) and Gerd Theissen (Heidelberg) both stress the socio-political threats that were implicit in Jesus' message and behavior.[41] All these scholars have painted relatively plausible portraits of Jesus, grounding him firmly in the *Jewish* world of his day.

This procedure has been followed with even more methodological rigor by the Oxford scholar A. E. Harvey. In his Bampton Lectures, Harvey stresses that there are certain historical constraints that any individual must follow if he or she wants to be understood in a given society. In the world of Jesus, these constraints would have compelled him to address major issues of the day—the volatile political climate, legal controversies, widespread expectation of the end of the present world order, the limitations set up by Jewish belief in monotheism, and so on. Harvey concludes that there are no convincing alternatives to the conclusion that Jesus combined an expertise in debating about issues of the law with the freedom and directness of a prophet. Only if Jesus saw himself as anointed by the Spirit can we understand the church's widespread messianic claims for him. He must have worked miracles, anticipated the imminent end of the age, and sufficiently challenged the authorities so as to provoke their execution of him.[42]

Indeed, major studies of almost every theme or segment of the Synoptic tradition have advanced plausible arguments for accepting *the historical reliability* of substantial portions of Matthew, Mark, and Luke, once they are interpreted in light of an early first-century Palestinian Jewish setting.[43] In fact, about the only sections of the Gospels consistently rejected are some of Jesus' more spectacular miracles over the forces of nature (e.g., stilling the storm or walking on water—Mark 4:35–41; 6:45–52 pars.), the most exalted claims he makes for himself, usually in the Gospel of John (consistent with prevailing skepticism about the Fourth Gospel more generally), and his resurrection. Charlesworth, quoting Sanders approvingly, concludes that "the dominant view today seems to be that we can know pretty well what Jesus was out to accomplish, that we can know a lot about what he said, and that those two things make sense within the world of first-century Judaism."[44]

The most significant observation about the third quest is that *none* of its major contributors are evangelical Christians, though some are recently joining in the undertaking.[45] Thus, they are not susceptible to the charge that they are simply reading their religious beliefs into their historical research and thereby skewing their results. Yet they come to conclusions greatly at odds with those of the Jesus Seminar. And they do so precisely by following the standard canons of the historical investigation of antiquity more generally: considering all of the data available about a particular figure and seeing how much of it can be plausibly fitted together to create a coherent picture of that individual—how he both resembles and differs from the beliefs and practices of his culture. Thus, the third quest tends to write books about *all* of Jesus' life and ministry, not merely atomistic analyses of individual sayings or deeds. No responsible historian would ever approach the biographies of Alexander, Augustus, or Apollonius with the approaches of Crossan or Funk. We should not treat Jesus this way either.

At the same time, it is important not to exaggerate the extent to which even the "third questers" are prepared to endorse the historical trustworthiness of the Gospels. Where parallel accounts of the same event differ considerably, many are still quick to speak of contradictions. Material found only in one Gospel often remains historically suspect. Even passages that appear more than once are often subdivided into a historical "core" overlaid with inauthentic "accretions." And few are prepared to return to a full-fledged Christian orthodoxy that affirms Jesus as wholly man and wholly God, at least not on the basis of historical research.[46]

Where Do We Go from Here?

What are the problems that remain? Can a serious-minded thinker acquainted with the issues offer *historically* credible reasons for affirming the substantial trustworthiness of the *entire* canonical accounts of the life of Christ? The rest of this chapter will address these questions. We will consider three major areas that are crucial in assessing the historicity of any ancient document. First, we will survey the evidence for the authorship and date of each of the Gospels. Second, we will look at the processes involved in their composition. Third, we will analyze the shape of the end-product, that is, the literary genre of Matthew, Mark, Luke, and John. Finally, we will examine the external evidence—from ancient non-Christian writers, from archaeology, and from later Christian writers—that corroborates material found in the four Gospels.

Who Wrote the Gospels and When Were They Written?

Outside of more conservative circles, few scholars believe that Matthew, Mark, Luke, or John wrote the Gospels attributed to them. Mark is usually dated in the 70s (occasionally in the late 60s), Matthew and Luke in the 80s or 90s, and John near the end of the first-century or even a little later. Space precludes a detailed consideration of the arguments advanced for these positions, but the major evangelical New Testament introductions have repeatedly provided appropriate replies.[47] Here we simply want to stress that a plausible case can still be made for the traditional conservative claims, and that those claims substantially advance the case that the Gospels were written by people in a position to report accurate historical information.

Evidence from outside the Gospels

To begin with, all of the external evidence—the witness of the early church fathers—uniformly supports the belief that Matthew (the tax collector turned disciple), Mark (the companion of Peter and Paul), and Luke (Paul's "beloved physician") penned the Gospels attributed to them. No competing traditions assigning these books to any other authors have survived, if any ever existed.[48] Why would Christians as early as the second century ascribe these otherwise anonymous Gospels to three such unlikely candidates if they did not in fact write them? Mark and Luke, after all, were not among Jesus' twelve apostles. Luke is particularly obscure, being mentioned by name only once in the New Testament (Col. 4:14), and Mark is best known for his abandoning Paul (Acts 13:13; cf. 15:37–40). Though an apostle, Matthew is also best known for a negative characteristic, his unscrupulous past as practitioner of a trade Jews considered traitorous to their nation (Matt. 9:9–13). The apocryphal Gospels consistently picked more well-known and exemplary figures for their fictitious authors—for example, Philip, Peter, James, Bartholomew, or Mary.[49] Even Thomas, despite his famous doubts about Jesus' resurrection (John 20:25), seems a more likely person to whom to attribute a Gospel than Matthew, Mark, or Luke (cf. John 20:28).

Second, the testimony of Christians as early as Irenaeus near the end of the second century attributes the writing of Matthew and Mark to the first generation of church history, that is, before the fall of Jerusalem to Rome in A.D. 70. According to this testimony, "Matthew produced his gospel written among the Hebrews in their own dialect, while Peter and Paul proclaimed the gospel and founded the church at Rome." This would have had to have been before the martyrdoms of these two apostles under Nero some time between 64 and 68. Concerning Mark, Irenaeus continues, "After the departure of these, Mark the disciple and interpreter of Peter also transmitted to us what he had written about what Peter had preached" (*Adv. Haer.* 3.1.38–41). Some take this to mean that Mark wrote after Peter's death, but "departure" may refer to his leaving Rome to travel somewhere else, prior to his death. But even if it does not, the perfect participle "what he had written" suggests that only the *transmission* and not the writing of Mark's Gospel took place after Peter's "departure."[50]

Evidence from inside the Gospels

Early external evidence does not enable us to date Luke, but internal evidence does give a hint. Despite a variety of other suggestions, the most plausible reason for the abrupt ending of Acts is that Luke was still writing at the time of the events he describes in Acts 28—Paul's two-year house arrest in Rome. No other explanation convincingly accounts for why Acts 19–28 devotes ten whole chapters to the events leading up to and including Paul's arrest and trials, only to leave us completely in the dark about the outcome of his appeal to Caesar. But if Luke did not know that outcome because Caesar had not yet tried Paul's case, then his omission is understandable. If, then, Luke wrote Acts while Paul was still awaiting the result of his appeal to Rome, we must date that book to no later than A.D. 62.[51] Then Luke's Gospel, as the first of his two-part work (cf. Luke 1:1–4 and Acts 1:1–2), must be dated to the same year or even earlier.

The internal evidence of the literary relationship among Matthew, Mark, and Luke has also suggested to most scholars that Mark wrote before the other two Synoptics.[52] *All of this adds up to a strong case that all three Gospels were composed within about thirty years of Christ's death (probably A.D. 30) and well within the period of time when people could check up on the accuracy of the facts they contain.* The most reliable early tradition suggests a date for John in about the 90s (Irenaeus, *Adv. Haer.* 2.22.5; Eusebius, *Hist. Eccl.* 3.23.1–4), and there is some uncertainty among the later Christian writers whether this is John the apostle or a different John called "the elder" (or "presbyter"), who was a disciple of John the apostle.[53] Either way, however, we are still far closer to the original events than with many ancient biographies. The two earliest biographers of Alexander the Great, for example,

Arrian and Plutarch, wrote more than four hundred years after Alexander's death in 323 B.C., yet historians generally consider them to be trustworthy. Fabulous legends about the life of Alexander did develop over time, but for the most part only during the several centuries *after* these two writers.[54]

Most scholars agree, however, that considerations of authorship and date do not comprise the most decisive part of our discussion. Accurate information can be transmitted over long periods of time from one person to the next, while falsification of reports can occur relatively rapidly even among eyewitnesses of events. Three other issues, in fact, stand out in many contemporary scholars' minds as the most crucial questions to answer in trying to assess the historical trustworthiness of the Gospels. (1) Were the first Christians *interested* in preserving reliable history? (2) Were the first Christians in a position to be *able* to preserve reliable history? (3) Does a comparison of the Gospel parallels themselves suggest that the first Christians *did* in fact preserve reliable history? Answers to these questions require us to explore the nature of the transmission of traditions about Jesus while they circulated orally and the nature of the editorial activity of the four Gospel writers themselves.

How Were the Gospels Put Together?

Were the first Christians interested in preserving reliable history?

The average first-time reader of the Gospels almost always gets the impression that their writers were very much interested in supplying an accurate account of the life of Christ. Luke, in fact, tells us this is part of his very purpose in writing:

> Many have undertaken to draw up an account of the things that have been fulfilled among us, just as they were handed down to us by those who from the first were eyewitnesses and servants of the word. Therefore, since I myself have carefully investigated everything from the beginning, it seemed good also to me to write an orderly account for you, most excellent Theophilus, so that you may know the certainty of the things you have been taught. (Luke 1:1–4)

But did previous Christians share Luke's interests and strategies? There are two main reasons many scholars believe that the first generation of Christians was *not* interested in preserving reliable history, so that, when the Gospel writers later wanted to record information about the historical Jesus, they were unable to do any better than mix together fact and fiction. (1) Many assume that the early Christians thought Jesus would come back within their lifetime, so that historical records about what he did and said would be unnecessary. (2) These initial believers, especially those who claimed to have the gift of prophecy, frequently understood the risen Lord to be speaking to them with important messages for their churches. These words were every bit as authoritative as what Jesus taught while he was alive on earth, so that no one felt any need to distinguish the sayings of the risen Lord from the words of the earthly Jesus. Our Gospel accounts thus mingle together both these categories somewhat indiscriminately.

Although each of these views has been widely promoted, there is little evidence on which either is based. In favor of the first point, it is noted that Jesus made only three cryptic references to his return in ways that could suggest he believed he would come back within the lifetime of his first followers (Matt. 10:23; Mark 9:1; 13:30). But a fair consensus today agrees that these texts are to be interpreted differently. In Mark 9:1, Jesus' prediction that some will not taste death before seeing the kingdom of God come in power probably refers to the next event narrated—his transfiguration—which provides a foretaste of the permanent glory associated with his return.[55] In Mark 13:30, the end-time events that must happen in his generation cannot include his return, because the "these things" of v. 30 must be the same as the "these things" of v. 29, which clearly refer to signs *preceding* Christ's second coming.[56] In Matthew 10:23, Jesus' promise that the disciples will not finish visiting the cities of Israel before the Son of Man comes probably refers to the perennially incomplete mission to the Jews prior to Christ's return.[57] Moreover, *the majority of Jesus' teaching presupposes a significant interval before the end of the world,* because Christ spends much time instructing his disciples on such mundane matters as paying taxes, marriage and divorce, dealing with one's enemies, stewardship of wealth, and so on.

Yet even if some of Jesus' disciples did think that he might come back fairly quickly, it is unlikely that this would have prevented them from preserving his teaching with care. The Jews had lived for eight centuries with the tension between the repeated pronouncements by the prophets that the Day of the Lord was at hand (e.g., Joel 2:1; Obad. 15; Hab. 2:3) and the continuing history of Israel. Such warnings did not discourage them from recording the words of the Old Testament prophets, and it is not likely that it would have hindered Jesus' followers from exercising remarkable care in transmitting the teachings of one whom they believed was even greater than a prophet (e.g., Matt. 12:41).[58]

The second argument—i.e., that the words of later Christian prophets are intermingled with the sayings of the historical Jesus on the pages of our Gospel—rests on even scantier evidence. This hypothesis was built up largely on a comparison with certain Greco-Roman prophecies, which prove to be questionable analogs. The only sayings of early Christian prophets actually recorded in the New Testament explicitly distinguish their teachings from those of the earthly Jesus (Acts 11:28; 21:10–11; Rev. 2–3). And Paul's insistence that churches weigh carefully what prophets declared (1 Cor. 14:29) suggests that no alleged prophecy would be accepted if it contradicted what Jesus had earlier taught.

The strongest argument against the idea that Christians felt free to invent sayings of Jesus, however, comes from what we *never* find in the Gospels. Numerous Christian controversies that surfaced after Jesus' ascension and threatened to tear the New Testament church apart could have been conveniently solved if the first Christians had simply read back into the Gospels solutions to those debates. *But this is precisely what never happens.* Not once does Jesus address many of the major topics that for the rest of the first century loomed large in the minds of Christians—whether believers needed to be circumcised, how to regulate speaking in tongues, how to keep Jew and Gentile united in one body, whether believers could divorce non-Christian spouses, what roles were open to women in ministry, and so on. In other words, the first Christians *were* interested in preserving the distinction between what happened during Jesus' life and what was debated later in the churches.[59]

Were the first Christians able to preserve reliable history?

But suppose the disciples of Christ *were* interested in preserving reliable history. Were they *able* to? Anyone who has played the child's game of "telephone" knows how easily even relatively straightforward messages get garbled when they are passed along orally in a room full of, say, twenty or thirty people. Are we seriously to imagine that the wealth of information found in the Gospels circulated entirely by word of mouth for up to thirty years without serious error creeping in? Yes, and for quite a number of reasons. To begin with, the ancient Jewish world (and to only a slightly lesser extent, the Greco-Roman world around it) was a culture that prized memorization skills highly. Rabbis were encouraged to memorize the entire Hebrew Scriptures (what we call the Old Testament), plus a sizable body of the oral laws that grew up around them. Elementary education, mandatory for many Jewish boys from ages five to twelve or thirteen, was entirely by rote memory; and only one topic was studied, the Bible.[60]

On the other hand, transmission of important traditions not written down in sacred Scripture often involved a substantial amount of flexibility in retelling those stories, in the inclusion or omission of certain incidental details, in the arrangement and sequence of episodes, and in paraphrasing and interpreting a person's teaching, *so long as the major events of the narrative and their significance were not altered.*[61] Recent studies undertaken in traditional Middle-Eastern villages today demonstrate that these same customs still prevail.[62] In other words, it is likely that a substantial amount of the similarities and differences among the Synoptic Gospels can be explained by assuming that the disciples and those whom they in turn instructed had committed to memory a sizable body of material about what Jesus did and said. Nevertheless, they felt free to recount this information in various forms, even while preserving the significance of Jesus' original teachings and deeds.

Six supporting arguments tend to confirm this hypothesis. *First, it is likely that written accounts of various portions of the Gospel record predate the appearance of the final form of the three Synoptic Gospels in the 60s and of the Gospel of John in the 90s.* "Q," the sayings source on which Matthew and Luke apparently drew, was probably composed by at least A.D. 50; even the Jesus Seminar agrees on that (although they unnecessarily postulate an abbreviated Q, which later overlaid original wisdom material with secondary apocalyptic traditions).[63] Matthew and Luke probably relied on additional written or oral sources unique to each of their Gospels, conventionally designated "M" and "L," which are at least as old as, if not older than, Q.[64] John may have relied on a "signs-source" for his accounts of Jesus' miracles that goes back at least to the 60s, and a plausible case can be made for dating it to the 40s or 50s.[65]

Second, although they disapproved of the public use of written notes, rabbis and their followers often used a kind of shorthand to record in private important information they wished to preserve. Jesus' disciples may have adopted this practice even while he was still alive to encapsulate the major contours of his longer discourses in writing. This could well have provided the primary material for their own preaching and teaching when Jesus sent them out (and later the Seventy-Two) to duplicate his ministry, even while he was still alive (Matt. 10; Luke 10).[66] And when one observes that over 80 percent of Jesus' teaching was poetic in form, even what they did not jot down would have been memorable and memorizable.[67]

Third, the existence of a center of apostolic leadership in Jerusalem, from at least A.D. 30–60, which periodically "checked up" on the spread of the Gospel (Acts 8:14; 11:1–3; 15:1–2; 21:17–25), means that the analogy of the child's game of telephone is inappropriate. In the analogy, each participant is left alone to do the best he or she can with the message to be transmitted. In early Christianity, however, the center of leadership would periodically have been available to correct any errant traditions, had they developed, and to restore the original, more accurate information about Jesus' life.[68] Rabbis regularly corrected each other in their care to preserve oral tradition, and even villagers had the right to correct storytellers in their midst when they erred in significant ways in recounting sacred tradition.[69] And, of course, the presence throughout the first generation of Christianity of unbelieving and at times even hostile eyewitnesses to Jesus' life would have acted as a corrective to the spread of inaccurate traditions. So there would have been numerous checks and balances to make it unlikely that widespread distortion entered into the church's message about what Jesus said and did.

Fourth is the argument based on the "hard sayings" of Jesus. Much of Jesus' ethical instruction as portrayed in the Gospels is so challenging that it is unlikely that it would have been invented. What later Christian, convinced of Christ's deity, would have made up an account in which Jesus denied knowing when he would return (Mark 13:32) or was unable to work a miracle because of people's unbelief (Mark 6:5–6)? Who would have made him ask, "Why do you call me good? ... No one is good—except God alone" (Mark 10:18), as if to deny either his goodness or his deity or both? Who would have had him forbid divorce (Mark 10:10–12) in an age when men found it easy to request and receive one? Who would create a large body of sayings demanding renunciation of wealth in one form or another? The list is so extensive that one recent book on Jesus' ethics is understandably entitled *Strenuous Commands*.[70] The entire history of the church is one of its inability to come to grips with these stringent teachings, so it is not likely to have created them.

Fifth, Paul later takes pains to preserve distinctions between what the earthly Jesus said and what he believed God was telling him to write to his congregations. When he could quote or allude to a tradition from the historical Jesus, he did; but he knew when the tradition did not teach on a particular topic, and he did not attempt to claim otherwise. So, for example, in 1 Corinthians 7:10, Paul cites Jesus' teaching on divorce (Mark 10:10) as "not I, but the Lord"; yet when he comes to a situation of mixed marriages, which Jesus did not address, he writes, "I, not the Lord."

Sixth, distinctions can be discerned within the pages of the Gospels themselves, when one compares the thrust of Jesus' teaching before his death and his words to his followers after his resurrection. Matthew summarizes John's and Jesus' preaching by focusing on the fact that the kingdom of heaven was drawing near (Matt. 3:2; 4:17; 10:5), but he epitomizes the apostles' postresurrection ministry as discipling nations in the observance of Jesus' commandments (28:18–20). Mark sums up Jesus' message as preaching the gospel (good news) about God and his government (Mark 1:14–15), but he recognizes that by his time it was appropriate to speak of the gospel *about* Jesus Christ (1:1). Luke highlights Christ's precrucifixion proclamation of release for the captives and his social concern (Luke 4:16–30), but his postresurrection command shifts more to the preaching of forgiveness of sins to the nations (24:46–47). None of these contrasts is inherently contradictory, but each reformulates the nature of discipleship and belief sufficiently to cast doubt on the notion that the Evangelists were reading post-Easter theology back into the pre-Easter portions of their narratives.[71] In sum, the Gospel writers *were able* to preserve reliable history.

Did the first Christians preserve reliable history?

What then of the final question about Gospel parallels? Regardless of the Gospel writers' interest or ability, how do we assess the similarities and differences among their finished products? Certainly there is substantial overlap and agreement on main points, with the type of diversity in details one would expect when different writers reflect on the same events from their unique perspectives. The German classical historian Hans Stier makes this observation even about the resurrection narratives: agreements over basic data, coupled with divergence of detail

> present for the historian for this very reason a criterion of extraordinary credibility. For if that were the fabrication of a congregation or of a similar group of people, then the tale would be consistently and obviously complete. For that reason every historian is especially sceptical at that moment when an extraordinary happening is only reported in accounts which are completely free of contradictions.[72]

But what of all the places where the differences (a better word in this context than Stier's "contradictions") seem greater than that? Can we look at the four Gospels as we now have them and avoid the charge of *bona fide* contradictions among parallel accounts? Again, I believe the answer is most certainly, yes. None of the so-called contradictions among the Gospels is a discovery of modern scholarship. The church has been aware of them throughout its history and usually has believed that there are plausible harmonizations. A survey of the leading evangelical commentaries on any one of the four Gospels will give a sampling of the most convincing of those harmonizations today.[73] Space precludes all but a handful of examples.[74]

Many of the seeming discrepancies vanish once we understand the literary conventions for writing history or biography in the ancient world. Neither Greek nor Hebrew had any symbol for our quotation marks, nor did people feel that a verbatim account of someone's speech was any more valuable or accurate than a reliable summary, paraphrase, or interpretation. The order of events described in a famous person's life was often arranged thematically rather than strictly chronologically. So we should not be surprised to find all kinds of minor variations in both the sequence of episodes in Jesus' life from one Gospel to the next and in the actual words attributed to him on any given occasion.

Other problems simply have to be examined one by one. Was the Last Supper celebrated on the night of the Passover meal (so apparently Mark 14:12–16 pars.) or before it (so apparently John 18:28 and 19:14)? Probably it was on Passover, since John 18:28 seems to allude to the week-long Passover festival and 19:14 can be taken as the Day of Preparation *for the Sabbath* during Passover week (as in the NIV).

Did the centurion himself come to Jesus to ask healing for his servant (Matt. 8:5–13) or did he send the elders of the Jews to make the request (Luke 7:1–10)? Probably the latter, since in the ancient world actions taken by one's emissaries could be considered one's own. We preserve the same convention today when the newspapers print, "The President today said that . . . ," when in fact his speech writers created the copy and his press secretary delivered the address.

Did Jesus send the demons into the swine in Gerasa (Mark 5:1; Luke 8:26) or in Gadara (Matt. 8:28)? Probably near Khersa—a city on the east bank of the Sea of Galilee, whose spelling in Greek could easily yield Gerasa—in the *province* of Gadara.

Additional examples abound. Not every proposed harmonization is as credible as every other, but enough are sufficiently credible that it is best to give the text the benefit of the doubt where we are less sure rather than immediately speaking of proven contradictions.

At this point some people will object. "It's all well and good to look for harmonizations between the accounts of two historians when you know they are trying to report the facts accurately. But aren't the Gospels an entirely different kind of literature than straightforward history or biography?" So we must look briefly at the question of the genre of the Gospels.

What Kind of Literature Is a Gospel?

It is certainly true that the New Testament Gospels in some ways look quite different from modern historical or biographical writing. Most notably, the four Evangelists have clear theological axes to grind. They believe that Jesus is the Messiah, the Son of God, and that people should believe in him as the only way to God. Surely this prevents them from functioning as psychologically objective biographers, it is alleged. Aren't the Gospels more theological than historical, and don't they reflect fairly biased theology at that?

Other reasons for assuming the Gospels to be something quite different from sober history involve the contents the Evangelists chose to include. Take Mark, for example. What kind of biography would omit all information about its hero's birth, childhood, adolescence, and early adulthood, present just a handful of teachings and actions of that individual from a three-year span of his career (without telling us it was three years), and then spend half of his book on the events that led up to and included the last week of this man's life?

This last question is relatively easy to answer. There are unique aspects of the Gospels, precisely because their authors believed there were unique aspects about Jesus' life. Compared to the period of his ministry after being baptized in water by John and by the Holy Spirit, his earlier life was uneventful. Because Christians believed that his death was no mere martyrdom but an atonement for the sins of the world, it was natural that they would focus a disproportionate amount of attention on the events leading up to it. The first Christian preachers, according to Acts, consistently appeal to the death and resurrection of Jesus as the key to understanding his significance (e.g., Acts 2:22–36; 10:36–43; 13:27–37). But such selectivity does not in and of itself impugn the trustworthiness of the events the Gospel writers did choose to include.[75]

Theological history

The larger issue of the relationship between theology and history requires a more detailed response. Perspectives that pit theology against history reveal a false dichotomy that unfortunately remains rampant in modern thought. Simply because a writer is passionately committed to promoting a particular cause does not at all mean he or she will falsify the facts. Often, such a person will work all the harder to tell the story straight. Personal commitment to and involvement with something does not mean that the person cannot present a truthful account of the topic in question. After all, often the truthfulness of something is what produced the personal commitment in the first place.

An excellent modern example involves the aftermath of the Nazi holocaust. Some of the most detailed and reliable reporters of that event were Jews who have been passionately committed to seeing that such atrocities never again occur.

Yet it is not they who are falsifying history but the later revisionist "historians" who play down the extent of the debacle or even deny it ever happened. And in the ancient world, there was virtually no such thing as dispassionate history. The attitude then was: Why bother to record and pass on the story of certain events unless there was a moral to be learned from them? *So if the Gospels were* not *ideological, they would have been unparalleled among ancient historical and biographical writing!* [76]

A good illustration of the way many biblical scholars or theologians are simply unfamiliar with how ancient history-writing worked has been exposed by University of Ottawa historian Paul Merkley. Many people have cited Julius Caesar's crossing of the Rubicon River as he returned from Gaul to Italy in 49 B.C. as a model of an incontrovertible historical fact from the ancient world that also had *historic* significance: with that deed Caesar committed himself to civil war, and the course of the Roman empire was forever altered. What is often overlooked is that we are not absolutely sure of the date of the crossing or the location of the Rubicon. And, as with the Gospels, we have four accounts of the event from later historians—Velleius Paterculus, Plutarch, Suetonius, and Appian. Only the first of these was even born before the mid-first century *after* Christ. All apparently relied on one eyewitness source, that of Asinius Pollio, which has disappeared without a trace. Yet the four accounts vary at least as much as the Gospels do when reporting the same event. One writer, Suetonius, attributes Caesar's decision to cross the Rubicon to seeing "an apparition of superhuman size and beauty," who was "sitting on the river bank, playing a reed pipe."

When this kind of miraculous detail appears in a Gospel account, the entire story is usually rejected as mythical. Here it appears in an account of an event that is regularly cited as one of the most well-established historical facts of antiquity! Clearly a double standard is at work here. *The Gospels deserve to be treated at least as generously as any other purportedly historical narrative from the ancient world.* [77] The words of the British historian of ancient Rome, A. N. Sherwin-White, though penned a generation ago, remain equally applicable to today's radical criticism: "It is astonishing that while Graeco-Roman historians have been growing in confidence, the twentieth-century study of the Gospel narratives, starting from no less promising material, has taken so gloomy a turn."[78]

In a separate chapter in this book, Gary Habermas discusses the problem of miracles in the Gospels (see chapter 5). But one comment is appropriate here. It is sometimes argued that the Gospels need to be treated more skeptically than other ancient histories or biographies because of the miraculous elements included. The example of Caesar crossing the Rubicon is just one of many that could be given to remind us that *most* ancient historians or biographers believed in supernatural causes of certain events. The Gospels are little different in this regard. In fact, a case can be made that the Gospel miracles are more integrated with and integral to the rest of their narratives than in most ancient history. Consistently, the miracles reinforce and illustrate Jesus' central message, widely accepted as authentic even by critical scholars, that the kingdom of God was invading human history.[79]

Once one is not overly distracted by the issue of miracles, *a careful comparison of the four Gospels with other ancient literature reveals that the greatest number of similarities appears in texts that are generally said to represent ancient historical and biographical genres.* One recent study finds the closest parallels to Luke's prologue (Luke 1:1–4) in the technical prose of medical and scientific treatises.[80] Another investigation finds the greatest number of similarities to the primary purposes of the Synoptic Gospels in such generally trustworthy works as the histories of Herodotus, Tacitus, Arrian, Dio Cassius, Sallust, and Josephus.[81] Even the Gospel of John, which differs markedly from the other three, compares favorably with such Greco-Roman biographies as those written by Isocrates, Xenophon, Plutarch, Suetonius, Lucian, and Philostratus.[82]

John versus the Synoptics

But what of the details of the Fourth Gospel? Why are so many things included in it that are not in the Synoptics, and vice-versa? What about the consistently exalted picture of Jesus with all of his claims to deity? What about the fact that the language of John as he narrates his story is often indistinguishable from the words he attributes to Jesus?

Undoubtedly John is more interpretive than the Synoptic Gospels. Much of Jesus' teaching is reworded in John's own idiom and contextualized for the Greek audience of Ephesus at the end of the first century (to which John wrote, at least according to several of the early church fathers). John had had a lifetime to meditate on the significance of Jesus' person and work. Whether he knew the Synoptics and decided not to duplicate much of what was already treated well there, or whether he was writing largely independently of them and so happened to choose a different set of events, we should not be surprised at the amount of variation.[83] What *is* surprising is how much Matthew, Mark, and Luke have in common—parallels that have led most to posit some literary relationship among them.

We must be careful, too, not to overestimate the exalted picture of Jesus that John paints or to underestimate the portrait of Jesus in the Synoptics. It is true that only John records Jesus' seven "I am" sayings and that John himself believes explicitly in Jesus as the Word of God made flesh (John 1:1–14). But, on the one hand, sayings like "I am the door" or "the living water" or "the bread of life" remain metaphors and would have been more cryptic to Jesus' original audience than they are to us. Late in Jesus' ministry the Jewish crowds pleaded with him to stop keeping them in suspense: "If you are the Christ, tell us plainly" (10:24). And even on the night before Christ's crucifixion, his disciples failed to understand him until they at last exclaimed, "Now you are speaking clearly and without figures of speech" (16:29). Unfortunately, their boast was premature, for they continued to fail to grasp the need for Jesus' death.[84]

On the other hand, the Synoptics implicitly present a portrait of Jesus from which one could surely derive the more explicit claims of John. It is Matthew and Luke who describe the Virgin Birth. All three Synoptic Gospels (like John) have Jesus calling himself the Son of Man, which, notwithstanding protracted debate as to its origin, almost certainly harks back to the human figure of Daniel 7:13–14, who is nevertheless present in God's divine throne-room receiving universal authority and an everlasting kingdom.[85] The Jesus of the Synoptics also accepts worship (Matt. 14:33), forgives sins (Mark 2:5), announces that people's final destinies will be based on their response to him (Mark 8:38; Luke 12:8–10), and applies metaphors to himself, particularly in his parables, that in the Old Testament are often applied to Yahweh (Lord of the harvest, shepherd, sower, vineyard owner, bridegroom, rock, etc.).[86]

Another interesting feature of John is that, when compared with the Synoptics, his Gospel consistently gives more references to chronology, geography, topography, and the like. It is only from John that we learn, for example, of Christ's three-year ministry. Yet this information emerges almost incidentally, in John's concern to show Jesus' going up to Jerusalem at the major Jewish feasts, thus demonstrating that he is the fulfillment of all of the Jewish hopes embodied in those festivals. The fact that John's chronology and geography are not his primary interests makes that information all the more valuable, since he is not likely to have distorted it in service of his main points.[87]

In sum, there is no doubt that the Gospels mix theology and history and that in some ways John is more theological than the Synoptics. But both of these phenomena are natural in light of historical and biographical writing in the ancient world. And neither disqualifies the Gospels from providing reliable history, since *all* history is interpreted history. Nor are the differences among the four Gospels so great as to call their general trustworthiness into question. What we have yet to consider, however, is whether data from sources *outside* the Gospels may contradict (or corroborate) these four books. In fact, this is the primary method modern historians generally apply to evaluate their sources.[88]

What Evidence Do We Have from Outside the Gospels?

Our final area of discussion, then, as we address the question of where to start in studying the historical Jesus, involves corroborating evidence for the details of the Gospels in outside sources (see also chapter 8 by E. Yamauchi). It is often pointed out that there is little information about Jesus that can be gleaned from other *non-Christian* historical reports from the ancient world. Requiring such non-Christian corroboration, of course, immediately reintroduces the false dichotomy, for it implies that *Christians* cannot be trusted for the information they record about Jesus. As long as someone who saw or heard about Jesus' ministry remains unconvinced by his claims, he or she is an objective reporter; but as soon as one becomes a disciple, nothing one says can be trusted! The logic is similar to requiring a journalist describing a physics experiment not to believe in the scientific method or a reporter commenting on a person's unconscious motives not to believe in modern psychology!

Non-Christian Historians

Nevertheless, even if we limit ourselves to the testimony of ancient Jews, Greeks, and Romans who never became Christians, there is enough external evidence to support the broad contours of Jesus' life similar to that of Perrin's summary of the second quest for the historical Jesus (see above, pp. 25–26).[89] From Greco-Roman sources we learn little more than that a teacher by the name of Jesus who founded the sect of Christians lived and died on a cross in first-century Palestine. The Jewish reports are more substantial. From the Talmud (the later comprehensive collection of originally oral traditions from the centuries surrounding the life of Christ), we learn that Jesus was conceived out of wedlock, gathered disciples, made blasphemous claims about himself, and worked miracles; but these miracles are attributed to sorcery and not to God. From Josephus (a Jewish historian from the second half of the first century A.D.), we learn that Jesus was a wise man who did surprising feats, taught many, won over followers from among Jews and Greeks, was believed to be the Messiah, was accused by the Jewish leaders, was condemned to be crucified by Pilate, and was considered to be resurrected.[90] Josephus also gives substantial information about Herod the Great and his various sons, a brief description of the ministry of John the Baptist, and numerous details that dovetail with information in the book of Acts.[91]

When we realize that ancient historians focused almost entirely on the exploits of political and military leaders or officially recognized religious and philosophical spokespersons, one should not be surprised that Jesus gets so little attention in ancient historiography. Indeed, one might be surprised that he and the Baptist get as much press as they do. For example, Apollonius of Tyana (in what today is central Turkey) was a late first-century teacher and wonder-worker with several striking parallels in his message and deeds to the life of Jesus. Yet we know about his life almost exclusively from the third-century Greek biographer Philostratus. The passing reference made to him in Dio Cassius' *Roman History* (68:17) is briefer than Josephus' accounts of Jesus.[92]

Archaeological finds

Further corroboration comes from the arena of archaeology. The Gospels do not contain nearly as much material susceptible to comparison with ruins, inscriptions, and artifacts as does, say, the book of Acts. Still, where the data of the Gospels can be tested, they consistently have proven to be remarkably accurate, especially in John. Archaeologists have unearthed the five porticoes of the pool of Bethesda by the Sheep Gate (John 5:2), the pool of Siloam (9:1–7), Jacob's well at Sychar (4:5), the "Pavement" (*Gabbatha*) where Pilate tried Jesus (19:13), and Solomon's porch in the temple precincts (10:22–23). As recently as 1961 an inscription was discovered in Caesarea, providing for the first time extrabiblical corroboration of Pilate as Judea's prefect during the time of Christ. Since then, discovery of an ossuary (bone-box) of a crucified man named Johanan from first-century Palestine confirms that nails were driven in his ankles, as in Christ's; previously some skeptics thought that the Romans used only ropes to affix the legs of condemned men to their crosses. And less than five years ago, in 1990, the burial grounds of Caiaphas, the Jewish high priest, and his family were uncovered in Jerusalem. These and numerous other details create a favorable impression of the Gospels' trustworthiness in the areas in which they can be tested.[93] Reasonable historians will therefore give them the benefit of the doubt in areas in which they cannot be tested.[94]

New Testament letters

Christian testimony outside of the four Gospels must also be taken into account. Paul's writings (especially Romans, 1 Corinthians, and 1 Thessalonians) and, to a lesser extent, the other New Testament letters (especially James), contain numerous allusions to and occasional quotations of the words of Jesus.[95] Yet the three Pauline letters were definitely written, and James was likely written, before any of the Gospels appeared—Paul's works between A.D. 50 and 57 and James probably as early as the late 40s. Their echoes of Jesus' words must therefore stem from the oral tradition, and they attest to its careful preservation during the first two decades of Christian history.

In *Romans*, examples of these echoes include Jesus' words on blessing those who persecute you (Rom. 12:14; cf. Luke 5:27–28), repaying no one evil for evil (Rom. 12:17; cf. Matt. 5:39), paying taxes and related tribute (Rom. 13:7; cf. Mark 12:17), loving one's neighbor as summarizing the whole law (Rom. 13:8–9; cf. Mark 12:31; also Gal. 5:14), and recognizing all foods as clean (Rom. 14:14; cf. Mark 7:19b; Luke 11:41). Three times in *1 Corinthians* Paul explicitly quotes the words of Jesus from the Gospel tradition: on divorce and remarriage (1 Cor. 7:10; cf. Mark 10:10–12), on receiving money for ministry (1 Cor. 9:14; cf. Luke 10:7; 1 Tim. 5:18), and extensively on the Last Supper (1 Cor. 11:23–25; cf. Luke 22:19–20). In *1 Thessalonians* fairly close quotations appear in 2:14–16 (on the persecution of Judean Christians by their kinfolk—cf. Matt. 23:29–38) and 4:15–5:4 (on the return of Christ—cf. Matt. 24, esp. v. 43). Moving to the letter of James, one finds allusions to the Synoptic tradition, and especially the Sermon on the Mount, in almost every paragraph,[96] and a more explicit quotation of the saying on letting your yes be yes and your no, no in James 5:12 (cf. Matt. 5:37).

A summary of the biographical information about Jesus' *deeds* that can be pieced together from just the Pauline letters includes his descent from Abraham and David (Rom. 1:3; Gal. 3:16), his upbringing in the Jewish law (Gal. 4:4), his gathering together disciples, including Cephas (Peter) and John, his having a brother named James (Gal. 1:19; 2:9), his impeccable character and exemplary life (e.g., Rom. 15:3, 8; 2 Cor. 8:9; Phil. 2:6–8), his Last Supper and betrayal (1 Cor.

11:23–35), and numerous details surrounding his death and resurrection (e.g., 1 Cor. 15:4–8; Gal. 3:1; 1 Thess. 2:15).

Later Christian testimony

When one turns to the oldest noncanonical Christian literature, vestiges of this early tradition still reappear from time to time.[97] In the late 90s a manual of Christian instruction on such matters as baptism, fasting, prayer, the Eucharist, and church leadership appeared, called the *Didache* (*The Teaching of the Twelve Apostles*). Abundant quotations or allusions to the Gospels regularly cite items found in the Gospel of Matthew—but only those sections paralleled in Luke but not in Mark or those portions unique to Matthew himself. This suggests that the *Didache* was not quoting from the complete Gospel as we know it but from the sources designated Q and M (see above, pp. 32–33) or from the oral traditions contained in them.

In the writings of Ignatius, the early second-century Christian bishop and martyr, virtually three-fourths of his references to the words of Jesus parallel material found only in Matthew's Gospel (even though that material comprises only one-quarter of the whole Gospel). Minor variations in wording from canonical Matthew suggest, again, that Ignatius was not following the written form of the Gospel but relied instead on persistent oral traditions, or possibly on written sources that predate its completion. Parallel phenomena have been observed in other writings of the second-century Church Fathers.

Early Christian poetry

A final line of argument focuses on early Christian creeds or hymns. At several places in Paul's and Peter's letters, compact confessions of faith appear, often poetic in form—sometimes referred to as though their audiences were already familiar with them—and often employing language different from the characteristic vocabulary of those letters' authors. These factors have convinced many scholars that such passages reflect well-known early Christian statements of belief about Jesus.[98] The clearest examples appear in Philippians 2:6–11; Colossians 1:15–20; and 1 Peter 3:18–22.[99] These letters were most likely written in the early 60s, so that the creeds predating them were probably written no later than the 50s. And those that show signs of *Jewish*-Christian origin probably come from the 30s or 40s, within twenty years of the crucifixion and during the heyday of Christianity in Palestine.

Yet it is precisely in this "credal" material that we often find some of the most exalted language about Jesus. He was "in very nature God" (Phil. 2:6), "the image of the invisible God" (Col. 1:15), and "has gone into heaven . . . at God's right hand—with angels, authorities and powers in submission to him" (1 Peter 3:22). Such beliefs thus emerged early in the history of the church; we may not chalk Christ's "deification" up to a late stage in the development of Christianity.

In 1 Corinthians 15:3–7 Paul explicitly informs his audience that he delivered to them what he had received from his predecessors—using technical Jewish terminology for the transmission of oral tradition. Here we come to the very heart of early Christian belief about Jesus—"that Christ died for our sins according to the Scriptures, that he was buried, that he was raised on the third day according to the Scriptures, and that he appeared to Peter and then to the Twelve," and then to James and over five hundred other witnesses. Stripping away language and contents that Paul or later tradition might have added, many scholars conclude that the core of this confession—concerning Christ's death, burial, and resurrection—must have been delivered to Paul soon after his conversion. One important study assigns the original creed to the Hellenistic Jewish Christian community in Jerusalem before Stephen's martyrdom, which pushes its date back to A.D. 32 or earlier.[100]

The earliest Christian preaching in Acts points in the same direction. Immediately from Pentecost on, the apostles preached Jesus no longer merely as Christ (Messiah) but as Lord (Yahweh-God)—see, for example, Acts 2:36. These sermons in the early chapters of Acts have at times been ascribed to Luke's creative imagination, but there is telling evidence against this notion. In several places, Peter and Stephen use titles for Jesus that do not figure significantly in the later church's teaching about him, or even in the later chapters of Acts. He is the "servant" (Acts 3:13—probably drawing on Isa. 52–53), the "Holy and Righteous One" (3:14), "the author of life" (3:15), and the "prophet" Moses had predicted (3:22; 7:37). Yet all of these titles ascribe to Jesus functions of deity.[101]

Within the first two years after his death, then, significant numbers of Jesus' followers seem to have formulated a doctrine of the atonement, were convinced that he had been raised from the dead in bodily form, associated Jesus with God, and believed they found support for all these convictions in the Old Testament. This is a far cry from hypotheses either of the gradual evolution of a simple Jewish rabbi into a Greek god or of the revolutionary transformation of a Cynic sage into a Jewish apocalypticist. Credible historians must find better explanations for the presence *within Judaism* of beliefs that struck at the core of Jewish monotheism at so early a date in Christian history. *The most plausible explanation is surely that the events surrounding the life of this remarkable man, Jesus of Nazareth, made any lesser beliefs about who he was and what he did inadequate to account for what had actually happened among them.*[102]

Summary and Conclusions

The Jesus Seminar and its friends do not reflect any consensus of scholars except for those on the "radical fringe" of the field. Its methodology is seriously flawed and its conclusions unnecessarily skeptical. Far more worthy of a claim to a responsible, historical interpretation of the available data is the third quest for the historical Jesus. Yet even here scholars often stop a little short of historic, Christian orthodoxy. Renewed attention needs to be devoted to issues that can support an even more positive assessment of the trustworthiness of the Gospels.

Traditional authorship claims are most likely correct, and the three Synoptics should probably all be dated to the early 60s or before. This places these documents well within a period to have been written by people able to preserve accurate historical information.

The conservative nature of oral tradition in ancient Judaism, particularly among disciples who revered their rabbis' words, makes it highly likely that Jesus' teaching would have been carefully preserved, even given a certain flexibility in the specific wording with which it was reported. Virtually all the so-called contradictions in the Gospels can be readily harmonized.

In almost every case in which the Gospels can be tested against external evidence, that evidence corroborates the details found in Matthew, Mark, Luke, and John. A small amount of this corroboration comes from non-Christian historians of the day; a significantly larger percentage comes from other New Testament letters and the writings of the early church fathers, particularly when they were not relying on the canonical form of the four Gospels for their information. Archaeology has also continued to substantiate increasingly sizable portions of the Gospel traditions.

I would like to close this chapter with a personal note. In the mid-1970s, I received my undergraduate education, including a degree in religion, at a fairly prestigious private liberal arts college associated with a mainline Protestant denomination. Despite its historic Christian roots, my college's religion department was trying hard to model itself along the lines of a secular university's program of religious studies. On the first day of a course on the Gospels, for example, we were asked to read various apocryphal stories of the playful and spiteful miracles Jesus allegedly worked as a child—breathing life into clay pigeons and withering up an obnoxious playmate. Our professor then explained how this was just the tail end of a process that began already in Scripture of distorting and embellishing the historical Jesus—turning a pious Jewish prophet into a divine wonder-worker.

Today's mythology, popular particularly in university circles, is different in certain ways. The Jesus Seminar, for example, proposes that Jesus was a good *sage*, who perhaps did work a few wonders, but was turned by his followers into a divine *prophet*. The faith of the unsuspecting Christian student may be powerfully challenged by such notions, and unfortunately many are not aware that there are equally respectable scholarly traditions that come to diametrically opposite conclusions. It is sad, too, that many university libraries, with huge collections for other subjects in the curriculum, have only a handful of works in the area of biblical studies, often representing only the skeptical viewpoints of the professors in the department. It is my hope that this chapter, indeed the whole book, will encourage students and scholars, laypersons and clergy, to realize that one does not have to sacrifice his or her intellect to believe what evangelicals do about the Jesus of the Bible, and that there is a huge volume of scholarship to support the picture of Christ that Matthew, Mark, Luke, and John portray.[103]

Notes

1. Robert W. Funk, Roy W. Hoover, and the Jesus Seminar, *The Five Gospels: What Did Jesus Really Say?* (New York: Macmillan, 1993), 36.

2. All Bible quotations in this chapter follow the NIV.

3. For a complete list of "Voting Records Sorted by Weighted Average," see *Forum* 6 (1990): 139–91. Counting paralleled sayings once for every gospel in which they appear, a total of 1544 items are catalogued: 31 red, 211 pink, 416 gray, and 886 black.

4. Their names, positions, and degrees are listed in an appendix in Funk, Hoover, and the Jesus Seminar, *Five Gospels*, 533–37.

5. Specifically, the January 1993 CD-ROM of the American Theological Library Association, which indexes all articles in journals or multiauthor works listed in *Religion Indexes One and Two*, two standard indexes of articles in the field; and the April 1994 edition of the On-Line Computer Library Center, the comprehensive database of books available for interlibrary loan in North America, including all major theological libraries.

6. Far more representative is the new anthology of essays: Bruce Chilton and Craig A. Evans, eds., *Studying the Historical Jesus: Evaluations of the State of Current Research* (Leiden: Brill, 1994).

7. E.g., Funk, Hoover, and the Jesus Seminar, *Five Gospels*, 62, 461.

8. E.g., ibid., 60, 70–71.

9. E.g., ibid., 42. Cf. Robert W. Funk with Mahlon H. Smith, *The Gospel of Mark: Red Letter Edition* (Sonoma, Calif.: Polebridge, 1991), 40, 48.

10. E.g., ibid., 126, 178.

11. E.g., ibid., 105, 124.

12. E.g., ibid., 180, 303.

13. E.g., ibid., 151, 181, 318.

14. Cf., e.g., James H. Charlesworth, *Jesus Within Judaism* (New York: Doubleday, 1988); and many of the volumes surveyed in his appendix, "A New Trend: Jesus Research," 187–207.

15. For a book-length unpacking of this kind of Jesus by one of the cochairs of the Jesus Seminar, see John D. Crossan, *The Historical Jesus* (San Francisco: Harper SanFrancisco, 1991). Crossan has popularized his findings in *Jesus: A Revolutionary Biography* (San Francisco: HarperSanFrancisco, 1994). Less radical but still more in this camp than in line with the rest of the "third quest" is Marcus J. Borg, *Jesus: A New Vision* (San Francisco: Harper & Row, 1987).

16. E.g., see Funk, Hoover, and the Jesus Seminar, *Five Gospels*, 180, 182, 354.

17. Cf., e.g., John K. Riches, *Jesus and the Transformation of Judaism* (London: Darton, Longman & Todd, 1980); Donald A. Hagner, *The Jewish Reclamation of Jesus* (Grand Rapids: Zondervan, 1984); Geza Vermes, *The Religion of Jesus the Jew* (London: SCM, 1993).

18. John P. Meier, *A Marginal Jew: Rethinking the Historical Jesus*, vol. 1 (New York: Doubleday, 1991), 177.

19. Funk, Hoover, and the Jesus Seminar, *Five Gospels*, 32–33; cf. Funk with Smith, *Mark*, 13. For a book-length explanation of how these two stages allegedly affected a substantial body of early traditions about Jesus' sayings, see John S. Kloppenborg, *The Formation of Q* (Philadelphia: Fortress, 1987). For more standard and widely accepted perspectives on the composition of this hypothetical document (Q is the term used to

designate the material that is common to Matthew and Luke and is not in Mark), see David R. Catchpole, *The Quest for Q* (Edinburgh: Clark, 1993).

20. Larry W. Hurtado, "The Gospel of Mark: Evolutionary or Revolutionary Document?" *JSNT* 40 (1990): 15–32.

21. Burton L. Mack, *A Myth of Innocence* (Philadelphia: Fortress, 1988); idem, *The Lost Gospel: The Book of Q and Christian Origins* (San Francisco: HarperSanFrancisco, 1993).

22. Funk with Smith, *Mark*, 15. For a book-length defense of this position, see Stevan Davies, *The Gospel of Thomas and Christian Wisdom* (New York: Seabury, 1983).

23. All translations of *Thomas* are taken from *The Nag Hammadi Library in English*, 3d ed., ed. James M. Robinson (Leiden: Brill, 1988). For a balanced introduction to Gnosticism and its relevance for New Testament studies, see Robert McL. Wilson, *Gnosis and the New Testament* (Philadelphia: Fortress, 1968). For a more recent report on the "state of the art," cf. Pheme Perkins, *Gnosticism and the New Testament* (Minneapolis: Fortress, 1993).

24. For a good introduction to *Thomas* and a reflection of this early consensus, see Robert M. Grant and David N. Freedman, *The Secret Sayings of Jesus* (New York: Doubleday, 1960).

25. Robert McL. Wilson, *Studies in the Gospel of Thomas* (London: Mowbray, 1960), 73.

26. Cf. Jacques É. Ménard, *L'Évangile selon Thomas* (Leiden: Brill, 1975), 173–75.

27. Cf. Klyne Snodgrass, *The Parable of the Wicked Tenants* (Tübingen: Mohr, 1983), 41–71.

28. A point demonstrated in detail, with only slight overstatement, by Wolfgang Schrage, *Das Verhältnis des Thomas-Evangeliums zur synoptischen Tradition und zu den koptischen Evangelien-Übersetzungen* (Berlin: Töpelmann, 1964).

29. Cf. further Hans-Werner Bartsch, "Das Thomas-Evangelium und die synoptische Evangelien," *NTS* 6 (1960): 249–61.

30. Grant and Freedman, *Secret Sayings*, 20.

31. See esp. Michael Fieger, *Das Thomasevangelium: Einleitung, Kommentar und Systematik* (Münster: Aschendorff, 1991); Christopher M. Tuckett, "Thomas and the Synoptics," *NovT* 30 (1988): 132–57; and James H. Charlesworth and Craig A. Evans, "Jesus in the Agrapha and Apocryphal Gospels," in Chilton and Evans, *Studying the Historical Jesus*, 496–503 (cf. 479–95 and 503–33 for related materials).

32. Representative of this balanced perspective is Bruce Chilton, "The Gospel According to Thomas as a Source of Jesus' Teaching," in *Gospel Perspectives*, vol. 5, ed. David Wenham (Sheffield: JSOT, 1985), 155–75.

33. Meier, *Marginal Jew*, 139.

34. Stephen Neill and Tom Wright, *The Interpretation of the New Testament: 1861–1986* (Oxford: Oxford University Press, 1988), 379–403.

35. Albert Schweitzer, *The Quest of the Historical Jesus* (New York: Macmillan, 1910).

36. For the fullest treatment of what Bultmann did accept as historical, see his *History of the Synoptic Tradition* (Oxford: Blackwell, 1963).

37. Norman Perrin, *The New Testament: An Introduction* (New York: Harcourt, Brace, Jovanovich, 1974), 287–88.

38. Ben F. Meyer, *The Aims of Jesus* (London: SCM, 1979).

39. E. P. Sanders, *Jesus and Judaism* (Philadelphia: Fortress, 1985); cf. idem, *The Historical Figure of Jesus* (London: Penguin, 1993).

40. Charlesworth, *Jesus*, 131–64.

41. Richard A. Horsley, *Jesus and the Spiral of Violence* (San Francisco: Harper & Row, 1987); Gerd Theissen, *The Shadow of the Galilean* (Philadelphia: Fortress, 1987).

42. A. E. Harvey, *Jesus and the Constraints of History* (Philadelphia: Westminster, 1982). Particularly significant is his discussion of "the intelligibility of miracle" (pp. 98–119), in which he points out the differences between the accounts of Jesus' miracles and those of other wonder-working activity in the ancient world—the restraint in their narration, the focus on exorcisms in a society in which charges of sorcery would most likely discredit a person, and the consistency between the meaning ascribed to Jesus' miracles and the rest of his ministry and message.

43. See the catalogue in René Latourelle, *Finding Jesus Through the Gospels* (New York: Alba, 1979), 238–39. For more recent literature, see the various surveys of scholarship in Chilton and Evans, *Studying the Historical Jesus*.

44. Charlesworth, *Jesus*, 205; citing Sanders, *Jesus and Judaism*, 2.

45. For book-length works, see esp. Ben Witherington III, *The Christology of Jesus* (Minneapolis: Fortress, 1990); and Markus Bockmuehl, *This Jesus: Martyr, Lord, Messiah* (Edinburgh: Clark, 1994).

46. For a good overview of the progress made by the third quest, see Craig A. Evans, "Life-of-Jesus Research and the Eclipse of Mythology," *TS* 54 (1993): 3–36.

47. Cf., e.g., Donald Guthrie, *New Testament Introduction*, 4th ed. (Downers Grove, Ill.: InterVarsity Press, 1990), with D. A. Carson, Douglas J. Moo, and Leon Morris, *An Introduction to the New Testament* (Grand Rapids: Zondervan, 1992).

48. The earliest and most important of these traditions come from an early second-century Christian, Papias, quoted and endorsed ca. A.D. 300 by the church historian Eusebius.

49. For the complete collection of apocryphal gospels, see Wilhelm Schneemelcher, ed., *New Testament Apocrypha*, vol. 1 (Philadelphia: Westminster, 1991).

50. Robert H. Gundry, *Mark: A Commentary on His Apology for the Cross* (Grand Rapids: Eerdmans, 1993), 1042–43.

51. Cf. esp. Colin J. Hemer, *The Book of Acts in the Setting of Hellenistic History*, ed. Conrad H. Gempf (Tübingen: Mohr, 1989), 365–410.

52. See, e.g., Robert H. Stein, *The Synoptic Problem* (Grand Rapids: Baker, 1987).

53. For details, see Martin Hengel, *The Johannine Question* (Philadelphia: Trinity, 1990).

54. Cf. further Robin L. Fox, *The Search for Alexander* (Boston: Little, 1980).

55. See C. E. B. Cranfield, *The Gospel According to St. Mark* (Cambridge: Cambridge University Press, 1977), 285–88.

56. Ibid., 407–9.

57. See F. F. Bruce, *The Hard Sayings of Jesus* (Downers Grove, Ill.: InterVarsity Press, 1983), 109.

58. For the details of this line of argument, see Richard Bauckham, "The Delay of the Parousia," *TynBul* 31 (1980): 3–36. On the early development of Jesus' teachings as "holy words" to be carefully preserved, see J. Arthur Baird, "The Holy Word: The History and Function of the Teachings of Jesus in the Theology and Praxis of the Early Church," *NTS* 33 (1987): 585–99.

59. Cf. David Hill, *New Testament Prophecy* (London: Marshall, Morgan & Scott, 1979); and David E. Aune, *Prophecy in Early Christianity and the Ancient Mediterranean World* (Grand Rapids: Eerdmans, 1983).

60. See Birger Gerhardsson, *Memory and Manuscript* (Lund: Gleerup, 1961); Rainer Riesner, *Jesus als Lehrer* (Tübingen: Mohr, 1981).

61. See esp. A. B. Lord, *The Singer of Tales* (Cambridge, Mass.: Harvard University Press, 1960). For his application of this model to Gospel criticism, see idem, "The Gospels as Oral Traditional Literature," in *The Relationships Among the Gospels*, ed. William O. Walker, Jr. (San Antonio: Trinity University Press, 1978), 33–91.

62. See Kenneth E. Bailey, "Informal Controlled Oral Tradition and the Synoptic Gospels," *AJT* 5 (1991): 34–54.

63. Funk with Smith, *Mark*, 13–14.

64. See, respectively, Stephenson H. Brooks, *Matthew's Community: The Evidence of His Special Sayings Material* (Sheffield: JSOT, 1987); and Stephen C. Farris, *The Hymns of Luke's Infancy Narratives* (Sheffield: JSOT, 1985).

65. See, respectively, Funk with Smith, *Mark*, 16; and Robert T. Fortna, *The Fourth Gospel and Its Predecessor* (Philadelphia: Fortress, 1988), 214–16.

66. Heinz Schürmann, "Die vorösterliche Anfänge der Logientradition," in *Der historische Jesus und der kerygmatische Christus*, ed. Helmut Ristow and Karl Matthiae (Berlin: Evangelische Verlagsanstalt, 1960), 342–70.

67. Riesner, *Jesus als Lehrer*, 393, 398. Cf. also idem, "Jesus as Preacher and Teacher," in *Jesus and the Oral Gospel Tradition*, ed. Henry Wansbrough (Sheffield: JSOT, 1991), 185–210.

68. Robert H. Stein, "An Early Recension of the Gospel Traditions?" *JETS* 30 (1987): 167–83.

69. The role of "teacher" in the ancient world, including early Christianity, would have further promoted this care and correction. See esp. A. F. Zimmermann, *Die urchristlichen Lehrer* (Tübingen: Mohr, 1984).

70. A. E. Harvey, *Strenuous Commands: The Ethic of Jesus* (Philadelphia: Trinity, 1990).

71. For elaboration, see Eugene E. Lemcio, *The Past of Jesus in the Gospels* (Cambridge: Cambridge University Press, 1991).

72. Hans E. Stier, in *Moderne Exegese und historische Wissenschaft*, 152, cited by Hugo Staudinger, in *The Trustworthiness of the Gospels* (Edinburgh: Handsel, 1981), 77.

73. See, e.g., the Word Biblical, New International, Expositors' Bible, Tyndale, New American, or Pillar Commentary Series.

74. I have discussed these and numerous other examples in more detail in my book, *The Historical Reliability of the Gospels* (Downers Grove, Ill.: InterVarsity Press, 1987), 113–89.

75. Cf. further Robert Guelich, "The Gospel Genre," in *The Gospel and the Gospels*, ed. Peter Stuhlmacher (Grand Rapids: Eerdmans, 1991), 206.

76. See Hemer, *Acts*, 63–100. One of the best discussions of a how a Gospel can be both history and theology remains I. Howard Marshall, *Luke: Historian and Theologian*, rev. ed. (Grand Rapids: Zondervan, 1989).

77. Paul Merkley, "The Gospels as Historical Testimony," *EvQ* 58 (1986): 328–36.

78. A. N. Sherwin-White, *Roman Society and Roman Law in the New Testament* (Oxford: Clarendon, 1963), 187.

79. See further Craig L. Blomberg, "The Miracles as Parables," in *Gospel Perspectives*, vol. 6, ed. David Wenham and Craig Blomberg (Sheffield: JSOT, 1986), 327–59; idem, "Healing," in *Dictionary of Jesus and the Gospels*, ed. Joel B. Green, Scot McKnight, I. Howard Marshall (Downers Grove, Ill.: InterVarsity Press, 1992), 299–307.

80. Loveday Alexander, *The Preface to Luke's Gospel* (Cambridge: Cambridge University Press, 1993).

81. Terrence Callan, "The Preface of Luke-Acts and Historiography," *NTS* 31 (1985): 576–81.

82. Richard A. Burridge, *What Are the Gospels? A Comparison with Graeco-Roman Biography* (Cambridge: Cambridge University Press, 1992), 220–39.

83. Cf. my article, "To What Extent Is John Historically Reliable?" in *Perspectives on John: Method and Interpretation in the Fourth Gospel,* ed. Robert B. Sloan and Mikeal C. Parsons (Lewiston, N.Y.: Mellen, 1993), 27–56.

84. On not overestimating John's high Christology, see esp. John A. T. Robinson, *The Priority of John* (London: SCM, 1985), 343–97, although Robinson swings the pendulum too far and underestimates even what is present.

85. See Seyoon Kim, *The Son of Man as the Son of God* (Grand Rapids: Eerdmans, 1985); Chrys C. Caragounis, *The Son of Man* (Tübingen: Mohr, 1986); John J. Collins, "The Son of Man in First-Century Judaism," *NTS* 38 (1992): 448–66.

86. Cf. R. T. France, "The Worship of Jesus: A Neglected Factor in Christological Debate," in *Christ the Lord,* ed. Harold H. Rowdon (Leicester: Inter-Varsity Press, 1982), 28; with Philip B. Payne, "Jesus' Implicit Claim to Deity in His Parables," *TrinJ* n.s., 2 (1981): 3–23.

87. See Ethelbert Stauffer, "Historische Elemente im vierten Evangelium," in *Bekenntnis zur Kirche,* ed. Ernst-Heinz Amberg and Ulrich Kuhn (Berlin: Evangelische Verlagsanstalt, 1960), 33–51.

88. See the discussions of the use of external evidence in Jacques Barzun and Henry F. Graff, *The Modern Researcher* (New York: Harcourt, Brace, Jovanovich, 1977), 87–92; and Robert J. Shafer, *A Guide to Historical Method* (Homewood, Ill.: Dorsey, 1969), 137.

89. For details, see R. T. France, *The Evidence for Jesus* (Downers Grove, Ill.: InterVarsity Press, 1986). See also Craig A. Evans, "Jesus in Non-Christian Sources," in Chilton and Evans *Studying the Historical Jesus,* 443–78.

90. The key passage from Josephus (*Antiquities,* 18.63–64) has been widely discussed, because the extant texts record this Jewish historian as claiming that Jesus *was* the Messiah and *was* resurrected. But Josephus never records anything else to suggest he became a Christian, and his writings were preserved later on in Christian circles. Thus it is likely that his text has been tampered with. This has led some skeptics to dismiss his entire statement about Jesus as inauthentic, but a fair consensus is emerging that such skepticism is unfounded. Removing "non-Josephan" stylistic intrusions yields a coherent passage that Josephus himself probably wrote, disclosing something along the lines of the information we have listed. See esp. Meier, *Marginal Jew,* 56–88.

91. See the helpful chart of information in Paul Barnett, *Is the New Testament History?* (London: Hodder & Stoughton, 1986), 159–63.

92. Cf. further B. F. Harris, "Apollonius of Tyana: Fact and Fiction," *JRH* 5 (1968–69): 189–99.

93. For more details, see, e.g., Rainer Riesner, "Archaeology and Geography," in Green, McKnight, and Marshall, *Dictionary of Jesus and the Gospels,* 33–46; E. M. Blaiklock, *The Archaeology of the New Testament* (Nashville: Thomas Nelson, 1984). On the Caiaphas find, see Bockmuehl, *This Jesus,* 70–71.

94. Cf. Stewart C. Goetz and Craig L. Blomberg, "The Burden of Proof," *JSNT* 11 (1981): 39–63.

95. For details, see my *Historical Reliability,* 223–31, and the literature there cited. Cf. now esp. Michael B. Thompson, *Clothed with Christ: The Example and Teaching of Jesus in*

Romans 12.1–15.13 (Sheffield: JSOT, 1991); and David Wenham's work *Jesus and Paul* (Grand Rapids: Eerdmans, 1995).

96. See the list in Peter H. Davids, *The Epistle of James* (Grand Rapids: Eerdmans, 1982), 47–48.

97. For the following, see my *Historical Reliability*, 202–8, and the literature there cited.

98. For an introductory discussion, see Ralph P. Martin, *New Testament Foundations*, vol. 2 (Grand Rapids: Eerdmans, 1978). For a good list of criteria for recognizing traditional material embedded in letters, see Markus Barth, *Ephesians 1–3* (Garden City, N.Y.: Doubleday, 1974), 6–10.

99. One may consider in this light also the five "faithful sayings" of the Pastoral Letters (1 Tim. 1:15; 3:1; 4:9; Titus 3:8; 2 Tim. 2:11). See esp. George W. Knight III, *The Faithful Sayings in the Pastoral Epistles* (Grand Rapids: Baker, 1979).

100. In part, because it refers to "all the apostles" (v. 7) as a group that is separate from and prior to Paul's apostolate (cf. Acts 6:2). Paul's consistent concern to number himself among the apostles would have made it unlikely that he would have preserved such a distinction in terminology unless it were well-established by the time of his conversion just after Stephen's death. See Peter J. Kearney, "He Appeared to 500 Brothers (1 Cor. XV 6)," *NovT* 22 (1980): 264–84.

101. See Richard N. Longenecker, *The Christology of Early Jewish Christianity* (Naperville: Allenson, 1970).

102. For details of how this process might have worked, see esp. Larry W. Hurtado, *One God, One Lord: Early Christian Devotion and Ancient Jewish Monotheism* (Philadelphia: Fortress, 1988).

103. A book not yet available at the time of the writing of this chapter, but one that surely will be a major evangelical contribution to this already large volume of scholarship, is N. T. Wright, *Jesus and the Victory of God* (Minneapolis: Fortress, 1994). Two works, potentially just as significant, became available only in the final stages of editing: Volume 2 of John Meier's *A Marginal Jew* (New York: Doubleday, 1994), and Ben Witherington III, *Jesus the Sage* (Minneapolis, Fortress, 1994).

Chapter 2

WHO IS JESUS?
AN INTRODUCTION TO JESUS STUDIES

SCOT MCKNIGHT

Scot McKnight (Ph.D., University of Nottingham) is
Associate Professor of New Testament at Trinity Evangelical
Divinity School. He is author of *Interpreting the Synoptic
Gospels*, *Galatians* in the NIV Application Commentary series,
and *A Light Among the Gentiles: Jewish Missionary Activity of
Second Temple Judaism*, and is editor of *Introducing New
Testament Interpretation* and *Dictionary of Jesus and the Gospels*.

I read books about Jesus—lots of them, because lots of them are published annually. In a corner of my study I have two bookcases, from floor to ceiling, each one about three feet wide; both cases are now almost filled with books about Jesus written during the modern era. Because I think historically, these books are arranged in chronological order by publication date. The first book is the infamous book of H. S. Reimarus, entitled *Fragments*.[1] The last book right now is N. T. Wright's *Who Was Jesus?*[2] The first book was published in a series of seven fragments in 1778; the last one was published in 1993. In other words, Reimarus raised the questions, and scholars have not answered them, in spite of having over two centuries to do so.

This scholarly quest and fascination appear to be gaining momentum and interest. I find each book about Jesus interesting, stimulating, and challenging. If it is reasonable to expect books about Jesus to adopt the broader trends of scholarship and, inevitably, modern culture, it is also a joy to discover that because scholars work so hard at understanding Jesus, something fresh is nearly always at hand. In fact, an observation to make about Jesus books is that virtually every writer is pro-Jesus; everyone enlists Jesus in his or her camp.[3]

The most recent splash in this nearly endless ocean of books was caused when the Jesus Seminar officially threw their findings about Jesus into the water.[4] To evaluate their conclusions and the Jesus they propose, it is important for us to back up a few paces to gain a perspective on the history of Jesus studies by sketching a few of the essential pictures that have been drawn of Jesus since the days of Reimarus.

But does all of this matter? Is this debate nothing more than another example of sophistication, of pedanticism, of intellectualism? Nothing could be further from the truth! What we have before our eyes and in the reading of the public is what could be the most critical issue of our day. Who is Jesus? If the current views of Jesus that I discuss below are accurate, millions of Christians have been deluded into thinking that Jesus was and is their Savior. They have bought into a myth that has no more roots in reality than the Wizard of Oz. They have trusted in a Christ who is not there and assumed a faith that is an illusion. Millions of Christians, throughout the world and throughout the history of the church, have begun their day, sustained their work, and laid their heads down at night in constant prayer to Jesus, the Lord; if that Jesus did not exist, then their faith is a psychological trick and their prayers are no more than fanciful coping mechanisms. Their hope for life with God is a vapor trail that was created in thin air.

In the following pages I will first survey the history of the quests for Jesus in order to set before the reader some general categories. I will then survey three recent approaches to Jesus and his mission and point out lines of appreciation. Finally, I will propose a short defense of the traditional Jesus, suggesting that Jesus was much more than these approaches permit.

The Quests for Jesus

Fundamental to the entire discussion about Jesus is the distinction drawn, as early as Reimarus, between the historical Jesus and the Christ of faith. The "historical Jesus" (or "Jesus of history" or "Jesus of Nazareth") is the Jesus whom modern-day historians hope to recover when they use scientifically designed historical methods. This Jesus, it is to be understood, is the one who really existed and is to one degree or another different from the Christ of faith. The "Christ of faith" is the Jesus Christ in whom people have believed throughout the history of the church and whose nature and person is discussed in Christian theology. Put differently, the "historical Jesus" (e.g., a Jewish sage) is much different from the "Christ of faith" (e.g., the second person of the Trinity) because the historical Jesus was much less than the Christ of faith.

One way of understanding this history is to realize that scholars have been trying to find just how much was originally there within Jesus (e.g., did the historical Jesus think he was actually the Messiah? the Son of God? in some sense divine?) and how much was attributed to him by later Christian theologians, including the authors of our Gospels.

When I was doing my doctorate at the University of Nottingham, our family visited Edwinstowe, advertised as the heart of the Sherwood Forest, erstwhile home of Robin Hood. We happened upon a bookstore in which I found a fascinating book entitled *Robin Hood*.[5] What intrigued me about this piece of history was that its purpose was to find the "historical Robin Hood" beneath the centuries of layers of myths attributed to him and about him. My first questions were about the author's methods (I was, after all, doing a doctorate in the Synoptic Gospels and was concerned about historical methods) and then only secondarily about his conclusion—which, by the way, make many skeptics in the historical Jesus discussion look overly generous. Holt's conclusion was that most, if not all, of the events and ideas about Robin Hood were later projections and that very little could actually be known about the "historical Robin Hood." In parallel, then, to our concerns about Jesus, there is a distinction between the "historical Robin Hood" and the "Robin Hood of our storybooks."

Discussions about Jesus have been divided into three general periods, as my friend Craig Blomberg noted in the preceding chapter. First, there is the period we might call the "Old Quest," beginning with Reimarus (around 1775) and extending to Rudolf Bultmann (around 1920). This period is noted by a concern with the religious personality of Jesus, the environments in which he was raised and how they influenced his beliefs, and the desire to throw off the veneer with which Christian theologians had covered him. This historical-critical quest climaxed in part with the beautifully written book of Albert Schweitzer,[6] whose contention that Jesus was a misguided Jewish visionary has gone down, with rare exceptions, as an assured result in the history of Jesus studies.[7]

During this period, studies about the historical Jesus were important because scholars believed theology rested ultimately on what could be demonstrated as historically reliable. That is, the theological framework rested on a historical foundation. And, it was argued, historians could get back to the real Jesus. Albert Schweitzer's book uniquely demonstrated that, in the history of scholarship on Jesus, one could demonstrate that, when a picture of Jesus was fully drawn by any given scholar, that picture so resembled the scholar himself that the entire project became a perverse comedy. Everybody simply claimed Jesus for his own cause.

With Rudolf Bultmann a new angle was attempted. He argued that theology did *not* rest on the vagaries of historical reconstruction. Rather, to demand that our theology be founded on history was theologically perverse. Furthermore, he contended that what we can actually know about Jesus and the development of his religious personality was so minimal that we could never build anything of any consequence theologically.[8] Bultmann's legacy is his thoroughgoing skepticism about both the possibility of finding Jesus and the sufficiency of our methods in finding who he was. As a result, this period of study has been described quite accurately as the "No Quest" period. That is, there was no quest for the historical Jesus because the historical Jesus could not be found; even if he could be, it would not matter. Faith was not dependent on historically verifiable items.

One of Bultmann's students, Ernst Käsemann, stood up at an annual gathering of former Bultmann students in 1953 and proposed, contrary to Bultmann, that their methods[9] could lead them to Jesus, and he went on to suggest that such conclusions did matter. This began what has been called the "New Quest" (some call it the "Third Quest"[10]). While there is clearly a tempered enthusiasm for what scholars can actually discover and while theological reasoning is only partly rooted in historical reconstruction, it is this phase of the quest that currently dominates scholarship. More importantly, the fashion designers of the Jesus Seminar are heavily indebted to the scholarship of the post-Bultmannian New-Questers.[11] In all fairness, I must mention that a great variety of scholarship can be located in this New Quest, from conservative historians like C. F. D. Moule, J. D. G. Dunn, and N. T. Wright to the more radical types like J. M. Robinson, R. W. Funk, and B. L. Mack.[12]

Tom Wright, in his useful review of recent literature about Jesus,[13] uses the image of a ditch that I will appropriate to illustrate these three quests for the historical Jesus. The effect of the Old Quest (Reimarus to Schweitzer) for Jesus was the digging of a massive ditch, dividing the historical Jesus from the Christ of faith. From Schweitzer until Käsemann the ditch remained unfilled, and any bridge that was attempted was hacked down in the name of uselessness. But Käsemann constructed a rope across the great ditch. Many scholars have been traveling across the ditch, back and forth and back and forth, so that the rope is no longer strong enough to hold the traffic. Therefore, scholars are now building bridges to span the ditch because more and more are convinced that the historical Jesus—what he did, what he said, why he did what he did, etc.—matters for Christian faith. In fact, recent studies contend that the Christian faith is rooted in the historical Jesus and that apart from those roots there is no Christian faith.

In this all-too-brief survey, it is unfortunately impossible to be nuanced; furthermore, we have had to be simplistic to get a full picture in view. In what follows I will sketch three dominant views of Jesus today, each of which emerges from the "New Quest" period. However, while it is fair to say that each is in some sense a part of this New Quest, each scholar interacts with the entire scope of scholarship (since Reimarus, at least) and each scholar often extends the plank of history in his or her own way.

Jesus: Which One Shall We Choose?

Like a smorgasbord dinner, the options for moderns today with respect to Jesus are numerous. How can this be, since there is only one Jesus? Simply put, the various reconstructions offered by scholars in the history of this discussion amount to different Jesuses. Some skeptics have said there are as many Jesuses as there are Jesus scholars! While this is clearly an overstatement, there are several major options. I will dip into the literature for three of them: Jesus the Sage, Jesus the Religious Genius, and Jesus the Social Revolutionary. Each of these portraits of Jesus fastens upon an important element of Jesus' life, and each thus presents something about Jesus that is vital for our understanding. Accordingly, there is no room for doubting that Jesus was a profoundly wise teacher, that he was a man of deep religious experience, or that he said and did things that had massive social or political ramifications. *What I will contest about each of these is that the picture drawn of Jesus from this emphasis is inadequate for describing the whole of Jesus' life and mission.*

A common thread that unites nearly all pictures of Jesus today is the refreshing rediscovery of the Jewishness of Jesus.[14] This historical anchoring of Jesus into the Jewish world of his day is the most important development in modern studies about Jesus. But this insight has only permitted a marginal congruence of views about Jesus.

I add that the particular reconstruction one chooses for Jesus matters greatly, both for one's belief system and for how one actualizes the Christian life. If, for example, we hold that Jesus was originally a peasant involved in a peasant revolt against the Jerusalem (and Roman) authorities, and if we think Jesus is significant for our lives as Christians, then the agenda for the Christian is to fight with might and mane against contemporary social injustices. Let us not pretend that our depiction of Jesus does not matter, for the picture we conceive of Jesus unfolds neatly into a blueprint for the Christian life.[15]

And let us not pretend that those of us who are evangelicals have no depiction of Jesus because we believe the Gospels are historically reliable. Actually, each of us constructs Jesus the best that we can—by reading, listening, and following him. If we were all honest and if we each submitted our pictures of Jesus to the acid-test of the evidence of the Gospels, we would each discover that our depictions are often nothing other than a reflection of our hopes and a projection of ourselves and our beliefs onto Jesus—at least in part. Our goal, as honest readers of the Gospels and genuine followers of Jesus, is to find the real Jesus and to submit to that Jesus. This, no doubt, involves the surrender of our own images of Jesus.[16]

Jesus the Sage

This attractive picture of Jesus narrows its focus on him to that of a wise teacher, a religious sage, a pious spinner of tales and proverbs. This is essentially the view of the Jesus Seminar and is as old as skepticism itself. Here we have a Jesus who has been virtually stripped of his uniqueness, his deity, his ability to work miracles, his atoning death, and his resurrection. At the same time he is tragically mistaken with respect to his predictions about his return and the arrival of the glorious kingdom of God. But, it is argued, once we get over his tragic humanness and see that he was no different than any other human being, we then discover that these "supernatural pieces to the puzzle" are really later myths, ideas foisted onto Jesus because the early church loved and worshiped him so much that only some kind of deification could contain their ideas. Once we have done this subtracting, we will find out just why Jesus was so "bloomin' attractive" to so many. That is, we discover that Jesus was a *wise sage.*

First, Jesus *told parables.* Surely the most memorable and distinctive trait of Jesus' teaching style was the way he told stories and parables. Few can contest the shrewdness of Jesus' telling others that the kingdom of God is like new wine poured into old wineskins (Mark 2:21–22)[17] in order to illustrate the complexity and power of his views of what God's performance among humans was actually like. And Jesus told a parable about the sower (Mark 4:3–8), which highlights that people respond in various ways to his message. Jesus' comparison of the kingdom to a mustard seed is similar: though it is made up now of the nobodies, eventually it will conquer social forces (Mark 4:30–32).

This small sketch of Jesus' parables demonstrates that his wisdom was subversive, for it attacked conventional wisdom and cultural norms. That the kingdom was comprised of nobodies is certainly unusual (though not unknown), and that Jesus' new ideas could not be contained within the parameters of the old system is provocative. What Jesus asked his hearers to do was to listen to his stories; in listening, they were being invited to understand reality and the religious-social world of his day in a new, unconventional way.

Second, Jesus *offered memorable one-liners into typical situations.* These one-liners are frequently arresting and stunning, so much so that to memorize them is to risk misunderstanding, for they have meaning only in their embedded context. No one can memorize "Let the dead bury their own dead" (Matt. 8:22) as a general rule of life, but few have not been challenged by Jesus' call to follow him whatever the cost. From the same passage, the call to follow him carries the piercing warning that foxes have dens and birds have nests but Jesus, the Son of Man, may have no place even to lay down his head at night (8:20). Who has not been warned about preoccupation with minor details when reminded that Jesus warned the Pharisees of straining out a gnat while gulping down a camel (23:24)?

Contrary to conventional wisdom, Jesus blessed the poor and the hungry (Luke 6:20–21) and urged his followers to love their enemies (6:27). I know of almost no one who does not understand "turning the other cheek" (6:29) or the importance of removing the plank from one's eye before examining the specks of dust in others' eyes (6:41–42).

Third, Jesus' wise sayings were _countercultural_. One of the most interesting, if not humorous, teachings of Jesus concerns the friend at midnight. Jesus told the story of a friend who stopped over at his neighbor's house at midnight to acquire a loaf of bread for a guest. He goes on to relate how the sleeping man did not want to get up but, to avoid being shamed in his culture and neighborhood, did finally get up and give him the bread (Luke 11:5–8). What is arresting here is that Jesus anchors God's answering prayer in God's desire to avoid shame among the nations, not because the neighbor (Israel) is his friend.[18]

The parable of the Good Samaritan is a similar piece of unconventional wisdom. Here Jesus holds out as supreme example a man who is unclean; at the same time, he castigates two "clean" classes as disgustingly unclean because of their refusal to act compassionately (Luke 10:30–37). I can think of no more unconventional a piece of wisdom than when Jesus declared that his true family members were those who, like him, did the will of God (Matt. 12:48–50).

Fourth, Jesus taught about God and the kingdom, _not about himself or his death or resurrection_. Fundamental to the sketch of Jesus as found in the Jesus Seminar is that Jesus taught about God, the kingdom, and social ethics, but not about himself. Thus, Funk and Hoover can say: "The Christian inclination to put its own affirmations on the lips of Jesus here overrides the distant memory that Jesus did not make such claims on his own behalf."[19] They argue that if the evidence is tested carefully, what emerges from the laboratory is a Jesus who taught wise things, not a Jesus who, as Son of God, came to give his life as a ransom and who, after his intended crucifixion, was raised by God as a vindication of his life. In short, anything that smacks of the orthodox view of Jesus as the Savior is a later Christianizing of the story and not actual things said by the historical Jesus. That story is the Christ of faith, not the historical Jesus.

In sum, the picture of Jesus here is one of a masterful sage who utters pithy sayings and tells artful stories. He is good and wise, and his sayings are full of wit and wisdom for our day as well. As is the case with the next two pictures of Jesus, I do not doubt for a moment that something true and valuable is being said of

Jesus in this depiction. I suggest, however, that this is far from being the whole story of Jesus, and half a story of Jesus is not fair to Jesus.

Jesus the Religious Genius

Since the days of Schleiermacher (1768–1834), many scholars have focused on the religious life of Jesus. Where Schleiermacher spoke of Jesus' "consciousness of utter dependence on God," modern scholars are speaking of Jesus' religious genius, of his unique experience of the kingdom of God, or of his special experience of God. In modern discussions, there are at least two emphases in seeing Jesus as a religious genius: (1) those focusing on his religious experience, and (2) those focusing on his eschatological enthusiasm.

Religious Experience

This view of Jesus focuses not on his role as Savior or Lord, but on his religious experience as the foundation of his ideas, mission, and success. He was, in other words, a holy man, a sacred person, a spirit person, a man who drew people to himself and his ideas by virtue of his integrity and superior experience. In his presence, people knew something was different, something was utterly real; there was a numinous quality about him that made people both want to be near him and away from him.

Jesus truly was a religious man. The normal features of his intense religious fervor can be inferred from the records about his life. Jesus *prayed* frequently (Luke 5:16) and fervently (Mark 1:35; 6:46), even all night (Luke 6:12). His baptism and transfiguration were accompanied by prayer (Luke 3:21; 9:28–29). In fact, Luke tells us that Jesus' prayers were so noticeable that his disciples asked him to teach them how to pray (Luke 11:1). The distinguishing characteristic of Jesus' prayers was that he addressed God as *Abba* (the Aramaic term for "father"; cf. Matt. 6:9; 11:25–26; Mark 14:36). Scholars have found a surprising and perhaps unique degree of intimacy with God in this form of address; at the minimum, it reflects how Jesus experienced God.[20]

Probably in conjunction with his prayers, Jesus *fasted* (cf. Matt. 4:1–11; cf. 6:16–18; 9:14–15). He also had *visions*. For example, he saw Satan fall like lightning (Luke 10:18), and the heavens opened up and the Spirit descended on him (Matt. 3:16–17); some have classed both Jesus' temptation (Luke 4:1–13) and transfiguration (Matt. 17:1–8) as visionary experiences. A decisive component of Jesus' religious experience was the *miraculous*. He performed exorcisms (Matt. 12:22–37; Mark 1:21–28; 5:1–20) and healed many (Matt. 8:1–17; 9:1–8), not to mention the so-called nature miracles (8:23–27; 15:29–39). All in all, Jesus was a religious man with all the traits of a religious genius.

A notable proponent of this view of Jesus is Marcus Borg,[21] himself a deeply religious man who believes in the spirit world.[22] Borg contends that we cannot understand anything about Jesus until we recognize his fundamental nature as a spirit person. That is to say, Jesus was "a person to whom the sacred is an experiential reality."[23] As such, Jesus both experienced more than the tangible world and mediated this sacred experience to others. Borg finds the experience of Jesus as the foundation for Jesus' view of God as a compassionate being and for the wisdom he was able to proclaim. True to its aim, Borg's work shows the significance of Jesus as spirit person for Christian life today.

This focus on the religious experience of Jesus, whether rooted in the so-called "charismatic events" of Jesus' life (baptism, temptation, transfiguration, exorcisms, and prayers), in his address of God as "Abba," or in his personal charisma of generating a great following, has been a singular note in the history of Jesus research. In the late 1930s T. W. Manson lectured and wrote about Jesus and the kingdom of God. One of his striking notes about Jesus was that the foundation of his message about the kingdom was his experience of God as the Father. In essence, Manson presented a Jesus who experienced the Father and whose mission in the world was to lead others into that same experience of God as the Father.[24] Once again we find the twin themes of this approach to Jesus: Jesus was a man of profound religious experience, and his life was shaped by seeking to lead others into the same experience.

Eschatological Religion

A second type of portrait of Jesus as a religious genius orients itself around his view of eschatology and how that view shaped his religious life. While the emphasis on Jesus' eschatology has been central to the quest for the historical Jesus, especially since Schweitzer, some more recent treatments have sought to wed Jesus' religious experience to his eschatology. A good example of this is Geza Vermes's recent completion of a trilogy of books about Jesus.[25]

Vermes shares the view of a multitude of scholars, taking their cues from Matthew 10:23; Mark 9:1; 13:30, who find in Jesus a belief that the kingdom of God was imminent.[26] These scholars argue that Jesus' religiosity was so absorbed by his eschatology that he could never have entertained the notion of a church, a movement established by him with the intention of continuing long into the future. It follows, then, that ethics became predominant in Jesus' religion, and that these ethics were "emergency ethics"—for a short period until the end came. Thus, the "religion of Jesus the Jew is a rare, possibly unique, manifestation of undiluted eschatological enthusiasm."[27] Because to Jesus the kingdom was imminent, his religion developed a high degree of individualism, emphasizing the present and its bearing on the kingdom, as well as the undiluted commitment required of those who prepare themselves for the kingdom (understood as commitment and the imitation of God).

In spite of Borg's claim that the eschatological Jesus has become "very much a minority position,"[28] this view of Jesus persists today in the majority of critical scholarship. Jesus is continually understood as an eschatological enthusiast and an apocalyptic, and his ethics, beliefs about God, and warnings about judgment for not responding to his message are all derived from his eschatology—so much so, some say, that hardly anything remains of relevance for our day.

Jesus the Social Revolutionary[29]

We turn now to a third popular presentation of Jesus—the revolutionary Jesus. "Revolutionary," of course, has more than one connotation. While some scholars have argued that Jesus was essentially a political Zealot, the trend in modern scholarship today is to see Jesus as a countercultural social prophet who proclaimed a new way of living, one that broke down the conventional borders and boundaries of Jewish and Roman culture.

Perhaps the easiest place to begin here is with the well-known writer, John Dominic Crossan.[30] His own words tell it all:

> The historical Jesus was a *peasant Jewish Cynic.* . . . His strategy, implicitly for himself and explicitly for his followers, was the combination of *free healing and common eating,* a religious and economic egalitarianism that negated alike and at once the hierarchical and patronal normalcies of Jewish religion and Roman power. And, lest he himself be interpreted as simply the new broker of a new God, he moved on constantly, settling down neither at Nazareth nor at Capernaum. He was neither broker nor mediator but, somewhat paradoxically, the announcer that neither should exist between humanity and divinity or between humanity and itself. Miracle and parable, healing and eating were calculated to force individuals into unmediated physical and spiritual contact with one another. He announced, in other words, the unmediated or brokerless Kingdom of God.[31]

Unlike John the Baptist, who was an apocalyptic prophet, Jesus was absorbed by an eschatology that led to world-negation, much like the culture-denying and ruthlessly critical Cynics punctuating the Roman landscape. For example, Jesus' biting words against family are Cynic-like (Matt. 10:34–36; Mark 3:31–35). What Jesus proposed in his cultural critique was "open commensality," or eating with people of all kinds without social distinctions (cf. Luke 14:15–24). Whereas eating with one another in the ancient Jewish world always reflected the social customs and hierarchies of the day, Jesus' "open commensality" refused such distinctions. This kind of egalitarianism is exactly what the kingdom of God, as taught by Jesus, was about.

Furthermore, Jesus' healings were hardly physical restorations; rather, they were resocializations of people who had been excluded. All of these actions and teachings of Jesus, then, are borderline acts of resistance to the orders of the day, and this vision of a brokerless society, where persons relate to God and to others without mediation, is what Jesus preached. He died a martyr's death; he was not raised from the tomb; his death was not atoning. Those ideas are later Christian impositions onto the original story of a wandering Jewish Cynic peasant who dared to think of a better society.

Along the same lines of thinking but with sufficiently differing orientations, Richard Horsley has proposed that we learn to think of Jesus more along the lines of a social critic,[32] fighting a serious war against priestly authorities and Roman impostors. Jesus was a social revolutionary who got his ideas from the apocalyptic milieu in which he was raised. His vision was that God would bring about an ultimate political revolution, a transformation of the social conditions, and in so doing would restore Israel and end the spiral of violence in Palestine.

Jesus' specific actions were designed to bring about, in a nonviolent manner, an egalitarian movement among the peasants to replace the breakdown of patriarchal oppression (e.g., Matt. 10:34–37; Mark 12:18–27) and the necessary social conditions that would anticipate God's completion of the political revolution. Furthermore, Jesus rejected the priestly institutions of Judea (cf. Matt. 17:24–27). His demands of discipleship fit in with this theme: the call to a social revolution allowed no time for dawdling and half-heartedness. Everything had to be cast aside to follow Jesus and to enter into the coming revolution (Luke 9:62).

In essence, these two views of Jesus as a social revolutionary are alike, even if one dips Jesus into the paint of Cynicism and the other into the hues of social revolutionary movements in Palestine. Both see Jesus as involved primarily at the socio-political level; neither finds the genius of Jesus in his religious experience or in his atoning death; both present a Jesus who is strangely similar to the currents of our modern social impulses.

While it is perhaps inappropriate to offer sweeping criticisms of scholars whose work I respect and from whom I have learned a great deal, I must say that the above treatments of Jesus are unfair in that each presentation limits the evidence of the Gospels to a handful of sayings or events and builds an entire picture of Jesus primarily from one strand of the Gospel tradition. Yes, Jesus was a wise sage and a deeply religious man, and his teachings were undoubtedly more socially revolutionary than many evangelicals imagine; each of these portraits says something truthful about Jesus. At the bare minimum, they need to be combined for a fuller presentation.

My fundamental disagreement with each of them is that *such a Jesus would never have been crucified, would never have drawn the fire that he did, would never have commanded the following that he did, and would never have created a movement that still shakes the world.* A Jesus who went around saying wise and witty things would not have been threatening enough to have been crucified during Passover when he was surrounded by hundreds who liked him. A Jesus who was a religious genius who helped people in their relationship with God and was kind, compassionate, and gentle would not have been crucified either. A social revolutionary would have been crucified (and this partly explains Jesus' death, in my view), but it is doubtful that such a revolutionary would have given birth to a church that was hardly a movement of social revolution. And if in the process of surviving, this movement had to shave off the socially revolutionary bits of Jesus, it is amazing that they decided to connect themselves, even root themselves, into a person who was a social revolutionary at heart. No, these pictures of Jesus will not do.

Who, Then, Is Jesus?

Who, then, is Jesus? A daunting question—especially after simply tasting the smorgasbord options to modern readers about Jesus in the pages above. In what follows I will sketch out a view of Jesus that, first of all, begins with evidence taken by most scholars to be reasonably authentic,[33] and secondly, is traditional enough to be considered classically orthodox. I will begin with some introductory remarks about actions in general and then proceed to analyze four specific actions of Jesus. I will then supplement this survey with a look at the "I have come" sayings of Jesus. Finally, I will look at the claims of Jesus.

The Actions of Jesus

How do we find out what Jesus was about? What was his goal? What were his intentions? Where do we begin? I will use an analogy. How would you try to find out if your neighbor was running for a mayoral office? Depending on your personality and your comfort level of invading someone else's private life, you might approach her (or him) and just ask. But you could also watch her (or his) behavior. Is she seeking pledges? Is she garnering votes? Is she applying for the position? This latter approach seeks to determine a person's intentions and goals on the basis of actions. Such is a fruitful method for discerning a person's orientation and intentions because behavior is often the best clue to discerning what a person is up to.

Elizabeth Anscombe, in her classic little book *Intention*, sought to answer the question of how to discern a person's intentions and concluded:

> Well, if you want to say at least some true things about a man's intentions, you will have a strong chance of success if you mention what he actually did or is doing. For whatever else he may intend, or whatever may be his intentions in doing what he does, the greater number of the things which you would say straight off a man did or was doing, will be things he intends. . . . we are interested, not just in a man's intention *of* doing what he does, but in his intention *in* doing it, and this can very often be seen from seeing what he does.

What I propose to do below is look at some things Jesus did, infer from them what he intended, and in a logical progression, infer items about the mission and person of Jesus.

Jesus calls twelve apostles: A new people

The Synoptic Gospels record Jesus' appointing and sending out twelve of his followers as special ambassadors in ministry (Matt. 9:35–11:1; Mark 3:13–19; 6:7–11; Luke 9:1–5). Furthermore, Jesus promises these twelve a special role in the coming end times (Matt. 19:28). Why did Jesus segregate twelve into a special group and not five, seven, nine, ten, or fifteen? The answer is not hard to discern. If Jesus called twelve to be apostles, then it follows that he thought they would be the new leaders, the new tribal heads as it were, for the restoration of Israel. And if this Israel is to be understood as the people of God in the last days whom Jesus brings into existence, then it follows that Jesus appoints twelve to be the leaders of this new people.

It was widely believed in Jesus' day that the lost tribes of Israel would be restored in the last days; and it was well known that the lost tribes would need new tribal leaders. Into this bed of hope Jesus placed his new disciples as the new shepherds for the new Israel. Note also that Jesus did not number himself in the Twelve; he was distinct from this group. This indicates, in my judgment, that he saw himself as superior to this group—its founder and leader.

Jesus performs miracles: A significant person

Scholars of all persuasions today contend, from one angle or another, that Jesus did perform some stupendous acts.[34] In fact, the Gospel accounts witness to Jesus' ability to exorcise demons and heal in every strand and at every layer. Mark 1:15, which may well be a Markan summary of Jesus' ministry (cf. Matt. 4:17; Luke 4:15), sounds the opening notes of Jesus' ministry: " 'The time has come,' he said. 'The kingdom of God is near. Repent and believe the good news!' " Jesus' message and ministry revolved around God, his kingdom and its power, and the response of faith and obedience to his call to the kingdom.[35] One essential feature of his ministry was his healing and restoring of people. When John the Baptist queried whether Jesus was the Messiah or not, Jesus replied, "Go back and report to John what you hear and see: The blind receive sight, the lame walk, those who have leprosy are cured, the deaf hear, the dead are raised, and the good news is preached to the poor" (Matt. 11:2–5).

Fundamental to understanding this charge of Jesus is that he saw his miraculous cures and the wondrous events of his ministry as fulfillments of prophecy. Three passages from Isaiah confirm this:

In that day the deaf will hear the words of the scroll,
and out of gloom and darkness
the eyes of the blind will see.
Once more the humble will rejoice in the LORD;
the needy will rejoice in the Holy One of Israel. (Isa. 29:18–19)

Then will the eyes of the blind be opened
and the ears of the deaf unstopped.

> Then will the lame leap like a dear,
>> and the mute tongue shout for joy. (Isa. 35:5–6)

> The Spirit of the Sovereign LORD is on me,
>> because the LORD has anointed me
>> to preach good news to the poor. (Isa. 61:1)

Put differently, what Isaiah predicted as signs of salvation when the kingdom of God dawned for the restoration of Israel, Jesus saw as taking place in his own ministry. Furthermore, Jesus connects these actions with the presence of the Spirit of God in his ministry (Matt. 12:28; Luke 11:20): "But if I drive out demons by the Spirit of God, then the kingdom of God has come upon you."

In summary, Jesus saw his miraculous cures and marvelous acts as evidence that he, Jesus of Galilee, was bringing the kingdom of God to bear on the people who responded to his message and mission. God's new people who followed Jesus were following what can only be described as a significant person. Pockets of Judaism knew of only one person for whom such a ministry would be notable: the Messiah. From the connection of Jesus with the Twelve and the eschatological nature of his miraculous deeds we can derive, at a bare minimum, the insight that Jesus should be seen as the end-time agent of God, the inaugurator of the kingdom of God.

Jesus sits at table with the unlikely: Pardon for the new people

Perhaps the most distinctive feature of Jesus' ministry, seized upon by nearly every scholar of Jesus,[36] is what Crossan calls "open commensality"—Jesus' regular practice of table fellowship with the unlikely. It was a common jibe by outsiders that Jesus shared a table with sinners, tax collectors, whores, and other social undesirables: "The Son of Man came eating and drinking, and they say, 'Here is a glutton and a drunkard, a friend of tax collectors and "sinners" ' " (Matt. 11:19).[37] Thus, when Jesus sat at table after his calling of Matthew (Mark 2:14–17), he was rejected, insulted, and questioned.

If Jesus knew that his regular practice of table fellowship with nobodies was provocative, or even inexcusable for certain Jewish authorities of purity, why did he do it? To begin with, eating with someone was an act of social integration, and the Jewish world, as with most ancient cultures, was a society rooted in purity boundaries, whether those boundaries were moral (e.g., adultery, murder, or theft), social (e.g., classes, rank, or power), or bodily (e.g., bodily fluids).[38] To eat with people of a different rank or class, to eat with murderers, or to eat with the unclean was to defile oneself and accept their status as either acceptable or equal to one's own. Thus, eating with such people was taboo and unacceptable.

This means that Jesus' decision to eat with undesirables was designed to form an "open commensality," a radical egalitarianism, or to break down the conventional wisdom of boundaries in Jewish culture. He was breaking down boundaries between people, tearing down the walls of division, and forming a society rooted in other principles. By eating with sinners, Jesus accepted them and shared his life with them.

In addition, sharing the table in Judaism, and especially in the case of Jesus, was not simply a social action; it had a religious dimension. It is well known that Jewish meals were religious: there were prayers and covenantal blessings. As an extension of table fellowship with Jesus, the early church developed the Lord's Supper, and this Supper was rooted more in the regular table fellowship of Jesus than in the institution of the Last Supper during Passion week (Mark 14:22–25; Luke 22:15–20). Notice how the early church broke bread "daily," not weekly or monthly or quarterly (Acts 2:42–47); this constant fellowship with one another was rooted in the constant fellowship with Jesus prior to the resurrection.

A religious context for the meal forces us to see in it a resolute religious action on Jesus' part. We are not far from the mark, then, to think that in sharing table with others, Jesus was visibly demonstrating forgiveness of God, acceptance by God, and fellowship with God for those who ate bread and drank wine with Jesus.

Finally, table fellowship with Jesus was probably also an anticipation of the final feast of God. Note what Jesus said in Matthew 8:11: "I say to you that many will come from the east and the west, and will take their places at the feast with Abraham, Isaac and Jacob in the kingdom of heaven." In addition to the final state being compared to a meal (Matt. 22:1–14), we should observe that one of Jesus' last promises to his specially chosen ones was that he would not eat with them again until he ate with them again in the kingdom (26:29). I take it as probable, then, that Jesus saw in the regular course of table fellowship with his followers an anticipation of the final meal in the glorious kingdom of God—an anticipation of final forgiveness and full acceptance with God.

Jesus cleanses the temple: Purification of the old system

Recently, scholars have been debating whether the action of Jesus in the temple (Matt. 21:1–17) was a purification of the temple from the pollutions caused by religious obstacles and exploitations, an acting out of its future destruction, or nothing more than a symbolic demonstration of the destruction of the temple with its probable restoration shortly thereafter. I am of the view that the action was both an act of purification as well as a symbolic action of its future destruction.[39] What concerns us here is that this action was preceded by the provocative public entry of Jesus into Jerusalem. Together, the entry and cleansing form a whole picture of Jesus: He is the Messiah who enters Jerusalem, warns of judgment, and calls people into the kingdom (notice the miracles at Matt. 21:14). In the words of Ben Meyer, "The entry into Jerusalem and the cleansing of the temple constituted a messianic demonstration, a messianic critique, a messianic fulfilment event, and a sign of the messianic restoration of Israel."[40]

To summarize: the various actions of Jesus demonstrate that he intended to call forth a new people with the Twelve as its leaders; that he saw himself as the agent of God (the Messiah), who inaugurated the kingdom as made visible in his marvelous deeds; that he surrounded himself with nobodies and invited anyone who responded to his call to typical Jewish meals, demonstrating God's acceptance and pardon; and that in entering Jerusalem and cleansing the temple he was showing himself to be the Messiah who would restore Israel by purifying God's temple. Who then is this man?

The "I Have Come to . . ." Sayings

One of the more interesting ways Jesus spoke was in a stereotyped formula: "I have come. . . ." Whether Jesus was simply clarifying something about himself (which is less likely) or responding to overt comments and criticisms (which seems more likely), Jesus occasionally announced the essence of his mission by using this phrase.

I mention six of them. Jesus said that he did not come to abolish the law but to fulfill it (Matt. 5:17); that he did not come to call the righteous but to call sinners to forgiveness (Mark 2:17); that he did not come to bring familial peace but familial discord (Matt. 10:34–35; Luke 12:49–51); that he came to eat and drink with the nobodies (Matt. 11:19); that he came to give his life as a ransom for many (Mark 10:45); and that he came to seek and save the lost (Luke 19:10).

Jesus had a robust self-consciousness and a clear sense of being called by God to do what he did (preach the kingdom, heal, include many in God's family, warn of judgment, etc.). Furthermore, Jesus saw his mission in various images and terms. When put together, these "I have come" sayings evince a clear sense of the intention of Jesus' mission: to bring and offer end-time salvation (the kingdom of God) to any who responded to him. If we combine the eucharistic words of Jesus (Luke 22:15–20) with the ransom saying (Mark 10:45), we must imagine that Jesus saw himself inaugurating the kingdom of God through his life, his ministry, his message, and his atoning death.

Perhaps the most distressing element of modern pictures of Jesus is that they portray the death of Jesus (understood in orthodoxy as an atonement) as tangential to his mission and to his church. Thus, Marcus Borg relegates this understanding of Jesus (which he calls the priestly picture) as having been subverted by both Jesus and the New Testament itself.[41] What he fails to recognize is that the "old priestly story" is replaced by Jesus and in the New Testament by a "new priestly story," with Jesus as the climactic sacrifice.[42]

The Claims of Jesus

I finish this chapter by looking at some of the self-claims of Jesus. Who did he say he was, and what do these statements mean? I begin with *Jesus' demand for others to follow him*. At a bare minimum this is a bit "cheeky"—to ask others to follow you is to invite criticism and to set yourself up as a model of behavior. Jesus did just that. He called two sets of brothers to abandon their vocations and their fathers, to leave their income and their social network, and to follow him (Matt. 4:18–22). He called others to forget their obligations to parents and to deny any need for physical or social protection (Matt. 8:18–22). He said that to look back after one has started following him makes one unfit for the kingdom (Luke 9:61–62). He maintained that those who loved others, even family, more than him were not fit for the kingdom of God (Matt. 10:34–36). Clearly, then, Jesus thought he was more than ordinary, for it was more important to follow him than to obey parents, love family, to protect life, and preserve one's religious and social status. This takes some real *chutzpah*.

Furthermore, Jesus claimed that if people did not *confess him* before others—that is, own up an allegiance to him and to him alone—this meant that they would not be accepted by God. He called people to declare their colors: either announce before others that they followed him or announce that they had nothing to do with him: "Whoever acknowledges me before men, I will also acknowledge him before my Father in heaven. But whoever disowns me before men, I will disown him before my Father in heaven" (Matt. 10:32–33). Jesus would have no "crypto-disciples," no one who would be private followers at home and not also be followers in the social world of Judaism. Either one followed him wholeheartedly, openly, and confessedly, or one did not follow him at all. It is not an extension of the Synoptic sayings of Jesus, for John also records Jesus as saying, "I am the way and the truth and the life. No one comes to the Father except through me" (John 14:6).

Finally, there is a consistent strain in the records about Jesus that he, in some way, claimed to be uniquely the Son of God.[43] I believe that this claim by Jesus is rooted in his experience of God as the Father, but I also believe that Jesus is, in fact (*ontically* is the theological word), uniquely the Son of God. Jesus called God "Father" (cf. Matt. 6:9), never included himself in the "our Father" kind of prayers, and addressed God as Father in moments of crisis (cf. Mark 14:32–42). In addition, he claimed to have special access to the Father's mysteries, and only those who learned from him would gain a similar access (Matt. 11:27–29; cf. also Mark 13:32). Jesus compared himself to a son in a parable that spoke of God's sending, his rejection, and the Father's vindication (Mark 12:1–9). Jesus conferred a kingdom on his followers as the Father had done to him (Luke 22:29). As is well known, this theme is greatly developed in the Gospel of John, where the divine Logos is the Son (John 1:1–18), the preincarnate one (8:56–58) who was sent to earth to obey his Father (4:34; 6:38) and bring life (10:10).

Say what you want, these claims by Jesus—to obey him, to confess him, and to perceive him as the revealer of God—are special claims. In the words of Robert Stein:

> On the lips of anyone else the claims of Jesus would appear to be evidence of gross egomania, for Jesus clearly implies that the entire world

revolves around himself and that the fate of all men is dependent on their acceptance or rejection of him. . . . There seem to be only two possible ways of interpreting the totalitarian nature of the claims of Jesus. Either we must assume that Jesus was deluded and unstable with unusual delusions of grandeur, or we are faced with the realization that Jesus is truly One who speaks with divine authority, who actually divided all of history into B.C.-A.D., and whose rejection or acceptance determines the fate of men.[44]

And who cannot finish with the stunning observations of C. S. Lewis:

> I am trying here to prevent anyone saying the really foolish thing that people often say about Him: "I'm ready to accept Jesus as a great moral teacher, but I don't accept His claim to be God." That is the one thing we must not say. A man who was merely a man and said the sort of things Jesus said would not be a great moral teacher. He would either be a lunatic—on a level with the man who says he is a poached egg—or else he would be the Devil of Hell. You must make your choice. Either this man was, and is, the Son of God: or else a madman or something worse. You can shut Him up for a fool, you can spit at Him and kill Him as a demon; or you can fall at His feet and call Him Lord and God. But let us not come with any patronising nonsense about His being a great human teacher. He has not left that open to us. He did not intend to.[45]

Students of Jesus today are faced with a multitude of options, ranging from the traditional Jesus who was Savior, Lord, and founder of the church, to a Jesus who was considerably different—a Jesus who was a sage, a religious genius, or a social revolutionary. These latter three portraits, though clearly drawing their energies from live wires in the Gospels, leave us with a Jesus who is not big enough to explain his crucifixion, his following, or the development of the church. If we today are going to be honest about Jesus, we have to choose a Jesus who satisfies all the evidence historians have observed and who will also explain why it is that so many people have found him to be so wonderful that they attend churches every week to worship him.

Notes

1. H. S. Reimarus, *Reimarus: Fragments*, ed. C. H. Talbert, trans. F. S. Fraser; Lives of Jesus Series (Philadelphia: Fortress, 1970). For the story, see C. Brown, *Jesus in European Protestant Thought, 1778–1860* (1985; reprint, Grand Rapids: Baker, 1988), 1–55; for a brief survey, see C. Brown, "Historical Jesus, Quest of," in *Dictionary of Jesus and the Gospels*, ed. Joel B. Green, et al. (Downers Grove, Ill.: InterVarsity Press, 1992), 326–41, esp. 326–27.

2. N. T. Wright, *Who Was Jesus?* (Grand Rapids: Eerdmans, 1993). This book evaluates the conclusions of three recent books about Jesus: those of B. Thiering, A. N. Wilson, and Bishop John Spong. Wright's fuller study is *Jesus and the Victory of God* (Minneapolis: Fortress, 1994). In a period of two weeks, between the time I submitted this chapter to the editors and the time I received their suggestions back, I found three new books on Jesus that I was unaware of when I wrote the chapter. By the time this chapter is published, probably ten more books will have appeared.

3. A nice book along this line is the survey of what Jewish scholars are now saying about Jesus; see D. A. Hagner, *The Jewish Reclamation of Jesus: An Analysis and Critique of Modern Jewish Study of Jesus* (Grand Rapids: Zondervan, 1984).

4. R. Funk, R. Hoover, and the Jesus Seminar, *The Five Gospels: What Did Jesus Really Say?* (New York: Macmillan, 1994).

5. J. C. Holt, *Robin Hood* (London: Thames and Hudson, 1982).

6. Albert Schweitzer, *The Quest of the Historical Jesus: A Critical Study of Its Progress from Reimarus to Wrede*, trans. W. Montgomery (1906; reprint, New York: Macmillan, 1968).

7. In fact, when E. P. Sanders published his book about Jesus in 1985, he spent several pages at the end of his book distinguishing his views about Jesus from those of Schweitzer. See E. P. Sanders, *Jesus and Judaism* (Philadelphia: Fortress, 1985), esp. 327–30.

8. Of Bultmann's many works, the most important for our purposes here are *The History of the Synoptic Tradition*, trans. J. Marsh (1921; reprint, New York: Harper & Row, 1963). On top of the skeptical conclusions of this book, Bultmann wrote *Jesus and the Word*, trans. L. P. Smith and E. H. Lantero (1926; reprint, New York: Scribner's, 1958).

9. Methods of studying the Gospels have been the dominant feature of this discussion.

10. Tom Wright reserves "Third Quest" for a new chapter in the "New Quest"; he sees the works of G. Vermes, E. P. Sanders, A. E. Harvey, and M. Borg in this Third-Quest phase.

11. This is particularly the case with James Robinson and Robert Funk, two leading voices in the Jesus Seminar.

12. See C. Brown, "Historical Jesus, Quest of," 337–41; see also M. Borg, *Jesus in Contemporary Scholarship* (Valley Forge, Pa.: Trinity Press, 1994).

13. Wright, *Who Was Jesus?* 7.

14. See J. H. Charlesworth, *Jesus Within Judaism: New Light from Exciting Archaeological Discoveries*, ABRL (New York: Doubleday, 1988).

15. I might add here that only a traditional Jesus, a Jesus who was indeed Lord and Savior, provides an adequate apologetic basis on which a construction can be built that requires that Jesus be followed. As such, it is not arbitrary to follow Jesus. The three views I discuss have no such basis—why, it might be asked, not follow Ghandi? or Buddha? or David Koresh? An answer to the question "Why follow Jesus?" is required if any justification for one's belief system is of any value.

16. An interesting adult Bible study exercise can begin with the question "What was Jesus really like?" As each person sketches Jesus, the various features of the sketch need to be subjected to the evidence of the Gospels. And then the Gospels need to be studied to see if our sketch is adequate. What I have found is that most views of Jesus are more often than not deeply embedded in one's culture.

17. In what follows I cite sayings of Jesus that are either red or pink (occasionally gray) in Funk, Hoover, and the Jesus Seminar, *Five Gospels*.

18. I follow, in general, the interpretation of this parable as found in K. E. Bailey, *Poet and Peasant* (Grand Rapids: Eerdmans, 1976), 119–33.

19. Funk, Hoover, and the Jesus Seminar, *Five Gospels*, 33.

20. The classical presentation of this is J. Jeremias, *The Prayers of Jesus* (London: SCM, 1967), 11–65. His views have been evaluated and improved by G. Vermes, *The Religion of Jesus the Jew* (Minneapolis: Fortress, 1993), 152–83. See also J. D. G. Dunn, *Jesus and the Spirit: A Study of the Religious and Charismatic Experience of Jesus and the First Christians as Reflected in the New Testament* (Philadelphia: Westminster, 1975), 21–26. The entire book is exceedingly helpful for sorting out the evidence and drawing conclusions with respect to Jesus and the early Christians.

21. Marcus Borg, *Jesus: A New Vision* (San Francisco: Harper & Row, 1987), and his more popular *Meeting Jesus Again for the First Time: The Historical Jesus and the Heart of Contemporary Faith* (San Francisco: HarperSanFrancisco, 1994).

22. I must observe here that Borg, confessedly, is hardly orthodox in his views of Spirit, God, or Jesus. His religious ideas are rooted in the panentheism of Huston Smith. Because his views have not been submitted to theological scrutiny elsewhere (so far as I know), I mention a thorough analysis of Borg's views by a student who did a master's thesis under my direction: see Dana K. Ostby, "The Historical Jesus and the Supernatural World: A Shift in the Modern Critical Worldview with Special Emphasis on the Writings of Marcus Borg" (Master's thesis, Trinity Evangelical Divinity School, 1991). The thesis contains a transcript of an interview with Borg. A more orthodox focus on this feature of Jesus can be found in G. E. Hawthorne, *The Presence and the Power: The Significance of the Holy Spirit in the Life and Ministry of Jesus* (Dallas: Word, 1991).

23. Borg, *Meeting Jesus*, 32.

24. See especially T. W. Manson, *The Teaching of Jesus* (Cambridge: Cambridge University Press, 1939), esp. 89–95 (father) and 116–41 (kingdom).

25. See Geza Vermes, *Jesus the Jew* (Philadelphia: Fortress, 1973); *Jesus and the World of Judaism* (Philadelphia: Fortress, 1983); *The Religion of Jesus the Jew* (Minneapolis: Augsburg Fortress, 1993). Our sketch relies mostly upon the last book, pp. 184–207.

26. While it cannot be defended or expounded here, I am of the view that Jesus' language about the future has been grossly misunderstood because it has been taken too restrictedly in a linear fashion—i.e., thinking that Jesus had a strict timetable in mind (cf. Luke 17:20–21). Jesus' predictions of what appears to us to be an "imminent" eschaton must be set in the context of Old Testament prophecy and Jewish apocalyptic in such a fashion that both literary genre and the nature of prophetic prediction are seen for what they are. Every Jewish prophet predicted that the "next event" would be the "end event," and it never materialized that way. We must remember that prophets were necessarily shortsighted, indeterminate, and ambiguous in their predictions, seeing the future without historical depth and dimension, and Jewish readers knew that prophets worked this way. A starting point for discussion, though not without some problems, is B. F. Meyer, *The Aims of Jesus* (London: SCM, 1979), 242–53. This book

is for me the most stimulating and satisfying of books I have read on Jesus (just slightly ahead of Jeremias).

27. Vermes, *Religion of Jesus*, 190. Oddly enough, the other view within the category of Jesus the religious genius has been led by Marcus Borg, who contends vigorously for a Jesus who was *not* eschatologically driven. See Borg, *Jesus: A New Vision*, 10–17.

28. See Borg, *Meeting Jesus Again*, 29. Several of the most influential scholars in Jesus research still contend for the eschatological Jesus. I am thinking here of E. P. Sanders, G. Vermes, N. T. Wright, J. D. G. Dunn, and D. C. Allison, Jr. Borg's views seem to be too influenced by those who are in the Jesus Seminar, demonstrating once again that the Jesus Seminar is hardly representative of the broad sweep of scholarship.

29. In what follows I will analyze the recent works of Crossan and Horsely. A much more satisfying work along this line is John Howard Yoder, *The Politics of Jesus: Vicit Agnus Noster*, 2d ed. (Grand Rapids: Eerdmans, 1994). Since Yoder's ultimate purpose in writing is more along the line of demonstrating that Christian political discussions must begin with Jesus (and not with some extrinsic discussions) and is less than complete with respect to discussing the broader aspects of the ministry and mission of Jesus, I have not engaged the discussion with Yoder. However, I find his book brilliant and penetratingly accurate in many details.

30. J. D. Crossan's largest work is *The Historical Jesus: The Life of a Mediterranean Jewish Peasant* (San Francisco: HarperSanFrancisco, 1991); a more popular version is *Jesus: A Revolutionary Biography* (San Francisco: HarperSanFrancisco, 1994).

31. Crossan, *Jesus: A Revolutionary Biography*, 198; cf. *The Historical Jesus*, 421–22.

32. Richard A. Horsely, *Jesus and the Spiral of Violence: Popular Jewish Resistance in Roman Palestine* (San Francisco: Harper & Row, 1987).

33. Such an approach to Christology is frequently called a "Christology from below." In dealing with the Jesus Seminar, a "Christology from above" breaks down nearly every line of communication. In what follows I shall not cite scholars for or against a piece of evidence as being authentic or inauthentic. The standard books on Jesus and commentaries have such listings; furthermore, debates occur at every point.

34. In ch. 5 Gary Habermas will discuss further the miracles of Jesus. Here we are making general remarks that aid us in discerning the identity of Jesus.

35. See J. D. G. Dunn, *Jesus' Call to Discipleship* (Cambridge: Cambridge University Press, 1992); M. J. Wilkins, *Following the Master: Discipleship in the Steps of Jesus* (Grand Rapids: Zondervan, 1992).

36. The first scholar to bring this feature of Jesus' ministry to the fore, so far as I know, was J. Jeremias, *New Testament Theology: The Proclamation of Jesus*, trans. J. Bowden (New York: Scribner's, 1971), 114–16; see also J. D. G. Dunn, *Jesus' Call to Discipleship*, 72–76; J. D. Crossan, *Jesus*, 66–74; M. Borg, *Meeting Jesus Again*, 55–56.

37. The point is surely that whereas John was rejected because he was ascetic (Matt 11:18), Jesus was the opposite, a festive kind of guy, and he was rejected for the opposite (Matt. 11:19). In other words, the messengers of God are rejected by the hard of heart regardless of their approach.

38. An anthropological study of this can be found in M. Douglas, *Purity and Danger: An Analysis of the Concepts of Pollution and Taboo* (London: Routledge & Kegan Paul, 1966).

39. An academic defense of this view can be found in C. A. Evans, "Jesus' Action in the Temple: Cleansing or Portent of Destruction," *CBQ* 51 (1989): 237–70.

40. Meyer, *The Aims of Jesus*, 199.

41. See Borg, *Meeting Jesus Again*, 119–40.

42. It will not do to think that this priestly story produces an inferior picture of the

Christian life; all one has to do is to think of St. Francis of Assisi (who is but one example) for a clear example of the beauty of sacrifice and love.

43. See D. R. Bauer, "Son of God," in *Dictionary of Jesus and the Gospels*, 769–75.

44. R. H. Stein, *The Method and Message of Jesus' Teachings* (Philadelphia: Westminster, 1978), 118–19.

45. C. S. Lewis, *Mere Christianity* (New York: Macmillan-Collier, 1960), 55–56.

Chapter 3

THE WORDS OF JESUS IN THE GOSPELS: LIVE, JIVE, OR MEMOREX?

DARRELL L. BOCK

Darrell L. Bock (Ph.D., University of Aberdeen) is Professor of New Testament studies at Dallas Theological Seminary. He is author of a two-volume commentary on *Luke* in the Exegetical Commentary on the New Testament series and of the *Luke* volume in the NIV Application Commentary series.

Introduction

In the beginning there were no tape recorders. In our twentieth-century high-tech world it is difficult to appreciate how communication took place in the first century. There were no printing presses, no cassette players, no newspapers, no printed page, no faxes, no dozen other devices by which we send and record information today. Two thousand years ago there were only individually produced, handwritten copies either on pieces of parchment or on reed paper known as papyri.

In fact, most information was not recorded; it was reported orally. The culture was not one of the written word but of the spoken word. Books were rare and precious. These cultural realities stand behind the reporting of Jesus' teaching and the formation of the Gospels.

This chapter considers how Jesus' words and teaching came to us from this first-century oral world. Just as Jesus lived as a first-century man reflecting the limitations of humanity, so the Gospels were produced in the context of the realities of the ancient world. God chose to express himself through means and forms that people of that time understood. Though we might have wished the Bible came to us like a video recording; it did not. We must let the biblical text reveal how it came to us and seek to understand it in that original setting.

Three Perspectives and One Key Distinction Concerning the Words of Jesus

It might be difficult for us to understand how an oral culture could have produced an accurate account of Jesus' life and words since they lacked our technological means for getting the story right. We feel this tension especially when we recognize that the Gospels present two seemingly contradictory phenomena. On the one hand, the Gospel writers present their accounts of Jesus' life and teachings as accurate and true (see Luke's careful statement in Luke 1:1–4). On the other hand, when we compare individual accounts to one another, we find striking differences, even in places where the same event is being described (e.g., the three accounts of the Father's words to Jesus at the baptism; Matt. 3:13–17; Mark 1:9–11; Luke 3:21–22).

Can that oral culture have produced an accurate record of Jesus' sayings, and if so, how do we know? How can his sayings be accurate when differences occur in the Evangelists' records? What kind of flexibility in recording Jesus' sayings was appropriate for this culture? Most importantly, what evidence do these records give themselves of how they work? What do the authors intend to give us, based on what they passed on to us? Put in theological terms, how did the Author work through these authors to give us what we have?

In recent years such questions have prompted intense scrutiny of and debate concerning the words of Jesus, producing a variety of approaches that cover a wide spectrum. I will discuss three points on the spectrum that reflect the basic options that today's reader can take to this issue. In modern parlance, are the words of Jesus to be taken as "live," "jive," or "memorex"?

"Memorex"

Some treat the words of Jesus like a "memorex" cassette tape. The red letters of the Gospels *are* the exact words Jesus spoke. This view of inspiration means that if the text claims that Jesus says something, then Jesus said exactly that (not a summary or the gist of that). People who hold this position suggest that since the Bible is the inspired word of God and is true, Jesus' words recorded in the Gospels must be exactly what he said. This approach takes the Word of God seriously as a true word from God. As I will show, however, it does not always adequately explain what the text itself shows about how it communicates Jesus' words. By looking at some biblical examples, I will show that the authors of the Gospels, though recording accurate and true accounts, did not always intend to give us a "memorex" tape. It is possible to have historical truth without always resorting to explicit citation.

"Jive"

The other end of the interpretive spectrum is represented by the Jesus Seminar. This approach emphasizes the loose oral roots behind the communication of Jesus' teaching and the Evangelists' need to adapt that teaching for their preaching. According to those who hold this position, the Gospel writers had *and took* the opportunity *to create* sayings. They felt perfectly free to put words in Jesus' mouth that did not reflect at all what he had taught, because of their intense desire to meet the needs of the churches they were addressing. They presented as Jesus' views those that they themselves had come to hold as a result of their resurrection faith. This development in the sayings usually took place when the church turned to discuss who Jesus was. They exalted him to a level far beyond what he himself taught and specified the nature of his work with regard to sin in more detail than he himself ever expressed it.

Though I admit to being a little cute in using street language to describe this second view, I suggest that this approach views the Gospels as containing significant portions of "jive" when it comes to history and the "historical Jesus." The Jesus Seminar only manages to rate 18 percent of the sayings of Jesus as being directly from him (in red letters) or something close to what he said (in pink letters).[1] They speak of the tradition's "christianizing Jesus" and of the Evangelists' using a "storyteller's license" to make their point. The image of a storyteller is a telling one, for it shows how important a loose oral approach is to this view. More than half of the sayings of Jesus are printed in black, thus not going back to Jesus at all.[2] I think the term "jive" fits how this approach views the Gospels as a historical repository for recovering the historical Jesus.[3] Their view of Jesus as sage and teller of parables of wisdom is far different from the portrait of Jesus as Savior and Lord that the Gospels portray.

"Live"

Placing "jive" on our spectrum of views next to the "memorex" approach, one can see how broad the range of opinions is about the words of Jesus in the Gospels. It is also easy to see how one approach emphasizes the accuracy of the accounts, while the other approach highlights the cultural setting and the nature of the differences. I contend that this is an artificial dichotomy. Both approaches, expecting more than the Gospels seek to give, come up short in explaining what the Gospels intend for us. A third approach—rooted in a careful understanding of how historical events and sayings were remembered and recorded in the first century and drawing on careful attention to the biblical texts themselves—leads us to recognize both the writers' accuracy and the nature of the differences in their accounts.

This third approach readily acknowledges that the text reports Jesus' sayings, even those that can be tied to the same setting, with variation of wording. Such variations, reported by authors who knew the tradition's wording, reveal their intent to summarize and explain, not merely to quote, as they sought to apply Jesus' teaching to their audiences, selected what to discuss, and sometimes arranged their material for topical reasons rather than by sequence.[4] So we do not necessarily have "memorex." This approach also recognizes that much of early tradition tied to Jesus' teaching circulated in an oral context.

But this oral tradition did not operate anywhere near as loosely as the "jive" view suggests. The Evangelists did not create sayings of their own free will; rather, they attempted to work responsibly with what they reported. By their own admission, they used resources the tradition made available to them. Luke writes in Luke 1:1–4, for example:

> Inasmuch as many have undertaken to compile a narrative of the things fulfilled among us, just as they were delivered to us by those who from the beginning were eyewitnesses and ministers of the word, it seemed good to me also, having followed all things carefully from the beginning, to write it out for you in an orderly manner, most excellent Theophilus, so that you might know the truth concerning the things of which you were instructed.[5]

According to this passage, the tradition was rooted in eyewitness accounts, and many such accounts about what Jesus did and said were available. Luke was fully aware of what others had said about Jesus. He himself intended to be careful in his account, for he desired accuracy as he sought to retell the story in a fresh way.

This is what the "live" approach is all about. Each Evangelist retells the living and powerful words of Jesus in a fresh way for his readers, while faithfully and accurately presenting the "gist" of what Jesus said. I call this approach one that recognizes the Jesus tradition as "live" in its dynamic and quality. We clearly hear Jesus, but we must be aware that there is summary and emphasis in the complementary portraits that each Evangelist gives to the founder of the faith. Jesus' teaching is both present in the Gospels and reflected on in light of the significance his teaching came to possess.

The rest of this essay will argue that this is what the Gospel writers intended to do: nothing more ("memorex") and nothing less ("jive"). I will also argue that the biblical writings themselves, the cultural milieu, and even our own styles of historical summarizing give evidence that such reporting is both common and capable of being fully trusted. However, merely to make a claim or to describe a view is not proof. Thus, we must discuss the basis for considering the Gospels as "live," rather than "memorex" or "jive."

Before I proceed with this central question, I must note a key distinction, held by many evangelical scholars, that frees one up from the accuracy versus differences dichotomy inherent in the "memorex" versus "jive" positions. It is the distinction between having the precise words of Jesus and having his voice in an accurate summary.

Ipsissima Vox, Not Always *Ipsissima Verba*

In examining the wording of Jesus' teaching in the Gospels, we must distinguish between the *ipsissima verba* of Jesus ("his very words") and the *ipsissima vox* ("his very voice," i.e., the presence of his teaching summarized).[6] One universally recognized reality makes assessing the presence of the exact words of Jesus difficult and argues for the distinction between *verba* and *vox*. It is that Jesus probably gave most of his teaching in Aramaic, the dominant public language of first-century Palestine where Jesus ministered, whereas the Gospels were written in Greek, the dominant language of the larger first-century Greco-Roman world to which the Gospels were addressed. In other words, most of Jesus' teaching in the Gospels is already a translation.

Though one could argue Jesus spoke Greek and that some of the tradition is not translated, that is unlikely for the whole tradition, particularly when Jesus ministered in a Semitic context. It would be like asking Jesus to speak in English to a Mexican audience on the Mexican side of the Rio Grande! Since a translation is already present in much of the tradition, we do not have "his very words" in the strictest sense of the term.

A second factor also argues for this distinction. Most accounts of Jesus' remarks are a few sentences long. In fact, even his longest speeches as recorded in the Gospels take only a few minutes to read (e.g., the Sermon on the Mount or the Olivet Discourse). Yet we know that Jesus kept his audiences for hours at a time (e.g., Mark 6:34–36). It is clear that the writers give us a reduced and summarized presentation of what Jesus said and did. John's Gospel says as much in hyperbole, noting that all the books in the world could not hold a full account of what Jesus did and said (John 21:25).

Third, the distinction between *verba* and *vox* is valuable when we look at the way the Bible cites itself—i.e., the way the New Testament uses the Old. Numerous New Testament citations of the Old are not word for word, even after taking into account translation from Hebrew into Greek (cf. Isa. 61:1–2 with Luke 4:16–20; Amos 9:11–12 with Acts 15:16–17; Ps. 40:7–9 with Heb. 10:5–7). If the Bible can summarize a citation of itself in this way, then to see the same technique in its handling the words of Jesus should come as no surprise.

With this distinction in place, I return to our basic question: On what grounds should we see the Gospels as "live," rather than "memorex" or "jive"? I will proceed in three sections. (1) One of the most important elements is to examine how history was recorded in the ancient world.

(2) Details within the Gospels themselves show why a "memorex" approach is not how the Evangelists handled issues of wording and historical presentation. Some of my examples will treat events, not just words, to show how consistently the Scripture takes a summarizing approach to Jesus' life and ministry. It is in this section I hope to show that the distinction between Jesus' words and Jesus' voice is clearly evidenced *within the biblical text itself*.

(3) But if there is summary, could it be that the Evangelists have simply presented their own theology and not that of Jesus? To pursue this question, I will examine the criteria scholars have used to determine what are the true words (or concepts) of Jesus. These are called *criteria of authenticity* because they assess whether a saying is authentic (i.e., whether it goes genuinely back to Jesus). They form the basis for why some scholars (especially in the Jesus Seminar) argue for the presence of "jive" in the tradition.

To evaluate their claims, we must first see how they attempt to get there. So, in the midst of evaluating the criteria, I will take two key examples of Jesus' teaching and attempt to show how the criteria are not always consistently applied by the Seminar's scholars themselves. Furthermore, key features of Jesus' teaching can be defended on the basis of such standards. If the two examples I treat are authentic in going back to Jesus, then the major teaching about his person and saving work do have roots in Jesus' ministry. Such findings show that the early church did not create their fundamental view of Jesus' person and work out of whole cloth. The early church believed about Jesus *what he personally taught them to believe*. The Gospels give us the true gist of his teaching and the central thrust of his message.

Is History in the Ancient World "Memorex"?

The Greco-Roman Historical Tradition

In asking how the ancients viewed the task of recounting historical events, we get help from the ancients themselves. A famous quotation that illustrates the problem of recording speech in an ancient culture comes from Thucydides (*History of the Peloponnesian War*, 1.22.1), who is representative of Greco-Roman historians generally. This Greek historian of the fifth century B.C. is candid about the speeches he reports in his work: "It was difficult for me to remember the exact substance of the speeches I myself heard and for others to remember those they heard elsewhere and told me of." But that does not mean that he felt free to have his history say anything he wanted. He continues:

> I have given the speeches in the manner in which it seemed to me that each of the speakers would best express what needed to be said about the ever-prevailing situation, but I have kept as close as possible to the total opinion expressed by the actual words.

In other words, the Greek standard of reporting speeches required a concern for accuracy in reporting the gist of what had been said, even if the exact words were not remembered or recorded.[7] The ancients also recognized an author's right to summarize and bring out the contemporary force of a speaker's remarks. In other words, the historian sought to report and edify.

This tradition became a standard for Greco-Roman history. In places where we can compare the reports of Claudias's speeches by Tacitus with the recording of those speeches on tablets, we can see how this standard lived on into the first century of the time of Jesus. Like Thucydides, Tacitus felt free to rearrange, condense, and summarize, but he still sensed a responsibility to present the speech's basic content. Charles Fornara, a modern historian, concludes: "The little evidence we possess indicates that he presented speeches responsibly, refused to invent them, and searched them out when it was possible to do so."[8] This procedure sounds much like that cited by Luke in Luke 1:1–4. The Evangelists were able to search out what Jesus did and said because they had access to people and communities who had been exposed to Jesus or his intimate followers.

Fornara goes on to say, "We are not entitled to proceed on the assumption that the historians considered themselves at liberty to write up speeches out of their own heads."[9] Fornara is not a biblical scholar. He has no ax to grind on theological questions. He is simply describing how careful ancient historians worked. In other words, though they worked at a disadvantage by living in an oral, non-high-tech culture, the ancients knew what good reporting was and tried to achieve it. We, as moderns, sometimes underestimate the "tenacity of oral tradition in a pre-literate society and the importance of reminiscence in such a society."[10]

The Jewish Culture of Remembering

If the role of oral tradition was important to the ancients in general, it was especially important to Jewish culture. As early as the book of Deuteronomy, the importance of oral instruction and memory regarding divine teaching is stressed (Deut. 6:4–9). Moreover, Jewish rabbis developed elaborate means by which to communicate the tradition orally from generation to generation, finally codifying it in writing about A.D. 170 in the *Mishnah*. Rabbinic schools, which majored in study of the law, taught the importance of careful memory work. To the Jew, if something reflected the Word of God or the wisdom of God, it was worth remembering.[11]

Three institutions reinforced this commitment to reflect on and remember teaching: the home, the synagogue, and the elementary school. In all three locations Jews worked with material they had learned carefully to recall. The Jewish historian Josephus was proud of his memory skills (*Life* 8). True, Josephus was prone to self-congratulation, but the fact that he boasted of such skill shows how culturally appreciated it was. Jews would read and repeat important points of the law to their children (4 Macc. 18:10–16). Or as Philo, another Jewish historian of Jesus' time, declared:

> For all men guard their own customs, but this is especially true of the Jewish nation. Holding that the laws are oracles vouchsafed by God and having been trained in this doctrine from their earliest years, they carry the likeness of the commandments enshrined in their souls. (*The Embassy to Gaius* 210)

All major Jewish groups had community prayers that they committed to memory, whether it be the *Shema* of Deuteronomy 6:4–9, the *Decalogue* (the Ten Commandments), or the *Eighteen Benedictions*. The Psalms and Scripture were sung. Another means of making sayings memorable was the use of graphic images and parallelism.[12] We know from the discoveries at Qumran that the Old Testament text was faithfully copied with such care that a thousand years of copying saw no substantial differences introduced into the wording of the text.[13] I am not trying to argue that the Jews did everything without error, but they did give great care in how they communicated and passed on events, especially divinely associated events. The culture was, to use Riesner's words, "a culture of memory."[14]

The New Testament shares this approach to the importance of what Jesus taught and how it was transmitted. I have already noted how Luke affirmed that the tradition he received had roots in those who were eyewitnesses and ministers of the word (Luke 1:1–4). When Paul writes about the gospel message or the tradition of the Last Supper that he passed on to the Corinthian church, he uses the language of tradition carefully passed on: "I preached to you [the gospel] which you received" (1 Cor. 15:1), and, "I received from the Lord what I also passed on to you" (11:23). The terms "received" and "passed on" are technical terms for hearing and passing on tradition.[15] In fact, Paul's version of this event reads virtually the same as how Luke recorded the event (Luke 22:14–23), showing that the church "passed on" events in much the way Judaism did.[16] Numerous other passages reflect the use of Jewish forms of tradition, suggesting the apostles' connection to the passing on of tradition; in some cases the oral tradition took on a fairly fixed form as it started to be passed on.[17]

In summary, whether one looks at Greco-Roman historiography or Jewish culture, one can see that oral culture of that society did not mean the kind of loose approach to the teaching of divine wisdom that the "jive" approach suggests, even though one cannot guarantee from the cultural practice that such writers would have always quoted material as if on a "memorex" tape. Their goal was to get the gist of the teaching and to reproduce it faithfully. This means that we have historical grounds for approaching the Gospels with the reasonable expectation that they faithfully preserve the sayings of Jesus in summarized form. However, the issue should not be left there. A detailed examination of the Gospel texts themselves shows that the Bible itself evidences this approach.

Is History in the Gospels "Memorex"?

In surveying cultural expectations in the first century, one cannot ignore the Gospels themselves. An examination of the texts should indicate how the Evangelists saw and performed their task. After considering how history works, I will quickly move through a series of examples that relate to the questions of order, detail, and wording in the Gospels. My point is simple. There is more to history than precise chronological sequence or always relating the exact same detail or reporting something in the same words. A Gospel writer wrote not only to tell the story of Jesus, but also to reveal additional perspectives about his story. Why else would one write on a topic someone else had already covered? Recorded history presents and explains. The Gospels do both as well.

How History Works

History is not a static entity. Neither are the sayings that belong to it and describe its events. Historical events and sayings do not just happen and then sit fossilized with a static meaning. As events in history proceed, they develop their meaning through the interconnected events that give history its sense of flow. Later events impact how previous events and sayings are understood, seen, and appreciated. Even when those earlier events had conscious intentions tied to them when they occurred, what takes place later influences how those earlier events and the things said about them are seen and understood.

Written history involves perspective and can be told from a variety of perspectives, both in terms of time frame and ideology. History also reflects the time frame from which it presents and perceives events. Because history in its essence involves a sequence, sayings and events have the capability of being pregnant with meaning. Sometimes events and sayings are understood better after reflection than when they first took place. The wording of a saying may not change, but what is perceived about it may change. On the other hand, a saying's meaning may be better summarized in descriptive terms because the events that follow it reveal its full import. We live, almost unconsciously, with such an appreciation of how history works.

Two recent events in my own life, both occurring within a month of one another, illustrate this point and show how common it is. A few weeks ago, the institution where I teach honored its retiring president's forty years of service. They did so by unveiling on our campus a statue of one of his favorite biblical scenes. Included with the statue was a large plaque in honor of Dr. Donald K. Campbell as the graduate school's third president. It was a grand occasion, and among the honoree's guests were two of his grandchildren—a five-year-old girl and a four-year-old boy. The two cousins were taking in the unveiling when the elder of the two became concerned that her younger relative might misunderstand what was taking place. Full of compassion and motherly instinct, she turned to her companion and said, "Don't worry. Grandpa's not dead. They just gave him a statue."

Now the event and the saying about it reflect the fact that this ceremony was inherently pregnant with meaning. What was being unveiled was a memorial to honor the life and service of a distinguished colleague. For as long as the statue remains, most viewers of it and its commemorative plaque will be looking back on the life of a significant historical figure in the life of our school. What had produced the potential for confusion was a mixture of perspectives that the event reflected. Though they were honoring Dr. Campbell in the present, while he was still alive, they were doing so for time immemorial. The event was so pregnant with significance that the granddaughter wanted to be sure the setting did not cause her less mature cousin too much trauma. In her simple, childlike way, she sensed what these occasions normally mean. Events often take on this kind of complex character, and so do the sayings that go with them.

My second example comes from the world of sports. As I write, the National Basketball Association is holding its playoffs. My favorite team, the Houston Rockets, have had a roller coaster week and a half in their quarterfinals series with the Phoenix Suns. They came into the series with home-court advantage, meaning that if the series went the full seven games, four games would be in Houston and three in Phoenix. Usually in professional basketball, home-court advantage means everything. For example, the home team has won the last fourteen consecutive decisive seventh games, a streak that goes back more than a decade. Houston has never won a major sports championship and came into the series with home-court advantage for the entire playoffs. That is, they were assured of more games at home than their opponents. So here was a great opportunity for a first, for Houston to win a championship.

The Rockets promptly lost the first two home games and threw away the home-court advantage. Worse than that, they lost the second game after having had a twenty-point lead in the fourth quarter! The loss was the worst in franchise history and set an NBA playoff record for squandering the largest fourth-quarter lead. Only once in all of NBA history has a team won a seven-game series after losing the first two games at home. So they headed for Phoenix, down 0–2, to play two games away from home against a team that had the league's best regular season home record. Rockets fans were devastated. The dream was gone.

The Houston papers' headlines read, "Choke City." Surely Game 2 would go down in Rockets history as a day of infamy.

But a funny thing happened on the way to the funeral. Subsequent events illustrate how a linked sequence of events can change one's perspective. The Rockets went to Phoenix and amazingly won two games in a row. They returned to Houston with the series tied at two, and Houston had regained the home-court advantage. They promptly won their next game at home, putting the series at 3–2. The newspapers now called the team "Clutch City." What a difference one week can make in a linked chain of events!

As I write, the drama is not over. But after Game 5 one of the Rockets' players said about the infamous Game 2 that it was the best thing that could have happened to the team, a feeling he certainly did not have in that same locker room a week earlier. The loss, he said, woke the team up. That remark recalled comments made by the team on the night of the Game 2 loss, that such a shocking loss had better wake the team up. Now nothing had changed about the contents of Game 2 except the sequence of events that followed it. The original wake-up remark, stated with uncertainty but reality on the night of the loss, had become a rally cry throughout the series. Seen in the light of subsequent events, the saying retains its basic content and yet takes on a freshness and significance that only the passage of time and subsequent events can give it. The illustration shows how dynamic, how alive, and how complex historical perspective can be.

One other point about historical perspective remains from this basketball illustration. By the time this article is published, we will know how the Rockets fared in their quest.[18] As a presenter of that event and with the possibility of editing my remarks in light of the history to follow, I have the choice of telling this story from a variety of perspectives. I could leave it as I wrote it, leaving the tension of being in the midst of the drama on the surface, even though much of that drama will have been resolved by what takes place subsequently; or I could update the illustration in light of the results of the series and the playoffs as a whole, telling the events more retrospectively. I could choose to present the "wake-up call" remark as "we had better wake up" or "that game was a wake-up call," depending on which perspective is chosen, *and both reports would be accurate in light of the dynamic nature of how events impact one another.*

This same kind of historical interaction and interconnectedness influences how the Gospels work. In an ancient oral culture where events surrounding Jesus involved great reversals of emotion and understanding, the variety of perspectives seen in the Gospels is nothing but a reflection of the presence of complementary perspectives that are inherent in a presentation of a linked sequence of events in history.[19] Though the Gospel writers wrote with a perspective that allowed them to look back on earlier events with a larger context for understanding, they often chose, while looking through that context, to retell the original story with some of the elements of emotional and intellectual ambiguity and uncertainty that the events possessed when they were originally experienced. One Evangelist might choose to cite the remark with its originally perceived ambiguity, while another might bring out its ultimate intended force, a force that became clear in light of subsequent events. Yet both presentations would be accurate to the event's historical thrust. This multitiered nature of historical meaning and portrayal is crucial in appreciating how the Gospels work.

History and the Gospels

How does this view of history work in the Gospels? What do these texts actually do? The principle of choice and arrangement in the Gospel materials is apparent. Whether involving order, detail, or wording of texts, the following examples reveal how the Gospels present Jesus. I cover events and order, because the issue of the setting of sayings and their chronological position within Jesus' ministry is a question one could assume is simply a matter of reading the text in its sequence. Though these texts present a general outline to Jesus' ministry, the choices involving arrangement of material reveal how difficult it is in some cases to determine an exact sequence. At some point, each Evangelist covered Jesus' teaching on a topical, not a chronological, basis.

Evidence of Gospel writers' intentions: Order and Gospel events

Issues of arrangement of order are easy to show. The account of Jesus' temptation is an example of rearrangement within a pericope.[20] Here is a chart comparing the order of the temptations in Matthew 4:1–11 and Luke 4:1–13.

Matthew 4	Luke 4
1. Stones to bread (vv. 3–4)	1. Stones to bread (vv. 3–4)
2. Jump from temple (vv. 5–7)	2. Kingdoms of the world (vv. 5–8)
3. Kingdoms of the world (vv. 8–9)	3. Jump from temple (vv. 9–12)

As one can easily see, the second and third temptations do not come in the same order in each Gospel. Now there was only one set of temptations, and it has the same location in each Gospel; thus, one of the Evangelists has rearranged this material.[21]

The Gospels can also reorder the sequence between events. The following chart shows the event distribution between Matthew 8–9 and its parallels, following the Matthean order.

Event	Matthew	Mark	Luke
Leper cleansing	8:1–4	1:40–45	5:12–16
Centurion	8:5–13	(no parallel)	7:1–10
Peter's mother-in-law	8:14–15	1:29–31	4:38–39
Sick healed	8:16–17	1:32–34	4:40–41
Following Jesus	8:18–22	(no parallel)	9:57–62
Stilling the storm	8:23–27	4:35–41	8:22–25

Gadarene demoniac	8:24–34	5:1–20	8:26–39
Paralytic	9:1–8	2:1–12	5:17–26
Matthew's call	9:9–13	2:13–17	5:27–32
Fasting question	9:14–17	2:18–22	5:33–39
Jairus and woman	9:18–26	5:21–43	8:40–56

Once again, a quick glance at the chart shows that some rearranging between events has taken place. Sometimes the Evangelist discusses issues on the basis of topical consideration rather than sequence. For example, the first three events in Matthew 8:1–15 are miracles, but Luke has the same events in a different order. Checking Luke 8:22–56, one can see a sequence of four miracles, an order Mark 4:35–5:43 also possesses, but Matthew 8–9 breaks this order up. This means that we cannot always know exactly where the sayings of Jesus fall in sequence within his ministry. It was more important for the Evangelists to give Jesus' teaching, and sometimes group it with related events, than to be concerned with sequence. These differences in order are not an example of error in reporting; rather, they reflect differences in theme and emphasis in terms of intended presentation. They give evidence of conscious choices in ordering events within the Gospel accounts.

Sometimes details *within* events are selected on a parallel basis. An examination of the healing of the centurion's servant (Matt. 8:5–13; Luke 7:1–10) shows a significant difference of detail. In Matthew the discussion occurs directly between the centurion and Jesus. However, in Luke a major point of the account is that the centurion never speaks directly to Jesus, for the soldier reveals his humility by insisting that Jesus need not come under his roof to facilitate a healing. Instead, Jewish messengers speak up for this Gentile, declaring he is worthy of Jesus' aid. This major detail allows Luke to make a point that Matthew is not concerned about: how Jews and Gentiles can respect one another. A common explanation for the difference is that Matthew has telescoped the account and made it simpler, since in the ancient world a messenger sent on someone's behalf was seen as equal to speaking to the person directly (much like an ambassador or press secretary speaks for the president today).

Thus, the text shows how details between the Gospels do not necessarily match within the same event.[22] Sometimes speaking is summarized rather than presented directly. But such differences should not be seen as errors, once the summarizing approach to the description is recognized. We do not get upset if a press secretary's message is reported as the president's communiqué! Sometimes this type of summarizing can involve the naming and numbering of the characters present at an event (e.g., the naming of the women at the empty tomb in the various resurrection accounts or the number of messengers present at the tomb).

Recognizing these choices of order actually removes confusion about the differences between accounts in the text. Once one sees that conscious reordering or summarizing has taken place, one can explain both the nature of the differences that are clearly present in the text, while also explaining the event's teaching and varied perspectives faithfully.

More evidence of Gospel writers' intentions: The gist of Jesus' sayings

We now turn to issues of wording. I will choose several examples involving different speakers to show the consistency of this "gist of the event" principle in handling dialogue. In considering the portrait of Jesus and his words, it is also important to see how what is said to him is handled, since that also helps to show how the Evangelists handle dialogue in general.

It is revealing to consider the report of Jesus' baptism (Matt. 3:13–17; Mark 1:9–11; Luke 3:21–22). The significant remark in the account comes from the voice from heaven. In comparing the accounts, I will retain touches of the Greek word order in the translation.

> Matthew 3:17: "This is my Son, the beloved, with whom I am well pleased."
> Mark 1:11: "You are my Son, the beloved; with you I am well pleased."
> Luke 3:22: "You are my Son, the beloved; with you I am well pleased."

What did the voice say exactly? Since this is a singular event and only one saying is reported by each Evangelist, it is clear that some summarizing or choice has taken place somewhere. We do not have a "memorex" tape in all three cases.[23] Mark and Luke portray the remark as made directly to Jesus, while Matthew has the feel of a general report of its significance. In other words, Mark and Luke presumably report the remark, while Matthew details the event's significance for his readers. What God did by speaking to Jesus was to endorse him, marking out the event as full of import, even if that remark was only heard by Jesus and the dove-like descent of the Spirit was only seen by Jesus and John (John 1:33–34).[24]

This difference is equal to our basketball illustration above. Two writers opt for a vivid presentation of the actual event, while the third by summary citation opens up its significance for the audience. What is implied as a public presentation in Mark and Luke is explicit in Matthew. Both portrayals are an accurate reflection of the meaning of the event and the saying.

Similar examples could be multiplied, but to show that the baptismal voice is not an exceptional case, I will note two more. Another key event, where another speaker is involved, is found in Peter's confession at Caesarea Philippi (Matt. 16:13–20; Mark 8:27–30; Luke 9:18–21). Here two points are illustrated at once. To open the unit Jesus asks the following question:

> Matthew 16:13: "Who do people say the Son of Man is?"
> Mark 8:27: "Who do people say I am?"
> Luke 9:18: "Who do the crowds say I am?"

Once again, the gist, but with variation, is present. Since Jesus called himself the "Son of Man," it is not surprising to see a change from "Son of Man" to "I." They mean the same thing—though Jesus probably uttered the enigmatic title originally, since the Gospel writers never introduce this term independently of Jesus. Second, did Jesus say "people" or "crowd"? Did the translation of remarks in distinct reports of the event merely use two similar Greek words to render one Aramaic one? Or did one writer put the question in language that was more like his own style? Or did one writer simply intend to summarize the event rather than to transcribe it? Any of these options is possible. What is crucial to note is that the texts themselves show no necessity to render each other word for word, even in dialogue.

Later in the passage comes Peter's answer to Jesus' question, "Who do you say that I am?" In this case, that question is rendered word for word the same in all three Gospels. But the reply has variation.

Matthew 16:16: "You are the Christ, the Son of the living God."
Mark 8:29: "You are the Christ."
Luke 9:20: "The Christ of God."

Matthew's reply is the fullest and Luke's the shortest. Matthew's is also the most ambiguous. While Mark and Luke highlight the messianic confession, Matthew has a note about the Son of God. Interestingly, Luke's summary notes the presence of God in the reply but simply links it to the Christ title. Most Christians reading Matthew probably jump to the conclusion that Peter has confessed Jesus as the only Son of God. But one must remember that sonship was also a term for a regal figure in Israel (2 Sam. 7:6–16; Ps. 2:7). There are two possibilities here. Either Mark and Luke have simplified a much deeper confession as recorded by Matthew, or Matthew has presented in ambiguous terms the fundamental messianic confession of Mark and Luke.

Matthew has worded Peter's confession in such a way that who the Messiah came to be revealed as is anticipated by the response. In other words, though Peter's confession recognized Jesus as a regal "son," Matthew has rendered this phrase, pregnant with meaning, in a way that suggests all that "Son of God" came to mean for the church. The rendering is accurate because regal Messiah and Son of God are uniquely combined in Jesus. One further point is important: The confessions in each version are fundamentally the same, for each presents Jesus as Messiah.

Our final illustration of wording comes from the scene at Jesus' trial (Matt. 26:57–68; Mark 14:53–65; Luke 22:54–71). There is some debate whether the Lukan scene is exactly the same as that in Matthew and Mark, since Luke alludes to a morning trial and Matthew and Mark describe a night examination. However, one of two things is happening here. Either Luke is relating the end of the trial before the council, whose decisive moments took place at daybreak, or the separate Lukan morning session was nothing but a replay of what had occurred earlier that evening. Either way, there is so much overlap between the accounts that they are worth comparing. Even if Luke is rendering a distinct scene, he still has made a choice to do so. Those who work with the Gospels must never forget that some sayings may have been repeated in similar types of settings—a point that is sometimes ignored when assessing parallels. Regardless, Matthew and Mark are certainly parallel.

The question that brings Jesus' response shows the same "gist" principle.

> Matthew 26:63: "I charge you under oath by the living God: Tell us if you are the Christ, the Son of God."
> Mark 14:61: "Are you the Christ, the Son of the Blessed One?"
> Luke 22:67: "If you are the Christ . . . tell us."

Jesus is asked about his messianic claim, though again the wording differs. So some of the Evangelists must be summarizing. Jesus' reply shows the same summarizing character:

> Matthew 26:64: "Yes, it is as you say. . . . But I say to all of you: In the future you will see the Son of Man sitting at the right hand of the Mighty One and coming on the clouds of heaven."
> Mark 14:62: "I am. . . . And you will see the Son of Man sitting at the right hand of the Mighty One and coming on the clouds of heaven."
> Luke 22:67b–70: "If I tell you, you will not believe me, and if I asked you, you would not answer. But from now on, the Son of Man will be seated at the right hand of the mighty God." They all asked, "Are you then the Son of God?" He replied, "You are right in saying I am."

What we have seen in the other texts also applies here. Though there is variation and difference in detail, the gist of the replies is the same. Whether Jesus said "I am" or used the idiom "You are right in saying I am"—an ancient expression that means, "It is as you say but not with the sense you mean"—he affirmed his identification as Messiah, Son of God. He also alluded to Psalm 110:1 in replying to indicate the extent of his authority. Interestingly Luke omits any reference to the return on the clouds, probably because for him Jesus' present authority made the point sufficiently.

Jesus' exact words or his exact voice?

It is texts like these that cause interpreters to distinguish between *ipsissima verba* ("the exact words" [of Jesus]) and *ipsissima vox* ("the exact voice" [of Jesus]). One can present history accurately whether one quotes or summarizes teaching, or even mixes the two together. To have accurate summaries of Jesus' teaching is just as historical as to have his actual words; they are just two different perspectives to give us the same thing. All that is required is that the summaries be trustworthy—a factor made likely not only by the character of the writers and the nature of their religious convictions, but also by the presence of opponents and eyewitnesses who one way or the other could challenge a fabricated report.[25]

I am reminded of our daily five-minute news broadcasts. Often the newscaster is faced with the choice of having to summarize in a minute or less a speech by the president that took anywhere from fifteen minutes to an hour. Today, he or she can simply run the tape of a sound bite, "memorex" style. But even today, the newsperson can also choose to summarize the message in a few sentences of his or her own and even preface them with the introduction, "The President said today as he addressed. . . ." Or he or she can mix the two.

The Evangelists had the same options, only the ability to be exhaustive or detailed in the ancient context was limited by the largely oral world in which they functioned. The Gospels are summaries of the teachings of Jesus. They may not always present the material "memorex" style, but that does not mean that they have given us "jive" either, as the proponents of the Jesus Seminar claim. The ancients knew how to summarize and how to do so accurately, with the "gist" of a teaching intact.

We are now ready to examine what the Seminar has done and why. I hope to show, even using their own standards of testing, how they have made too much of the limitations of oral culture and the nature of these differences within the Gospels.

Why Did the Seminar Say So Much Was "Jive," and Is It?

What criteria did the Jesus Seminar scholars use to assign a color to the words of Jesus? If red means exact quotation, pink means something pretty close to what he said, gray means the saying may have roots in something Jesus said though these are not his words, and black means no contact with Jesus at all, then how did they decide?[26] We turn our attention to the criteria applied to Jesus' sayings by the Seminar and offer a critique of them and of the Seminar's application of them. Why did they say so much of Jesus' teaching in the Gospels is "jive"?

I have already treated the assumption of the Seminar about the fluid nature of orality. This is a major blow against their approach, but it is not the only problem. What about the tests the Seminar applied in specific cases to conclude that over 50 percent of teachings attributed to Jesus in the Gospels are not from him? I will begin by examining briefly their use and estimation of extrabiblical Gospel accounts like *Thomas*. Then I will treat and assess three criteria they used to rate the authenticity of Jesus' words: dissimilarity, multiple attestation, and coherence. Do these criteria really argue that Jesus said less than half of what the Gospels say he said?

The Use of Other Gospels' Material

The database that the Jesus Seminar Fellows used to assess the Jesus tradition is important. They examined not only the canonical Gospels of Matthew, Mark, Luke, and John, but also included the Gospels of *Thomas* and *Peter*.[27] The Jesus Seminar worked with Thomas so seriously that they entitled their book *The Five Gospels*. All of these Gospels do give evidence of a strand of development within the history of the transmission of Jesus' teaching, so they are relevant. However, key members of the Seminar have treated the Gospels of *Thomas* and *Peter* as of equal importance to the tradition as the canonical texts.

But these works are overrated when they are equated with the canonical Gospels in the discussion. I underscore several basic points here. *Thomas* and *Peter* are late works. Though the Seminar treats *Thomas* as though it were at least as old a source as the teaching material shared by Matthew and Luke (a source tradition called "Q"), that position is unproven. Richard Hays called this position "an extraordinarily early dating," "a highly controversial claim," and "a shaky element in their methodological foundation."[28] The Seminar's evaluation of the worth of *Thomas* is hardly a consensus view. Since *Thomas* and *Peter* show more variation in how they handle the Jesus material, they distort the assessment of how orality works, especially if they are perceived as typical of the earliest period of the written tradition.

Criteria of Authenticity

In evaluating the sayings of Jesus, scholars have worked for most of this century with various criteria to determine their authenticity.[29] It is important to recognize that some of these criteria can only test the conceptual level of Jesus' teaching—i.e., did Jesus teach about this theme with this emphasis? These criteria cannot prove that he used a specific wording to make his point. Such tests are almost impossible to create for any ancient document. The absence of tape recorders in the ancient world cuts both ways. It not only allows for orality, but it also makes proving the presence of specific wording difficult to establish on the basis of formulated criteria.

In fact, one of the problems in such a discussion is called "the burden of proof." Should the benefit of the doubt go to a saying unless it can be shown to be inauthentic, or should it be doubted unless proved authentic? The loose orality view of the Seminar takes the position: Prove it to be true! On this approach, single testimony is almost automatically excluded as being of any value; one witness is not enough to establish a saying as tied to Jesus.[30] If we were to apply such standards to other documents, whole shelves of ancient history would have to be excluded. Most of the events we know about from ancient history are attested only in one ancient source. One could argue that the burden of proof should be the reverse, since Greco-Roman historiography and the Jewish culture of memory attempted to be careful in presenting the thrust of this material.

The burden of proof often exposes the presuppositions of the person examining the text, but people who take opposite positions on burden of proof still work with the criteria of authenticity.[31] I will now define, illustrate, and evaluate each of the three dominant criteria.

Dissimilarity

This standard argues that only if what Jesus said is unlike Judaism and unlike the practice that emerged from the early church, then it must go back to Jesus.

In fairness, usually it is the difference from Judaism that receives the bulk of the attention when this criterion is used in broader New Testament circles. If there is evidence of reform from Jewish teaching, then the teaching under discussion most likely goes back to Jesus. For example, when Jesus teaches love for one's enemy, the Seminar rates this red, calling it "close to the heart" of Jesus' teaching. It cuts "too much against the social grain," so it is original with Jesus.

This criterion is actually a helpful one in determining where Jesus differs from his cultural heritage. But two problems exist with its rigorous application. First, if both sides of the dissimilarity are affirmed, so that Jesus differs from *both* Judaism *and* the early church, then Jesus becomes a decidedly odd figure, totally detached from his cultural heritage *and* ideologically estranged from the movement he is responsible for founding. One wonders how he ever came to be taken seriously. He becomes an eccentric if only that which makes him different is regarded as authentic. The criterion may help us understand where Jesus' teaching is exceptional, but it can never give us the essential Jesus.

Second, the Seminar does not consistently apply the principle. On the debate over Jesus' lack of fasting in Luke 5:33–39 and parallels, the Seminar argues that although Jesus' remark is distinct from Judaism and the early church's known practice, that remark cannot go back to Jesus with any kind of certainty.[32] Apparently even dissimilar sayings must pass some additional, unexpressed criteria. Moreover, the church presumably could not follow Jesus' hesitation to fast and so chose to go back to fasting, despite the fact that other practices that deviated from Judaism, like refusing circumcision, were not resumed.

Another key example of a dissimilar set of sayings not being accepted as authentic is the extensive "Son of Man" saying tradition in the Gospels. Most scholars regard this expression as not an established title for the Messiah in Judaism at Jesus' time, nor did the early church use it as a title for Jesus. Yet, despite this acknowledged double dissimilarity, the "Son of Man" sayings are excluded as being authentic, except when they describe humans as the son of man, a usage attested to in Judaism through its use in the Psalter and Ezekiel! The reason why the title "Son of Man" is excluded is the fact that it expresses such a high Christological view of Jesus.

What this "Son of Man" example reveals perhaps is a hidden criterion—a Christological standard—in the Seminar's evaluation of sayings: If a saying says Jesus is more than a sage and a teller of parables, then it is not authentic. But this approach begs the question. If, on the one hand, the critical criteria are not consistently applied by the Seminar's scholars, then certainly a claim of bias may be justified. On the other hand, if Jesus was merely a sage and teller of parables, then why all the fuss over him? Where did the severe animosity surrounding him come from?[33] How can they explain his rejection, given their slight portion of authentic sayings on mostly proverbial topics?

In sum, the Jesus that emerges from the Seminar's extreme and inconsistent use of the criterion of dissimilarity is not a Jesus whom Judaism would have crucified. Their deduced portrait of the Jewish teacher cannot match what we know about the origin of his demise. Since virtually everyone acknowledges that Jesus was crucified because of Jewish frustration with his teaching and claims, perhaps what should be adjusted is not the Gospel's portrait of Jesus, but the way in which this criterion is used to yield a picture of Jesus that cannot adequately explain why he was treated to such an end.

Multiple attestation

Multiple attestation occurs when a saying appears either in multiple sources (M, L, Q, Mark) or in multiple forms (i.e., in a miracle account, a parable, and/or apocalyptic settings).[34] The Seminar's evaluation of Jesus' sayings about John the Baptist in Matthew 11:7–8 in pink appeals to this criterion. Since this saying appears in Q as well as in *Thomas*, it likely goes back to Jesus. This criterion is helpful for what it includes, though one must be careful not to suggest that failure of a saying to be attested in multiple sources is adequate reason for rejecting it.

Like the previous one, this criterion is not consistently applied by the Seminar. Scot McKnight's essay in this volume treats this criterion when he evaluates the "I have come" sayings. To this expression could be added the "I am sent" sayings, which are conceptually similar in form. This kind of expression appears at various levels of the tradition ("I have come": Matt. 5:17 [M]; 9:13 is like Mark 2:17; Luke 5:32 [Mark and/or Q]; 10:34–35 is like Luke 12:45 [Q]; "I am sent": Matt. 15:24 [M]; Luke 4:43 [L]). If we include statements like "the Son of Man has come" in this motif, then the selection of material broadens (Matt. 11:19 is like Luke 7:34 [Q]; Luke 19:10 is like Mark 10:45 [Mark]). One can see that this kind of statement is attested in multiple sources, since M, L, Q, and Mark all contain it.

But apparently Jesus' tendency to express his mission in "I have come" terms is not sufficient to consider a text like Mark 10:45 as authentic: "For even the Son of Man did not come to be served, but to serve, and to give his life as a ransom for many."[35] The Seminar regards much of this famous line as "Mark's creation," printed in gray.[36] Why do they reject it? The original saying in their view was about service, not redemption. The service concept belongs to Jesus, but not the redemptive idea. They argue that Luke's shorter version indicates that Mark made the change and supplied the more theological version of what originally was just a proverb, even though Mark, in this case, is recognized by all as the earlier Gospel!

Again the real criterion applied to this saying is not multiple attestation but the hidden Christological standard of the Seminar that is applied even when the source evidence goes the other direction. In fact, one can suggest that Christology is the *real* issue in the debate over many sayings, much more so than history or the objective application of abstract criteria. In an almost circular kind of way, a saying is accepted because it reflects a certain circumscribed Christology formed on an impression not created by the consistent application of the criteria, but by the preconceived, limited Christology. This Christology is affirmed because Jesus was only, it is argued on the basis of the accepted sayings, a sage and teller of parables.

It would be unfair to suggest that the consensus of New Testament critical studies embraces the authenticity of Mark 10:45.[37] In fact, its authenticity is heavily debated. But what should not be debated is that the form of the saying is very much a reflection of the way Jesus talked. One can make a strong case for its authenticity. The idea that Jesus died "for many" is attested in several levels of the Gospel tradition and in the tradition that grew from it (Matt. 26:24; Mark 14:24; Luke 22:19–20; 1 Cor. 11:24–25). Not every "Son of Man" saying that discusses Jesus' death makes this "he died for many" point, a fact that shows the tradition distinguished different kinds of suffering sayings and did not creatively insist on making them all refer to how Jesus' death paid for sin (e.g., Mark 8:31; 9:12, 31; 10:33–34). But if Jesus, sensing the rejection growing around him, was aware of his approaching death, certainly he would have reflected on his suffering's value as a basis for continuing his mission. Why would he continue to pursue his ministry in the way he did? Moreover, in Judaism, there was already precedent for a representative martyr's death, so that cultural and theological categories did exist that could be drawn upon (2 Macc. 7:37–38; 8:2–7; 4 Macc. 6:26–30; 9:21–25; 17:20–22; 18:10–16).[38]

In sum, as with the "Son of Man" sayings, there is good reason to defend the authenticity of the ransom concept in the ministry of Jesus himself, even on the basis of the criterion for authenticity the Seminar uses! As one examines these criteria individually, it becomes clear that even by these more discriminating standards a case can be made for the major redemptive and Christological themes of Jesus' ministry. The judgments of the Seminar are suspect even by their own limiting standards.

Coherence

This criterion is dependent on the application of the previous two. It argues that whatever coheres or "jives" with the application of the other criteria should be accepted as authentic. This process is hard to illustrate, since it requires a detailed working through all the sayings to establish a base of teaching from which to judge those sayings that cannot be evaluated as easily by the other criteria. If, as the Seminar has done, the teaching base of Jesus is reduced by more than half using the other criteria, then there is much less authentic data to serve as a ground of coherence for the sayings that are left. In fact, it is the rigorous application of the criterion of coherence that has led the Seminar to see Jesus as only a sage and teller of parables.

In the few examples I have treated in this essay, one can easily defend the Son of Man concept, reflecting a high Christology, as going back to Jesus himself, as well as the view of his death as a sacrificial ransom for many. These aspects of his teachings show a much larger base of coherence than the Seminar allows, and the number of additional sayings that cohere with this larger base is far greater in our judgment as well. Jesus' remarks in Mark 14:24 (one that the Seminar treats as probably inauthentic, i.e., gray) about his self-sacrifice instituting the covenant in his blood at the Last Supper coheres, since Jesus did see his life offered as a ransom for many. In fact, it is likely that the covenant mentioned here is the new covenant as Luke 22:20 argues, a text the Seminar rejects by printing in black. What other covenant could Jesus mean? If one applies the gist and summary principle argued for above, then it is easy to make sense of how one moves from Mark to Luke's rendering.

What our survey of critical methods shows is that the sayings of Jesus need not be viewed as "jive," even though they are not always "memorex" tapes either. A more balanced use of these criteria can argue for the authenticity of major strands of Jesus' redemptive and Christological teaching. With these themes in place, it is easier to understand and explain why Jesus was seen to be a challenge to the Jewish authorities and why he ended up on the cross, crucified for claiming to be sent from God.

Conclusion

In the beginning there were no tape recorders, but that does not mean that the oral transmission of Jesus' words in the Gospels was haphazard and uncontrolled. This essay has surveyed issues tied to orality in a non-high-tech first-century world. Greco-Roman historiography, the Jewish culture of memory in working with divine teaching, and the Gospel texts themselves expose the shortcomings of any view that argues that orality in ancient culture means that major fabrication of key Christian teachings took place.

In sum, the portrait of the Jesus Seminar in their work, *The Five Gospels*, is much too black in its assessment of Jesus' teaching. Too little of the real, live Jesus shows through their work. So little emerges that one wonders how their Jesus ever generated the level of hostility he received from the Jews or the total loyalty he procured from his disciples. The Jesus tradition may not always be exactly like "memorex," but neither is it anything remotely like "jive." The voice of Jesus comes through the Gospels, "live and in color." It is summarized discourse that has faithfully preserved the gist of Jesus' teaching.

The Gospels' portrait of the words of Jesus reveals a figure whose teaching required a choice to follow him or reject him, a figure who claimed to reveal the way to God in no uncertain terms. He did not bring wisdom; he was wisdom (Matt. 7:24–27). That is why people were either for him to the point of death or against him to the point of death. His words presented the choice between life or death (Luke 9:18–26). Anyone who reads his words in the Gospels should realize that the voice that is present is neither muffled nor created; it is loud and clear.

The Words of Jesus in the Gospels: Live, Jive, or Memorex?

Notes

1. This color scheme is present in Robert Funk, Roy Hoover, and the Jesus Seminar, *The Five Gospels; What Did Jesus Really Say?* (New York: Macmillan, 1993). The two other colors are gray and black. Black means Jesus did not say this or anything like it. Gray means Jesus probably did not say this, but that something he taught may have some connection with that saying; thus one can use the material in determining who Jesus was (see p. 36 for their description of the color-scheme philosophy). As other essays in this volume explain, the fifth Gospel for the Jesus Seminar is the Gospel of *Thomas*, a Gnostic text that the Seminar has elevated to a status equal to if not above the canonical Gospels in its historical value (see note 3 below, premises 24–25).

2. Ibid., *The Five Gospels*, 30.

3. A list of sixty-four premises opens another key work published by the Jesus Seminar, *The Gospel of Mark: Red Letter Edition*, ed. Robert Funk and Mahlon Smith (Sonoma, Calif.: Polebridge Press, 1991). This book does for Mark what *The Five Gospels* did for Matthew, Mark, Luke, John, and *Thomas*. To their credit, the Jesus Seminar has been honest about their presuppositions and has tried to list and defend them. Some of their premises show that my description of this approach as a "jive" approach to the Gospels is fair. I list some of the key, and most questionable, ones here.

   "Premise 1: The historical Jesus is to be distinguished from the Gospel portraits of him."

   "Premise 4: Oral tradition is fluid."

   "Premise 9: Jesus' disciples were oral and itinerant: they moved around and revised his sayings and parables as the situation demanded."

   "Premise 10: The oral tradition exhibits little interest in biographical data about Jesus."

   "Premise 20: Matthew and Luke have no independent knowledge of the order of events in the story of Jesus."

   "Premise 24: Thomas represents an earlier stage of the tradition than do the canonical Gospels."

   "Premise 25: Thomas represents an independent witness to the Jesus tradition."

   "Premise 47: The greater part of the sayings tradition was created or borrowed from common lore by the transmitters of the oral tradition and the authors of the Gospels."

   In surveying this list, two things are clear: the stress placed on the freedom of orality and the significant role given to the Gospel of *Thomas* in making assessments (*Thomas* is given an independence that Matthew and Luke are not granted as witnesses to Jesus). These are two severe flaws in the Seminar's approach.

4. All the approaches to this question argue that the later Gospel writers had some knowledge of what earlier Gospels writers had written and drew on traditions that recalled these events. They may not agree on which Gospel was first (either Mark or Matthew), but the amount of agreement both in wording and in event order makes it clear that some events, including most of the key events of Jesus' ministry, circulated and were well known within the church. This suggests that some, if not most, variations in wording were conscious. The variations help to explain what kind of report the Evangelists were giving.

5. The translation is the author's, but a comparison to any accepted translation yields the same basic points: Luke had sources, he examined them, yet he still felt a need to write his own version. As I have argued elsewhere, Luke sought "to carefully follow precedent" (Darrell L. Bock, *Luke 1:1–9:50*, Baker Exegetical Commentary on the New Testament [Grand Rapids: Baker, 1994], see exegesis on Luke 1:1–4).

6. For a clear explanation of this distinction by a conservative evangelical, see Paul

Feinberg, "The Meaning of Inerrancy," *Inerrancy*, ed. Norman L. Geisler (Grand Rapids: Zondervan, 1979), 267–304, esp. 298–304.

7. For a helpful discussion of this passage and topic in Greco-Roman historiography, see Charles Fornara, *The Nature of History in Ancient Greece and Rome* (Berkeley: University of California Press, 1983), 143–68.

8. Ibid., 153–54.

9. Ibid., 154–55.

10. Ibid., 163.

11. A summary of Jewish instructional technique appears in the article by Rainer Riesner, "Jüdische Elementarbildung und Evangelienüberlieferung," *Gospel Perspectives: Studies of History and Tradition in the Four Gospels*, vol. 1, ed. R. T. France and David Wenham (Sheffield: JSOT, 1980), 209–23. This article, though it is in German, summarizes the parallels between Jewish instructional technique in the culture at large and the recording and remembering of the tradition that found its way into the Gospels. I summarize its contents in this subsection. The names associated with this approach to the background for the Gospels are Birger Gerhardsson and Harold Riesenfeld. A second article making some of the same points in English is R. Riesner, "Jesus as Preacher and Teacher," *Jesus and the Oral Gospel Tradition*, JSNTMS 64, ed. Henry Wansbrough (Sheffield: Sheffield Academic Press, 1991), 185–210.

12. Riesner, "Jesus as Preacher," 197–208. Riesner stresses Jesus' vivid style and his memorizable speech, given that about 80 percent of his teaching is structured in parallelism of one type or another. Moreover, the disciples ("disciple" itself means "learner") were gathered by Jesus to learn from him and then to undertake mission work; thus, his teaching was important to them. Riesner goes on to challenge the views of orality espoused by Werner Kelber, a view like that reflected in the Jesus Seminar, arguing that orality in the Gospel tradition is not as flexible as Kelber suggests. Riesner notes three conditions when verbatim transmission might occur: (1) if the author is viewed as divinely inspired; (2) if the text has a recognized form, like poetry or parallelism; and (3) if the material is handed down by a group with specialized training. Jesus and his disciples fit all three. One final point: Those who work with the Gospels know that the *teachings* of Jesus exhibit the least amount of variation in the way they are presented. Although the settings in which the sayings appear sometimes vary, the contents themselves show little variation.

13. The text of the prophet Isaiah found at Qumran is almost identical to that of the rabbis a thousand years later.

14. Riesner, "Jüdische," 218.

15. G. Fee, *The First Epistle to the Corinthians*, NICNT (Grand Rapids: Eerdmans, 1987), 548; G. Delling, "παραλαμβάνω," *The Theological Dictionary of the New Testament*, ed. G. Kittel and G. Friedrich, trans. G. W. Bromiley (Grand Rapids: Eerdmans, 1964), 4:11–14.

16. Interestingly the Lukan form of this event differs slightly from the Matthean and Marcan versions (Matt. 26:26–29; Mark 14:12–17), showing the "differences" issue I noted at the beginning of the essay. Anyone reading the three versions, however, can see that the fundamentals of the report of what was said contains the same gist of the event, reflecting the principle argued for here in the ancient handling of such events.

17. The examination of Jewish forms of tradition within the New Testament is a more recent attempt to correct the excessive claims of older form critics who modeled their observations on the distant and much later cultural setting of Icelandic folklore. Two essays by E. Earle Ellis are key to this fresh and more historically sensitive perspective on how tradition was communicated in the early church: "Gospels Criticism," *The*

Gospel and the Gospels, ed. P. Stuhlmacher (Grand Rapids: Eerdmans, 1991), 26–52; and "New Directions in Form Criticism," *Prophecy and Hermeneutic*, ed. E. Earle Ellis (Tübingen: Mohr, 1978), 237–53. Ellis cites numerous examples of the traces of Jewish forms of tradition in the whole of the New Testament. Among the key points made in these essays is that major teaching would not have remained in exclusively oral form for long (see Ellis, "Gospels Criticism," 39, and the article by Stuhlmacher in the same volume, "The Theme: The Gospel and the Gospels," 1–25, esp. 2–12).

The classic essay arguing for evidence of the early fixing of parts of the Gospel tradition is H. Schürmann, "Die vorösterlichen Anfänge der Logientradition," in his *Traditionsgeschichtliche Untersuchungen zu den synoptischen Evangelien* (Düsseldorf: Patmos, 1968), 39–65. The essay's title refers to the "pre-Easter origins of the Sayings tradition." This body of work shows that much of the tradition did not remain in a loose, floating position for very long, as well as discussing the care with which such tradition was passed on.

18. In fact, the Rockets won the Phoenix series 4–3 and went on to win Houston's first major professional championship in another seventh-game victory at home. My footnote has a different historical perspective than the body of my article!

19. One can hardly think of a greater death-to-life reversal than the one the Gospels portray. It would be naive to expect the Evangelists to ignore what they had come to understand about Jesus as a result of his resurrection as they wrote their accounts of his ministry. But that does not mean that such reflection required fabrication of events. What is amazing about the Gospels is their honest portrayal of the disciples' confusion during Jesus' life. Surely if the Gospels were as "creative" as some make them out to be, then these disciples would have been portrayed in more flattering ways than they are. If Jesus' portrait can be enhanced to such a great degree, why not that of his followers? Those who are skeptical about the Gospels' portrayal of Jesus and his disciples have to explain two realities: (1) the unflattering portrayal of the disciples during Jesus' ministry, if the Gospel writers really did enhance the portrait of Jesus, and (2) the amount of courage the disciples showed in Jesus' absence after his crucifixion that led them to risk their lives for him. What brought about this change, even reversal, of character? The Gospels make it clear that what the resurrection revealed to the disciples was Jesus' identity and what he had really been about. Their transformation and the resurrection's role in it is one reason why the resurrection is seen as such a hub event by the Christian faith.

20. Pericope is the technical name for a unit of tradition in a Gospel. It usually is a paragraph unit.

21. Although who is responsible for the shift in order is a matter for discussion, most see Luke doing the rearranging here because for him the city of Jerusalem is so central in Jesus' ministry; thus he makes the Jerusalem temptation the climactic one. Tighter temporal markers and explicit dismissal language also appear in Matthew (4:5, 10), which also suggests the likelihood of this explanation.

22. Matthew 8 and Luke 7 are the same event, since they occupy nearly parallel positions in each Gospel. Both come immediately following Jesus' ethical teaching in the Sermon on the Mount (Matthew)/Plain (Luke). Note one other feature. A reading of Matthew alone leaves one impression about how the event occurred, while Luke leaves another impression. The differences in choice leave slightly different perspectives on the event, which give it a distinct force in each account. Yet the basic event remains the same. As we shall see, the Gospels handle event and sayings in a similar manner. Such differences do not impact that thrust of an event; rather, they reflect literary choices made by the author. In this case, literary compression has probably influenced

Matthew's account, as his intention was to highlight the healing, not supply every detail about it.

23. Interestingly, the apocryphal *Gospel of the Ebionites* solves the wording dilemma by having the voice utter both sentences in the one setting, something none of the canonical Gospels opt to do.

24. Note how Mark 1:10 and Matthew 3:16 are explicit in identifying only Jesus as seeing the dove. In none of the accounts is there any indication that the crowd present saw or heard anything. Only John 1 indicates that the Baptist was aware of what took place.

25. In making this conclusion, I remind readers of the points made above about summary (*vox*) versus citation (*verba*). An account need not be detailed in its precision to be accurate and true. Summary can be as historical and true as citation. They are simply different forms of presenting history. What I have argued is that the Gospel writers intended to summarize, and the texts themselves reveal the ways in which these summaries were done. So they should be evaluated for what they attempted to do, not for attempting to do anything more or less. Saying this more theologically, one can say that the biblical texts reveal how God inspired the Evangelists to present their account of Jesus. In John 14–16, Jesus promised that those who passed on his story would be led into all the truth by the Spirit. These texts show how that was done.

26. By what has been said so far, it should be clear that had a significant number of evangelical moderates been included in the Seminar and had it represented a real cross-section of current scholarship, the percentage of red, pink, gray, and black sayings would be radically different, with a much higher number of sayings falling into the first three color groupings. It would be fair to argue that the results of the Jesus Seminar are not a consensus of current scholarship, but reflect a minimalist position. For a critique of the Seminar or its failure to really represent a cross-section of current scholarship, in contrast to how the Seminar portrays itself, see Richard Hays' review of the Seminar's work, "The Corrected Jesus," *First Things* 43 (1994): 43–48, esp. 47–48. Hays, who teaches at Duke, cannot be accused of possessing any evangelical bias, so his critique is a particularly significant one.

27. See Craig Blomberg's essay in this volume for an analysis of the Gospel of *Thomas*.

28. Hays, "The Corrected Jesus," 44–45.

29. A full listing of all these proposed criteria is present in Robert Stein's "The Criteria for Authenticity," *Gospel Perspectives*, 225–63. Among the criteria he mentions that are less often used than the three this essay treats are: evidence of Aramaic linguistic phenomena, presence of Palestinian environmental phenomena, an appeal to tendencies within tradition to develop (a negative criterion designed to *exclude* saying material), an appeal to tendencies in Jewish Christianity to soften the tradition's bolder statements, and traditions whose patterns do not match the editorial style of the Evangelist. Of his secondary list, the most helpful are Aramaic linguistic tendencies and appeals to Palestinian environment, but all these criteria show is that the tradition can fit within a setting involving Jesus.

30. This largely unexpressed standard alone ends up removing almost all the *Gospel of John* from serious consideration. This "single witness" exclusion criterion is hidden in the Seminar's claim that "only sayings that can be traced back to the oral period, 30–50 C.E., can possibly have originated with Jesus" (Funk, Hoover, and the Jesus Seminar, *The Five Gospels*, 25). Since John is regarded by most to date from 90 and his material is largely unique, it cannot be connected to earlier sources, and so it becomes excluded almost by definition. One must grant that John's Gospel is more explicit in its Christological teaching than the Synoptics and that its style of Jesus' discourse is unique, but much of this Christology emerges from debate over the meaning of his

works and what they imply. John makes explicit what these events showed, and certainly debate over Jesus' work is attested throughout the tradition. Given the kind of multiple perspectives possible within a portrayal of history, these sayings and discourses too can represent authentic summaries of Jesus' teaching. They should not be excluded merely because they are unique. For a careful discussion of the issues John's Gospel raises that are peculiar to it, see D. A. Carson, *The Gospel According to John* (Grand Rapids: Eerdmans, 1991), 40–68.

31. Sometimes how the criteria are named reveals a great deal. To call them the criteria *for* authenticity suggests that a saying needs to pass these tests to be seen as authentic. To speak of criteria *of* authenticity simply notes that these tests can help us argue for a saying's authenticity without arguing that passing such a test is a necessary qualification to establish authenticity. For a careful discussion of burden of proof from a more philosophical angle, see S. C. Goetz and C. L. Blomberg, "The Burden of Proof," *JSNT* 11 (1981): 39–83.

32. Funk, Hoover, and the Jesus Seminar, *The Five Gospels*, 285–87.

33. For more on this, see ch. 1 by Craig Blomberg.

34. A source refers to a document or stream of tradition that the Evangelists used in writing their Gospels. They are what Luke alludes to in his mention of his awareness of other accounts (Luke 1:1–4). In Gospel studies, the siglum "M" stands for material unique to Matthew, "L" for material unique to Luke; "Q" for teaching shared between Matthew and Luke, while Mark refers to material originating in that Gospel. These are treated as four different strands of tradition that make up the bulk of the Synoptic Gospel tradition.

35. One might ask how this saying could be considered an "I have come" saying when it refers to the Son of Man, not Jesus. The answer is that Jesus only referred to himself as "Son of Man," so it is an indirect reference to himself. As such, it is semantically and conceptually equivalent to "I have come."

36. Funk, Hoover, and the Jesus Seminar, *The Five Gospels*, 95.

37. For the details of this debate pro and con, see Robert Gundry, *Mark: A Commentary for His Apology for the Cross* (Grand Rapids: Eerdmans, 1993), 587–93. The same kind of debate rages over the "Son of Man" sayings as well. On this debate, see Darrell L. Bock, "The Son of Man in Luke 5:24," *BBR* 1 (1991): 109–21. Our point in both cases is that something other than a consistent application of these criteria is at work in rejecting these sayings.

38. Gundry, *Mark*, 588, 590, also notes two other key factors. First, the saying has Semitic touches in that it reveals its age and roots in a Palestinian setting. At the least, it comes from the earliest church. Second, sixteen epistolary texts express this idea in varied terminology. So such a saying had an impact. Where did such a view come from, if not from Jesus? As Gundry says, "It seems unlikely that a saying dealing simply with service and set in a pericope dealing only with service should have been given a soteriological twist without dominical [i.e., a saying associated with Jesus] support, especially since indisputably Christian formations concerning Jesus' death do not use the vocabulary of service."

Chapter 4

WHAT DID JESUS DO?

CRAIG A. EVANS

Craig A. Evans (Ph.D., Claremont Graduate School) is
Professor of biblical studies at Trinity Western University. He
is an active participant in the Society of Biblical Literature
Historical Jesus Section. He is editor of *Jesus, Life of Jesus
Research: An Annotated Bibliography*, and (with Bruce Chilton)
of *Studying the Historical Jesus: Evaluation of the State of Current
Research*.

The Jesus Seminar has reported its findings with respect to what Jesus said;[1] it is now addressing the question of what Jesus did.[2] This is a serious issue, for the latter is just as important as the former. After all, even if (contrary to what the Jesus Seminar has concluded) Jesus said most of the things that the Gospels say he did, this fact is of little significance if he did not do the things described in the Gospels. Did Jesus perform miracles? Did he enter Jerusalem as Israel's messianic king? Did he confront Israel's religious leaders? Did he predict coming judgment on Jerusalem and the temple? Was he seized by the religious leaders, interrogated, and handed over to Pontius Pilate, the Roman governor of Judea? Did Pilate crucify Jesus as "king of the Jews," and was this execution the result of his teachings and activities?

Members of the Jesus Seminar have expressed doubts about several of these questions. Perhaps the most controversial thesis to date comes from Burton Mack in his recently published book, *A Myth of Innocence: Mark and Christian Origins*.[3] According to Mack, the factors that led to Jesus' execution are unclear:

> One can only speculate about what happened. . . . Jesus must have gone [to Jerusalem] on some occasion, most probably during a pilgrimage season, was associated with a demonstration, and was killed. . . . Some of his followers apparently saw a connection between Jesus' activity in Galilee and his fate in Jerusalem. How they put these pieces together, however, and what they concluded from them are hardly reconstructible.[4]

Mack believes that the linkage of Jesus' public teachings to the story of his death as presented in Mark, the earliest of the New Testament Gospels, is no more than narrative fiction.[5] Impressed by this analysis, David Seeley, one of Mack's students, has asserted that "Mark concocted the Jewish conspiracy against Jesus for his own, redactional reasons."[6]

Such skepticism is hard to justify. What gives Mark's linkage of Jesus' Galilean preaching and Judean execution an unhistorical appearance? Does not logic alone suggest a close link between the execution of a man as "king of the Jews" and the memories of that man talking about the coming "kingdom of God"? Almost all biblical scholars accept these data as historical. Moreover, as we shall see shortly, this link is attested in sources independent of Mark's Gospel.

In a major study that appeared a decade ago, E. P. Sanders identified the "almost indisputable facts" of Jesus' life as follows:

1. Jesus was baptized by John the Baptist.
2. Jesus was a Galilean who preached and healed.
3. Jesus called disciples and spoke about twelve of them.
4. Jesus confined his activity to Israel.
5. Jesus engaged in a controversy about the temple.
6. Jesus was crucified outside Jerusalem by the Roman authorities.
7. After his death Jesus' followers continued as an identifiable movement.
8. At least some Jews persecuted at least parts of the new movement (Gal. 1:13, 22; Phil. 3:6), and it appears that this persecution endured at least to a time near the end of Paul's career (2 Cor. 11:24; Gal. 5:11; 6:12; cf. Matt. 10:17; 23:34).[7]

To these facts one can add a few complementary details. I think that it is highly probable that Jesus was viewed by the public as a prophet, that he spoke often of the kingdom of God, that his temple controversy involved criticism of the ruling priests, and that the Romans crucified him as "king of the Jews." We shall find that many of the sayings of Jesus cohere with these historical elements, often either explaining them or being explained by them.

The most important of Jesus' activities can be gathered into two major groupings: (1) the proclamation of the kingdom of God and the appointment of the twelve apostles; and (2) controversy with the ruling priests and a Roman execution. The evidence for these activities is strong enough, as we shall see, that they may with confidence be designated "facts." It will also become clear that these two groupings of activities are closely related, with the first leading inexorably to the second.

My purpose in focusing on these two groups of facts and their connection to Jesus' execution is twofold. First, the historicity of these items is important for its own sake and worthy of serious reflection. But second and more broadly, if it can be shown that these facts are, indeed, reasonably established, then the skepticism of critics like Mack and Seeley, who doubt the essential historicity of the Gospels' portrait of Jesus' public ministry and death in Jerusalem, has been in large measure answered. If this is so, then we should exercise caution in following the (un)critical skepticism with respect to other reported activities and deeds of Jesus. Let us, then, begin with the two major groupings that have been proposed.

The Proclamation of the Kingdom of God and the Appointment of the Twelve Apostles

Of all of Jesus' teachings, the parables are viewed by critical scholars with the greatest amount of confidence. With respect to the question of authenticity, they have been called the "bedrock" of the tradition.[8] Recent critical studies echo this sentiment,[9] while major, comprehensive works proceed on the assumption that most, if not all, of the parables originated with Jesus.[10] The significance of this scholarly consensus lies in the observation that approximately one-half of Jesus' parables speak of the kingdom of God. These parables attempt to describe what the kingdom is like, on what basis one may expect to enter it, and how one should be prepared for the kingdom's appearance. On any reading, Jesus' kingdom parables clearly imply that he anticipated a change in his society. The human way of doing things, of running the state and society, was in the process of giving way to God's way of doing things.

One saying of Jesus that scholars have with a high degree of confidence traditionally regarded as authentic is found in Luke 11:20: "But if I drive out demons by the finger of God, then the kingdom of God has come to you."[11] It seems clear from this utterance that Jesus not only anticipated the coming of the kingdom, as though still future, he also believed that the kingdom had in some sense arrived. This is best explained by understanding the kingdom of God as the power and presence of God.[12] Jesus did not have in mind a kingdom with traditional political and territorial boundaries, but a sphere of power in which God reigned and transformed society. This sphere had begun so small that it was hardly noticeable, but it would eventually engulf the world (cf. Mark 4:30–32).

The exorcism saying quoted above probably explains in part Jesus' statements on faith, which sometimes accompanied other healings. "Your faith has healed you" (Mark 5:34; 10:52; Luke 7:50) was not simply an explanation of how the sufferer had become healed, but implied that the healed person was now fit to enter the kingdom of God.[13] In other words, just as the exorcisms demonstrated the power and presence of the kingdom, so the other acts of healing demonstrated the same. Jesus' ministry of healing and exorcism was not simply motivated out of compassion for the ill and oppressed, but was part of the restoration of Israel and preparation for the dawning of the kingdom of God. The association of Jesus' miracles with the kingdom of God explains why blind Bartimaeus cried out to Jesus, "Jesus, Son of David, have mercy on me!" (Mark 10:47–48).

Closely related to Jesus' proclamation of the kingdom of God was his appointment of the twelve apostles. That there were twelve and that he called these disciples "apostles" are two important facts. "Twelve" is best understood as a deliberate correspondence to the twelve tribes of Israel.[14] This does not mean that the twelve apostles were themselves members of the twelve tribes.[15] Nor does this mean that there never was any fluctuation in the membership of the twelve.[16] Rather, the number twelve was to be understood in a symbolic sense; it implied the restoration of Israel—all of Israel.

Perhaps the saying of Jesus that expresses this hope in the clearest fashion is his promise to his apostles: "I tell you the truth, at the renewal of all things, when the Son of Man sits on his glorious throne, you who have followed me will also sit on twelve thrones, judging the twelve tribes of Israel" (Matt 19:28 = Luke 22:28–30).[17] Such a promise is in all probability what prompted James and John to request the privilege of sitting on Jesus' right and left (Mark 10:35–45).[18] These eager disciples were hoping for the top assignments in Jesus' new government.

By dubbing the Twelve as "apostles," Jesus underscored his own regal authority. By sending out ambassadors, he was acting as a king.[19] His apostles (from the word meaning "one sent") were to act as heralds proclaiming both the dawning of the kingdom of God and the one who was to sit on a throne of glory in this new kingdom. The people of Israel were called on to repent and to prepare for the kingdom.[20]

Jesus' kingdom preaching and healing resulted in the attraction of large crowds.[21] Many of these people followed Jesus to Jerusalem to celebrate the Passover and there greeted him with shouts of "Hosanna" and excited talk about the coming kingdom of David (Mark 11:1–10). Talk of the kingdom of God, complete with Jesus mounted on a donkey (something that Solomon son of David had done; cf. 1 Kings 1:38–40), set the stage for the conflict that would develop between Jesus and the religious authorities of Jerusalem.

Controversy with the Ruling Priests and a Roman Execution

According to all four New Testament Gospels, Jesus engaged in controversy with the Jewish religious leaders based in Jerusalem, as a result of which he was handed over to the Roman governor for execution. As mentioned above, David Seeley thinks that this presentation is nothing more than a literary concoction. He suspects that Mark, whose narrative is followed by Matthew and Luke (and possibly John as well), wished to tell the story this way in order to shift blame to the Jews and away from the Christians. Or (thinking again of Burton Mack) the Marcan evangelist, in his anxiety to exculpate Christians, created an imaginative story that would distance the Christian movement from Jewish revolutionary ideas and activities.

Of course, interpreters have for at least a century observed that the Gospels tend to exonerate Pilate by showing that he did not take the initiative against Jesus and that he was passive and easily influenced. At the same time the Gospels tend to emphasize the active role played by Jerusalem's religious leadership. But have these tendencies obliterated the record so that we, in Mack's words, "can only speculate about what happened"?

In my judgment, Mack, Seeley, and others have not given Mark and the other Gospels due consideration, especially in view of the relevant extracanonical sources and in view of what we do know of Roman policy. In the paragraphs that follow we will consider three passages found in the writings of the first-century Jewish historian Josephus, who is our most important extracanonical source. We are interested in his accounts of two Jesuses, the well-known one from Nazareth and the lesser-known son of Ananias.[22]

Josephus on Jesus of Nazareth

The most important non-Christian source for the historical Jesus is found in Josephus' *Jewish Antiquities*, penned sometime in the final decade of the first century. Jesus is mentioned in two passages. The first is the so-called *Testimonium*

Flavianum. According to this controversial and disputed text, Josephus describes Jesus in the following terms (*Ant.* 18.3.3 §63–64):

> At this time there appeared Jesus, a wise man, *if indeed one ought to call him a man*. For he was a doer of amazing deeds, a teacher of persons who receive truth with pleasure. He won over many Jews and many of the Greeks. *He was the Messiah*. And when Pilate condemned him to the cross, the leading men among us having accused him, those who loved him from the first did not cease to do so. *For he appeared to them the third day alive again, the divine prophets having spoken these things and a myriad of other marvels concerning him*. And to the present the tribe of Christians, named after this person, has not disappeared.

This passage has aroused a great deal of academic debate. Some scholars have argued that the passage is inauthentic in its entirety and is nothing more than a Christian insertion, perhaps authored by the fourth-century church historian Eusebius. Others have argued that the passage is wholly authentic. Today, however, most agree that the passage was authored by Josephus, with the exception of the three italicized sections.[23]

The principal support for the authenticity of the passage lies in a second passage that refers to Jesus, albeit only incidentally. The reference is found in *Antiquities* 20.9.1 §200–201:

> He (Ananus) convened the council of judges and brought before it the brother of Jesus—the one called "Christ"—whose name was James, and certain others. Accusing them of transgressing the law he delivered them up for stoning. But those of the city considered to be the most fair-minded and strict concerning the laws were offended at this and sent to the king secretly urging him to order Ananus to take such actions no longer.

There are no compelling reasons for rejecting this shorter passage as inauthentic. There is nothing Christian, or positive, in the reference to James and Jesus. The whole point is to explain why Ananus was deposed as high priest. Furthermore, the designation "brother of Jesus" contrasts with Christian practice of referring to James as the "brother of the Lord" (cf. Gal. 1:19; Eusebius, *Hist. Eccl.* 2.23.4). It is not surprising, therefore, that, in the words of Josephus scholar Louis Feldman, "few have doubted the genuineness of this passage on James."[24]

The authenticity of the second, shorter passage lends further support to the authenticity of the earlier passage. The reference to "Jesus the one called 'Christ' " clearly implies a prior reference; in all probability the *Testimonium Flavianum* is that prior reference.[25]

The significance of this passage lies in its corroboration of the basic narrative outline found in the New Testament Gospels. According to Josephus, Pilate condemned Jesus to the cross after the "leading men" (lit., "first men," i.e., the religious leaders; cf. *Ant.* 11.5.3 §140–141; 18.5.3 §121; Luke 19:47) among the Jews accused him. This reflects exactly the sequence and causal development narrated in Mark and the other canonical Gospels. Thus Josephus provides us with an important point of agreement with the New Testament account of the Passion, which tells us that the ruling priests had Jesus arrested and handed over to Pilate.

One may wonder from what source Josephus gathered his information concerning Jesus and James. Since Josephus says nothing about Jesus' resurrection, John Meier has concluded, rightly in my judgment, he probably did not learn of Jesus and James from Christian sources.[26] Because what he relates has to do with the execution of both, it is possible that his sources were official records. Feldman also entertains this possibility, but that can be no more than a conjecture.[27] In any case, the source of the *Testimonium* was in all probability not a Christian one.

Josephus on Jesus ben Ananias

A second discussion in Josephus, one that does not mention Jesus of Nazareth but is important for Jesus research, concerns Jesus ben Ananias, who uttered a prophetic oracle before and during the First Great War with Rome (*J.W.* 6.5.3 §300–309):

> But a further portent was even more alarming. Four years before the war, when the city was enjoying profound peace and prosperity, there came to the feast at which it is the custom of all Jews to erect tabernacles to God, one Jesus, son of Ananias, a rude peasant, who, standing in the temple, suddenly began to cry out, "A voice from the east, a voice from the west, a voice from the four winds; a voice against Jerusalem and the sanctuary, a voice against the bridegroom and the bride, a voice against all the people." Day and night he went about all the alleys with this cry on his lips. Some of the leading citizens, incensed at these ill-omened words, arrested the fellow and severely chastised him. But he, without a word on his own behalf or for the private ear of those who smote him, only continued his cries as before. Thereupon, the magistrates, supposing, as was indeed the case, that the man was under some supernatural impulse, brought him before the Roman governor; therefore, although flayed to the bone with scourges, he neither sued for mercy nor shed a tear, but, merely introducing the most mournful of variations into his ejaculation, responded to each stroke with "Woe to Jerusalem!" When Albinus, the governor, asked him who and whence he was and why he uttered these cries, he answered him never a word, but unceasingly reiterated his dirge over the city, until Albinus pronounced him a maniac and let him go. During the whole period up to the outbreak of war he neither approached nor was seen talking to any of the citizens, but daily, like a prayer that he had conned, repeated his lament, "Woe to Jerusalem!" He neither cursed any of those who beat him from day to day, nor blessed those who offered him food: to all men that melancholy presage was his one

reply. His cries were loudest at the festivals. So for seven years and five months he continued his wail, his voice never flagging nor his strength exhausted, until in the siege, having seen his presage verified, he found his rest. For, while going his round and shouting in piercing tones from the wall, "Woe once more to the city and to the people and to the temple," as he added a last word, "and woe to me also," a stone hurled from the *ballista* struck and killed him on the spot. So with these ominous words still upon his lips he passed away.[28]

This account is valuable because it helps us understand the sequence of Jesus' arrest, interrogation, and execution, as well as the motives for doing so. There is a remarkable correspondence between what is related of Jesus of Nazareth and what Josephus says happened to Jesus ben Ananias. Both entered the precincts of the temple (Mark 11:11, 15, 27; 12:35; 13:1; 14:49; *J.W.* 6.5.3 §301) at the time of a religious festival (Mark 14:2; 15:6; John 2:23; *J.W.* 6.5.3 §300). Both spoke of the doom of Jerusalem (Luke 19:41–44; 21:20–24; *J.W.* 6.5.3 §301), the sanctuary (Mark 13:2; 14:58; *J.W.* 6.5.3 §301), and the people (Mark 13:17; Luke 19:44; 23:28–31; *J.W.* 6.5.3 §301). Both apparently alluded to Jeremiah 7, where the prophet condemned the temple establishment of his day ("den of robbers": Jer 7:11 in Mark 11:17; "a voice against the bridegroom and the bride": Jer 7:34 in *J.W.* 6.5.3 §301). Both were "arrested" by the authority of Jewish,[29] not Roman, leaders (Mark 14:48; John 18:12; *J.W.* 6.5.3 §302). Both were beaten by the Jewish authorities (Matt. 26:68; Mark 14:65; *J.W.* 6.5.3 §302). Both were handed over to the Roman governor (Luke 23:1; *J.W.* 6.5.3 §303), who interrogated them (Mark 15:4; *J.W.* 6.5.3 §305). Both refused to answer the governor (Mark 15:5; *J.W.* 6.5.3 §305) and were consequently scourged (John 19:1; *J.W.* 6.5.3 §304). Governor Pilate may have offered to release Jesus of Nazareth, but did not; Governor Albinus did release Jesus son of Ananias (Mark 15:9; *J.W.* 6.5.3 §305).[30]

In other words, Josephus provides important corroboration of the major components relating to Jesus' fate in Jerusalem. From him we learn not only that his arrest was initiated by the religious authorities, as the Gospels claim, but also that the judicial and penal process itself, again as described in the Gospels, was apparently in step with practice in Roman Palestine. Other texts from Josephus could also be adduced that help in various ways to clarify Jesus' actions and the priestly establishment's reactions. One thinks of the devoted people who threw lemons at the high priest (and "king") Alexander Jannaeus, just as he was about to offer sacrifice (*Ant.* 13.13.5 §372–373), and of the young men incited by teachers to cut down the golden eagle that adorned the gate of the temple (*J.W.* 1.33.2–4 §648–655; *Ant.* 17.6.2–4 §149–167). In all of these cases, a particular understanding of temple policy led to public demonstration and deadly retaliation.[31]

In other words, there are no compelling reasons for rejecting the narrative presented by the New Testament Gospels, that Jesus was handed over by the religious leaders to Pilate. Why the leaders did this is clarified in part by Josephus' description of their response to Jesus ben Ananias, who during the Feast of

Tabernacles predicted the destruction of the city and the temple. The religious leaders seized him, beat him, and brought him before the Roman governor. The governor scourged him and interrogated him. Only when convinced that Jesus ben Ananias was a harmless lunatic did he release him. The parallels with Jesus of Nazareth are striking and strongly suggest that the Gospels' accounts, which testify of Jesus criticism of the religious establishment and his warning of its destruction, are true to history and practice.

How Did Jesus Provoke the Authorities?

We have concluded that Jesus of Nazareth provoked the religious authorities with his pronouncements against the temple establishment. But why would Pontius Pilate crucify Jesus for criticizing the temple establishment, whereas he let the son of Ananias go? Why especially did he crucify Jesus as "king of the Jews"? Here we have important differences between Jesus of Nazareth and Jesus ben Ananias. (1) Whereas the latter was little more than a prophet of doom, who may or may not have viewed the temple establishment as corrupt and deserving of criticism, the former was much more vehement in his denunciation. (2) Jesus of Nazareth had a sizable following; the son of Ananias did not. (3) In contrast to the son of Ananias, Jesus of Nazareth spoke of the kingdom of God, (4) Jesus of Nazareth performed miracles, attesting the present power of the kingdom of God; not so the son of Ananias. (5) Finally, Jesus of Nazareth publicly demonstrated in the temple precincts and criticized its authorities; the son of Ananias did not.

In my view, Jesus' criticism of the temple authorities may or may not have been sufficient to provoke these authorities in seeking his death. It may or may not have been sufficient to persuade Pilate, the Roman governor, to comply with their wishes. But had criticism of the temple authorities, even with a prediction of the temple's description, led to Jesus' death, it still would not explain the crucifixion of Jesus *as "king of the Jews"* (Mark 15:26 and parallels), a tradition that most scholars are prepared to accept as genuine.[32] But because the religious authorities recognized the importance of the wording of the inscription placed on, above, or in the vicinity of Jesus' cross, they most likely handed Jesus over to Pilate not simply because he criticized and perhaps even threatened them, but because he acknowledged that he was Israel's Messiah, the king of the kingdom that he had proclaimed throughout his ministry.

The messianic dimension of Jesus' visit to Jerusalem is attested at many points. We see it in the Triumphal Entry (Mark 11:1–10), where Jesus mounted a donkey and the crowd shouted, "Blessed is the coming kingdom of our father David." We see it in his temple action (11:15–18), where Jesus criticized high priestly polity, possibly as called for and anticipated by the author of the *Psalms of Solomon* 17:21–18:9, who expected the son of David, the "Lord Messiah," to cleanse Jerusalem.[33] The question of corruption is treated further in the denunciation of the scribes (Mark 12:38–40) and in the example of the widow who gave her last penny to an oppressive temple establishment (12:41–44).[34]

The fact that the very next passage (Mark 13:1–2) predicts the destruction of the temple, implies that the corruption of high priestly polity would result in divine judgment. Jesus' *messianic* authority is probably what lay behind the questions put to him by the ruling priests (11:27–33). We see it again in the parable of the vineyard tenants (12:1–12), where Jesus implied that he was the son (i.e., the Davidic Son of God), who although rejected by the "builders" (i.e., the religious authorities) would become the principal figure in the coming kingdom. The messianic dimension surfaced in the question of paying taxes to Caesar (12:13–17). If Jesus was Messiah, Israel's king, then surely it was wrong, as Jesus' opponents hoped he would affirm, to pay taxes to Caesar, a rival king; they should be paid to Messiah Jesus. The question about the interpretation of Psalm 110:1 (Mark 12:35–37) highlighted further the messianic dimension. The messianic identity of Jesus also probably motivated an unnamed woman to anoint Jesus with perfume (Mark 14:3–9). Jesus interpreted her action as foreshadowing his own death and burial, but her intention was to express her faith in and allegiance to Israel's long-awaited king.

All of these elements cohere with Jesus' arrest, hearings before the Jewish Sanhedrin and the Roman governor, and execution as "king of the Jews." As Israel's awaited Messiah, Jesus assumed the prerogative to pronounce judgment against what he regarded as improper temple polity.[35] As Messiah, Jesus was God's Son (as was David; cf. 2 Sam. 7:12–16; Ps. 2:7) and so was empowered to speak of new temple polity and a new social order.

It is probable that the false charges brought against Jesus ("We heard him say"; Mark 14:58) related in some way to his prophecy of the temple's destruction (13:2) and perhaps to his promise to raise up a new order (12:10–11).[36] The messianic dimension of Jesus' actions and pronouncement during his visit to Jerusalem, as well as talk of his authority over the temple precincts, led Caiaphas to ask Jesus directly if he was "the Christ, the son of the Blessed One" (14:61). To this question Jesus responded: "I am. . . . And you will see the Son of Man sitting at the right hand of the Mighty One and coming on the clouds of heaven" (14:62). The expression "right hand" alludes to Psalm 110:1; the expressions "Son of Man" and "coming on the clouds of heaven" allude to Daniel 7. Jesus said that he was indeed the Messiah, the Son of God, and that he was the human being of Daniel 7 ("son of man" = human being), who receives kingdom and power. "*Sitting* at the right" and "*coming* on the clouds" are not contradictory, even though the former implies being stationary while the latter implies motion, for these words allude to Jesus' enthronement on God's chariot throne (see Dan. 7:9, where God's throne has burning wheels). Jesus had asserted that he would sit on God's throne and come in judgment on his accusers.

Caiaphas recoiled in horror at Jesus' stunning assertion. He had uttered blasphemy and was worthy of death.[37] All agreed. Jesus had not only affirmed his messianic actions and innuendoes; he had shocked the religious sensibilities of his judges. Thus Jesus provided the grounds for a sentence of death from both the Jewish authorities (i.e., capital blasphemy) and the Roman authorities (i.e., treason and sedition).

The details provided by Mark and the other Gospels fill out the bare outline provided by Josephus. Jesus, the one called Messiah, was accused by the leading men among the Jews and was put to death by Pontius Pilate. There is no reason to conclude, as Mack has done, that we "can only speculate about what happened" and that pieces of the story of Jesus' passion "are hardly reconstructible." The messianic dimension of Jesus' activities is unmistakable. His crucifixion as "king of the Jews" was the inevitable result of his prior teachings and activities, in which he sought to proclaim and advance the kingdom of God.

The credibility of the Gospels' account of Jesus' death should increase our confidence in the essential reliability of these documents. Although the four Evangelists have edited their materials—materials that had admittedly already undergone a certain amount of editing and recontextualizing by Christians who preserved them and passed them on—there is no justification to adopt a skeptical stance with respect to what the Gospels report concerning Jesus' activities and deeds. The Gospels' presentation of Jesus' ministry and subsequent execution is coherent and entirely credible.

Notes

1. As seen in its recently published "red letter" edition of the New Testament Gospels plus the Gospel of *Thomas*; cf. R. W. Funk, R. W. Hoover, and the Jesus Seminar, *The Five Gospels: What Did Jesus Really Say?* (New York: Macmillan, 1993). For discussion and criticism of this book, see the preceding chapter by Darrell Bock.

2. The Seminar's first installment is W. B. Tatum's *John the Baptist and Jesus: A Report of the Jesus Seminar* (Sonoma, Calif.: Polebridge, 1994). This book is primarily devoted to what can be known of the historical John the Baptist (or Baptizer). The part that is particularly relevant for the present purposes is the chapter entitled "John the Baptist and Jesus" (145–57). The Seminar has concluded that John and Jesus did minister in the same time and place, but it expresses doubt about whether Jesus began his proclamation after John's imprisonment. The Seminar has also concluded that John did baptize Jesus, though it rejects the Gospels' reports of Jesus' vision of heaven and of the descent of the dove. The Seminar further concludes that in all probability Jesus had been a disciple of John, that he deliberately separated his movement from John's, and that some of John's disciples, believing Jesus to be John's successor, became Jesus' disciples. These conclusions are not particularly remarkable or objectionable.

   The one conclusion with which I disagree strongly concerns the question that the imprisoned John put to Jesus: "Are you the one who was to come, or should we expect someone else?" (Matt. 11:3 = Luke 7:19). Tatum reports (153–55) that the Seminar gave this tradition a "gray" rating, thus indicating a great deal of doubt (see also Funk, Hoover, and the Jesus Seminar, *The Five Gospels*, 177–78, 301–2). Several of the members of the Seminar believe that John's question and Jesus' answer derive from early Christian apologetic reflecting the rivalry between the followers of John and of Jesus. In my judgment, however, this exchange has a strong claim to authenticity, for I find it difficult to believe that early Christians, anxious to have Jesus claim fulfillment of ancient prophecies (such as Isa. 35:5–6; 62:1–2; cf. Matt. 11:4–6 = Luke 7:22–23), would invent a question in which John gives expression to doubts about Jesus' identity and calling. This potentially embarrassing tradition is in all probability authentic: John had doubts, and Jesus attempted to dispel them by claiming that his ministry of healing was fulfilling certain scriptural expectations. Whether this answer satisfied John, we do not know. Were this exchange between John and Jesus no more than an early Christian fiction, why not report that John was persuaded?

3. B. L. Mack, *A Myth of Innocence: Mark and Christian Origins* (Philadelphia: Fortress, 1988). Mack is not a member of the Jesus Seminar but has attended some of the Seminar's meetings and expresses his appreciation for insights that he has gained from these meetings.

4. Ibid., 88–89.

5. Ibid., 282.

6. D. Seeley, "Was Jesus Like a Philosopher? The Evidence of Martyrological and Wisdom Motifs in Q, Pre-Pauline Traditions, and Mark," in *Society of Biblical Literature 1989 Seminar Papers*, ed. D. J. Lull (Atlanta: Scholars Press, 1989), 548.

7. E. P. Sanders, *Jesus and Judaism* (London: SCM / Philadelphia: Fortress, 1985), 11.

8. J. Jeremias, *The Parables of Jesus* (London: SCM / New York: Scribner's, 1963), 11.

9. See P. B. Payne, "The Authenticity of the Parables of Jesus," *Gospel Perspectives: Studies of History and Tradition in the Four Gospels*, ed. R. T. France and D. Wenham (Sheffield: JSOT, 1981), 329–44; B. B. Scott, "Essaying the Rock: The Authenticity of the Jesus Parable Tradition," *Forum* 2, no. 3 (1986): 3–53; R. W. Funk, et al., *The Parables of Jesus: Red Letter Edition* (Sonoma, Calif.: Polebridge, 1988).

10. See B. B. Scott, *Hear Then the Parable: A Commentary on the Parables of Jesus* (Minneapolis: Fortress, 1989); C. L. Blomberg, *Interpreting the Parables* (Downers Grove, Ill.: InterVarsity Press, 1990).

11. The Jesus Seminar has given this saying a "pink" rating; cf. Funk, Hoover, and the Jesus Seminar, *The Five Gospels*, 329.

12. See B. D. Chilton, "Regnum Dei Deus Est," *SJT* 31 (1978): 261–70.

13. Some of the documents from Qumran illustrate the idea that the infirm and disabled were unqualified for certain privileges and activities associated with the kingdom.

14. See Sanders, *Jesus and Judaism*, 95–106.

15. Since some of the apostles were related to one another, this would not have been possible.

16. This seems to be the case, since there are some fourteen or fifteen names.

17. The Jesus Seminar assigns a "black" rating to this saying, indicating that they think it was produced by the early church (cf. Funk, Hoover, and the Jesus Seminar, *The Five Gospels*, 222–23, 389). The saying is rejected because it is "alien to the authentic thought of Jesus," which (in their estimation) did not include ideas of future judgment or the appearance of the "Son of Man." This conclusion, however, is the result of an egregious misunderstanding of eschatology and its relation to Jesus' teaching. See the helpful clarification offered by B. D. Chilton, "The Kingdom of God in Recent Discussion," in *Studying the Historical Jesus: Evaluations of the State of Current Research*, ed. B. D. Chilton and C. A. Evans, NTTS 19 (Leiden: Brill, 1994), 255–80, esp. 265–70. Sanders (*Jesus and Judaism*, 98–102) rightly argues that the early church, painfully aware that one of the Twelve (i.e., Judas Iscariot) had betrayed Jesus, would not be inclined to invent a saying in which Jesus tells the Twelve that they would some day sit on twelve thrones judging Israel. There is no compelling reason to deny the saying to Jesus.

18. Again the Jesus Seminar rejects the authenticity of the passage in question ("black" for Mark 10:36–40, "gray" for 10:42–45); cf. Funk, Hoover, and the Jesus Seminar, *The Five Gospels*, 94–95. Unfamiliar with the Jewish idioms and ideas, members of the Seminar imagine that the dialogue between Jesus and his disciples is the product of the early church. Again the Seminar's prejudice against and misunderstanding of eschatology plays a role in its negative decision. In support of the authenticity of the tradition, one must wonder why the early church would invent a dialogue that puts the disciples in a poor light—requesting seats of honor and disputing among themselves who was the greatest. This potentially embarrassing material has been preserved because of the importance attached to Jesus' reply.

19. The imagery was not lost on the apostle Paul, who describes himself and the other apostles: "We are . . . Christ's ambassadors" (2 Cor. 5:20; cf. Eph. 6:20). See Luke 14:32, where in one of his parables Jesus describes a king sending forth his ambassadors to sue for peace.

20. See ch. 2, "Who Is Jesus?" by Scot McKnight.

21. See the helpful discussion in Sanders, *Jesus and Judaism*, 157–73.

22. In addition to the writings of Josephus, there is a host of other writings that refer to Jesus and the origin of Christianity. Among the most important is Tacitus' reference (ca. 110 C.E.) to Jesus' execution by authority of Pontius Pilate (*Annals* 15.44). In a letter to Emperor Trajan, Pliny the Younger (ca. 110 C.E.) describes his interrogations of Christians who assembled and sang to "Christus as to a god" (*Epistles* 10.96). In *Divus Claudius* 25.4, Suetonius (ca. 120 C.E.) probably refers to Jesus when he tells of one "Chrestus" who caused unrest among the Jews. In many places in *Contra Celsum*

Origen attempts to refute the writings of the second-century Celsus who claimed, among other things, that Jesus performed his miracles by means of black magic. In his account of the death of Peregrinus, Lucian of Samosata (ca. 165 C.E.) refers to Christian faith in "the man who was crucified in Palestine" (*Passing of Peregrinus* 11). The rabbinic writings contain several critical references to Jesus. He is viewed as a sorcerer and false teacher who finally met his end: "And it is tradition: On the eve of Passover they hanged Yeshu ha-Nosri [Jesus the Nazarene]" (b. Sanh. 43a). For a critical assessment of these traditions, see C. A. Evans, "Jesus in Non-Christian Sources," in *Studying the Historical Jesus*, 443–78. See also ch. 8 by E. M. Yamauchi.

23. For a succinct and fair review of the evidence, see J. P. Meier, "Jesus in Josephus: A Modest Proposal," *CBQ* 52 (1990): 76–103; idem, *A Marginal Jew: Rethinking the Historical Jesus*, ABRL (New York: Doubleday, 1992), 56–69.

24. L. H. Feldman, *Josephus X*, LCL 456 (London: Heinemann / Cambridge: Harvard University Press, 1965), 108, n. a, cited with approval by Meier, *A Marginal Jew*, 59.

25. See the discussion in Meier, *A Marginal Jew*, 57–59.

26. Ibid., 67–68.

27. L. H. Feldman, "The Testimonium Flavianum: The State of the Question," *Christological Perspectives*, ed. R. F. Berkey and S. A. Edwards (New York: Pilgrim, 1982), 179–99, 288–93 (here 194–95).

28. Translation from H. St. J. Thackeray, *Josephus*, vol. 3, LCL 210 (London: Heinemann; Cambridge: Harvard University Press, 1928), 463–67.

29. R. A. Horsley (" 'Like One of the Prophets of Old': Two Types of Popular Prophets at the Time of Jesus," *CBQ* 47 [1985]: 435–63, esp. 451) rightly draws our attention to the fact that it was only the priestly aristocracy that tried to silence Jesus, son of Ananias.

30. Are these verbal parallels evidence of some sort of literary relationship between *J.W.* 6.5.3 and the Passion tradition found in the New Testament Gospels? For two reasons I think that a literary relationship is improbable. (1) The "parallels" comprise no more than nouns of place and context and verbs that mark the various steps in the judicial and penal process. In other words, the parallels are precisely what one would expect in cases where routine actions are being described. (2) Aside from the single parallel cluster where we have a common verbal root, preposition, and Roman governor as object, there are no instances of parallel sentences or phrases. Literary relationships are suspected when there is a high concentration of common vocabulary, especially phrases and whole sentences. In short, I think that the common vocabulary adduced above indicates common procedure, but not literary relationship. There is no indication that the story of the one Jesus influenced the telling of the story of the other Jesus. For further discussion of the parallels and their implications, see C. A. Evans, "Jesus and the 'Cave of Robbers': Toward a Jewish Context for the Temple Action," *BBR* 3 (1993): 93–110.

31. For a recent and compelling assessment of these traditions and others, see Chilton, *The Temple of Jesus* (University Park, Pa.: Pennsylvania State University Press, 1992), 100–111.

32. N. A. Dahl, "The Crucified Messiah," *The Crucified Messiah and Other Essays* (Minneapolis: Augsburg, 1974), 1–36; E. Bammel, "The Titulus," *Jesus and the Politics of His Day*, ed. Bammel and C. F. D. Moule (Cambridge: Cambridge University Press, 1984), 353–64; R. H. Gundry, *Mark: A Commentary on His Apology for the Cross* (Grand Rapids: Eerdmans, 1993), 958–59.

33. Qumran's expectation that the Messiah would assist the rightful high priest in the

purging of the temple establishment may also be relevant for understanding Jesus' disposition.

34. Contrary to popular interpretation of the story of the widow's two copper coins, I do not think that Jesus intended to applaud the widow. I think he pointed her out as an example of a marginalized person whose "house" had been "devoured" by the religious establishment (as warned of in the preceding passage). The temple establishment offered her no relief; instead it had taken her last penny or, as Jesus put it, "all she had to live on."

35. This probably involved (1) oppression of the marginalized and (2) disagreements involved in the buying and selling of the sacrificial animals.

36. Perhaps also in reference to his own resurrection (Mark 8:31).

37. For a discussion of the legal aspects of Jesus' blasphemy, see Gundry, *Mark*, 914–18.

Chapter 5

DID JESUS PERFORM MIRACLES?

GARY R. HABERMAS

Gary R. Habermas (Ph.D., Michigan State University) is
Distinguished Professor of philosophy and apologetics at
Liberty University. He is coauthor of *Why Believe? God Exists:
Rethinking the Case for God*, and has written numerous articles
and books on historical aspects of Jesus and his resurrection.

The Gospel miracles are a crucial ingredient in a historical examination of the life of Jesus. Jarl Fossum begins his study on the subject by asserting, "That Jesus was a miracle worker is central to the Christology of the New Testament Gospels and Acts."[1] This chapter will investigate whether it can still be said that Jesus actually performed miracles.

We will begin with some background to the question, followed by a consideration of certain ancient, non-Christian parallels to the New Testament claims. Then we will treat the Gospel data themselves, including both worldview and historical considerations.

The Critical Stance

A brief historical survey of critical approaches to miracles will help set the stage for what follows. A major feature of the German liberalism of the nineteenth century[2] was the large number of lives of Jesus that were produced. This was the heyday of the search for the historical Jesus, but the inquiry was usually at the expense of two elements in the Gospels: the supernatural and theology. In other words, the older liberal approach constructed a life of Jesus that was a great example for living but was devoid of miraculous and many doctrinal components.

Regarding miracles, the predominant approach in early liberalism was rationalistic. Heinrich Paulus, for example, whose life of Jesus was published in 1828, accepted a fair amount of the New Testament text but offered natural explanations for miracles instead of supernatural ones. But with the publication of David Strauss' *Life of Jesus* in 1835, this approach was radically challenged. Strauss used a mythical approach, which questioned much of the Gospel teachings concerning the historical Jesus. He interpreted myth as the clothing of religious ideas in seemingly historical garb in order to express essentially inexpressible truths.

We should not underestimate the difference between the rational and the mythical interpretations. By denying the basic historicity of the Gospel texts, the latter method undermined even the former's factual approach to Jesus. The Jesus of history was being separated from, and even changed into, the more theological Christ of faith. Albert Schweitzer noted: "The distinction between Strauss and those who had preceded him upon this path consists only in this, that prior to him the conception of myth was neither truly grasped nor consistently applied."[3]

The twentieth century has witnessed various approaches to the historicity of Jesus—pro, con, and in between. One movement, for example, rejected the earlier historical quest but also presented a modest critique of contemporary mythical strategies.[4] A recent more positive trend in its assessment of the historical Jesus emphasizes the Jewish background and context of his life and teachings.[5] On the other hand, most of the more critical scholars remain close to Strauss' mythical method. Throughout many of the discussions from the end of the nineteenth through the twentieth century, as we will see, the question of ancient similarities to New Testament narratives has contributed much to the modern outlook.

Ancient Parallels

The question of early, non-Christian miracle claims is an intriguing one. These descriptions are plentiful in the ancient world, and comparisons to Jesus are only natural, especially since incidents similar to those of Jesus were reportedly performed by other religious figures (e.g., Jewish holy men, magicians, and Hellenistic "divine men"[6]). Some critics have charged that these ancient parallels provide different levels of influence—either on the Gospel portrayals of Jesus' miracles (perhaps even providing the inspiration for entire episodes) or in motivating Jesus' own ideas and actions.

What is to be made of these parallels? We now turn to this issue, with examples revealing some of the variety of ancient miracle claims.

Jewish Holy Men

Josephus writes about a righteous man named Onias (or Honi, as he is usually called), who prayed to God to send rain in order to end a drought, and God answered that prayer by granting the request.[7] Providing more detail, the *Mishnah* reports that God did not answer the prayer at first. So Onias the Circle-maker drew a circle and stood within it, telling the Lord that he would not leave until it rained—and it did.[8]

On another occasion, Josephus relates watching a Jew named Eleazar cast demons out of people by holding a root up to the person's nose and drawing the demon out through the nostrils! Then Eleazar forbade the demon to return, citing Solomon as his authority and repeating an incantation. Finally, he commanded the demon to overturn a nearby water container in order to prove that it had, indeed, left the possessed individual. The purpose of this was to show Solomon's greatness.[9]

Many Jews about the time of Jesus believed that some rabbis could perform miracles. Hanina ben Dosa, for example, could heal, even over a distance. Once he prayed in order to cure a boy who had a high fever and afterwards pronounced him well. This was later confirmed by the lad's father.[10]

Could the Gospel accounts of Jesus' miracles have been inspired (or even invented) because of the influence of such Jewish holy men?[11] We cannot fail to note how Hanina ben Dosa's healing at a distance is reminiscent of Jesus' curing the centurion's servant (Matt. 8:5–13; Luke 7:1–9). On the other hand, these examples also indicate dissimilar aspects, such as Eleazar's employing a root, pulling the demon through the nostrils of the possessed, and uttering the Solomonic incantation, and Honi's magical circle-drawing.

Needless to say, the Gospels do exhibit influence from the Old Testament and reflect Jewish tradition. Jesus himself was referred to as a rabbi.[12] But can the similarities we see in Josephus and the *Mishnah* actually account for Jesus' miracles or the records of them? To begin, we have no concrete evidence of any mimicry of these Jewish traditions, the written forms of which date after the Gospels.[13] Furthermore, the Jewish leaders in the Gospels actually acknowledged Jesus' miracles,[14] which is understandable in light of the wonders that they also performed.[15]

The major issue here is the historicity of Jesus' miracles. Jesus was a Jew, and Jewish concepts exerted influence on the Gospel writers. But unless it can be shown that Jesus' miracles were either invented wholesale or the supernatural element significantly colored by such a bias, this Jewish element is not a major problem. We will return to this issue below, when we discuss reasons for the historicity of the Gospel miracles.

Magicians

The two examples from Josephus indicate some overlap between the category of Jewish holy men and that of magicians. The holy men seem to have employed means often connected with magic in order to accomplish their ends (e.g., the use of special roots and Solomonic incantations). Note also that in the case of Onias, Josephus continues by reporting that Simeon b. Shetah made a complaint against him, charging him with unorthodoxy in his use of magical circle-drawing.[16]

Other magical accounts abound in the ancient world. For example, Edwin Yamauchi reports the existence of a thousand cuneiform texts in ancient Mesopotamia that depict the healing of diseases by magic. Many diseases were attributed to demons, and the cure resulted in casting out the demons by specific formulas.[17] Is there perhaps credible evidence that such non-Christian cases inspired, or even led to the creation of, certain of the Gospel miracles? For example, can Jesus' miracles and exorcisms as reported in the Gospels be understood as the work of a magician?

Yamauchi's detailed study sufficiently addresses the major concerns here. A crucial roadblock to understanding Jesus as a magician is the ancient concept of magic itself, which was quite negative. Both Christians and non-Christians characterized magic as including elements like sorcery, demons, incantations, spells, and trickery. It involved people of questionable moral character.[18] Even Morton Smith, who argues that Jesus was a magician, states that "cannibalism, incest, and sexual promiscuity were reported of magicians."[19] He links Jesus and early Christianity to magic primarily because of Jesus' being a miracle-worker, as well as his claims to be divine. But Smith also includes the early Christian belief in mutual love, the use of "brother" and "sister," the practice of having all things in common, and the custom of the Lord's Supper (which some critics of Christians in the ancient world considered a form of cannibalism).[20]

It is difficult to understand how any of these items *require* one to be a magician! If all miracle-workers, people who claim to love one another in a special way, and those who share their material possessions qualify as devotees of magic, then we have robbed the word of all crucial meaning! And while it is true that some unbelievers understood the Lord's Supper in a perverse way, this is hardly evidence for Christian cannibalism!

Smith's tangential arguments are even more questionable. He proposes that Jesus went to Egypt in order to study magic, that the marks on Paul's body (Gal. 6:17) were magical tattoos, that the Roman historian Tacitus's comment that Christians were charged with "hatred for the human race" probably referred to their practicing magic, and so on![21] Such arguments hardly need a response. Each one stretches beyond any normal meaning, lacks crucial evidence, and is opposed to the clear and early data we do have. For example, there is no early testimony that Jesus studied magic in Egypt or anywhere else,[22] and the marks on Paul's body are plainly due to the extraordinary physical sufferings that he explicitly enumerates (2 Cor. 11:23–28).

Thus, if one defines magic as was done in ancient times, then Jesus is not a magician, for none of the unique concepts connected with the subject can be applied to him. If, on the other hand, the notion of magic is defined so broadly that Jesus is included, as Smith does, then the concept loses any distinctive meaning.[23] Still, we need to ask whether ancient accounts of magic somehow inspired Jesus' miracles or their reports. We will shortly face squarely this issue of their historicity.

Hellenistic "Divine Men"

Besides Jewish holy men and magicians, one of the best-known parallels to the Gospel miracles is from the Hellenistic "divine men." To the extent that criteria to describe these ancient "superheroes" can be established at all, they seem to have been concerned mostly with two types of phenomena: divination and miracles.[24]

The best known of the Hellenistic divine men was Apollonius of Tyana, a first-century traveling Neo-Pythagorean bard who was said to have exhibited special powers, including miracles.[25] On one occasion, Apollonius ordered a demon to leave a young man and to prove he had done so by visible sign. The demon responded that he would knock down a nearby statue, which promptly fell to the ground. The young man rubbed his eyes as if he had just awakened, being totally healed.[26] While Apollonius' exorcism is not far removed from the Gospel story of Jesus' casting out the demon from the Gadarene man (Mark 5:1–20), Graham Twelftree argues that the demons' entering the pigs should not be understood as the confirmation of their exit, but simply as Jesus' granting the request of the demons to inhabit other bodies.[27]

On another occasion, while visiting Alexandria, Apollonius watched as twelve men were being led away to execution. He identified one as being innocent, which was confirmed by a messenger who reported new evidence that this was indeed the case.[28] This special cognizance of an innocent man facing execution reminds one of the many times Jesus exhibited supernatural knowledge.[29] But in no way do the Gospels hint that Jesus' abilities are connected with divination or using the occult. Since divination was "the most prevalent power" displayed by the Hellenistic divine men, Blackburn notes the stark contrast here with the Gospel accounts.[30]

Could the Gospel picture of Jesus' miracles have been inspired by the Hellenistic divine men?[31] For one thing, we should point out that these classical wonder-workers were not a group that can be easily defined; there was no fixed type or list of common characteristics.[32] They were ancient "super-heroes," who claimed healings and the power of divination. It is difficult to support the contention that Jesus' miracles were patterned after such an ill-defined class. Even if such a concept is honed, the Gospel accounts are still distinguished from it in several ways. They exhibit a reserve in their description of miracles and a lack of the magical traits that characterize the Hellenistic accounts.[33]

In addition, while there may be some similarities between the Gospel accounts and Hellenistic sources, almost all the Gospel motifs are also paralleled in the Old Testament, Palestinian Jewish, or rabbinic literature. This fact alone makes it difficult to prove that any particular Gospel miracle must have come from Hellenistic genre.[34] Furthermore, most of the alleged parallels postdate the New Testament. Reginald Fuller declares: "Now it cannot be denied that most of the evidence adduced for the Hellenistic concept of the divine man by the History of Religions school is later than the NT."[35] And after an extensive study of Hellenistic miracles, Blackburn concludes: "In fact, among the undoubtedly pre-Christian traditions I can adduce only three stories formally reminiscent of the Gospel accounts."[36]

Finally, the very center of Christianity—the atoning death and resurrection of Jesus Christ—is unique and cannot be accounted for by referring to Hellenistic motifs. After speaking about the vastly different nature of the death and resurrection of Jesus, Fuller states: "The idea of resurrection in the biblical sense appears to be foreign to antiquity."[37] Similarly, I. Howard Marshall concludes concerning the deity of Christ, "the influence of pagan ideas is minimal."[38]

We must conclude, therefore, that the Evangelists' records of the miracles of Jesus cannot be explained by influence from the Hellenistic stories. The lack of clarity in the concept of the divine man, the areas of divergence from the Gospels, the Old Testament and Jewish parallels to the Gospels, the very absence of clear, pre-Christian Hellenistic accounts, and the inability to explain the most crucial components of the Christian gospel all seriously militate against the thesis. As

Blackburn concludes, belief in the "pervasive assimilation" of Hellenistic sources into the Gospel accounts, as is often claimed, is "without justification." That such influence can be proven even in particular cases is "questionable" and ought not be concluded with any confidence.[39]

It must also be remembered that to challenge the perceived origin of an idea instead of addressing the concept itself is to commit the informal logical falsehood known as the genetic fallacy. Even if some relationship could be proved, this still does not mean that the reports of Jesus' miracles are false.

Historicity of Ancient Non-Christian Miracle Claims

We have just surveyed three alleged sources for the miracles of Jesus. The historicity of these ancient miracle claims is an often-overlooked aspect of contemporary studies. Even if it cannot be proven that non-Christian accounts are the cause of Jesus' miracles or the Gospel descriptions of them, this is not the end of the matter. It still remains to be seen if the New Testament texts correctly report these events. Before turning to a direct examination of this topic, a few comments about the historicity of the non-Christian parallel stories are in order.

Few (if any) of these sources can provide good grounds regarding the veracity of the miracles they record. Note especially one of the best-attested examples of such miracle stories, Philostratus' *Life of Apollonius of Tyana*. This work is problematic on several counts:

- Philostratus' third-century account dates more than one hundred years after the end of Apollonius' life. While this is not a horrible gap for ancient history, it is enough to require a cautious examination of the author's reports.
- There are serious historical inaccuracies over significant portions of Philostratus' work, like Apollonius' lengthy journeys to cities such as Nineveh and Babylon. Not only were these places lying in ruins during the first century, but at least Nineveh had been destroyed hundreds of years earlier. This also raises serious questions about Apollonius' dialogues with the kings in each of these locations.
- Philostratus' major source of information, a disciple of Apollonius named Damis, may be a fictitious person. We are told that Damis came from the nonexistent city of Nineveh, thus raising doubt about whether he existed.[40]
- Many scholars think that Philostratus' work is primarily romantic fiction, a popular literary form in the second century A.D. There are a number of indications that his primary intent was other than an accurate presentation of Apollonius' life.[41] This does not undermine the recording of ancient history as a whole because, as Darrell Bock has shown in his chapter, ancient historians were able to write accurate, factual reports. It just seems that Philostratus was attempting to do otherwise.
- The similarities between Apollonius and Jesus may well be more than

coincidence. Philostratus was commissioned to write this work by Julia Domna, the wife of Roman emperor Septimius Severus, and it is popularly held that she did so in order to orchestrate "a counterblast to Jesus."[42]

- Philostratus' source is known to have embellished Apollonius' life, especially in regard to the supernatural claims. Miracles were among the fictitious items that were added. In this sense, the text is "not altogether . . . credible."[43] Perhaps more crucial, we find no other historical data to validate the miracle claims in Apollonius' life.

To be sure, problems with the example of Apollonius of Tyana do not invalidate miracle stories in other ancient sources. But just as critical scholars inquire about the nature of the New Testament text, the same questions need to be addressed concerning the non-Christian sources. It is insufficient simply to *claim* that a miracle occurred in any tradition. All the data must be examined, including the date and circumstances of the writing, the position and sources of the author, what evidence is presented, and whether alternative proposals better explain the data.[44] We now proceed to the Gospel accounts.

The Miracles of Jesus

It is customary to divide Jesus' miracles into three categories: healings, exorcisms, and nature miracles. The first two are viewed more positively in contemporary studies, although they are not treated synonymously. As Marcus Borg explains: "The gospels consistently distinguish between exorcisms and healings; not all healings were exorcisms, and not all maladies were caused by evil spirits."[45] In contrast, the accounts that report Jesus' controlling nature are of another character, the chief example being the resurrection of Jesus.[46]

The somewhat positive attitude toward Jesus' healings and exorcisms in twentieth-century critical theology ranges from general affirmation to explicit acceptance. Rudolf Bultmann himself declares that there is "no doubt" that Jesus really "healed the sick and expelled demons."[47] Günther Bornkamm agrees: "It would be difficult to doubt the physical healing powers which emanated from Jesus, just as he himself interpreted his casting out of demons as a sign of the dawning of the kingdom of God."[48] A. M. Hunter's careful wording provides more detail on the healing miracles:

> No Christian with a respect for his intellectual integrity need doubt that Jesus restored sight to the blind, helped deaf men to hear again, enabled lame men to walk, cleansed lepers, cured those thought to be possessed by evil spirits, and brought back to life those apparently dead. For these miracles the historical evidence is excellent.[49]

Critical theologians have continued this basic attitude of acceptance. Marcus Borg, a member of the Jesus Seminar, asserts: "Despite the difficulty which miracles pose for the modern mind, on historical grounds it is virtually indisputable that Jesus was a healer and exorcist."[50] Jesus Seminar cofounder John Dominic Crossan adds: "You cannot ignore the healings and the exorcisms," and "throughout his life Jesus performed healings and exorcisms for ordinary people."[51]

Yet when critical scholars affirm Jesus' healings and exorcisms to have occurred, they generally do not affirm them as supernatural events. Rather, they qualify these events in two significant ways.[52] (1) While Jesus definitely healed people, the cure was cognitive or psychosomatic rather than biological. According to Bultmann, since truly supernatural events do not occur, "sickness and the cure of disease are likewise attributable to natural causation."[53] Hunter ascribes Jesus' healings to the part played by the power of the mind—in short, faith-healing.[54] For Crossan, Jesus never produced any physical changes, but cured the social illnesses that accompanied the actual diseases.[55] And while he rejects the existence of demons, an exorcism could heal the very real symptoms, especially in one who does believe in them.[56] (2) Other ancient persons both healed and exorcised "demons," perhaps even frequently (see Matt. 12:27–28; Mark 9:38–40). Thus, Jesus' miracles were not even unique.[57]

These scholars do not, however, treat the nature miracles in the same way, presumably because they more directly involve the supernatural. Fossum sums up the typical disposition here: "They are not intended to recount history, an actual event, but to convey a religious message."[58] Thus, such stories as the stilling of the storm and Jesus' walking on water indicate that God is in control of our lives and that the pious ought not be afraid, and that Jesus is "the Lord of salvation as well as the Lord of creation." The feeding miracles point to "Jesus' followers as partakers in the coming messianic feasts."[59]

Crossan interprets the predeath nature miracles in conjunction with the postdeath appearance accounts as conveying a message concerning ecclesiastical authority. He thinks these texts are chiefly interested in the spiritual power of specific leaders, leadership groups, and the general community.[60]

In a different vein, Borg is not dogmatic, suggesting that the purpose of these events "may be symbolic rather than historical." According to him, we "do not know" if the nature wonders really occurred. "A clear historical judgment is impossible," and these "mighty deeds" must remain in suspense. To Borg, even Jesus' healings are not quite so simple. While many think of them as faith-healings, in some cases "the faith of the healed person was not involved at all." Jesus' healings were performed by "power," and it is difficult to know exactly its extent and range.[61]

Defense of Jesus' Miracles

So what can be said about the historicity of Jesus' supernatural wonders, and the nature miracles, in particular? We turn to this topic now, looking at two areas of investigation—worldview concerns and the factual data.

Worldview Considerations

Scholars sometimes speak as if the factual data can be divorced from world-view concerns—as if we can look at history in a dispassionate, totally objective manner or apart from any overarching beliefs. Yet it is undeniable that everyone generally operates within his or her own concept of reality and usually views information through multicolored lenses.

Having said this, however, the factual data are still equally crucial. Even if we generally tend to decide issues based upon our predispositions, this does not nec-essarily justify those preconceptions. We do need to be informed by the data we receive. And sometimes this is precisely what happens—the evidence on a subject convinces us against our indecisiveness or even contrary to our former position.[62]

The influence of our worldviews

We begin by making some comments on how worldviews affect our attitudes toward Jesus' miracles. Many commentators, both pro and con, readily agree that the issue of Jesus' miracles will at least partially be viewed according to one's understanding of reality. As the Jesus Seminar asserts, "The contemporary reli-gious controversy . . . *turns* on whether the worldview reflected in the Bible can be carried forward into this scientific age and retained as an article of faith."[63] And this conviction is immediately applied to Jesus:

> Jesus figures prominently in this debate. The Christ of creed and dogma . . . can no longer command the assent of those who have seen the heavens through Galileo's telescope. The old deities and demons were swept from the skies by that remarkable glass. Copernicus, Kepler, and Galileo have dismantled the mythological abodes of the gods and Satan, and bequeathed us secular heavens.[64]

In this statement, the Jesus Seminar identifies its radical approach to the Gospel records. As far as they are concerned, the advances of science have ruled out the possibilities of viewing Jesus Christ as deity or of postulating a super-natural world of demons and spirits.[65] The Seminar is, of course, correct that such discussions depend to a large extent on which worldview is correct. But they are mistaken if they think that the advances of science make supernatural belief obsolete.

In fact, Hunter is one among an equally large and growing number of criti-cal scholars who think that, far from ruling out the supernatural, scientists are more open to it than they have been in the past: "Gone are the days when scien-tists could dogmatically declare that miracles, because they were 'violations of the laws of nature,' were therefore impossible."[66] He declares that our conclusions on miracles will depend on our worldview and our appraisal of Jesus:

> All *turns* on what we think of him. . . . If Jesus was, and is, what Christians have always believed him to be, the Son of God . . . there is

nothing inherently incredible in the belief that such a person as Jesus may have had control over the great frame of nature itself.

In a word, grant "the grand miracle" of the Incarnation, grant that God became man in Jesus, and most of the objections to his miracles fall to the ground.[67]

Interestingly, the Jesus Seminar and Hunter both agree that the issue "turns" on the truth of one's overall stance.[68] But each one heads toward different conclusions!

So whose perspective is correct? Is belief in the supernatural really passé, or could the New Testament portrait of Jesus' miracles still be accurate? We can perhaps agree on two things. (1) It solves nothing to simply *state* one's views to be correct, no matter how vociferously the claim is made. (2) To reject another's evidence or overall position in an *a priori* manner is likewise illegitimate; there can be no substitute for a careful investigation of the possibilities. Both of these inadequate approaches fail to address the data and are thus detrimental to reaching a reasoned conclusion. Although we obviously cannot settle here the worldview issue, we can at least attempt to avoid some of the more apparent pitfalls.

We need to be fair, too; all sides stumble into such errors on occasion. But it seems that radical critics frequently make comments that reveal an *a priori* rejection of at least Jesus' nature wonders. It has long been a hallmark of certain commentators to dismiss the miraculous without an investigation. For example, after asserting that modern science has ruled out belief in spirits and demons, Bultmann gets more specific about Jesus' resurrection: "But what of the resurrection? Is it not a mythical event pure and simple? Obviously it is not an event of past history. . . ."[69]

John Macquarrie, a leading commentator on Bultmann, critiques this German theologian's rejection of the miraculous, calling it "an entirely arbitrary dismissal . . . because of some prior assumption in his mind." He continues:

> The fallacy of such reasoning is obvious. The one valid way in which we can ascertain whether a certain event took place or not is not by bringing in some sweeping assumption to show that it could not have taken place . . . . But Bultmann does not take the trouble to examine what evidence could be adduced to show that the resurrection was an objective-historical event. He assumes that it is a myth.[70]

The Jesus Seminar and the supernatural

After a theological hiatus, views like Bultmann's seem to be returning to vogue. Crossan asserts that Jesus "did not and could not cure that disease or any other one. . . ."[71] Later he adds: "I do not think that anyone, anywhere, at any time brings dead people back to life."[72] Fossum continues this last thought, complete with a poke at conservatives: "Or it can be asserted that Jesus really did raise the girl from the dead—which would only reflect fundamentalist naiveté."[73]

The Jesus Seminar likewise makes a number of comments against the occurrence of supernatural events. For example: "Whenever scholars detect detailed knowledge of postmortem events in sayings and parables attributed to Jesus, they are inclined to the view that the formulation of such sayings took place after the fact."[74] But there is more than this mere "inclination" to rule out any postdeath phenomena from the life of Jesus. The Seminar *as a matter of principle* does not consider a single Gospel teaching from the resurrection narratives as a genuine Jesus saying. Why not? "By definition, words ascribed to Jesus after his death are not subject to historical verification."[75]

As mentioned above, Macquarrie thought that Bultmann's view was arbitrary and *a priori*. Do the conclusions of the Jesus Seminar fare any better? It is true that they provide more than three dozen of what they term "rules of written evidence"[76] and often report that such-and-such sayings are editorial summations. It is also unfair to require that they provide, in every instance, the reasons for their conclusions. Furthermore, they are also honest enough to share "up front" that Jesus can no longer be considered deity and that modern science has "dismantled the mythological abodes of the gods and Satan, and bequeathed us secular heavens."[77]

However, seldom do the Jesus Seminar Fellows provide *reasons* for their opinions or otherwise vindicate their own worldview. Only rarely do they attempt to justify their rules of evidence beyond reporting that certain things are assumed. And those who reject supernatural events such as Jesus' resurrection often do so with a flare for the *a priori*. Throughout, like Bultmann, their theological method is assumed, and these assumptions are wide open to alternative interpretations.

For instance, frequently we are told that because a certain passage fits the particular writer's motif and theological agenda, a particular saying was not uttered by Jesus.[78] But does the presence of a certain theme *require* that Jesus never said these things? According to the critical method itself, such might only show that the writer is taking an actual teaching of Jesus and paraphrasing it or otherwise making it conform to his own style. Why are we required to make a leap from authorial motif to the subsequent invention of the message?

And we dare not forget the fallacy mentioned above. To note the possible origin of a particular saying or event without addressing whether or not it is factual does not necessarily explain it away. In other words, if one attributes a Gospel report to ancient beliefs, parallels, or the author's style and believes that this in and of itself explains it away, this is a logical mistake.[79] Such charges do not necessarily rule out historicity.

But we should also note that not all the scholars of the Jesus Seminar respond this way. Although Crossan states his disbelief in demons,[80] Bruce Chilton, without commenting on his own belief, perceptively remarks that while rejecting the existence of demons sounds attractively rational, "it would seem to reduce history to *a priori* notions of what is possible."[81] And while Crossan asserts that Jesus never really healed a disease or changed the physical world, and that no one has ever raised the dead,[82] Borg is not quite so sure. In fact, Borg specifically uses the example of raising the dead to say that we cannot know whether or not Jesus actually performed the nature miracles.[83]

Our chief purpose in this section has been to note the importance of our worldviews and their influence on us. The truth or falsity of worldviews is far too large a topic to address here. Still, we cannot settle the miracles question by simply asserting our views or by rejecting other possibilities *a priori*. We need to address other areas of data as well, to ascertain whether there is some actual evidence for Jesus' miracles as taught in the Gospels. And if we find such, it ought not be dismissed due to prior assumptions. This is the subject to which we now turn.

Evidence for Miracles

Borg lists three reasons why the historicity of Jesus' healings and exorcisms is virtually undisputed by the vast majority of critical scholars. These occurrences are attested in the "earliest sources." In addition, they were "relatively common in the world around Jesus." Finally, not only did Jesus' opponents not challenge the assertion that he did miracles, but "they claimed that his powers came from the lord of the evil spirits." Thus, both followers and foes alike admitted his abilities.[84]

But this applies only to the healings and exorcisms. What can we say about Jesus' nature miracles, which are rejected by many of these same scholars? We will list seven evidences in favor of the miracles of Jesus, and for the nature wonders in particular.

Source attestation

First, Jesus' miracles are attested in each of the Gospel sources. The Jesus Seminar recognizes four major, independent sources behind the Synoptic Gospels: the sayings document Q, Mark, M (material peculiar to Matthew), and L (material peculiar to Luke).[85] In each of these Jesus is a miracle worker.

Furthermore, Jesus' *nature* miracles are mentioned in each of these sources, including a passage in the pre-Gospel source Q, where Jesus alludes to several of his healing miracles for John the Baptist's disciples. At the end of this list Jesus includes "the dead are raised."[86] The other three major sources (Mark, M, and L) include multiple examples of Jesus' nature wonders.

Jesus' opponents

Second, Jesus' opponents and critics in the Gospels not only witnessed his healings and exorcisms (Mark 2:1–12; 3:22; Luke 13:10–17), but they also knew about his nature miracles (Matt. 28:11–15; Mark 5:40–42; John 11:47–48). These observers did not differentiate between the two types of miracles, nor did they try to explain away either type.[87]

Before proceeding further, let us compare our first two evidences to two of Borg's reasons given above. If pre-Gospel sources and testimonies of opponents are two reasons that make Jesus' healings and exorcisms "virtually indisputable" among scholars, why shouldn't they serve as evidences for the nature miracles as well? In other words, if the attestation of all the major Gospel sources counts for the former miracles, why do they not count heavily for the latter? And if we are to accept the opposition witnesses for the former, as Borg does, then it is difficult to exclude them in the case of the latter.[88] Protests at these two points easily take on an *a priori* slant and begin to look like special pleading.

The historicity of Jesus' healings and exorcisms

Third, a number of researchers have noted various marks of historicity in the narratives of Jesus' healings and exorcisms. While it is true that these episodes are seldom questioned, further reasons may also be helpful beyond the three already listed by Borg.

Some scholars are impressed with the coherence of the total Gospel picture—how Jesus' miracles fit with his person and message. Fuller addresses this blend of Jesus' authoritative words and mighty acts: "God is directly present in the words of Jesus" as he offers salvation and judgment; his healings and exorcisms indicate the presence of God's kingdom.[89]

Bornkamm also argues for a congruence between Jesus' preaching and his actions. In particular, the miracles drew people to him, but so did the authority he manifested in his words. Word and deed fit together and account for Jesus' influence.[90]

Taking a different route but ending up at a similar conclusion, Graham Twelftree notes several marks of authenticity in Jesus' exorcisms. Jesus used no material devices, in contrast to other ancient cases. Neither did he require the departing demon to give proof of his exit. Furthermore, he did not use the common formula, "I bind you." Finally, he did not pray in order to remove the spirit or otherwise invoke authorities beyond himself. Twelftree then concludes that, while Jesus' methods are not without some parallel, he did make a unique appeal to his own authority in casting out demons. As with Fuller and Bornkamm, Twelftree takes this power as an indication of the presence of God's kingdom. He sums up the matter this way: "Jesus was the first to believe that in the ordinary events of exorcism Satan was being destroyed and the Kingdom of God was arriving."[91]

Jesus Seminar Fellow Bruce Chilton notes elements in the exorcism account in Mark 1:21–28 that indicate its pre-Markan status; in particular, the demon's attempt to gain control over Jesus by using his name and the violence it exhibited before leaving the possessed point to authenticity.[92]

130

The historicity of Jesus' nature wonders

Fourth, scholars have also isolated numerous historical elements in the accounts of Jesus' nature miracles. In a study of Jesus' raising the dead, Murray Harris records such components. While raising the widow's son at Nain (Luke 7:11–17), Jesus found the mother walking in front of the funeral bier, which was the custom in Galilee but not in Judea! Other hints are the specific location being provided, unlike other places in Luke, and the fact that the account is exceptionally restrained, for the son makes no comments about the nature of the afterlife.[93]

In raising the daughter of Jairus,[94] Harris notes the presence of additional, unneeded details: Jairus's prostrating himself before Jesus, the pressing throng, Jesus' overhearing the message of Jairus's servants, Jesus' twice telling the mourners to leave the room, the derision of those present, Jesus' report that the girl was asleep, and his order to give her food. Harris cautiously urges authenticity because of the presence of such elements in the absence of the wild features often found in miracle accounts in the apocryphal Gospels.[95]

In the raising of Lazarus (John 11:1–44), Harris suggests that historicity is favored by the wealth of circumstantial details, such as geography, personal names, and family background. In addition, this report is also brief and simple, without reports from Lazarus concerning what he experienced during his four days of death or comments from the bystanders.[96]

In a similar vein, Stephen Davis lists three factors that argue for the rationality of believing another nature miracle, Jesus' changing water to wine (John 2:1–11). It is odd, he says, that the early church would invent or otherwise utilize a story that might encourage those who criticized Jesus for being a glutton and a drunkard (Matt. 11:19). Furthermore, it is difficult to explain the seemingly harsh way that Jesus addressed his mother, and Jesus himself plays a rather unobtrusive part throughout.[97]

Paul Barnett presents a study of the feeding of the five thousand, carefully comparing Mark's account (Mark 6:30–46 and parallels) to that of John (John 6:1–15). After listing both similarities and differences, he sides with a number of contemporary scholars in his decision that the two versions derive from separate renditions, "with each resting in all probability on independent eyewitness recollection."[98]

Craig Blomberg begins his article with the almost unanimously accepted kingdom parables of Jesus. Then he applies the widely attested principle of coherence, whereby the best test of authenticity is "that which is fully consistent with material authenticated by the other recognized criteria." The bulk of his essay consists of showing how the nature miracles symbolize the inbreaking kingdom of God. He concludes: "In short, the nature miracles and the parables closely cohere with each other. . . . It therefore follows that the earliest forms of these miracle stories should be recognized as most probably historical."[99]

Thus, like Jesus' healings and exorcisms, there are also marks of historicity that indicate the credibility of the nature miracles.

The trustworthiness of the Gospels

Fifth, many critical scholars dismiss the nature miracles because they doubt the Gospels as sources. Sometimes they charge that the Gospel authors were not eyewitnesses,[100] or that the accounts themselves are not based on eyewitness reports.[101] While this is not the place to argue for the trustworthiness of the Gospels (Craig Blomberg does so in his chapter, above), we can simply note here that any evidence that backs the reliability of Gospels in general and of the miracle texts in particular supports our case for the historicity of the miracles.[102]

It should also be noted that these efforts do not turn on whether all of the Gospel authors were eyewitnesses or writing under the control of eyewitnesses, although such a conclusion would further the case for Jesus' miracles. Even though he says he would argue for the traditional Gospel authors, R. T. France makes the point that it is not essential whether their identity is known. These books should be judged the way most historians judge historical accuracy—by their early date and the tradition behind them.[103]

The resurrection of Jesus

Sixth, although reasons such as these for Jesus' miracles can stand on their own, William Lane Craig will argue in the next chapter that there is exceptionally strong evidence in favor of one particular miracle: the resurrection of Jesus. If this is the case, the remainder of Jesus' miracles become both less problematic and more likely.

The resurrection is a nature wonder—what Crossan calls "the supreme 'nature' miracle."[104] If this grand nature miracle did in fact occur, this presents a positive answer to the question addressed in this chapter about the possibility of Jesus' miracles in general.[105]

Modern scientific confirmation

Seventh, it is often assumed that if modern medical science could investigate the Gospel miracles, perhaps the verdict would oppose supernatural causation. Furthermore, some charge that since we do not witness miracles today like those the biblical writers describe, we should be even more skeptical of such wonders.[106]

But perhaps we should ask a different question: Could modern studies actually change our perspective and increase our openness to the New Testament reports? Is it possible that we do not hear of such wonders today simply because we do not look in the right places? Two examples may provide some hints.

A recent double-blind medical experiment examined how prayer might affect physical healing. The intriguing outcome indicated a statistically positive effect on the recuperation of those who were prayed for, who did better in twenty-one of twenty-six monitored categories. Yet none of the almost four hundred coronary care patients knew whether they were actual recipients of prayer. Because of this experimental design, the results cannot be explained by references to the patient's faith healing alone.[107]

Moreover, Borg reminds his readers of the provocative nature of certain contemporary "possession" cases. He cites the testimony of psychiatrist M. Scott Peck, who became involved with two examples of possession and exorcism that he and a team of professionals could not account for within purely medical parameters.[108]

Summary and Conclusion

Miracles were integral to the life of Jesus as presented in the Gospels. But critics have responded variously to these occurrences. In comparing them to claims on behalf of other ancients (Jewish holy men, magicians, and Hellenistic "divine men"), we found both similarities and differences, with the latter being more important than the former.

We also studied two other aspects of these parallel claims—their influence and historicity. We argued that it cannot be proven that ancient parallels account for the Gospel reports. Not only are there numerous problems involved with each category, but it is illegitimate to imply that similarities can explain the origin of the Gospel accounts. Further, we considered the historical factor. It is insufficient simply to claim that miracles occurred or did not occur; we must examine all the data concerning non-Christian as well as Christian claims.

Our chief purpose in this chapter has been to explore the basis for believing that Jesus indeed performed miracles. Critical scholars generally recognize the historicity of Jesus' healings and exorcisms, often without believing that they were genuinely miraculous occurrences. The nature wonders are frequently rejected outright, presumably because they more readily indicate supernatural events.

We examined the case for miracles in two parts: worldview concerns and the historical evidence itself. This issue cannot be settled by simply asserting one's views or by rejecting another's position *a priori*. We must address the factual data too, in order to ascertain whether there are actual evidences for Jesus' miracles. And if there are such data, it is insufficient to dismiss them due to prior assumptions.

Finally, we enumerated seven evidences for Jesus' miracles, and for his nature wonders in particular. They are present in all of the Gospel sources, and Jesus' opponents readily admitted them. There are a number of marks of historicity not only in Jesus' healings and exorcisms, but also in the accounts of his nature miracles. Other evidence for the reliability of the Gospels in general and the miracle texts in particular furthers this case. If Jesus' resurrection is a historical miracle, then the grand nature miracle occurred, and Jesus' other miracles are immediately on better ground. Lastly, medical studies of certain "miraculous" phenomena today indicate that we are still not able to account for all such incidents in purely naturalistic terms.

The cumulative case shows that the Gospels are correct in reporting that Jesus performed miracles. The texts do not distinguish among the three types; basically the same sorts of evidence characterize all of them. Thus, just as scholars are essentially agreed that Jesus was both a healer and an exorcist (Borg calls this "virtually indisputable"[109]), so should they recognize that he performed miracles that affected nature. Not to do so appears to reflect more of one's biases and worldview rather than being a response to the data. And if Jesus did perform these miracles, we should also be open to the worldview he taught.

Notes

1. Jarl Fossum, "Understanding Jesus' Miracles," *BR*, 10:2 (April 1994): 17.

2. Briefly, the liberalism of the last century often followed various aspects of German idealistic philosophy. Its time span is usually dated from Friedrich Schleiermacher's treatise *On Religion: Speeches to Its Cultured Despisers* (1799) to Karl Barth's theological critique in *The Epistle to the Romans* (1918).

3. The classic overview of nineteenth-century liberalism is Albert Schweitzer's *The Quest of the Historical Jesus: A Critical Study of Its Progress from Reimarus to Wrede*, trans. W. Montgomery (1906; reprint, New York: Macmillan, 1968), 78.

4. Representative of this strategy is James M. Robinson, *A New Quest of the Historical Jesus: Studies in Biblical Theology* (London: SCM, 1959). Another example is Günther Bornkamm, *Jesus of Nazareth*, trans. Irene and Fraser McLuskey with James M. Robinson (New York: Harper & Row, 1960).

5. A bit more diverse, some of the key volumes include: Geza Vermes, *Jesus the Jew: A Historian's Reading of the Gospels* (New York: Macmillan, 1973); E. P. Sanders, *Jesus and Judaism* (Philadelphia: Fortress, 1985); James H. Charlesworth, *Jesus Within Judaism* (Garden City, N.Y.: Doubleday, 1988); John P. Meier, *A Marginal Jew: Rethinking the Historical Jesus*, vol. 1 (Garden City, N.Y.: Doubleday, 1991).

6. In this chapter we do not consider the fantastic feats attributed to Jesus in the apocryphal Gospels, especially since they are neither earlier nor contemporary parallels to the miracles of Jesus. In general, these writings are much later than the canonical Gospels, as well as being of a different quality. In addition, there is a decided lack of historical attestation to the claims being made.

7. Josephus, *Antiquities of the Jews*, 14:2, 1, in *Complete Works*, trans. William Whiston (Grand Rapids: Kregel, 1960).

8. *Mishnah*, Taanith 3:8. This text is also found in C. K. Barrett, ed., *The New Testament Background: Selected Documents* (New York: Harper and Brothers, 1956), 150–51.

9. *Antiquities*, 8.2.5.

10. Israel W. Slotki, ed., *The Babylonian Talmud*, trans. S. Daiches (n.p.: Rebecca Bennet Publications, 1959), Berakot 34b; cf. Fossum, "Understanding Jesus' Miracles," for another example (p. 18).

11. Vermes, *Jesus the Jew*, describes Jesus as a popular Jewish rabbi and holy man from Galilee.

12. John 1:38, 49; 3:2; 6:25. John the Baptist was also called by this title (John 3:26).

13. The earliest of these writings, Josephus' *Antiquities*, dates from late in the reign of Roman Emperor Domitian, perhaps A.D. 93–94. This places it after the Synoptic Gospels and from about the time of John's Gospel. The earliest portions of the *Mishnah* date from no earlier than about 200, when it was completed by Rabbi Judah, later becoming part of the *Talmud*. For details, see Barrett, *New Testament Background*, 141, 143, 145, 190.

14. See Mark 2:1–12; 3:22; Luke 13:10–17; John 11:47.

15. Besides the accounts by Josephus and the *Talmud*, see Matt. 12:27–28.

16. See Barrett, *New Testament Background*, 150–51, for both the original text and the comments.

17. See Edwin Yamauchi's impressive chapter, "Magic or Miracle? Diseases, Demons and Exorcisms" in *Gospel Perspectives*, vol. 6, *The Miracles of Jesus*, ed. David Wenham and Craig Blomberg (Sheffield: JSOT, 1986), 89–183. Barrett, *New Testament Background*, 31–35, includes an example of an ancient incantation from the Paris Magical Papyrus.

18. Yamauchi, *Miracle of Jesus*, 89–91, 97.

19. Morton Smith, *Jesus the Magician* (New York: Harper & Row, 1978), 66.

20. Ibid., 46, 64–67.

21. Ibid., 47–48, 50–53.

22. For an investigation of what I term the "Jesus as international traveler" thesis, see Gary R. Habermas, *Ancient Evidence for the Life of Jesus: Historical Records of His Death and Resurrection* (Nashville: Thomas Nelson, 1984), 72–78.

23. For other issues that we cannot cover here, see the remainder of Yamauchi's well-documented essay.

24. See the excellent essay by Barry L. Blackburn, " 'Miracle Working ΘΕΙΟΙ ΑΝΔΡΕΣ' in Hellenism (and Hellenistic Judaism)," *The Miracles of Jesus*, 185–218. Blackburn includes a helpful chart listing pre- and post-Christian representatives (p. 187).

25. His life is detailed in a major biography, written in the first half of the third century A.D., by Flavius Philostratus, *The Life of Apollonius of Tyana*, trans. F. C. Conybeare, 2 vols., LCL (Cambridge, Mass.: Harvard University Press, 1912).

26. Ibid., 4.20. Actually, exorcisms were quite rare among the Hellenistic divine men. This case is one of the only such reports.

27. See Graham H. Twelftree, " 'ΕΙ ΔΕ . . . ΕΓΩ ΕΚΒΑΛΛΩ ΤΑ ΔΑΙΜΟΝΙΑ . . . ,' " in *The Miracles of Jesus*, 381–84.

28. Philostratus, *Life of Apollonius of Tyana*, 5.24.

29. See Luke 5:4–10; John 1:47–49; 2:24–25; 4:17–19; 6:64; 11:11–15; 18:4.

30. Blackburn, "Miracle Working," 190.

31. The classic expression of a positive connection between the divine men and Jesus is W. Bousset's *Kyrios Christos* (1913; reprint, Nashville: Abingdon Press, 1970). A slightly earlier forerunner from the History of Religions (*Religionsgeschichte*) school is Otto Pfleiderer's *The Early Christian Conception of Christ: Its Significance and Value in the History of Religion* (London: Williams and Norgate, 1905), with ch. 3 addressing parallels to Jesus' miracles. The best-known recent supporter is Rudolf Bultmann, in *Theology of the New Testament*, vol. 1, trans. Kendrick Grobel (New York: Scribner's, 1955), 128–33. For an evaluation and critique of some of these and related positions, see Reginald Fuller, *The Foundations of New Testament Christology* (New York: Scribner's, 1965), 68–72, 86–101; Oscar Cullmann, *The Christology of the New Testament*, rev. ed., trans. Shirley C. Guthrie and Charles A. M. Hall (Philadelphia: Westminster, 1963), 195–99, 239–45, 270–72.

32. Blackburn, "Miracle Working," 188–92, 205; cf. Fuller, *Foundations*, 97.

33. See Rudolf Bultmann, "The Study of the Synoptic Gospels," *Form Criticism: Two Essays on New Testament Research*, trans. Frederick C. Grant (New York: Harper & Row, 1962), 38, where, interestingly, Josephus' case of Eleazar is one of the comparisons.

34. Blackburn, "Miracle Working," 196–99; Fuller, *Foundations*, 70–72, 97–98; Cullmann, *Christology*, 199–217, 241–45, 272–75.

35. Fuller, *Foundations*, 98. On a related topic, Fuller judges that the Gnostic redeemer myth "is not directly attested in pre-Christian sources. It is no more than a reconstruction" (p. 93). Later he adds, "But there is no evidence for a pre-existent redeemer who becomes incarnate. Only in second-century 'Christian' gnosticism does the incarnate redeemer figure finally penetrate the gnostic tradition" (p. 97).

36. Blackburn, "Miracle Working," 199–202.

37. Fuller, *Foundations*, 90; cf. 142–43. On the atonement, see Martin Hengel, *The Atonement: The Origins of the Doctrine in the New Testament*, trans. John Bowden

(Philadelphia: Fortress, 1981), 31–32, 65–75. For more on the uniqueness of the resurrection, see Hengel, *The Atonement*, 34–39, and Sir Norman Anderson, *Christianity and World Religions: The Challenge of Pluralism* (Downers Grove, Ill.: InterVarsity Press, 1984), 48–81.

38. I. Howard Marshall, *The Origins of New Testament Christology*, updated ed. (Downers Grove, Ill.: InterVarsity Press, 1990), 128; see 112–23, 126–29. On the deity of Jesus Christ vis-à-vis the Hellenistic options, see Cullmann, *Christology*, 203–37, 270, 275–90; cf. 150–64; Martin Hengel, *The Son of God* (Philadelphia: Fortress Press, 1976). Blackburn, "Miracle Working," 189, knows of no example where a pagan miracle worker was called the Son of God, nor where his divinity was argued from his miracles. Fuller, *Foundations*, 69–72, adds that the title "Son of God" is never used in Hellenistic Judaism for the divine man but has its chief roots in the Old Testament.

39. Blackburn, "Miracle Working," 198–99, 205–6.

40. See Howard Kee, *Miracle in the Early Christian World* (New Haven: Yale University Press, 1983), 256; James Ferguson, *The Religions of the Roman Empire* (Ithaca, N.Y.: Cornell University Press, 1970), 182; Charles Bigg, *The Origins of Christianity* (Oxford: Clarendon, 1910), 306.

41. For details, see Kee, *Miracle*, 253; S. A. Cook, ed., *The Cambridge Ancient History*, vol. 12 (Cambridge: Cambridge University Press, 1965), 611.

42. Ferguson, *Religions of the Roman Empire*, 51; cf. Cook, *Cambridge Ancient History*, 613.

43. For these problems, see Conybeare, "Introduction" to Philostratus' *The Life of Apollonius of Tyana*, 1.vii–x.

44. For details on this last point, as well as further issues regarding both Philostratus's text and other parallel sources, see Gary R. Habermas, "Resurrection Claims in Non-Christian Religions," *Religious Studies* 25 (1989): 167–77.

45. Marcus J. Borg, *Jesus: A New Vision: Spirit, Culture, and the Life of Discipleship* (San Francisco: HarperSanFrancisco, 1987), 61–62.

46. John Dominic Crossan, *The Historical Jesus: The Life of a Mediterranean Jewish Peasant* (San Francisco: HarperSanFrancisco, 1991), 404.

47. R. Bultmann, *Jesus* (Tübingen: Mohr, 1926), 146 (as quoted by Fossum, "Understanding Jesus' Miracles," 23).

48. Bornkamm, *Jesus of Nazareth*, 130–31.

49. A. M. Hunter, *Jesus: Lord and Saviour* (Grand Rapids: Eerdmans, 1976), 63.

50. Borg, *Jesus, A New Vision*, 61.

51. John Dominic Crossan, *Jesus: A Revolutionary Biography* (San Francisco: HarperSanFrancisco, 1994), 93 and 177, respectively. (This book will be referred to below as *Jesus*, distinguishing it from Crossan's *The Historical Jesus*.)

52. For other examples besides Borg and Crossan, see Bultmann, *Theology of the New Testament*, 1.7; Fuller, *Foundations*, 105–7; Reginald Fuller, *Interpreting the Miracles* (London: SCM Press, 1963), 18–29; Wolfhart Pannenberg, *Jesus—God and Man*, trans. Lewis L. Wilkens and Duane A. Priebe (Philadelphia: Westminster, 1968), 63–65; Fossum, "Understanding Jesus' Miracles," 23. In the opinion of the Jesus Seminar, Jesus' words reflect his exorcisms in at least one text (Matt. 12:27–29 = Luke 11:17–22); see Robert W. Funk, Roy W. Hoover, and the Jesus Seminar, *The Five Gospels: What Did Jesus Really Say?* (New York: Macmillan, 1993), 186, 330.

53. Rudolf Bultmann, "New Testament and Mythology," *Kerygma and Myth: A Theological Debate*, ed. Hans Werner Bartsch, rev. trans. by Reginald H. Fuller (New York: Harper & Row, 1961), 4–5.

54. Hunter, *Jesus: Lord and Saviour*, 63.

55. Crossan differentiates between diseases, which are biological in nature, and illnesses, which are sociological (*Jesus*, 80–82). To him, while Jesus did not actually cure diseased persons, such as lepers and those with related problems, he "healed the poor man's illness by refusing to accept the disease's ritual uncleanness and social ostracization. . . . But miracles are not changes in the physical world so much as changes in the social world" (82).

56. Crossan introduces a modern case to show how a psychiatrist advised exorcism, leading to the complete recovery and "healing" of a teenage girl (*Jesus*, 85).

57. Borg, *Jesus, A New Vision*, 60–62, 70.

58. Fossum, "Understanding Jesus' Miracles," 21.

59. Ibid., 21–23.

60. Crossan, *The Historical Jesus*, 404; *Jesus*, 169–70, 175, 181, 186, 190.

61. Borg, *Jesus, A New Vision*, 66–71.

62. For some thought-provoking books that address criteria for establishing and choosing worldviews, including the relationship between facts and presuppositions, see Ronald H. Nash, *Worldviews in Conflict: Choosing Christianity in a World of Ideas* (Grand Rapids: Zondervan, 1992); Norman L. Geisler and William D. Watkins, *Worlds Apart: A Handbook on World Views*, 2d ed. (Grand Rapids: Baker, 1989); J. P. Moreland, *Scaling the Secular City: A Defense of Christianity* (Grand Rapids: Baker, 1987); Winfried Corduan, *Reasonable Faith: Basic Christian Apologetics* (Nashville: Broadman & Holman, 1993), esp. chs. 4–5.

63. Funk, Hoover, and the Jesus Seminar, *The Five Gospels*, 2, emphasis added.

64. Ibid., 2.

65. One is reminded of a related comment by Bultmann in "New Testament and Mythology," 5: "It is impossible to use electric light and the wireless and to avail ourselves of modern medical and surgical discoveries, and at the same time to believe in the New Testament world of spirits and miracles."

66. A. M. Hunter, *Bible and Gospel* (Philadelphia: Westminster, 1969), 93.

67. Ibid., 93, emphasis added.

68. Other scholars concur. For example, in *The Miracles of Jesus*, see the comments by Edwin Yamauchi, "Magic or Miracle? Disease, Demons and Exorcisms," 143–44, 147; B. D. Chilton, "Exorcism and History: Mark 1:21–28," 263; Murray J. Harris, " 'The Dead are Restored to Life': Miracles of Revivification in the Gospels," 310; Stephen T. Davis, "The Miracle at Cana: A Philosopher's Perspective," 435; Craig L. Blomberg, "Concluding Reflections on Miracles and Gospel Perspectives," 445.

69. Bultmann, "New Testament and Mythology," 38.

70. John Macquarrie, *An Existentialist Theology: A Comparison of Heidegger and Bultmann* (New York: Harper & Row, 1965), 185–86.

71. Crossan, *Jesus*, 82.

72. Ibid., 95.

73. Fossum, "Understanding Jesus' Miracles," 50.

74. Funk, Hoover, and the Jesus Seminar, *The Five Gospels*, 25.

75. Ibid., 398.

76. Ibid., 19–35.

77. Ibid., 2.

78. Ibid., 199–200, 270, 399–400, 439, 468–69.

79. After his comment concerning "fundamentalist naïveté" mentioned above, Fossum explains that "raising the dead was not considered impossible in the ancient world" ("Understanding Jesus' Miracles," 50), apparently thinking that this is an adequate explanation of Jesus' raising the dead. But whatever one concludes about Jesus' miracles, this is an instance of what is called a genetic fallacy. For all we know, all the ancient reports could be true, or some false and others true. Similarities do not disprove either case. (It should be noted that Fossum's response is used only as an example; he is not listed as a Fellow of the Jesus Seminar.)

80. Crossan, *Jesus*, 85.

81. B. D. Chilton, "Exorcism and History: Mark 1:21–28," in *The Miracles of Jesus*, 263.

82. Crossan, *Jesus*, 82, 95.

83. Borg, *Jesus, A New Vision*, 66–67, 70–71.

84. Ibid., 61. Borg's second point, that healings and exorcisms were common in the ancient world, depends on what one concludes about the parallels, which we have already addressed. Perhaps surprising to some, we need not hold that all such non-Christian reports are false, for too many other options are available. For instance, Scripture records God's performance of miraculous acts among those who were neither Israelites nor Christians, and it could be the same today.

85. They also include additional important sources such as the Gospel of *Thomas*, John (which they think "contributes little to the search for the authentic sayings of Jesus"), as well as the letters of Paul and the *Didache*. Each of these is also considered an independent source (Funk, Hoover, and the Jesus Seminar, *The Five Gospels*, 16, 18, 128). For more on the Seminar's use of Gospel sources as a criterion of authenticity, see Darrell Bock's chapter.

86. This passage is numbered QS 16 in the reconstruction of Q as suggested by Burton Mack, *The Lost Gospel: The Book of Q and Christian Origins* (San Francisco: HarperSanFrancisco, 1993), 86. The reader should be aware that both Q and its reconstruction are also questioned by many scholars. William Farmer asserts in his "The Church's Stake in the Question of 'Q,' " *The Perkins Journal of Theology*, 39:3 (July 1986): 14:

    The existence of Q, the fount of all these speculations, is not proven and today is more hotly contested in gospel scholarship than at any other time in our century. . . . In our view the present spectacle of theologians writing books about the theology of the "Q" community is like children making castles in a sandbox.

    See also Farmer's "Order Out of Chaos," *The Perkins Journal of Theology* 40:2 (April 1987): 1–16.

87. Interestingly, at times Crossan is reminiscent of some of the old liberal attempts to find a natural explanation for Jesus' miracles (*The Historical Jesus*, 405, 407).

88. The charge by his adversaries that Jesus cast out demons by the power of the prince of the demons is contained in QS 28, but there are no further opposition claims in Q concerning the cause of Jesus' miracles. So with this one exception, the case for critical attestation to Jesus' miracles is similar with regard to both the healing and the nature miracles.

89. Fuller, *Foundations*, 103–8.

90. Bornkamm, *Jesus of Nazareth*, 54–63, 64–69, 130–32, 169–70.

91. Twelftree, "'ΕΙ ΔΕ . . . ΕΓΩ ΕΚΒΑΛΛΩ ΤΑ ΔΑΙΜΟΝΙΑ . . . ,' " 361–400. For his conclusion, see 383–86, 393.

92. B. D. Chilton, "Exorcism and History: Mark 1:21–28," 260–61.

93. Murray J. Harris, "The Dead Are Raised," 298–99.

94. This is the only time that all three Synoptics record the same incident of Jesus' raising the dead (Matt. 9:18–19, 23–26; Mark 5:21–24, 35–43; Luke 8:40–42, 49–56).

95. Harris, "The Dead Are Raised," esp. 310.

96. Ibid., 313–14.

97. Stephen T. Davis, "The Miracle at Cana," 429.

98. P. W. Barnett, "The Feeding of the Multitude," 273–93.

99. Craig Blomberg, "The Miracles as Parables," 327–59. Blomberg's succinct conclusion is found on pp. 347–48.

100. Funk, Hoover, and the Jesus Seminar, *The Five Gospels*, 16.

101. Fossum, "Understanding Jesus' Miracles," 23.

102. For some treatments of this subject, see Craig Blomberg, *The Historical Reliability of the Gospels* (Downers Grove, Ill.: InterVarsity Press, 1987), ch. 3; F. F. Bruce, *The New Testament Documents: Are They Reliable?* 5th ed. (Grand Rapids: Eerdmans, 1960), ch. 5. For shorter treatments, see Hunter, *Jesus: Lord and Saviour*, ch. 5; Moreland, *Scaling the Secular City*, ch. 5; Corduan, *Reasonable Faith*, ch. 10.

103. R. T. France, *The Evidence for Jesus* (Downers Grove, Ill.: InterVarsity Press, 1986), 124–25.

104. Crossan, *The Historical Jesus*, 404.

105. In *Miracles and the Critical Mind* (Grand Rapids: Eerdmans, 1984), 289, Colin Brown argues that the New Testament witness is not from the resurrection of Jesus to his other miracles, but rather that the resurrection showed that all of Jesus' activities were the works of God. Initially, this distinction is difficult to maintain in strict terms, since the truth of the second proposition tends to evidence the first, at least to some degree. But even if the New Testament writers do not argue in the first manner, that, of course, does not mean that such is not a legitimate option. Neither is it apparent that Brown would argue otherwise at this point.

106. See Crossan, *Jesus*, 80–82, 84–86; cf. Borg, *Jesus, A New Vision*, 63.

107. Randolph C. Byrd with John Sherrill, "On a Wing and a Prayer," *Physician*, 5:3 (May–June, 1993): 14–16. The original study was published by Randolph C. Byrd, M.D., in the *Southern Medical Journal* (July 1988).

108. Borg, *Jesus, A New Vision*, 72, n.16; M. Scott Peck, *People of the Lie* (New York: Simon and Schuster, 1983), 182–211.

109. Borg, *Jesus, A New Vision*, 61.

Chapter 6

DID JESUS RISE FROM THE DEAD?

WILLIAM LANE CRAIG

William Lane Craig (Ph.D., University of Birmingham) is currently Visiting Scholar at Emory University. He is author of *Assessing the New Testament Evidence for the Historicity of the Resurrection of Jesu*s and *The Historical Argument for the Resurrection of Jesus.*

Introduction

I was more than mildly surprised last year, while reading an account of the Jesus Seminar in *Time* magazine, to learn that according to John Dominic Crossan, the cochairman of the Seminar, after the crucifixion Jesus' corpse was probably laid in a shallow grave, barely covered with dirt, and subsequently eaten by wild dogs; the story of Jesus' entombment and resurrection was the result of "wishful thinking."[1]

Having carried out fairly extensive research into the historicity of Jesus' resurrection,[2] I was well aware that the wide majority of New Testament critics affirm the historicity of the Gospels' assertion that Jesus' corpse was interred in the tomb of a member of the Jewish Sanhedrin, Joseph of Arimathea. Thus it puzzled me why a prominent scholar like Crossan would set his face against the consensus of scholarship on this question. What hitherto undetected or unappreciated evidence had he discovered, I wondered, that had escaped the notice of critical scholarship and made it probable that Jesus' body was dispatched in the way he alleged, and how did he nullify the evidence that has led most critics to regard the Gospel accounts of Jesus' entombment as fundamentally historically reliable?

You can imagine my sense of disappointment when, consulting Crossan's works, I found that he had no particular evidence, much less compelling evidence, for his allegation; rather, it was just his hunch as to what happened to the body of Jesus.[3] Since he does not accept the historicity of the discovery of the empty tomb (not to speak of the resurrection), Crossan merely surmises that Jesus' corpse was laid in the graveyard reserved for executed criminals. Moreover, he does not engage the evidence that prompts most scholars to accept the historicity of Jesus' entombment; instead, he seeks to undercut the credibility of the Gospel accounts of Jesus' burial and resurrection by means of a general analysis of the Gospel texts and traditions that is so bizarre and contrived that the overwhelming majority of New Testament critics find it wholly implausible.[4] It is sobering to think that it is this sort of idiosyncratic speculation that thousands of lay readers of magazines like *Time* have come to believe represents the best of contemporary New Testament scholarship concerning the historical Jesus.

Testing Historical Explanations

The Nature and Assessment of Historical Explanations

What evidence is there, then, for the resurrection of Jesus, and what is the best explanation of that evidence? Before we can answer these questions, we must say something about the nature of historical explanation and the testing of historical hypotheses. In seeking the best historical explanation of the evidence concerning the resurrection of Jesus, we employ a model of inference common to all inductive reasoning, including the natural sciences, known as *inference to the best explanation.*[5] According to this approach, we begin with the evidence available to us. Then out of a pool of live options determined by our background beliefs, we select the best of various competing explanations to give an account of why the evidence is as it is and not otherwise. For the scientist, the chosen explanation constitutes his theory; for the historian, his proposed reconstruction of the past. The scientist then tests his proposed theory by performing various experiments; the historian tests his historical reconstruction by seeing how well it elucidates the evidence.

The task of judging which historical reconstruction is the best explanation involves the historian's craft. In his recent book, *Justifying Historical Descriptions,*[6] C. Behan McCullagh lists the factors that historians typically weigh in testing a historical hypothesis:

(1) The hypothesis, together with other true statements, must imply further statements describing present, observable data.

(2) The hypothesis must have greater *explanatory scope* (that is, imply a greater variety of observable data) than rival hypotheses.

(3) The hypothesis must have greater *explanatory power* (that is, make the observable data more probable) than rival hypotheses.

(4) The hypothesis must be more *plausible* (that is, be implied by a greater variety of accepted truths, and its negation implied by fewer accepted truths) than rival hypotheses.

(5) The hypothesis must be *less ad hoc* (that is, include fewer new suppositions about the past not already implied by existing knowledge) than rival hypotheses.

(6) The hypothesis must be *disconfirmed by fewer accepted beliefs* (that is, when conjoined with accepted truths, imply fewer false statements) than rival hypotheses.

(7) The hypothesis must so exceed its rivals in fulfilling conditions (2) through (6) that there is little chance of a rival hypothesis, after further investigation, exceeding it in meeting these conditions.

Since some reconstructions fulfill some conditions but are deficient in others, the determination of the best explanation requires skill and is often difficult.

But if an explanation has great scope and power, so that it accounts for a larger number and greater variety of facts than any other competing explanation, then, advises McCullagh, it is likely true.

Historical Explanation and the Supernatural

In applying all this to the case of the resurrection of Jesus, one immediately encounters a watershed issue: will one's explanations be limited to exclusively naturalistic explanations? Naturalism, in contrast to supernaturalism, holds that every effect in the world is brought about by causes that are themselves part of the natural order (the space-time world of matter and energy). Thus no naturalist as such can accept the historicity of the miracles of the Gospels, such as Jesus' resurrection; he must deny either their miraculous nature or their historicity. The presupposition of naturalism will thus affect the historian's assessment of the evidence of the Gospels. The British New Testament critic R. T. France has commented:

> At the level of their literary and historical character we have good reasons to treat the gospels seriously as a source of information on the life and teaching of Jesus, and thus on the historical origins of Christianity. . . . Beyond that point, the decision as to how far a scholar is willing to accept the record they offer is likely to be influenced more by his openness to a "supernaturalist" world-view than by strictly historical considerations.[7]

We have seen, for example, that inferring to the best explanation, one chooses from a pool of live options a candidate that serves as the best explanation of the evidence. For the naturalistic New Testament critic confronted with evidence concerning the empty tomb, the hypothesis that Jesus rose from the dead would not even be a live option. And if a supernaturalist critic were to offer such an explanation of the evidence, his naturalistic colleague would no doubt find it incredible.

Here is a fundamental divide separating the Fellows of the Jesus Seminar from critics whose minds are open to a supernaturalist worldview. The implicit naturalism of the Seminar's methodology surfaces briefly in the Introduction to *The Five Gospels*:

> The contemporary religious controversy . . . turns on whether the worldview reflected in the Bible can be carried forward into this scientific age and retained as an article of faith. . . . The Christ of creed and dogma . . . can no longer command the assent of those who have seen the heavens through Galileo's telescope.[8]

This statement expresses scientific naturalism, which holds that a supernaturalist worldview is untenable in light of the advance of modern science.

To the Jesus Seminar, the historical Jesus of Nazareth *by definition* must be a nonsupernatural Jesus. Tracing modern biblical criticism back through D. F. Strauss, the Introduction correctly notes:

> Strauss distinguished what he called the "mythical" (defined by him as anything legendary or supernatural) in the gospels from the historical. . . . The choice Strauss posed in his assessment of the gospels was between the supernatural Jesus—the Christ of faith—and the historical Jesus.[9]

The Jesus Seminar Fellows have clearly aligned themselves with Strauss: "the distinction between the historical Jesus . . . and the Christ of faith" is deemed the first pillar of "scholarly wisdom" and "modern biblical criticism."[10] For them, Jesus' resurrection from the dead is not a live option even to be considered as a possible explanation for the relevant data;[11] a naturalistic explanation, no matter how outlandish, will *always* be preferred over a supernaturalist explanation (on the basis of criterion 4 above). But is such a verdict justified?

In a fascinating comment on the criteria for assessing historical hypotheses, McCullagh actually considers the Christian hypothesis of the resurrection of Jesus and observes: "This hypothesis is of greater explanatory scope and power than other hypotheses which try to account for the relevant evidence, but it is less plausible and more *ad hoc* than they are. That is why it is difficult to decide on the evidence whether it should be accepted or rejected."[12] A discussion of whether the resurrection hypothesis is more *ad hoc* than its rivals can be deferred until later, but for now we ask why this hypothesis should be considered less plausible than rival hypotheses.

Degree of plausibility is defined by McCullagh as the degree to which a hypothesis is implied by accepted knowledge, including (1) our *background knowledge* (that is, the whole body of knowledge that we bring to an inquiry) and (2) the *specific relevant evidence* for the hypothesis. With respect to our *background knowledge alone*, the supernaturalist agrees with the naturalist that the resurrection hypothesis has virtually zero plausibility in McCullagh's sense, for nothing in our background information implies that Jesus' resurrection took place.[13] But by the same token, the hypotheses that the disciples stole the body or that Jesus was not really dead also have zero plausibility with respect to the background information, for nothing in that information implies that any of these events took place either. That means that the greater plausibility must derive, not from the background information, but from the *specific evidence itself*. But the specific evidence does not confer greater plausibility on any naturalistic hypothesis than on the resurrection hypothesis; on the contrary, these rival hypotheses are usually thought to be made implausible by the specific evidence.

Perhaps McCullagh's claim, then, should have been that the resurrection hypothesis is more *implausible* than rival hypotheses. *Degree of implausibility* is defined as the degree to which our present knowledge implies the falsity of a hypothesis. Now, again dividing present knowledge into background information and specific evidence for the hypothesis, it cannot be that the *specific evidence* renders the resurrection hypothesis more implausible than its competitors, for that specific evidence in no way implies the falsity of the resurrection hypothesis. Hence, there must be something in our *background knowledge* that renders the resurrection hypothesis more implausible than its rivals. I suspect that the reason the naturalist finds the resurrection implausible is because included in our background knowledge of the world is the fact that *dead men do not* rise, which he takes to be incompatible with Jesus' resurrection.

We may agree that our background knowledge does make the hypothesis of the natural revivification of Jesus from the dead enormously implausible, in that the causal powers of nature are insufficient to return a corpse to life; but such considerations are simply irrelevant to assessing the implausibility of the hypothesis of the resurrection of Jesus, since according to that hypothesis God raised Jesus from the dead. I should say that the hypothesis that God raised Jesus from the dead has about zero implausibility with respect to our background knowledge. Only if the naturalist has independent reasons to think that God's existence is implausible or his intervention in the world implausible could he justifiably regard the resurrection hypothesis as implausible.

The bottom line is that what the Jesus Seminar calls the first pillar of scholarly wisdom is nothing more than a philosophical prejudice that actually impedes a fair assessment of the evidence relevant to the resurrection of Jesus. In what follows, then, I leave open the possibility of adopting a supernatural explanation if the facts should so warrant.

Evidence for the Resurrection of Jesus

What, then, is the relevant body of evidence pertinent to the alleged resurrection of Jesus? It can be conveniently grouped under three main headings: (1) Jesus' empty tomb, (2) the postmortem appearances of Jesus, and (3) the origin of the disciples' belief in Jesus' resurrection. In the following I shall concisely summarize the positive evidence concerning each one and then, because of limitations of space, interact with critical objections in the endnotes.

The Empty Tomb

We begin with ten lines of evidence that support the fact of Jesus' empty tomb. We shall then consider briefly naturalistic explanations of that fact.

The historical fact of the empty tomb

What evidence supports the historical fact of Jesus' empty tomb?

1. *The historical credibility of the burial story supports the empty tomb.* If the burial story is basically reliable, then the inference that Jesus' tomb was found empty lies close at hand. For if the burial story is fundamentally accurate, the site of Jesus' tomb would have been known to Jew and Christian alike. But in that case, it would have been impossible for the resurrection faith to survive in the face of a tomb containing the corpse of Jesus. The disciples could not have believed in

Jesus' resurrection; even if they had, scarcely anyone else would have believed them as they preached Jesus' resurrection; and their Jewish opponents could have exposed the whole affair, perhaps even by displaying the body, as the medieval Jewish polemic portrays them doing (*Toledot Yeshu*). Hence, as Crossan recognizes, no one can affirm the historicity of the burial story and plausibly deny the historicity of the empty tomb.

But, in fact, the burial story is widely recognized as a historically credible narrative, for the following reasons:

(a) *Paul's testimony provides early evidence for the historicity of Jesus' burial.* In 1 Corinthians 15:3–5, the tradition he received and passed on refers to Jesus' burial:

> . . . that Christ died for our sins in accordance with the Scriptures,
> and that he was buried,
> and that he was raised on the third day in accordance with the Scriptures,
> and that he appeared to Cephas, then to the Twelve. (pers. tr.)

The grammatically unnecessary fourfold "and that," the chronological succession of the events, and particularly the remarkable concordance between this tradition and both the preaching of Acts 13 and the Gospel narratives regarding the order of events (death - burial - resurrection - appearances) shows that the tradition's mention of the burial is not meant merely to underscore Jesus' death,[14] but refers to the laying of Jesus in the tomb, as recorded in the Gospels. This makes it difficult to deny the historicity of Jesus' burial in the tomb, for (i) given the age of the tradition (A.D. 30–36), there was not sufficient time for legend concerning the burial to accrue; (ii) the women witnesses (see below) to the burial were known in the early Christian fellowship in which the tradition was formulated, and their testimony stands behind it; (iii) Paul himself undoubtedly knew the stories that stood behind the traditions he delivered (see, for example, 1 Cor. 11:23–26), including the story of Jesus' burial. His two-week visit to Jerusalem in A.D. 36 (Gal. 1:18) makes this conclusion firm.

(b) *The burial story was part of the pre-Markan Passion story and is therefore very old.* It is generally acknowledged that the burial account is part of Mark's source material for the story of Jesus' passion.[15] This gives good reason to accept the burial as historical, on grounds similar to those listed above: (i) insufficient time for a legendary burial of Jesus to arise; (ii) the presence of eyewitnesses who could affirm the story; and (iii) Paul's probable knowledge of at least the pre-Markan Passion story.

(c) *The story itself is simple and in its basic elements lacks theological reflection or apologetic development.* Most scholars concur with Bultmann's judgment to this effect.[16] The simple story of Joseph's begging the body of Jesus and his laying it, wrapped in linen, in a tomb has not been significantly overlaid with theology or apologetics.

(d) *Joseph of Arimathea is probably historical.* Even the most skeptical scholars agree that it is unlikely that the figure of Joseph, as a member of the Sanhedrin, could have been a Christian invention.[17] Raymond Brown, one of the greatest New Testament scholars of our day, explains that Joseph's being responsible for burying Jesus is "very probable," since a Christian fictional creation of a Jewish Sanhedrist doing what is right for Jesus is "almost inexplicable," given the hostility toward the Jewish leaders responsible for Jesus' death in early Christian writings.[18] In particular, Mark would not have invented Joseph in view of his statements that the whole Sanhedrin voted for Jesus' condemnation (Mark 14:55, 64; 15:1).

The Gospels' descriptions of Joseph receive unintentional confirmation from incidental details, such as his being rich (rendered plausible by the type and location of the tomb) and his coming from Arimathea (a town of no importance and with no scriptural symbolism). His being a sympathizer of Jesus is not only independently attested by Matthew and John, but is likely in view of Mark's description of his special treatment of Jesus' body as opposed to those of the thieves.

(e) *Joseph's laying the body in his own tomb is probably historical.* The consistent descriptions of the tomb as an *acrosolia*, or bench tomb, and archaeological discoveries that such tombs were used by notables during Jesus' day makes it credible that Jesus was placed in such a tomb. The incidental details that it was new and belonged to Joseph are also probable, since Joseph could not have placed the body of a criminal in just any tomb, especially since this would defile the bodies of any family members also reposing there.

(f) *Jesus was buried late on the Day of Preparation.* The time of Jesus' interment, given what we know from extrabiblical sources about Jewish regulations concerning the handling of executed criminals and burial procedures, must have been on Friday before the evening star appeared. The body could not have been allowed to remain on the cross overnight without defiling the land, and since the Sabbath was impending, the body had to be buried before nightfall. With help, Joseph should have been able to complete a simple burial prior to the beginning of the Sabbath, just as the Gospels describe.

(g) *The observation of the burial by women is historical.* The Gospels report women as witnesses of the crucifixion, burial, and empty tomb. Unless that was actually so, it is inexplicable why they should play this role and not the disciples themselves (see below). Moreover, their roles in the burial and empty tomb stories are mutually confirmatory, since it is unlikely that they would be involved in one event but not the other. So if any of the lists of female witnesses (Mark 15:40, 47; 16:1) is reliable, the others probably are reliable as well. It is difficult to see how the names of these women who were known in the early Christian fellowship could be associated with such events unless this was in fact the case.

(h) *The graves of Jewish holy men were carefully preserved.* During Jesus' time there was an extraordinary interest in the graves of Jewish martyrs and holy men, and these were scrupulously cared for and honored. This suggests that the grave of Jesus would have also been noted. The disciples had no inkling of any resurrection prior to the general resurrection at the end of the world, and they would therefore not have allowed the burial site of the Teacher to go unnoted. This interest also makes plausible the women's lingering to watch the burial and their subsequent intention to anoint Jesus' body with spices and perfumes (Luke 23:55–56).

(i) *No other burial tradition exists.* If the burial of Jesus in the tomb by Joseph of Arimathea is legendary, then it is strange that conflicting traditions nowhere appear, even in Jewish polemic. That no remnant of the true story or even a conflicting false one should remain is hard to explain unless the Gospel account is substantially the true account.[19]

Taken together these nine considerations allow us to assert the historical credibility of Jesus' burial, a fact recognized by the majority of New Testament critics. According to Wolfgang Trilling, "It appears unfounded to doubt the fact of Jesus' honorable burial—even historically considered."[20] But then the conclusion that the tomb was found empty lies close at hand. Even if the disciples left for Galilee and did not return to Jerusalem preaching the resurrection until later, the prospect of a closed tomb would have silenced them effectively.

2. *Paul's testimony implies the fact of the empty tomb.* We come now to the second line of evidence that supports the historicity of the empty tomb. There is little doubt that Paul accepted not only the burial but also the empty tomb of Jesus, as is evident (a) from the sequence in 1 Corinthians 15:3–5 (death - burial - resurrection); (b) from the Jewish concept of resurrection itself; (c) from his Pharisaic background and language; (d) from the expression "on the third day"; (e) from the phrase "from the dead" in Romans 4:24; (f) from his doctrine of the resurrection and transformation of the body (1 Cor. 15:35–50); and (g) from his belief in the personal return of Christ (1 Thess. 4:14–17). All these imply a physical resurrection and therefore an empty tomb. It seems nearly certain, then, that Paul believed in the empty tomb.[21]

But now the question presses: how could the apostle Paul have believed in the empty tomb of Jesus if in fact the tomb were not empty? Certainly Peter, James, and the other Christians in Jerusalem with whom Paul spoke shortly after his conversion (Gal. 1:18) must also have believed that the tomb was empty and had been empty from the moment of the resurrection. Were this not so, Pauline theology would surely have taken a different route, trying to explain how resurrection could still be possible though the body remained in the grave. But neither Christian theology nor apologetics ever had to face such a problem.

Moreover, the third element in the tradition Paul preached (1 Cor. 15:3–5) corresponds to the empty tomb story in the Gospels, the phrase "that he was raised" mirroring the phrase "he is risen." The empty tomb tradition stands behind this element, just as the burial tradition stands behind the second. Two conclusions follow. (a) The tradition that the tomb was found empty is reliable. There would not have been enough time for an empty tomb legend to accrue by the date of the drafting of the formula, and the presence of witnesses in the early Christian fellowship would have prevented it. (b) Paul no doubt knew the tradition of the empty tomb as summarized in the formula of 1 Corinthians 15 and thus lends his own testimony to its reliability. If the discovery of the empty tomb is not historical, then it is inexplicable how both Paul and the early formulators could accept it.

3. *The presence of the empty tomb narrative in the pre-Markan Passion story supports its historical credibility.* That the empty tomb story (Mark 16:1–8) was part of the pre-Markan Passion story is evident from the fact that (a) the empty tomb story is bound up with the immediate context of the burial account and the Passion story; (b) verbal and syntactical similarities bind the empty tomb story to the burial narrative; (c) the Passion story would not have circulated without victory at its end; and (d) the correspondence between the events of the Passion and the formula of 1 Corinthians 15:3–5 confirms the inclusion of the empty tomb account in the pre-Markan Passion story.

From the nature of the events themselves, this conclusion makes good sense. There was no continuous account of Jesus' appearances because they were unexpected and sporadic and occurred to different people at various locations and occasions. The empty tomb story, on the other hand, related a fact that was, so to speak, "common property" of the early Christian fellowship.

According to Rudolf Pesch,[22] geographical references, personal names, and the use of Galilee as a horizon all point to Jerusalem as the source of the pre-Markan Passion story. Pesch argues that Paul's Last Supper tradition (1 Cor. 11:23–25) presupposes the pre-Markan Passion account; hence, the latter must have originated in the first years of existence of the Jerusalem fellowship. Confirmation of this is found in the fact that the pre-Markan Passion story speaks of the "high priest" without using his name (14:53, 54, 60, 61, 63). This suggests that Caiaphas was still the high priest when the pre-Markan Passion story was being told, since then there would be no need to mention his name. Since Caiaphas was high priest from A.D. 18–37, the latest possible date for the origin of the tradition is A.D. 37.[23]

4. *The use of "the first day of the week" (Mark 16:2) instead of "on the third day" points to the primitiveness of the tradition.* The tradition of the discovery of the empty tomb must be very old because it lacks altogether the "third-day" motif prominent in the earliest Christian preaching, as it is summarized in 1 Corinthians 15:3–5. If the empty tomb narrative were a late and legendary account, then, as Bode points out in his important study of the empty tomb, it could hardly have avoided being cast in the prominent, ancient, and accepted third-day motif.[24] In other words, the empty tomb tradition antedates the third-day motif itself.

5. *The nature of the narrative itself is theologically unadorned and nonapologetic.* The resurrection is not described, and later theological motifs that a late legend might be expected to incorporate are lacking. A comparison of Mark's account with those in later apocryphal Gospels like the *Gospel of Peter* underlines the simplicity of the Markan story. The *Gospel of Peter* inserts between Jesus' being sealed in the tomb and the visit of Mary Magdalene early Sunday morning an account

of the resurrection itself. In this account, the tomb is not only surrounded by Roman guards but also by the Jewish Pharisees and elders, as well as a multitude from the surrounding countryside. Suddenly, in the night there rings out a loud voice in heaven, and two men descend from heaven to the tomb. The stone over the door rolls back by itself, and they go into the tomb. Then three men come out of the tomb, two of them holding up the third man. The heads of the two men reach up into the clouds, but the head of the third man reaches up beyond the clouds. Then a cross comes out of the tomb, and a voice from heaven asks, "Have you preached to them that sleep?" And the cross answers, "Yes."

This is how legends look: they are colored by theological and other developments.[25] By contrast, Mark's account of the discovery of the empty tomb is a simple, straightforward report of what happened.

6. *The empty tomb was discovered by women.* Given the relatively low status of women in Jewish society and their lack of qualification to serve as legal witnesses, the most plausible explanation, in light of the Gospels' conviction that the disciples were in Jerusalem over the Easter weekend, why women and not the male disciples are described as discoverers of the empty tomb is that the women were in fact the ones who made this discovery.[26] Moreover, why would the Christian church humiliate its leaders by having them hiding in cowardice in Jerusalem, while the women boldly carry out their last devotions to Jesus' body, unless this were in fact true? Finally, the listing of the women's names weighs against their discovery being a legend, for these persons were known in early Christian fellowship and could not be easily associated with a false account.

7. *The investigation of the empty tomb by Peter and John is historically probable.* Behind the fourth Gospel stands the witness of the beloved disciple (John 21:24), who is most likely John the son of Zebedee, whose reminiscences fill out the traditions employed. The visit of the disciples to the empty tomb is therefore attested both in tradition (Luke 24:12, 24; John 20:3) and by John himself. The historicity of the disciples' visit is also made likely by the credibility of the story of Peter's denial (Mark 14:66–72), for since he was in Jerusalem, he would certainly want to check out the women's story of the empty tomb. The absence of any evidence for the disciples' flight to Galilee also implies that they were in Jerusalem, which makes the visit to the tomb plausible.[27]

8. *It would have been virtually impossible for the disciples to proclaim the resurrection in Jerusalem had the tomb not been empty.* The empty tomb is a *sine qua non* of the resurrection. The notion that Jesus rose from the dead with a new body while his old body still lay in the grave is a modern conception. Jewish mentality would never have accepted a division of two bodies. Even if the disciples failed to check the empty tomb, the Jewish authorities could have been guilty of no such oversight. When therefore the disciples began to preach the resurrection in Jerusalem and people responded, and when the religious authorities stood helplessly by, the tomb must have been empty.[28] The simple fact that the Christian fellowship, founded on belief in Jesus' resurrection, came into existence and flourished in

the very city where he was executed and buried is powerful evidence for the historicity of the empty tomb.

9. *The earliest Jewish polemic presupposes the empty tomb.* From information incidentally furnished by Matthew (Matt. 28:15b), we know that the Jewish opponents of Christianity did not deny that Jesus' tomb was empty. Instead, they charged that the disciples had stolen Jesus' body. From here the controversy over the guard at the tomb sprang up. Notice the response of the earliest Jewish polemic to the disciples' proclamation, "He has been raised from the dead" (27:64). Did the Jewish antagonists respond, "His body is still in the tomb in the garden," or "Jesus was thrown into the criminals' graveyard and eaten by dogs"? No. They responded, "His disciples came during the night and stole him away" (28:13). The earliest Jewish polemic was an attempt to explain away the empty tomb. This constitutes persuasive evidence that Jesus' tomb was in fact empty.[29]

10. *The fact that Jesus' tomb was not venerated as a shrine indicates that the tomb was empty.* We noted earlier that it was customary in Judaism for the tomb of a prophet or holy man to be preserved or venerated as a shrine. This was so because the bones of the prophet lay in the tomb and imparted to the site its religious value. If the remains were not there, then the grave would lose its significance as a shrine. Now in the case of Jesus' tomb, we find, in Dunn's words, "absolutely no trace" of any veneration of Jesus' burial place.[30] In light of the disciples' reverence for Jesus, the reason for this absence of veneration for his burial place was because his grave was empty.

Taken together, these ten considerations furnish good evidence that the tomb of Jesus was found empty on Sunday morning by a small group of his women followers. As Van Daalen has remarked, it is difficult to object to the fact of the empty tomb on historical grounds; most objectors do so on the basis of theological or philosophical considerations.[31] But these cannot change empirical facts. New Testament scholars seem to be increasingly recognizing this; according to Jacob Kremer, an Austrian specialist in resurrection research, "By far, most exegetes hold firmly . . . to the reliability of the biblical statements about the empty tomb."[32]

Explaining the historical fact of the empty tomb

But if the tomb of Jesus was found empty on the first day of the week, the question must be: How did this situation come to be? Although the empty tomb may have proved at first ambiguous and puzzling to the disciples, today we know that most alternative explanations are more incredible than the resurrection itself (for example, the disciples' stealing the body, Jesus' not being dead, the women's going to the wrong tomb, etc.). The old rationalistic explanations have thoroughly failed to provide plausible historical explanations that fit the facts without bruising them.[33] There is simply no plausible naturalistic explanation available today that accounts for the empty tomb of Jesus.

The Postmortem Appearances

Turning to the second category of evidence for the resurrection of Jesus, namely, his postmortem appearances, we now ask what evidence there is that Jesus appeared alive after his death to his disciples. Again we shall look first at the evidence for the historicity of the appearances and then examine briefly naturalistic explanations of them.

The historical fact of the appearances

There are four lines of evidence for the historicity of Jesus' appearances.

1. *The testimony of Paul shows that the disciples saw appearances of Jesus.* Paul's citation of the traditional formula in 1 Corinthians 15:3–5 includes references to appearances to Peter and the Twelve. He then goes on to say in verses 6–8:

> After that, he appeared to more than five hundred of the brothers at the same time, most of whom are still living, though some have fallen asleep. Then he appeared to James, then to all the apostles, and last of all he appeared to me also, as to one abnormally born.

The early date for the traditions in 1 Corinthians 15, which reach back to within the first five years after the crucifixion, precludes the hypothesis that the appearances in this list are legendary.[34] Also important is Paul's own early, personal contact with Peter and James and his acquaintance with some of the five hundred fellow believers. It is nothing short of amazing that we have here information from a man who spoke with both Jesus' younger brother and his chief disciple, each of whom claimed to have seen Jesus alive from the dead and who went to his death because of that conviction.

The appearance to the five hundred believers, which in itself sounds unbelievable because of the number involved, possibly harks back to a historical incident, not only because of Paul's personal acquaintance with them, but also because most of them were still alive and could be questioned. And, of course, the appearance to Paul himself, which changed his whole life to the point that he also went to his death for faith in the risen Jesus, is historically certain. We may try to explain these appearances as hallucinations if we choose, but we cannot deny that they occurred. As Norman Perrin remarks, "The more we study the tradition with regard to the appearances, the firmer the rock begins to appear upon which they are based."[35] Paul's list makes it clear that on separate occasions different individuals and groups saw appearances of Jesus alive from the dead.

2. *The Gospel accounts of the resurrection appearances are fundamentally reliable historically.* Though it may be impossible to prove any single appearance narrative as historically accurate, there are good grounds for holding to the historicity of

the Gospels in general and of the appearance stories in particular, given their breadth of tradition in the Gospel records. Trilling explains:

> From the list in 1 Cor. 15 the particular reports of the gospels are now to be interpreted. Here may be of help what we said about Jesus' miracles. It is impossible to "prove" historically a particular miracle. But the totality of the miracle reports permit no reasonable doubt that Jesus in fact performed "miracles." That holds analogously for the appearance reports. It is not possible to secure historically the particular event. But the totality of the appearance reports permits no reasonable doubt that Jesus in fact bore witness to himself in such a way.[36]

Indeed, the evidence for the historicity of the Gospels in general is strong enough that we may affirm that appearance traditions they contain, far from being basically legendary, are substantially credible from a historical standpoint. At least three basic considerations support this conclusion.

(a) *There was not enough time for legends to accrue significantly.* Ever since D. F. Strauss broached his theory that the Gospel accounts of Jesus' life and resurrection are the products of legendary and mythical development, the unanswered difficulty for this viewpoint has been that the temporal and geographical distance between the events and the accounts is insufficient to allow for such extensive development.

Roman historian A. N. Sherwin-White remarks that in classical historiography the sources are usually biased and removed at least one or two generations or even centuries from the events they narrate, but historians still reconstruct with confidence what happened.[37] In the Gospels, by contrast, the tempo is "unbelievable" for the accrual of legend; more generations are needed.[38] The writings of Herodotus enable us to test the tempo of myth-making, and the tests suggest that *even two generations are too short a span to allow the mythical tendency to prevail over the hard historic core of oral tradition.*[39] Such a gap with regard to the Gospel traditions would land us in the second century, precisely when the apocryphal Gospels began to originate.

(b) *The controlling presence of living eyewitnesses would retard significant accrual of legend.* Related to the first consideration is the controlling presence of living eyewitnesses who knew what did and did not happen. The eminent Markan commentator Vincent Taylor has twitted skeptical New Testament scholars for their neglect of this factor, observing that if these critics were right, then the disciples "must have all been translated into heaven immediately after the Resurrection."[40] The witnesses listed in 1 Corinthians 15 continued to live and move in the early community and would exercise a control over the appearance traditions. Similarly, if persons like Mary Magdalene and the women did not see Jesus, it is difficult to see how the early tradition could arise and continue in opposition to the better knowledge of first generation believers.

(c) *The authoritative control of the apostles would have helped to keep legendary tendencies in check.* Since the apostles were the guardians of the Jesus tradition and directed the Christian community, it would have been difficult for fictitious appearance stories incompatible with the apostles' own experience to arise and flourish so long as they were alive.[41] Discrepancies in secondary details could exist, and the theology of the Evangelists could affect the traditions, but the basic traditions themselves could not have been legendary. The substantially unhistorical accounts of Jesus did not arise until the second century, and even then they were universally rejected by the church.

These three considerations ensure that the central traditions underlying the Gospel narratives are not unhistorical legends. Therefore, the appearance stories of the Gospels, which play such an important role in the Gospels, are substantially accurate accounts of what took place.

3. *Particular resurrection appearances have historical credibility.* In addition to the general consideration above, several of the resurrection appearances have in themselves marks of historical credibility. By way of summary:

(a) *The appearance to the women.* The fact that women and not male disciples were chosen for the first appearance lends credibility to this incident. It would seem purposeless to make unqualified women the first witnesses of the risen Jesus, were this not the case. Indeed, Paul's formula probably omitted them because of their lack of legal status. So why have such a story at all recorded in the Gospels? Any conceivable purpose for such an appearance would have been better served by, say, an appearance to Peter at the tomb.

(b) *The appearance to Peter.* Although we have no Gospel narrative of this appearance, its historicity is granted by nearly all New Testament scholars. It is attested in the early tradition quoted by Paul and in another early tradition cited by Luke (Luke 24:34). Moreover, Paul had personal contact with Peter during his visit in A.D. 36, and in citing the formula he vouchsafes its accuracy in this regard.

(c) *The appearance to the Twelve.* The reference to this appearance in the pre-Pauline tradition, as well as Paul's personal contact with the disciples, prevents it from being a late legend. Both Luke and John hand on independent traditions of this event. Behind the Johannine account stands the witness of the Beloved Disciple, one of the Twelve, which serves as a guarantee of the fundamental accuracy of that tradition. In light of Luke and John's agreement, this appearance probably occurred in Jerusalem on the first Sunday after the crucifixion.

(d) *The Lake of Tiberias appearance.* The disciples' fishing (John 21) soon after Christ's resurrection and commissioning of them is unusual and bespeaks an early and probably accurate tradition of an appearance by the Lake of Tiberias. Moreover, the witness of the Beloved Disciple also stands behind this appearance and vouches for the traditions contained therein.

(e) *The appearance in Galilee.* An appearance of Jesus to the disciples in Galilee is referred to in the pre-Markan Passion story through Jesus' and the angel's predictions. Since Mark's source arose so early in the Christian fellowship, it probably preserves the memory of an actual incident.

(f) *The appearance to the five hundred believers.* As in the case of (b), we have no narrative in the Gospels of this event, but it must have taken place, for Paul had firsthand contact with some of these people and appeals to them as eyewitnesses for Jesus' resurrection. The appearance probably occurred in Galilee under open air, prior to the disciples' return to Jerusalem.

(g) *The appearance to James.* Given James' antipathy to Jesus during his lifetime (Mark 3:21, 31–32; John 7:1–5) and his leadership of the church thereafter (Acts 15:13ff.; Gal. 1:19; 2:9), his turnabout was most likely due to a resurrection appearance of Jesus to him. Paul's personal contact with James in Jerusalem in A.D. 36 and his naming James among the list of witnesses make this a firm conclusion.

(h) *The appearance to Paul.* We have in Paul's letters firsthand information concerning the appearance of Jesus to him, an event that revolutionized the life of this learned Pharisee. No one can doubt that this event occurred, and most scholars are willing to recognize the fundamental historical credibility of the account of this incident in Acts 9:1–9.

Hence, wholly apart from the support springing from the general historical credibility of the Gospel appearances stories, these individual incidents have in themselves positive marks of historical credibility. From these we may conclude that the disciples witnessed appearances of Jesus first in Jerusalem and then in Galilee, that these appearances were witnessed by both groups and individuals, and that they occurred under varying conditions. The nature of these appearances is considered more closely in the fourth and final point.

4. *The resurrection appearances were physical, bodily appearances.* There is a widespread consensus among New Testament critics that the disciples did see "appearances of Jesus" after his death, and a considerable number interpret these appearances in terms of the bodily resurrection and appearances of Jesus. But at the same time, a great many critics hold that because the body was "spiritual," the appearances of the risen Christ were heavenly visions involving no physical reality. For example, McDonald asserts, "Taken by themselves, experiences of 'seeing the risen Christ' would probably represent psychic phenomena of significance to the experiencing subject but otherwise of direct moment only to the psychical researcher."[42] Sometimes the appearances are described as "objective visions" in order to differentiate them from mere hallucinations (or subjective visions). Hence, according to this widespread viewpoint, the *physical* resurrection appearance stories are historically unreliable.

There are, however, two good reasons for affirming the truth of physical resurrection appearances of Jesus:

(a) *Paul implies that the appearances were physical events.* Those who take the appearances to be merely visionary in nature typically propose a sharp division between Paul and the Evangelists concerning the nature of Christ's resurrection body. Seeking to align themselves with what they perceive to be Paul's position, they reason that since Paul teaches that our future resurrection bodies will be modeled after Jesus' resurrection body and our future resurrection bodies will be spiritual (1 Cor. 15:42–49), it follows that Jesus' resurrection body was a spiritual body (that is to say, his body was immaterial, intangible, unextended, invisible, etc.).

But while it is true that Paul teaches that our resurrection bodies will be modeled after Jesus' body and that they will be spiritual, it does not follow that these bodies will be nonphysical. Such an interpretation is not supported by an exegesis of Paul's teaching. If by *soma pneumatikon* ("spiritual body") one understands a body that is intangible, unextended, or immaterial, then it is false to assert that Paul taught that we shall have *that* kind of resurrection body. New Testament commentators agree that *pneumatikos* means "spiritual" in the sense of orientation, not substance (cf. 1 Cor. 2:15; 10:4). The transformation of the earthly body to a *soma pneumatikon* accordingly does not rescue it from materiality, but from mortality.[43]

A *soma* ("body") that is unextended and intangible would have been a contradiction in terms for the apostle. The resurrection body will be an immortal, powerful, glorious, Spirit-directed body, suitable for inhabiting a renewed creation. All commentators agree that Paul did not teach the immortality of the soul alone; but his affirmation of the resurrection of the body becomes vacuous and indistinguishable from such a doctrine unless it means the tangible, physical resurrection.[44] The exegetical evidence does not, therefore, support a bifurcation between Paul and the Evangelists with regard to the nature of the resurrection body.

More than that, however, there are positive grounds to believe that Paul implies physical appearances of Jesus. (i) Paul, along with the whole New Testament, makes a conceptual (if not a linguistic) distinction between an appearance and a vision of Jesus. While visions continued in the church, the resurrection appearances were unrepeatable and confined to a brief initial period. A vision, whether "subjective" (nonveridical) or "objective" (veridical), was wholly in the mind, while a resurrection appearance involved something happening in the external world. If this is the case, then Paul, in listing the resurrection appearances in 1 Corinthians 15, implies that they were extramental events, not visions. Because Paul's own Damascus Road experience, though semivisionary in character, included extramental phenomena (audible speech and a bright light; cf. Acts 9:7; 22:9; 26:13–14), he can add himself to the list in good conscience. Moreover, since Paul evidently believed in a physical resurrection body, then in stating that Jesus "was raised" and "appeared" (1 Cor. 15:4–5), he meant appeared physically and bodily, just as he was raised physically and bodily. Thus to Paul, Jesus' appearances were physical, bodily appearances.

(ii) We see a second indication of Paul's belief in this regard when we consider the reverse side of the coin. If originally there were no physical, bodily appearances of Jesus but only visions, then the development of Paul's teaching on the resurrection becomes difficult to explain. He could not have taught that we will have resurrection bodies patterned after Christ's, for Christ apparently had no resurrection *soma*. Indeed, as we shall see, it is doubtful that such visionary experiences would have led Paul to speak of resurrection at all. In other words, mere visions of Jesus after his death are not sufficient to explain the direction and development of Paul's doctrine of the resurrection body.

(b) *The Gospels confirm that the appearances were physical and bodily.* Although the Gospels' discussion of Jesus' physical appearances is often alleged to be an antidocetic apologetic, the grounds for this assertion are weak, and there are positive considerations mitigating against it.[45] Indeed, Paul's doctrine shows an early belief in a physical resurrection body of Christ that cannot be written off to an antidocetic apologetic, since that would have been counterproductive against his Corinthian opponents, who seemed repulsed by the notion of a physical resurrection.

In addition, there are positive reasons to affirm the historical credibility of the Gospel narratives in this regard. (i) Every resurrection appearance narrated in the Gospels is a physical, bodily appearance. The unanimity of the Gospels on this score is impressive when one remembers that the appearance accounts were originally more or less separate, independent stories, which the different Evangelists collected and arranged. All the separate traditions agree that Jesus appeared physically and bodily alive to the various witnesses. There is no trace of nonphysical visions in the traditions, a remarkable fact if *all* the appearances were really visionary. A series of heavenly visions could not have become so thoroughly corrupted or recast as to produce a uniform tradition of physical appearances.

(ii) The decisive point is, as we have already seen, that the Gospel resurrection narratives are fundamentally historically reliable. The physicalism of the appearance stories is so prominent, though often inadvertent, a feature of these narratives that it could not fall through the net of this general consideration. It is inexplicable how a sequence of visions could be so thoroughly materialized into the unanimous physicalism of the Gospel appearance stories in so short a time, in the very presence of the witnesses to those appearances themselves, and under the eyes of the apostles responsible for preventing such corruption.

Hence, the evidence of the Gospels confirms Paul's perspective. Incredible as it may seem, the evidence for the physical, bodily appearances cannot be plausibly rejected on historical grounds.

Explaining the historical fact of the resurrection appearances

In sum, the evidence shows that the disciples witnessed physical, bodily appearances of Jesus after his death. What is the best explanation for this remarkable fact? Although some scholars regard the appearances as mere subjective visions or hallucinations, such a hypothesis faces insuperable difficulties. (1) The hypothesis is undermined by points 2, 3, and 4 just discussed. (2) The number and various circumstances of the appearances attested to by Paul alone make the subjective vision hypothesis unlikely. (3) Subjective visions would have led at most to the disciples' belief in Jesus' translation and exaltation, not in his resurrection, since the latter belief did not fit Jewish conceptions of resurrection (see below). (4) The hypothesis fails to account for the full scope of the evidence in that it provides no explanation of the empty tomb.

Having examined the evidence concerning the empty tomb and the post-mortem appearances of Jesus, we turn now to the final category of evidence for the resurrection.

Origin of the Disciples' Belief in Jesus' Resurrection

The fact of belief in the resurrection

Whatever they may think of the historical resurrection, even the most skeptical scholars admit that at least the *belief* that Jesus rose from the dead lay at the very heart of the earliest Christian faith. In fact, the earliest believers pinned nearly everything on it. The resurrection was the *sine qua non* for their belief in Jesus as Messiah and in his death as the basis for forgiveness of sins.

It is difficult to exaggerate what a devastating effect the crucifixion must have had on the disciples. They had no conception of a dying, much less a rising, Messiah, for the Messiah would reign forever (cf. John 12:34). Without prior belief in the resurrection, belief in Jesus as Messiah would have been impossible in light of his death. The resurrection turned catastrophe into victory. Because God raised Jesus from the dead, he could be proclaimed as Messiah after all (Acts 2:32, 36). Similarly for the significance of the cross—it was his resurrection that enabled Jesus' shameful death to be interpreted in salvific terms. Without it, Jesus' death would have meant only humiliation and accursedness by God; but in view of the resurrection it could be seen to be the event by which forgiveness of sins was obtained. Without the resurrection, the Christian Way could never have come into being. Even if the disciples had continued to remember Jesus as their beloved teacher, they could not have believed in him as Messiah, much less deity.[46]

Explaining the belief in the resurrection

The question now becomes: What caused that belief? Though Bultmann protests against any further historical probing behind the faith of the first disciples, even the most skeptical critic must posit some mysterious X to get the movement going.[47] But what was that X?

If one denies that the historical event of the resurrection was that mysterious X, then one must find something in antecedent Judaism to account for the origin of the disciples' belief and proclamation that Jesus was risen from the dead.[48] The Jewish doctrine of resurrection is attested at least three times in the Old Testament (Isa. 26:19; Ezek. 37; Dan. 12:2) and flowered during the intertestamental period. During Jesus' day belief in bodily resurrection had become a widespread hope, being championed by the Pharisees, with whom Jesus sided on this score against the Sadducees (Matt. 22:23–33). Thus, the concept of bodily resurrection from the dead was part of Jewish religious mentality.

But the Jewish conception of resurrection differed from the belief in Jesus' resurrection in two fundamental respects:

(1) *Jewish belief always concerned a resurrection at the end of the world, not a resurrection in the middle of history.* There were, to be sure, instances in the Old Testament of revivifications of the dead; but these dealt with a return to the earthly life, and those so resuscitated would eventually die again. The resurrection to glory and immortality did not occur until after God had terminated world history. This traditional Jewish conception was the prepossession of Jesus' own disciples (Mark 9:9–13; John 11:24). The notion of a genuine resurrection occurring prior to God's bringing about the world's end would have been foreign to them. Confronted therefore with Jesus' crucifixion and death, the disciples would at most have looked forward to the resurrection at the final day and carefully honored their Master's tomb as a shrine, where his bones could rest until the resurrection. It is most unlikely that they would have come to believe that he was already raised.

(2) *Jewish belief always concerned a general resurrection of the people, not the resurrection of an isolated individual.* Whether it was the righteous, or all of Israel, or the entire human race, the resurrection in Jewish thinking always referred to the general resurrection of the dead. Moreover, no one believed that the people's resurrection in some way hinged on the Messiah's prior resurrection. In this respect, the Jewish conception contrasts sharply with the disciples' belief in Jesus' resurrection. Once again, in light of Jewish religious mentality, the disciples after the burial of Jesus would have waited with longing for that day when Jesus, along with all the righteous of Israel, would be raised by God to glory.

The disciples' belief in Jesus' resurrection cannot, therefore, be explained in terms of the beliefs of antecedent Judaism. According to C. F. D. Moule of Cambridge University, the disciples' belief in the resurrection of Jesus cannot be accounted for in terms of previous historical factors.[49] "The birth and rapid rise of the Christian Church ... remain *an unsolved enigma for any historian who refuses to take seriously the only explanation offered by the Church itself.*"[50] The resurrection of Jesus is therefore the most plausible explanation of the origin of the Christian Way.

But, it might be argued, perhaps the disciples were led to that conclusion by certain events following Jesus' crucifixion and burial. Some scholars have suggested, for example, that the disciples experienced visions of the eschatological Son of Man, which they interpreted in terms of the Jewish anticipation of the resurrection of the dead, and that the story of the empty tomb is a legend that arose as a consequence of their belief that Jesus had been raised. Such a scenario contradicts the evidence; but putting that aside, could such experiences have caused the disciples' belief in the resurrection?

In order to answer this question, we need to take up again the issue of hallucinations. As projections of the mind, hallucinations can contain nothing that is not already in the mind. So if the disciples were to experience visions, they would have projected them on the Jewish model of the afterlife. But we have just noted that Jesus' resurrection involved at least two aspects not part of the Jewish frame of thought: it was a resurrection within history, and it was the resurrection of an isolated individual. What this seems to imply, therefore, is that even if the disciples projected hallucinatory visions of Jesus, they would not have projected him as literally risen from the grave. Rather, given first-century Judaism's beliefs concerning immortality, they would have projected visions of him in glory—that is, in Paradise or in Abraham's bosom. That is where the souls of the righteous dead went to await the final resurrection.

But in that case, it needs to be seriously questioned whether the disciples would have arrived at the doctrine of Jesus' resurrection.[51] Even given the prior discovery of the empty tomb, they would most likely have inferred that Jesus had been translated directly into heaven on the model of Enoch and Elijah (Gen. 5:24; 2 Kings 2:11–18). *Testament of Job* 40 shows that translation was a category applicable to recently deceased persons as well as to the living. For Jewish mentality a translation and a resurrection were different phenomena. A translation is the assumption of an individual out of this world into heaven, while a resurrection is the raising up of a dead person in the spatio-temporal world to eternal life. Therefore, even if the disciples saw hallucinatory visions of Jesus in glory after finding his tomb empty, it is unlikely that they would have concluded that he had been raised from the dead; rather, they would have concluded that God had translated him into heaven, from where he appeared to them.

It is intriguing to observe that some scholars, perhaps feeling the weight of these considerations, have actually argued that the death-exaltation model was in fact primitive and that the death-resurrection model developed from it. The empty tomb story is thus interpreted as a translation story and the appearances are understood as visions of Christ in heavenly glory. But this hypothesis of last resort cannot be sustained. Had a death-translation scheme been primitive, then the development of the disciples' belief in and proclamation of Jesus' resurrection becomes unintelligible. Besides, there is no evidence that a death-exaltation model that did not include a literal resurrection was primitive. Gerald O'Collins, a specialist in resurrection studies, writes:

> The resurrection claim was not derived from the less specific assertion that God has exalted Jesus in his death. . . . we fail to find that death-exaltation texts occur *early* in the NT, while the pattern of death-resurrection (or death-resurrection-exaltation) surfaces only *later*. In fact, if a pattern does exist, it is rather the opposite.[52]

The fact that the disciples proclaimed, not the translation of Jesus (in accord with a common Jewish category suited to explain their experience), but his resurrection (contrary to the mode of Jewish thinking) strongly suggests that the origin of their belief in Jesus' resurrection cannot be derived from an experience of visions of Christ. According to the strictest use of the dissimilarity criterion, the only reasonable explanation for the disciples' faith is the historical fact of Jesus' resurrection, for that belief cannot be explained from the side of Judaism nor from the side of the church.

Concluding Assessment

Evidence for the Resurrection and Criteria of Authenticity

We have summarized the evidence for the historicity of Jesus' resurrection. As one reflects on this evidence, it is striking how successfully the historical material undergirding the physical resurrection of Jesus passes the received tests of authenticity employed by the Fellows of the Jesus Seminar. Evans has recently argued that the same criteria used to establish the authenticity of the sayings of Jesus can also be used to establish the miraculous deeds of Jesus.[53] What is intriguing is that a glance at the evidence for the historicity of Jesus' resurrection reveals that much of it is based on an implicit application of precisely the same criteria. For example:

1. *Multiple attestation.* The resurrection appearances enjoy multiple attestation from Pauline and Gospel traditions, and the latter themselves attest to appearances in various traditions (both Synoptic and Johannine). And, of course, the fact that the first disciples came to believe in Jesus' resurrection is attested throughout the New Testament.

2. *Dissimilarity.* The origin of the disciples' belief in Jesus' resurrection is a clear example of the application of this criterion, for their belief cannot be explained either as the result of antecedent Jewish influences or as a retrojection of Christian theology.

3. *Embarrassment.* The force of the argument based on the discovery of the empty tomb by women derives in large part from this criterion, for their role in the story was useless, not to say counterproductive, for the early church and would have been much better served by men.

4. *Context and expectation.* Again, the disciples' faith cannot be explained as an outgrowth from any expectation in Judaism of a dying, much less rising, Messiah, for there was no such belief.

5. *Effect.* According to this criterion, an adequate cause must be posited for some established effect. The conversion of James and Paul, the earliest Jewish polemic concerning the disciples' alleged theft of the body, and the disciples' transformation after the crucifixion all constitute effects that point to the resurrection appearances, the empty tomb, and the disciples' coming to believe that Jesus was risen as their sufficient causes.

6. *Principles of embellishment.* The Markan account of the empty tomb, in contrast to the apologetically and theologically embellished account in the *Gospel of Peter*, should not be regarded as a legend, precisely on the basis of this criterion.

Did Jesus Rise from the Dead?

7. *Coherence.* The three independently established facts pointing to the resurrection of Jesus—namely, the empty tomb, the resurrection appearances, and the origin of the disciples' belief that he was raised—cohere together and form a powerful argument for the historicity of the resurrection. Moreover, there is also coherence between Paul's teaching on the nature of the resurrection body, Jesus' physical postmortem appearances, and the empty tomb.

Thus, the complex of facts that we have examined in support of the historicity of Jesus' resurrection passes the same tests for authenticity employed by the Jesus Seminar to establish the authentic sayings of Jesus. It therefore deserves to be accorded no less degree of credibility than those utterances.

Assessing the Resurrection as the Best Historical Explanation

But is the resurrection of Jesus the best explanation of this body of evidence? We cannot automatically assume that just because all naturalistic explanations are implausible, therefore the resurrection hypothesis is, by default, the best explanation. In order to answer this question, let us return to McCullagh's seven criteria for testing a historical hypothesis and apply them to the hypothesis that God raised Jesus from the dead.

1. *The hypothesis, together with other true statements, must imply further statements describing present, observable data.* The present, observable data is chiefly the historical texts in the New Testament that form the basis of the historian's reconstruction of the events of Easter. Moreover, there exists the Christian faith itself, whose origin must be accounted for. The resurrection hypothesis, if true, explains all of this.

2. *The hypothesis must have greater explanatory scope than rival hypotheses.* The resurrection hypothesis exceeds counterexplanations like hallucinations or the women's visiting the wrong tomb precisely by explaining all three of the facts at issue (the empty tomb, the resurrection appearances, and the origin of the disciples' belief in Jesus' resurrection), whereas these rival hypotheses explain only one or two.

3. *The hypothesis must have greater explanatory power than rival hypotheses.* This is perhaps the greatest strength of the resurrection hypothesis. The conspiracy theory or the apparent death theory just do not convincingly account for the three facts at issue. On these theories, established facts such as the transformation in the disciples, the conversion of James, and the physicality of the resurrection appearances become improbable. By contrast, on the hypothesis of the resurrection the established facts are probable.

4. *The hypothesis must be more plausible than rival hypotheses.* We have already seen that once one abandons the philosophical prejudice against the miraculous, the resurrection is just as plausible as its rivals.

5. *The hypothesis must be less* ad hoc *than rival hypotheses.* Recall that while McCullagh thought that the resurrection hypothesis possessed great explanatory scope and power, he nevertheless felt that it was *ad hoc,* which he defines in terms

of the number of new suppositions made by a hypothesis that are not already implied by existing knowledge. So defined, however, it is difficult to see why the resurrection hypothesis is extraordinarily *ad hoc*. It requires only one new supposition: that God exists. Surely the rival hypotheses require this many new suppositions. For example, the conspiracy theory requires us to suppose that the moral character of the disciples was defective, which is not implied by existing knowledge. The apparent death theory requires the supposition that the soldier's lance thrust into Jesus' side was just a superficial poke or is unhistorical, which again goes beyond existing knowledge. The hallucination theory requires us to suppose some sort of emotional preparation of the disciples that predisposed them to project visions of Jesus alive, which is not implied by our existing knowledge. Such examples could be multiplied. Moreover, for the person who is already a theist, the resurrection hypothesis does not even introduce the new supposition of God's existence, since that is already implied by his existing knowledge. So the resurrection hypothesis cannot be said to be *ad hoc* simply by virtue of the number of new suppositions it introduces.

Scientific hypotheses regularly include the supposition of new, often unobservable entities, such as quarks, strings, gravitons, black holes, and the like, without those theories being characterized as *ad hoc*. Why should the supposition of God's existence be any different? Philosophers of science have found it notoriously difficult to explain exactly what makes a hypothesis *ad hoc*. There is a certain air of artificiality about a hypothesis deemed to be *ad hoc* that can be sensed, if not defined, by seasoned practitioners of the relevant science. Many persons, *including theists*, feel a certain discomfort about appealing to God as part of an explanatory hypothesis for some phenomenon in the world precisely because doing so has this air of artificiality. It just seems too easy when confronted with some unexplained phenomenon to throw up one's hands and say, "God did it!" The universal disapprobation of the so-called "God of the gaps" and the impulse toward methodological naturalism in science and history spring from the sense of illegitimacy attending such appeals to God. Is the hypothesis that "God raised Jesus from the dead" *ad hoc* in this sense?

I think not. One of the most important contributions of the traditional defenders of the Gospel miracles was their drawing attention to the religio-historical context in which a purported miracle occurs. A supernatural explanation of the facts of the empty tomb, the resurrection appearances, and the origin of the disciples' belief in Jesus' resurrection is not *ad hoc* because those events took place in the context of and as the climax to Jesus' own unparalleled life, ministry, and personal claims, in which a supernatural hypothesis readily fits.[54]

It is also precisely because of this historical context that the resurrection hypothesis does not seem *ad hoc* when compared to miraculous explanations of other sorts: for example, that a "psychological miracle" occurred, causing normal men and women to become conspirators and liars who would be willingly martyred for their subterfuge; or that a "biological miracle" occurred, which prevented Jesus' expiring on the cross or his dying of exposure in the tomb. It is these miraculous hypotheses that strike us as artificial and contrived, not the resurrection hypothesis, which makes abundantly good sense in the context of Jesus' entire ministry and radical personal claims.

6. *The hypothesis must be disconfirmed by fewer accepted beliefs than rival hypotheses.* I cannot think of any accepted beliefs that disconfirm the resurrection hypothesis—unless one thinks that "Dead men do not rise" is disconfirmatory. But then we are just back to the problem of miracles again. This belief would disconfirm a naturalistic revivification hypothesis, but it does nothing to disconfirm the hypothesis that God raised Jesus from the dead. By contrast, rival theories are disconfirmed by accepted beliefs about, for example, the instability of conspiracies, the likelihood of death as a result of crucifixion, the psychological characteristics of hallucinatory experiences, etc.

7. *The hypothesis must so exceed its rivals in fulfilling conditions (2)-(6) that there is little chance of a rival hypothesis exceeding it in meeting these conditions.* There is certainly little chance of any of the extant rival hypotheses exceeding the resurrection hypothesis in fulfilling the above conditions. The stupefaction of contemporary scholarship when confronted with the facts of the empty tomb, the resurrection appearances, and the origin of the disciples' belief in Jesus' resurrection suggests that no better rival is anywhere on the horizon. It is hard to deny that the resurrection is the best explanation of the facts.

Therefore, it seems to me that the sort of skepticism expressed by members of the Jesus Seminar like Crossan with respect to the resurrection of Jesus not only fails to represent the consensus of scholarship, but is quite unjustified.

Concluding Remarks

"There ain't gonna be no Easter this year," a high school friend once remarked to me.

"Why not?" I asked incredulously.

"They found the body."

Despite his irreverent sense of humor, my friend displayed a measure of insight that is apparently not shared by the Fellows of the Jesus Seminar. They seem perfectly willing to maintain that although Jesus died and rotted away, the resurrection still has value as a symbol of Christ's "continuing presence" with us, so that Christianity can go on quite nicely as if nothing were changed. My friend's joke, on the other hand, implied that without a literal resurrection, the Christian faith is worthless.

The earliest Christians would have agreed with my friend (1 Cor. 15:14, 17, 19). Without the historical resurrection, Jesus would have been at best just another prophet who met the same unfortunate fate as others before him, and faith in him as Messiah, Lord, or Son of God would have been stupid. It would be no use trying to save the situation by interpreting the resurrection as a symbol. The cold, hard facts would remain: Jesus was dead, and that's it.

I suspect that the average layperson today also has too much common sense to be impressed by theological salvage operations like that advocated by the Jesus Seminar. After all, why should I let a Christian myth about a dead man be determinative for the meaning of my life today? Why not a non-Christian myth? Why follow myths at all?

Fortunately, the Christian faith does not call for us to put our minds on the shelf, to fly in the face of common sense and history, or to make a leap of faith into the dark. The rational person, fully apprised of the evidence, can confidently believe that on that first Easter morning a divine miracle took place.

Notes

1. Richard N. Ostling, "Jesus Christ, Plain and Simple," *Time*, 10 January 1994, 32–33.

2. From 1978 to 1980, I had the privilege of spending two years as a fellow of the Alexander von Humboldt Foundation, studying the historicity of the resurrection of Jesus with Wolfhart Pannenberg at the University of Munich. I continued my research into the 1980s, which led to the publication of two companion volumes, *The Historical Argument for the Resurrection of Jesus*, Texts and Studies in Religion 23 (Lewiston, N.Y.: Edwin Mellen, 1985); and *Assessing the New Testament Evidence for the Historicity of the Resurrection of Jesus*, Studies in the Bible and Early Christianity 16 (Lewiston, N.Y.: Edwin Mellen, 1989). Detailed discussion and documentation of the issues summarized in this article may be found there. A popularization for laypeople is my book, *The Son Rises* (Chicago: Moody Press, 1981).

3. John Dominic Crossan, *Jesus: A Revolutionary Biography* (San Francisco: Harper SanFrancisco, 1994), ch. 6; idem, *The Historical Jesus: The Life of a Mediterranean Jewish Peasant* (Edinburgh: Clark, 1991), 392–93; idem, *The Cross That Spoke: The Origins of the Passion Narrative* (San Francisco: Harper & Row, 1988), 21, 235–40; idem, *Four Other Gospels* (Minneapolis: Winston Press, 1985), 153–64.

4. For this reason it is difficult to engage Crossan in a conversation concerning the evidence for the resurrection of Jesus, since the presuppositions from which he works are so at odds with the consensus of New Testament criticism concerning the development of the Gospels in general. Unless these more fundamental issues are resolved first, a discussion of specific points of evidence is all but impossible.

   Crossan's theory of the Gospels' formation is that the second-century apocryphal *Gospel of Peter*, which is largely a compilation of elements from the four canonical Gospels, has embedded within it the most primitive Gospel of all, which he dubs the Cross Gospel—the story of Jesus' crucifixion, entombment, and resurrection. The author of the Gospel of Mark had no other source for Jesus' passion and resurrection than the Cross Gospel, but he invented additional details of the passion and burial, based on Old Testament passages, which Crossan calls "historicized prophecy." For the resurrection narratives, virtually nothing was available from the Old Testament, but out of his theological conviction that Jesus' passion was to be followed immediately by his coming again in glory, without any intermediate manifestation of the resurrection, Mark retrojected the Cross Gospel's resurrection appearance back into his Gospel in the form of Jesus' transfiguration. But canonical Mark was not the original form of this Gospel. Crossan accepts Morton Smith's claim that canonical Mark is based on an earlier "Secret Gospel of Mark," which Crossan believes ended with the centurion's confession in 15:39 (itself a retrojection of the guard at the guard's confession in the Cross Gospel). Canonical Mark, in addition to cleaning up the potentially offensive texts in *Secret Mark*, also created 15:40–16:8. The other canonical Gospels are based on both the Cross Gospel and canonical Mark. On the basis of this reconstruction, Crossan identifies several strata of tradition and, in reconstructing the historical Jesus, adopts the methodological principle of refusing to allow as authentic any passage not attested by multiple, independent sources, even if that passage is found in the first stratum of tradition. This ensures agnosticism concerning Jesus' burial and resurrection since, on Crossan's view, we lack multiple independent accounts of the exact sequence of what happened at the end of Jesus' life.

   Given this idiosyncratic approach to the Gospels, it is small wonder Crossan comes to conclusions so radically diverse from the majority of critics, who deny the existence of the hypothesized "Cross Gospel," reject any dependence of canonical Mark on a *Secret Mark*, hold that the Gospel traditions concerning the burial and empty tomb of Jesus are rooted in history rather than the Old Testament, regard the *Gospel of Peter*, even if it contains some independent tradition, as a composition basically compiled from the canonical Gospels, and maintain that multiple attestation is not a necessary condition of judging a passage to be authentic. It would be a hopeless undertaking to provide in the limited space of this article a critical analysis of Crossan's presuppositions, but I think it is salutary at least to mention them because (1) it exposes the pretension of the Fellows of the Jesus Seminar to represent the mainstream of New Testament scholarship, and (2) it shows that Crossan's skepticism vis-à-vis the resurrection of Jesus is predicated on presuppositions that most critics regard as dubious. The extremity of Crossan's skepticism is perhaps best illustrated by his remark that he firmly believes that Jesus was crucified under Pontius Pilate because his crucifixion is attested by Josephus (A.D. 93–94) and Tacitus (A.D. 110/120), two "early and independent non-Christian witnesses" (*Historical Jesus*, 372)! This is quite amazing. We have on the one hand a New Testament chock full of early and independent references to Jesus' crucifixion, including Paul's citation of the early tradition in 1 Cor. 15:3, and on the other hand a doctored reference a half century later in Josephus and a reference no doubt dependent on Christian tradition by Tacitus; yet Crossan accepts the crucifixion on the basis of the latter! This evinces a prejudice against the New Testament documents that can only be described as historically irresponsible.

On the purported *Secret Mark* as a pastiche of elements drawn from the canonical Gospels, see F. F. Bruce, *The "Secret" Gospel of Mark* (London: Athlone Press, 1974); for a critique of Crossan's hypothesis that canonical Mark revises *Secret Mark*, see Robert H. Gundry, *Mark: A Commentary on His Apology for the Cross* (Grand Rapids: Eerdmans, 1993), 613–23; on the *Gospel of Peter*'s being a late compilation containing no primitive "Cross Gospel," see Raymond E. Brown, "The Gospel of Peter and Canonical Gospel Priority," *NTS* 33 (1987): 321–43, which is expanded in Appendix 1, "The Gospel of Peter—A Noncanonical Passion Narrative," of Brown's magisterial *The Death of the Messiah: A Commentary on the Passion Narratives in the Four Gospels*, 2 vols., ABRL (New York: Doubleday, 1994).

5. For a discussion, see Peter Lipton, *Inference to the Best Explanation* (London: Routledge, 1991).

6. C. Behan McCullagh, *Justifying Historical Descriptions* (Cambridge: Cambridge University Press, 1984), 19.

7. R. T. France, "The Gospels as Historical Sources for Jesus, the Founder of Christianity," *Truth 1* (1985): 86.

8. R. W. Funk, R. W. Hoover, and the Jesus Seminar, *The Five Gospels: What Did Jesus Really Say?* (New York: Macmillan, 1993), 2.

9. Ibid., 3.

10. Ibid., 2–3.

11. This fact becomes explicit when the Seminar comes to words of the risen Jesus: "By definition, words ascribed to Jesus after his death are not subject to historical verification" (ibid., 398). But since words spoken during Jesus' life are sometimes transferred to the resurrected state, "the Jesus Seminar decided in some instances to evaluate such words *as though they were spoken by a historical figure*" (ibid., my emphasis). It could not be plainer that the Seminar rules out the risen Jesus as a historical figure and that it does so not on the basis of the evidence, but *by definition*.

12. McCullagh, *Justifying Historical Descriptions*, 21.

13. For the sake of argument, I am leaving out of account Christians' experience of the presence of the risen Lord. The Danish philosopher Søren Kierkegaard maintained that it was precisely this experience that frees believers from the tyranny of the his-

torical method and makes every generation in effect contemporaneous with the disciples.

14. As the Archbishop of Perth, Peter Carnley, proposed in his *The Structure of Resurrection Belief* (Oxford: Clarendon, 1987), 52. J. C. O'Neill, professor of New Testament at Cambridge University, points out that Paul would have said merely "he was buried and on the third day appeared to Cephas," if no empty tomb were contemplated and the burial only served to underscore the death (J. C. O'Neill, "On the Resurrection as an Historical Question," *Christ, Faith and History*, Cambridge Studies in Christology, ed. S. W. Sykes and J. P. Clayton (Cambridge: Cambridge University Press, 1972), 208.

15. Even Crossan's imagined Cross Gospel includes Jesus' being sealed in a tomb, not buried in the criminals' graveyard (*Gosp. Pet.* 8:30–33). Apart from his methodological requirement of multiple attestation, Crossan provides no reason why this presumed pre-Markan source is not to be trusted in this regard.

16. Rudolf Bultmann, *The History of the Synoptic Tradition*, 2d ed., trans. John Marsh (Oxford: Basil Blackwell, 1900), 274. Crossan, on the other hand, thinks that the burial story is a fictitious account manufactured out of Deut. 21:22–23 and Josh. 10:26–27. This hypothesis, however, is rendered awkward by the fact that the supposed Cross Gospel contains no burial story at all, since Crossan attributes *Gosp. Pet.* 6:23–24 (Joseph's entombment of Jesus) to a later stratum based on the canonical Gospels. So is Mark's account supposed to be manufactured out of these Old Testament texts plus the Cross Gospel? Wholly apart from the question of whether the early Christians felt free just to invent incidents without any historical basis, two problems with Crossan's hypothesis arise: (1) Such an approach to the Gospels is in danger of repeating with Jewish texts the same error committed by the old History of Religions movement with pagan texts. That nineteenth-century movement sought to find parallels to Christian beliefs in pagan religions, and some scholars sought to explain Christian beliefs as the product of pagan influences. The movement collapsed, however, largely because no genealogical link could be shown between pagan beliefs and Christian beliefs. Crossan's Jewish parallels are similarly devoid of significance unless a causal connection to incidents narrated in the Gospels can be shown. In the case at issue, it is doubtful that this can be done, since one only notices the parallels if one reads the relevant texts in the light of and with full knowledge of the Gospel narratives. The parallels are too distant to think that a first-century Christian with knowledge only that Jesus was crucified would find such texts relevant to Jesus' fate. (2) The dissimilarities between the burial story and Josh. 10:26–27 suggest that Mark's account is not based on the latter. Joshua speaks of a cave, whereas Mark makes a point of the man-made, rock-hewn sepulcher in which Jesus was laid (cf. Isa. 11:16); Joshua has a guard at the cave, whereas Mark has no guard; Mark's reference to Joseph of Arimathea, the scene with Pilate, and the linen shroud have no parallel in Joshua. Details like the stone over the entrance and burial before nightfall are features that belong to the attested historical Jewish milieu and so provide no genealogical clue. Crossan thinks that the Cross Gospel simply took it for granted that the Jews buried Jesus, but that the Joshua passage provided the buried body, the great rolled stone, and the posted guards for the Cross Gospel's guard at the tomb story. But surely the buried body is already provided by the fact of the crucifixion and Jewish customs with respect to burial of the dead; the stone is an archaeologically confirmed feature of tombs of notable persons in first-century Palestine; and the guard is more plausibly derived from Matthew than Joshua, particularly in light of the *Gospel of Peter*'s heightening of the guard story by identifying it clearly as a Roman guard (complete with the name of the commander), having it posted on Friday rather than on Saturday so that the tomb is never left

unguarded, and emphasizing that the soldiers did not fall asleep but were constantly on watch.

17. Again, Crossan disagrees, asserting that Mark invented Joseph of Arimathea to take Jesus' burial from his enemies to his friends. Unfortunately, Crossan gives no evidence for this assertion. Against it stands the fact that neither the Cross Gospel nor Mark say clearly that Jesus was buried by his enemies or that Joseph was a friend of Jesus. Even more simply, if Mark was so inventive, why would he create a figure like Joseph rather than just have the disciples bury Jesus? If he wanted more historical verisimilitude, he could have had Jesus buried by his enemies or his family.

18. Brown, *Death of the Messiah*, 2:1240.

19. Crossan attempts to find other burial traditions in the *Epistula Apostolorum* 9.20 (a Coptic document from the second century) and Lactantius's *Divine Institutes* 4.19 (from the early fourth century). That Crossan thinks that these late, derivative, and sometimes fanciful sources are more trustworthy purveyors of historical tradition than the New Testament documents is a comment on his methodology. In any case, these sources do not offer alternatives to the Gospel account. The *Epistula Apostolorum* speaks of Jesus' body being taken down from the cross along with those of the thieves, but then singles him out as being buried in a place called "skull," where Sarah, Martha, and Mary Magdalene went to anoint him. The summary nature of the passage no more excludes burial by Joseph of Arimathea than does the Apostles' Creed. The same is true of Lactantius' summary, in which he says in reference to the Jews, "They took his body down from the cross, and enclosing it safely in a tomb, they surrounded it with a military guard." The desire to polemicize against the Jews leads Lactantius to include Joseph under the general rubric "the Jews." The same motive governs Acts 13:27–29, to which Crossan also appeals. Finally John 19:31 has to do only with a request, not with actual burial. That Crossan has to appeal to passages such as the above only serves to underline how desperate is the attempt to find other burial traditions.

20. Wolfgang Trilling, *Fragen zur Geschichtlichkeit Jesu* (Düsseldorf: Patmos Verlag, 1966), 157. See also Raymond E. Brown, "The Burial of Jesus (Mark 15:42–47)," *CBQ* 50 (1988): 233–45.

21. Carnley denies this, arguing: (1) 1 Cor. 15:4 is meant only to underscore the reality of Jesus' death; (2) 2 Cor. 5:1 shows that Paul conceivably did not hold to a reanimation of the body in the resurrection; (3) 1 Cor. 15:51 precludes an empty tomb since the resurrection body is not composed of "flesh and blood"; and (4) Baruch 49–51 shows that the restoration of flesh and bones was not part of the current Jewish concept of the resurrection (Carnley, *Structure of Resurrection Belief*, 52–53). I have already dealt with (1). Concerning (2), the present tense verb "have" in 2 Cor. 5:1 does not imply that the resurrection body is already waiting in heaven for us; rather it expresses certainty of future possession, as when one says that he has an inheritance in heaven. The notion of an unanimated resurrection body, stored up in the closets of heaven, is a contradiction in terms, since as a spiritual body (cf. 1 Cor. 15:44), it is imbued with life. As Paul goes on to intimate in 2 Cor. 5:4, the earthly body will be transformed into the resurrection body (cf. 1 Cor. 15:54). Both (3) and (4) are beside the point, since even if the resurrection body were immaterial, in both the passages cited it is the product of the transformation of the earthly body, so that an empty grave would be left in its wake. On the materiality of the resurrection body, see below.

22. Rudolf Pesch, *Das Markusevangelium*, 2 vols., HTKNT 2 (Freiburg: Herder, 1977), 2:21; cf. 2:364–77.

23. If this is the case, it is futile to construe the empty tomb account as an unhistorical

legend. It seems astounding that Pesch himself (ibid., 2:522–36) tries to convince us that the pre-Markan empty tomb story is an unhistorical fusion of three literary forms from the history of religions: door-opening miracles, epiphany stories, and stories of seeking but not finding persons who have been translated to heaven. He considers the account of the stone's being rolled away to be the product of door-opening miracle stories. When it is pointed out that no such door opening is narrated in Mark, Pesch gives away his case by asserting that it is a "latent" door-opening miracle! The angelic appearance he attributes to epiphany stories, though without showing the parallels. Finally he appeals to a story-form of seeking but not finding someone for the search for Jesus' body, adducing several largely irrelevant texts (e.g., 2 Kings 2:16–18; Ps. 37:36; Ezek. 26:21) plus a spate of post-Christian or Christian-influenced sources (*Gospel of Nicodemus* 16:6; *Testament of Job* 39–40) and even question-begging texts from the New Testament itself. He does not come to grips with his own early dating of the tradition and does not show how legend could develop in so short a span in the presence of those who knew better.

24. Edward Lynn Bode, *The First Easter Morning* (Rome: Biblical Institute Press, 1970), 161. Brown agrees: "The basic time indication of the finding of the tomb was fixed in Christian memory before the possible symbolism in the three-day reckoning had yet been perceived" (Raymond C. Brown, *The Gospel According to John*, ABRL 29A [Garden City, N.Y.: Doubleday, 1970], 980). The fact that "on the first day of the week" is probably a Semitism also points to the early origin of the phrase.

25. Crossan agrees that this account in the Cross Gospel (=*Gosp. Pet.* 9:35–10:42) is theologically determined, but he thinks that Mark's account is too. Mark's linking of Jesus' passion and return in glory leads Mark to suppress the Cross Gospel's colorful account of the resurrection and the guard, so that his simple narrative results. For Mark, "the resurrection was simply the departure of Jesus pending a now imminent return in glory" (Crossan, *Historical Jesus*, 296). The retrojected appearance from the Cross Gospel became the Transfiguration, which functions as a foretaste of Jesus' glorious return, not his resurrection. Crossan's hypothesis hinges crucially on the widely rejected idea that Mark implies no resurrection appearances, but only Jesus' appearance at his return (Mark 13:26; 14:62). Clearly, Jesus' predictions of his glorious return do not *preclude* resurrection appearances after he rises from the dead, also predicted (Mark 8:31; 9:9, 31; 10:34). And in 14:28; 16:7, Mark suggests clearly that such resurrection appearances will take place. Jesus' going before the disciples to Galilee and the restricted circle of the witnesses make it clear that Mark is not envisioning Jesus' second coming in Galilee (not to mention the problem that Mark knows that such did not occur). Crossan cannot retreat to the position that these verses were not part of the original *Secret Mark*, for the issue is the simplicity of Mark 16:1–8, which was supposedly added by canonical Mark. But if canonical Mark contemplates resurrection appearances, then no reason remains for him not to have given a resurrection narrative akin to that of the *Gospel of Peter*. As for the Transfiguration, most critics regard this narrative as so firmly embedded in its context that it cannot be considered to be a retrojected resurrection narrative. Crossan confesses that the parallels between Mark's Transfiguration narrative and the *Gospel of Peter*'s resurrection story (e.g., the height of the heads reaching to heaven becomes the high mountain) are "not very persuasive" in themselves, but he blames this on Mark's having "completely recast" the narrative (Crossan, *Four Other Gospels*, 173). In any case, Mark 16:1–8 lacks any theological reflection on Jesus' glorious return or other theological motifs, like his descent into hell and victory over his enemies, which in turn bespeaks its primitiveness.

26. At this point Crossan's speculations go off the rails. To him, *Secret Mark* lent itself to an erotic interpretation that the author of canonical Mark wished to avoid. Rather

than simply remove the offending text, Mark dismembered it and scattered its parts throughout his Gospel. For example, the angelic figure of the young man in the tomb (Mark 16:5) derives from the young man in *Secret Mark* who comes to Jesus for instruction in the mystery of the kingdom of God. More relevant to the point, the three women who discover the empty tomb (Mark 16:1) are the dismembered residue of *Secret Mark* 2r 14–16, which followed canonical Mark 10:46a and reads: "And the sister of the young man whom Jesus loved and his mother and Salome were there, and Jesus did not receive them." Why, one might ask, would Mark scatter these various figures and motifs throughout his Gospel, rather than just delete them if he found them potentially offensive? Crossan's ingenious answer is that Mark did this so that if someone should come upon a copy of *Secret Mark* with the offending passages, ortho- dox Christians could claim that the passages were just a pastiche assembled from dis- parate elements in the Gospel of Mark! This answer is just scholarly silliness. Not only does it ascribe to Mark prescience of redaction criticism, but, more importantly, it tends to render Crossan's hypothesis unfalsifiable, since evidence that does not con- firm his theory is reinterpreted in terms of the theory to be actually confirmatory— cf. Freudian psychology, which takes someone's claim not to have experienced Oedipal desires as evidence that that person is, in line with the theory, suppressing such expe- riences. That is, to critics who assert that the *Secret Mark* passages are not primitive but look like amalgamations drawn from other Gospel stories, Crossan would say, "Aha! that's just what Mark wanted you to think!" In any case, the answer will not work because some elements of the pastiche are drawn from John's Gospel (the beloved disciple, the raising of Lazarus), which *Secret Mark* is supposed to antedate. With respect to the women at the tomb, the hypothesis still fails to explain why Mark would insert them rather than elsewhere in the Gospel, when he could have made male disciples (perhaps even the young man!) discover the empty tomb. For a critique of Crossan's claim that the supposedly dismembered elements intrude unnaturally in canonical Mark, see Gundry, *Mark*, 613–21.

27. Crossan embraces without argument the hypothesis of the flight of the disciples, who knew nothing more than the fact of the crucifixion, a hypothesis most scholars today would regard, in von Campenhausen's words, as "a fiction of the critics" (Hans F. von Campenhausen, *Der Ablauf der Osterereignisse und das leere Grab*, 3d ed. [Heidelberg: Carl Winter, 1966], 44–49). Intriguingly, the Jesus Seminar also endorses this hypoth- esis (Funk, Hoover, and the Jesus Seminar, *The Five Gospels*, 468). Carnley is reduced to adopting the flight to Galilee hypothesis to explain why women are made the dis- coverers of the empty tomb (Carnley, *Structure of Resurrection Belief*, 60). His claim that their presence at the crucifixion and burial drew them into the empty tomb story is unconvincing, not merely because it arbitrarily selects which roles of the women are historical, but even more because if Mark felt free to invent the denials of Peter despite the historical flight to Galilee, he would have been free to make Peter or another male disciple discover the empty tomb. Crossan says that Peter's visit to the tomb is Luke's creation (from which he presumably infers nonhistoricity). For a cri- tique of Lukan creation, see William Lane Craig, "The Disciples' Inspection of the Empty Tomb (Luke 24,12. 24; John 20,2–10," in *John and the Synoptics*, BETL 101 (Leuven, Belgium: Leuven University Press, 1992), 614–19.

28. Carnley objects that this argument assumes that the proclamation of the resurrection was soon enough after the burial to allow Jesus' tomb to be identified; but perhaps this was not so (Carnley, *Structure of Resurrection Belief*, 55). If one grants the reliabil- ity of the burial tradition, however, as Carnley apparently does, this objection cannot even get off the ground, since the burial site was known. In any case, it is not evident that Jesus' grave could not be identified. Carnley thinks that one may infer from Matt.

Did Jesus Rise from the Dead?

27:61; Mark 15:47; Luke 23:55 that the Jewish response to the disciples' proclamation was that the women had gone to the wrong tomb. But these verses show no trace of polemical context (cf. Matt. 27:63; 28:15), serving rather to prepare for the women's visit to anoint the body; furthermore, appealing to the worthless testimony of women (point 6 above) would be counterproductive as a response to such a Jewish allegation. Besides, the authorities' alleging that the women had gone to the wrong tomb does not show that the real site was unknown, for even if the site of the corpse were known, the authorities could say that the women visited the wrong tomb. Indeed, this allegation would be most effective only if one could point to the actual (occupied) tomb. And Carnley admits that the Jewish authorities could not do that. This militates against the view that they made any such allegation, since alone it would not be maximally effective.

29. Again, Carnley tries to explain the Jewish polemic by the hypothesis that the location of the tomb was unknown or forgotten (*Structure of Resurrection Belief*, 55–56). What this fails to appreciate is that the allegation of body snatching made by the polemic actually *implies* (not merely fails to deny) the empty tomb. Contrary to Carnley, the polemic did not assert that "the emptiness of a grave . . . would not prove anything more than that the body had been stolen"; rather, it asserted that as a matter of fact the body had been stolen, which implies the factuality of the empty tomb.

30. James D. G. Dunn, *Jesus and the Spirit* (London: SCM, 1975), 120.

31. D. H. Van Daalen, *The Real Resurrection* (London: Collins, 1970), 41.

32. Jacob Kremer, *Die Osterevangelien: Geschichten um Geschichte* (Stuttgart: Katholisches Bibelwerk, 1977), 49–50. Perhaps most remarkable of all, two Jewish scholars, Vermes and Lapide, are convinced on the basis of the historical evidence that Jesus' tomb was found empty.

33. Craig, *Historical Argument for the Resurrection*, 321–50, 522–24.

34. Crossan himself states that it would take five to ten years just to discover the Old Testament motifs necessary to invent the Passion story alone (Crossan, *Jesus*, 145); yet the tradition delivered by Paul antedates even the lower limit assigned by Crossan and already includes, not only the Old Testament warrant for the Passion, but also the resurrection with its scriptural warrant. Incredibly, Crossan scarcely touches on 1 Cor. 15:1–11 (see *Historical Jesus*, 397–98), and he adopts the old interpretation of von Harnack that the list of witnesses reflects rival factions looking to Cephas and James as their respective leaders. It is noteworthy that the Jesus Seminar adopts Crossan's interpretation to explain away the denials of Peter tradition (Funk, Hoover, and the Jesus Seminar, *Five Gospels*, 119). Of the resurrection appearances, Crossan says, "None . . . was an illusion, hallucination, vision, or apparition. Each was a symbolic assertion of Jesus' continued presence to the general community, to leadership groups, or to specific and even competing individual leaders" (*Historical Jesus*, 507). The interpretation of the list as reflecting competitive leadership has been rejected by virtually all contemporary commentators, not only because there is no evidence of first-generation factions centered on Peter and James, but also because the chronological ordering of the list as well as the great age of the tradition Paul hands on precludes such an interpretation. Virtually every contemporary New Testament scholar agrees that the original disciples had apparitional experiences of Jesus alive after his death. On the resurrection as a symbolic assertion, see below on the origin of the disciples' belief in Jesus' resurrection.

35. Norman Perrin, *The Resurrection According to Matthew, Mark, and Luke* (Philadelphia: Fortress, 1977), 80.

36. Trilling, *Geschichtlichkeit Jesu*, 153. According to Trilling, the fact that miracles in

general belong to the historical Jesus is widely recognized and no longer disputed. He refers here not to the interpretation of miracles as a supernatural event, but to the historical factuality of the Gospel miracles attributed to Jesus.

37. A. N. Sherwin-White, *Roman Society and Roman Law in the New Testament* (Oxford: Clarendon, 1963), 188–91.

38. Ibid., 189. This consideration becomes especially forceful if one follows critics such as Guthrie, Reicke, and Robinson in a pre–70 dating of Luke-Acts (Donald Guthrie, *New Testament Introduction*, 3d ed., rev. [London: Inter-Varsity Press, 1970], 340–45; Bo Reicke, "Synoptic Prophecies on the Destruction of Jerusalem," in *Studies in New Testament and Early Christian Literature*, ed. D. E. Aune [Leiden: Brill, 1972], 121–34; John A. T. Robinson, *Redating the New Testament* [London: SCM, 1976], 13–30, 66–117).

39. Sherwin-White, *Roman Society*, 190.

40. Vincent Taylor, *The Formation of the Gospel Tradition*, 2d ed. (London: Macmillan, 1935), 41.

41. See Walther Künneth, *The Theology of the Resurrection*, trans. J. Leitch (London: SCM, 1965), 92–93.

42. J. I. H. McDonald, *The Resurrection: Narrative and Belief* (London: SPCK, 1989), 29.

43. Crossan tries to play off Paul's assertion that "flesh and blood cannot enter the kingdom of God" (1 Cor. 15:50) against a physical resurrection (Crossan, *Historical Jesus*, 404–5). But such an opposition is spurious. "Flesh and blood" is a typical Semitic word-pair connoting frail, mortal human nature (cf. Gal. 1:16; Eph. 6:12), so that the second half of verse 51 expresses in parallel form the same idea: "nor does the perishable inherit the imperishable." Paul is not talking about anatomy.

44. McDonald thus errs in appealing to Hellenistic Judaism's belief in the immortality of the soul in order to deny a material resurrection body; he also confuses resurrection with translation (see below; McDonald, *Resurrection*, 141). McDonald believes that "the corporeal aspect of the risen Jesus finds expression in the concept of 'the body of Christ' in which believers participate, rather than in the notion of a reanimated corpse" (ibid.). Here his reduction of the resurrection to the immortality of Jesus' soul seems unavoidable. For to state that we are *literally* Christ's body makes no sense of Paul's description of that body in 1 Corinthians 15 and implies a sort of modalism that denies our individual personhood. But if believers are only *metaphorically* the body of Christ, which is doubtless Paul's intent, then it follows on McDonald's view that Christ literally has no resurrection body, which contradicts Paul.

45. For example, Carnley writes off Luke and John's "materializing tendencies" as due to "apologetic developments," but provides no evidence for this assertion (Carnley, *Structure of Resurrection Belief*, 68). Contrary considerations include: (1) Docetism was the theological reaction to the physicalism of the Gospels, not vice versa. (2) Docetism denied the physical incarnation, not the physical resurrection. (3) The Gospel traditions antedate the rise of Docetism. (4) The appearance stories do not evince the rigor of an apologetic against Docetism. (5) Had visionary experiences been original, then Docetism would not have presented any threat vis-à-vis the appearances.

46. Crossan's position on this issue is ambiguous. On the one hand he seems to agree with the undeniable fact that the earliest disciples proclaimed the resurrection of Jesus and that that doctrine was crucial to the origin of the Christian faith. On the other hand, he reinterprets the belief in Jesus' resurrection to be the symbolic assertion of Jesus' continued presence. He writes, "That *is* the resurrection, the continuing presence in a continuing community of the past Jesus in a radically new and transcendental [*sic*] mode of present and future existence" (Crossan, *Historical Jesus*, 404); the problem the

disciples faced was "how to *express* that phenomenon." Crossan thinks that in order to express their sense of Jesus' ongoing invisible presence with them, Christians appropriated the language of resurrection from the dead. He explains:

> Those who had originally experienced divine power through his vision and example still continued to do so after his death. Jesus' followers, who initially fled from the danger of the crucifixion, talked eventually of not just continued affection, but of resurrection. They tried to express what they meant by telling, e.g., of the journey to Emmaus. They were disappointed and in dejected sorrow. Jesus joined them unrecognized and explained that Hebrew scripture "should have prepared them for his fate." Later they recognize him by the meal, as of old. Then they go back to Jerusalem in high spirits. The symbolism is obvious, as is the metaphoric condensation of the first years of Christian thought and practice into one parabolic afternoon (ibid., xii).

Thus, on Crossan's view, in a literal sense the first disciples did not really believe in the resurrection of Jesus.

Crossan's view raises two questions: (1) When the earliest Christians said Jesus was raised from the dead, did they mean it literally or not? (2) Can the origin of their belief be explained as a result of their reflection on Hebrew Scripture? With respect to (1), there can be no doubt that the earliest Christians asserted a literal resurrection of Jesus. Paul's earnest declarations in 1 Cor. 15:12–23, 29–32 about the essentiality of Jesus' being raised from the dead and especially his linking it with our own resurrection from the dead (which cannot be interpreted in terms of continuing presence) show how literally and seriously this event was taken. So do Paul's disquisitions about the nature of the resurrection body in answer to the questions "How are the dead raised? With what kind of body will they come?" (1 Cor. 15:35). The sermons in the book of Acts also present Jesus' resurrection as a literal event, which could only present gratuitous obstacles to their hearers if no such event were being asserted (e.g., Acts 17:31–32). Moreover, the empty tomb tradition would be superfluous and pointless were not a literal event in view, since mere continuing spiritual presence does not require an empty tomb. Furthermore, early Christians were perfectly capable of expressing the idea of Jesus' spiritual presence with them without recourse to the language of resurrection from the dead (cf. 1 Cor. 5:3; Col. 2:5). Indeed, in the notion of the Holy Spirit of Christ the Christians had the perfect vehicle for expressing in a theologically rich way the idea of Jesus' continuing, numinous presence with and in them (e.g., Rom. 8:9–11). But they were not content merely to assert the presence of Christ through the Spirit with them; they also believed in Jesus' resurrection from the dead, the harbinger of their own resurrection (Rom. 8:11, 23).

As for (2), it is now widely agreed that the disciples' belief in Jesus' resurrection cannot be explained as the result of their reflection on the Old Testament. As Crossan himself admits (Crossan, *Four Other Gospels*, 174), the Old Testament furnishes little that could be construed in terms of Christ's resurrection, much less prompt such a belief in the absence of any experiences of appearances or an empty tomb. When Crossan says the Hebrew Scripture should have prepared the disciples for Jesus' fate, what that refers to is his death; but there is almost nothing there to prepare them for his resurrection. Most critics concur that Old Testament proof texts of the resurrection could be found only *after* the fact of the disciples' coming to believe that Jesus was risen, not before.

In his more recent *Jesus*, 163, 165, Crossan takes an even more radical line: the primitive Christians did not express their sense of Jesus' continuing presence in terms of his resurrection, but held simply to belief in Jesus' passion and second coming. "Where, then did all the emphasis on resurrection come from? In a word, from

Paul.... For Paul ... bodily resurrection is the only way that Jesus' continuing presence can be expressed." But in light of the early tradition received and delivered by Paul in 1 Cor. 15:3–5 alone, this view is incredible, as is the claim that Paul was at a loss to express the notion of Jesus' continuing presence other than through the language of resurrection.

47. See Reginald H. Fuller, *The Formation of the Resurrection Narratives* (London: SPCK, 1972), 2.

48. The only other alternatives would seem to be Greek or Christian influences. But it is now widely recognized that belief in Jesus' resurrection cannot be traced to pagan factors (see Künneth, *Theology of the Resurrection*, 50–63), nor can it be ascribed to the influence of the church, since the resurrection is itself the cause of the church's coming into being.

49. C. F. D. Moule and Don Cupitt, "The Resurrection: A Disagreement," *Theology* 75 (1972): 507–19.

50. C. F. D. Moule, *The Phenomenon of the New Testament*, SBT 2d ser., 1 (London: SCM, 1967), 13.

51. Crossan's insistence that the Jewish mind *had to* express Jesus' victory over death by resurrection language is simply inaccurate, for we know of several other models current in Judaism that might have been employed. On the contrary, since there was no expectation of an isolated resurrection within history, the choice of the category of resurrection must be explained (Raymond E. Brown, *The Virginal Conception and Bodily Resurrection of Jesus* [London: Geoffrey Chapman, 1973], 76). Cf. Dunn, *Jesus and the Spirit*, 132.

52. Gerald O'Collins, *The Easter Jesus*, 2d ed. (London: Darton, Longman & Todd, 1980), 50–51.

53. Craig A. Evans, "Life-of-Jesus Research and the Eclipse of Mythology," *TS* 54 (1993): 21–33.

54. See Wolfhart Pannenberg, *Jesus—God and Man*, trans. L. L. Wilkens and D. A. Priebe (London: SCM, 1968), 67; idem, "Jesu Geschichte und unsere Geschichte," *Glaube und Wirklichkeit* (München: Chr. Kaiser, 1975), 92.

Chapter 7

IS JESUS THE ONLY WAY?

R. DOUGLAS GEIVETT

> *"You believe in God; believe also in Me."*
> *(Jesus, in John 14:1, NKJV)*

R. Douglas Geivett (Ph.D., University of Southern California) is Associate Professor of philosophy at Talbot School of Theology. He is author of *Evil and the Evidence for God: The Challenge of John's Hick's Theodicy* and coeditor of *Contemporary Perspectives on Religious Epistemology*.

The Jesus Question

Is Jesus the only way to obtain a saving relationship with God? The question needs to be asked with renewed sincerity and gravity. What prevents many people today from asking the question honestly and patiently is that the assumptions behind the question have already been flatly rejected. What are these assumptions? First, the question assumes the possibility of a singularly right way to organize our religious lives and the way we think about them. This is the force of the word "only" in our question. Second, the question assumes that, if there is a singularly right way, it is possible also for us to find that way. It would be pointless to entertain the question if we did not accept this second assumption—that there is such a thing as religious *knowledge*.

The trouble is, these two assumptions are not much at home among the unrefined relativists that populate our modern world. The mere suggestion that Jesus might be the *only* way to achieve authentic religious fulfillment smacks of bigoted narrowness and rigid exclusiveness. While these are qualities that we have come to expect from obtuse religious zealots, they surely are unworthy of the general run of humanity, if not of God himself—if he should happen to exist. And the idea that humans can acquire specific religious knowledge that holds the key to the entire human condition is, well, pretentious at the least. The attitude is simply incompatible with enlightened awareness of our cognitive limitations.

In a climate of suspicion about truth and reticence about claims to have the truth, exclusivist religious claims are bound to seem intolerant and unyielding. The claim that Jesus Christ is the way, the truth, and the life, the uniquely adequate remedy to the human spiritual condition, will almost certainly be met with suspicion and resistance by many who have not experienced the personal spiritual liberation that comes with acceptance of this claim. And in the present intellectual and religious climate, even those who *have* experienced such liberation often feel considerable pressure from the surrounding culture to eschew all forms of religious exclusivism.

This chapter may be the most controversial in the book, for it poses a question about the religious significance of Jesus. But many people may also ignore this chapter because they are prepared to answer the question without looking into the evidence. Almost always, when the question is answered without concern for the evidence, it is answered in the negative. Perhaps, after reading the other chapters leading up to this one, the reader will be sufficiently impressed with the evidence concerning Jesus to risk a closer inspection of the problem raised here: Is Jesus the only way? Let us call this "the Jesus Question."

178

By now the reader will be familiar with the basic contours of two very different perspectives on Jesus. One perspective adopts, in a straightforward manner, the portrayal of Jesus found in the undeconstructed pages of the Bible. This is the Jesus of orthodox Christian faith. This conviction concerning Jesus has a long and prestigious history and currently enjoys the support of an able body of defenders both inside and outside the academy. The other perspective, represented (among others) by the Jesus Seminar, interposes a contrasting picture. Their strategy is to eliminate many of the lines of text in the Bible and then read between the relatively few lines that are left in order to reconstruct a "historically responsible" picture of Jesus. Unfortunately, the resulting picture is neither historically responsible nor religiously adequate.

Since other contributors to this book have exposed the deficiencies in the methodology of the Jesus Seminar, I will concentrate on the question of Jesus' religious significance. In particular, I will develop an argument for answering the Jesus Question in the affirmative. There is, however, one point about which I am in agreement with the Jesus Seminar. If their portrayal of Jesus is historically accurate, then it is not plausible to believe that Jesus is the only way. On the other hand, if their handling of the evidence is flawed, then it remains an open question whether Jesus is the only way. And if the presentation of Jesus in the Gospels is, on the whole, historically reliable, then the chances that Jesus is the only way are greatly improved. Indeed, the powerful evidence for the historical reliability of the New Testament should encourage people to take the Jesus Question seriously and to answer it in the affirmative.

The God Question

We need to be realistic about the factors that play a role in our assessment of the Jesus Question. Whatever we decide concerning the historical Jesus, our beliefs about other matters will inevitably influence our judgment about the *religious significance* of Jesus. In particular, our understanding of Jesus depends fundamentally upon what we believe about God.

This is of great consequence, and it is relatively easy to illustrate. Consider the atheist. For anyone who denies the existence of God, it does not make much sense to embrace Jesus as the Son of God. An atheist might, however, indulge a measure of respect for Jesus if Jesus is understood as a morally exemplary peasant who just happened to suffer the indignity of deification by confused first-century admirers (who in turn accepted severe persecution for their unruly imaginations and deceptive caricatures of Jesus). Alternatively, a person might believe in God without affirming the deity of Jesus Christ. It is no surprise to find Jews and Muslims adopting this point of view.[1] Perhaps we may be permitted mild surprise, however, when we meet a self-described Christian whose view of Jesus closely parallels that of the respectful atheist or the traditional Jew or Muslim. And that is what we do find in some quarters, notably, among the Fellows of the Jesus Seminar.[2]

But let us not lose sight of the main point. What we believe about God and his relationship to the world sets the conditions for what it is both psychologically possible and rationally permissible for us to believe about Jesus. And let's face it. When we are told by a perfect stranger that he believes in God, we still don't know much about the person. That is partly because the word "belief" is used all too flippantly these days. For some, to say "I believe in God" means little more than "I haven't gotten around yet to denying the existence of God." But there is another reason why a person's assertion of belief in God is seldom very illuminating about that person. That is because two people who believe in God may believe radically different and incompatible things about God; or, to put it another way, one person's theism is another person's atheism. To say "I believe in God," then, is to say almost nothing.[3]

That is why Christians in the apostolic tradition do not stop there. Whether or not the apostles themselves directly sponsored the Apostles' Creed hardly matters; the Creed does distill the outline of a total package of orthodox New Testament belief:

I believe in God the Father almighty,
maker of heaven and earth;
and in Jesus Christ
his only Son, our Lord,
who was conceived by the Holy Ghost,
born of the Virgin Mary,
suffered under Pontius Pilate,
was crucified, dead, and buried:
he descended into hell;
the third day he rose again from the dead;
he ascended into heaven,
and sitteth on the right hand of God the Father almighty;
from thence he shall come to judge the quick and the dead.
I believe in the Holy Ghost;
the holy catholic church;
the communion of saints;
the forgiveness of sins;
the resurrection of the body,
and the life everlasting.

Affirming the existence of God is only the tip of the iceberg. That is, believing in God is only the beginning, though it is an apt beginning to be sure. Christian faith moves on to confess, among other things, the Lordship of Jesus Christ. Some conceptions of God are quite at home with this confession about Jesus Christ; others are much less so (e.g., polytheism or New Age religion).[4] Thus, we should never assume that two people who affirm God's existence are entitled to the same verdict concerning the significance of Jesus. While person

A might have a concept of God that is completed and confirmed by the biblical view of Jesus, person B might entertain a concept of God that requires the repudiation of Jesus as he is presented in the Bible.[5]

So the Jesus Question is inextricably connected with the God Question. Does God exist, and if he does, how are we to think about his nature and his relationship to our world and our concerns? If we desire to have religious beliefs that are true, then we must be careful about how we arrive at those religious beliefs. If we prefer to have theological reality rather than some religious placebo, we need to consider the manner in which we conduct our investigation. And the first order of business is to be clear about our starting-point and the logical progression of our inquiry. Therefore, before we assess the possible significance of Jesus, we must first consider what concept of God it is most reasonable for us to hold. A faulty conception of God could lead to a mistaken judgment about the religious significance of Jesus. And a mistaken judgment about the significance of Jesus for our religious lives could be spiritually risky, to say the least. We cannot answer the Jesus Question with any confidence, either positively or negatively, until we take stock of our specific beliefs about God.

The Jesus Question remains the fulcrum of debate regarding three related sets of issues. The first set pertains to the existence and nature of God. The second has to do with the historical data concerning Jesus of Nazareth. A final issue is the Jesus Question itself and the challenge of personal religious commitment it represents. In light of the crucial connections between these three issues, the remainder of my discussion will proceed as follows. In the next section we will examine the concept of God as affirmed by a prominent member of the Jesus Seminar. We will consider with special interest the way his concept of God has defined the aims and methodology of his project as a "Jesus scholar." Following that, I will offer a contrasting approach to the God Question, an approach that paves the way for a more historically realistic and religiously and intellectually satisfying answer to the Jesus Question—an answer that takes the form of a confident, "Yes, Jesus is the only way!"

The Jesus Question and the Jesus Seminar

"A fairy tale is something that never happened a long time ago."[6] The student responsible for this classroom blunder will probably never know that he had stumbled upon the verdict of some contemporary scholars concerning the biblical Jesus. To the Jesus Seminar, the Jesus of history, who lived nearly twenty centuries ago, is not the Jesus of the Bible (at least not without qualification). The biblical Jesus is by and large a fabrication—one that is perfectly innocent and understandable perhaps, but still a fabrication. The alleged Gospel writers—Matthew, Mark, Luke, and John—describe a series of events that never happened a long time ago, in the life of a person that never lived a long time ago.[7] In short, the Jesus of the Bible is a fantasy, and the Christ of faith is not the Jesus of history. As one of the Seminar's official publications announces:

The distinction between the two figures is the difference between a historical person who lived in a particular time and place and was subject to the limitations of a finite existence, and a figure who has been assigned a mythical role, in which he descends from heaven to rescue humankind and, of course, eventually returns there.[8]

After six years of investigating the question "What did Jesus really say?" the Jesus Seminar has concluded that a full "eighty-two per cent of the words ascribed to Jesus in the gospels were not actually spoken by him."[9] Can there be any doubt that their recondite assessment of the deeds of Jesus over the next few years will likewise result in a streamlined catalogue of activity? The vessel whose delicate cargo is a Jesus of historically obscure proportions is calculated to sail through the stormy waters of critical scholarship with the absolute minimum of resistance. While the lowest common denominator of a selective liberal critical consensus about Jesus cannot be expected to reflect scholarly objectivity, that is what the Jesus Seminar claims to do.[10] Moreover, they imagine a grass-roots readership awaiting with bated breath the results of their "scientific" efforts to vote into the collective consciousness a reliable picture of the Jesus of history.

A Modern Profile of the Historical Jesus

The professed aim of the Jesus Seminar is to determine who Jesus was.[11] What have they concluded so far? Their book *The Five Gospels* does not offer a summary profile of the Jesus that emerges by liberal consensus. Such a profile can, however, be found in the writings of individual members of the Seminar.[12]

In a book entitled *Meeting Jesus Again for the First Time*, Marcus Borg, one of the more celebrated figures of the group, presents a sketch of the "pre-Easter Jesus" that he thinks can be reconstructed from the available historical data.[13] His label "pre-Easter Jesus" refers not to the preresurrection Jesus of biblical record, but to the Jesus of history who underwent radical transformation through the Christianizing influence of several layers of tradition some time after Jesus died, was buried, and—well, some time after Jesus died and was buried.

To Borg, if there is an Easter event, the historical Jesus did not have anything to do with it. Easter was not the event of a single day, but a series of events over a period of time when Jesus' followers began to experience him "as a spiritual reality, no longer as a person of flesh and blood, limited in time and space, as Jesus of Nazareth had been."[14] According to this view, the preresurrection Jesus of biblical record is a product of post-Easter consciousness. Borg is willing to allow that what Christians of all generations have experienced as the living risen Christ is real; but we must not imagine that this Christ is the same figure as Jesus of Nazareth. This amounts to the trivial concession that when Christians describe their experience of the resurrected Lord, they are describing a real experience, and what they are describing has religious significance for them.

Perhaps an illustration will help. Suppose there are no flying saucers. But suppose, further, that a group of well-meaning individuals report experiences, not only of seeing flying saucers whisking about, but of close encounters with extraterrestrial intelligences. In other words, they have an experience of some kind, and they take their experience to be an experience of extraterrestrials and their flying machines. Moreover, they seem to be prepared to organize their lives around messages they believe they have received from these apparently higher and trustworthy intelligences. Now someone like Marcus Borg might be willing to humor his fellow humanoids by admitting that they are perfectly sincere in their belief and that their belief is rooted in some experience they have had. And if their lifestyle changes are harmless enough or for the better, he might even find himself thinking, "more power to them." But their reports will not be taken to be literally true. Nevertheless, something is gained by the experience even if it is not real in the sense our UFO enthusiasts themselves believe it to be. Their testimony is like that of the Gospel of John: "John's gospel is a powerful testimony to the reality and significance of the post-Easter Jesus, the living Christ of Christian experience. John's gospel is 'true,' even though its account of Jesus' life story and sayings is not, by and large, historically factual."[15]

It is interesting to note that, even though "the gospels are not straightforward historical documents,"[16] a reconstruction of the historical Jesus depends upon what is historically dependable in the Gospels. But because the percentage of historically reliable material is so small to Borg, any developed reconstruction requires a generous amount of surmising. And by "surmising" I do mean "going beyond the evidence." Borg's own surmising follows a two-stage trajectory. He first isolates and accumulates historical data using the available sources—primarily the canonical Gospels. He then constructs a hypothesis in terms of which the data might be coherently understood and embellished within the limits of responsible scholarly imagination. Just think of the work that some paleontologists do in reconstructing the whole skeleton of a fossil hominid (to say nothing of musculature, surface hair, and skin tone) from a single bone fragment discovered in a layer of sediment in the Rift Valley, and you get the basic idea. A fair amount of guesswork is involved.[17]

Borg's own reconstruction of Jesus' adult life can be outlined in six points, two negative and four positive.[18] (1) Jesus did not think of himself in messianic terms. (2) It cannot be claimed that Jesus expected "the supernatural coming of the Kingdom of God as a world-ending event in his own generation." In other words, the earlier liberal shibboleth of "realized eschatology" has been overturned by more recent scholarship. Following these are four broad positive features that Borg ascribes to the historical persona of Jesus: he was (3) a spirit person, (4) a teacher of wisdom, (5) a social prophet, and (6) the founder of a movement.

Included within the ambit of these four points are several impressions garnered about Jesus: his intelligence and verbal skills were on a very high order; he regularly acted with deliberate symbolic significance to much public acclaim; he boldly challenged the social and political institutions of his day, usually on behalf of the disenfranchised; he had a profound effect on people, seeming to heal many and certainly attracting a large following; and he managed to achieve this influence during a short life that ended perhaps within only one year of his emergence as a public figure.

Now what, according to Marcus Borg, is the religious significance of a figure portrayed in this way? Before we can appreciate his account of the religious significance of Jesus, we must examine his approach to the question of God's existence and nature.

Borg on the God Question

Borg explains that as a youth he held fairly traditional beliefs about God, Jesus Christ, and the Bible. While in a state of "precritical naiveté," as he puts it, Borg believed that "Jesus is the divine savior in whom one is to believe for the sake of receiving eternal life."[19] Borg's belief in God, however, not his belief in Jesus, was the first casualty in his progression toward general unbelief. With the onset of adolescence, he began to have doubts about the existence of God. Curiously, this did not immediately affect his beliefs about Jesus. Only later, as a student at a Lutheran college, was he prepared to abandon his childhood images of Jesus and Christianity. He subsequently enrolled in seminary, where, to his delight, he "discovered" that the New Testament picture of Jesus was the product of layers of developing tradition. Meanwhile, Borg's general attitude of religious unbelief deepened. He quietly shifted from "closet agnostic" to "closet atheist." At the same time, he became fascinated with the quest for the historical Jesus and embarked upon a lifelong study of the Christian tradition.

Borg candidly acknowledges that his "uncertainty about God affected the focus of [his] research on Jesus."[20] But Borg did not remain uncertain about God, for within a few years he had a number of mystical experiences that transformed his understanding of God and in turn affected his understanding of Jesus and Christianity. As he explains, these experiences "gave me a new understanding of the meaning of the word *God*. I realized that *God* does not refer to a supernatural being 'out there' (which is where I had put God ever since my childhood musings about God 'up in heaven'). Rather, I began to see that the word *God* refers to the sacred at the center of existence, the holy mystery that is all around us and within us."[21] Notice Borg's confidence in his new-found *knowledge*: by means of his own *experience*, he gained "a new understanding" of God, he came to realize what the term *God* refers to.

Buttressed by the impressive authority of his own experience, Borg went on to study the religious experiences of others within various cultures and religious traditions. When he thought he could discern a common conception of God across the diverse range of mystical and nonmystical experiences of "God," he concluded that this common core of religious experience picks out the true nature of God. In other words, "God" is reduced to whatever is common to the religious experiences of men and women across cultures and religious traditions.

Since religious experiences associated with disparate traditions are the source of Borg's conception of God, it is hardly surprising that his description of God is highly amorphous and inexact: God is "the sacred at the center of existence, the holy mystery that is all around us and within us."[22] Intoned in the right way, of course, his descriptions may convey the impression that Borg has laid hold of something definite and liberating about God's nature. But upon inspection, what Borg offers as a description of God is pretty weak stuff: "God is more than everything, and yet everything is in God."[23]

Being told that this is all that can really be known about God leaves one a little high and dry, religiously speaking. But Borg's method of inquiry is not only religiously inadequate; it is also intellectually impulsive. He offers an experience-based religious reductionism, entirely devoid of the external controls of publicly accessible evidence. It is not clear why Borg himself, when he had reached the nadir of his "closet atheism," deemed his own religious feelings to be reliable; it is even less clear why *others* should trust his type of religious feeling.

Borg on the Jesus Question

At any rate, both the form of Borg's new belief in God and the methodology he employed in his rediscovery of God influenced his views about the religious significance of Jesus. Just as his earlier agnosticism/atheism compelled him to limit his research on Jesus to "those parts of the tradition that made sense apart from the God question,"[24] the latest transformation in his understanding of God affects his understanding of Jesus.[25]

In order to move beyond the limiting conditions of sparse historical material concerning Jesus to a historically probable figure who also has contemporary religious significance, Borg relies on two basic considerations. First, he notes that Jesus inspired a movement of amazing scope and duration, which has included the transformation of innumerable lives across the centuries. Surely this provides a basis for inferring the greatness of this man. Second, Borg infers that Jesus' greatness is centered in his capacity as a spirit person—a person of unusual spiritual power and awareness and of moral superiority. Jesus is therefore typecast as a member of a spiritually elite class of individuals that includes the founders of the other great religious traditions of the world.

A "typology of religious figures" dominates Borg's appraisal of the religious significance of Jesus. This typology allows him to construct an interpretive framework within which he can then tease out, on the basis of relatively few historical facts, further details about the person of Jesus.[26] His analysis boils down to an investigation of the religious experience of Jesus and the formulation of a profile of Jesus' religious consciousness. This method requires a comparison of the religious life of Jesus with the lives of other noteworthy religious figures. This approach portrays Jesus as a figure so in touch with religious reality that his experience can mediate the sacred for us.

While Borg is plenty vague about how it is that Jesus functions as a mediator of the sacred for us, he is clear about what his account denies.

> Imaging Jesus as a particular instance of a type of religious personality known cross-culturally undermines a widespread Christian belief that Jesus is unique, which commonly is linked to the notion that Christianity is exclusively true and that Jesus is "the only way." The image I have sketched views Jesus differently: rather than being the exclusive revelation of God, he is one of many mediators of the sacred. Yet even as this view subtracts from the uniqueness of Jesus and the Christian tradition, it also in my judgment adds to the credibility of both.[27]

In sum, Borg produces a "credible" account of Jesus (and the Christianity he founded) by recasting the "historical Jesus" in the image of a 1990s politically correct ideologue. Jesus was a radical social visionary and reformer, driven by a "politics of compassion" to subvert existing social structures that repressed the poor and kept women in their place. He is portrayed as the arch-egalitarian of first-century Palestine, an iconoclast bent on reshaping public policy.[28] Borg imagines he can discern in the public persona of Jesus an "ethos of compassion" that implies the acceptance of homosexuality and the advocacy of gay rights.[29] With the transformation of the compassion of Jesus into a social paradigm, Borg suggests that following the example of Jesus in our day "clearly implies universal health care as an immediate goal."[30] Jesus is further characterized as the teacher of a "world-subverting wisdom," like that reflected in such Eastern religious sages as Lao-tzu and Buddha. His message was one of seeking personal spiritual transformation by means of enlightenment experiences in which God is encountered as the nonjudgmental compassionate one.[31] This is the image of Jesus that sets him apart as unique in his time and culture.[32]

Still, as remarkable as Jesus is, Borg thinks it is possible to go too far in stressing the uniqueness of Jesus.

> In the sense that Jesus is not exactly like any other religious figure, he is unique (and so are the Buddha, Muhammed, Lao-tzu, and, for that matter, every person). But in popular Christian usage, the "uniqueness" of Jesus is most commonly tied to the notion that he is the uniquely and exclusively true revelation of God. It is this meaning of his uniqueness that I deny.[33]

In other words, Jesus cannot be regarded as the mediator between God and humanity as that role has traditionally been understood by Christians.

> The notion that God's only son came to this planet to offer his life as a sacrifice for the sins of the world, and that God could not forgive us without that having happened, and that we are saved by believing this story, is simply

incredible. . . . taken literally, it is a profound obstacle to accepting the Christian message. To many people, it simply makes no sense.[34]

Borg willingly acknowledges that within the flow of Jesus' own personal history he became an almost ideal spiritual figure. Unfortunately, within the flow of consciousness among his followers, Jesus came to be identified with God himself. It is this threshold of traditional Christian belief that Borg refuses to cross. And the reasons he gives are illuminating. As it turns out, *they have less to do with the limitations of historical research about Jesus and more to do with Borg's own beliefs about the nature of God.*

Why are the religious experiences of others so important to Borg for assessing the religious significance of Jesus? Because, according to him, these experiences provide us with *our only access to an understanding of divine reality.* Only within the framework of our larger religious worldview can we make assessments about the religious significance of particular persons and events familiar to us from history. Borg explicitly rejects the possibility of confidently inferring the existence and nature of God from evidence at our disposal. And he recognizes that this leaves us in a fog about the details of religious reality. "Candor compels me to acknowledge that experiences of the sacred do not prove the reality of God (though I find them far more interesting and convincing than any of the 'proofs' for the existence of God)."[35]

Unfortunately, even if the collective religious experiences of persons does point to a divine reality, the evidence of religious experience alone does not permit a precise account of the nature of divine reality. Indeed, the religious experiences of different individuals and communities yield conflicting accounts of religious reality. Relying exclusively upon the data of religious experience, however, Borg tries to construct a frame of reference for understanding the specific nature of religious reality. He therefore neglects a far wider range of evidence, also presented in experience, that might prove relevant to forming a religious view of reality generally, and for understanding the religious significance of Jesus in particular.

Borg's strategy ignores the fact that we bring conceptual frameworks to our experience of the numinous (that is, of putative religious reality), and that we come to understand the specific significance of that religious experience in terms of our conceptual frameworks. While two individuals might encounter the same reality in religious experience, they may form strikingly different beliefs about that reality. This can be explained in terms of differences in the background beliefs about religious reality that each brings to religious experience.[36] Thus, one measure of a person's religious convictions based on personal religious experience is the prior justification he or she has for the background beliefs brought to the experience. By denying a role for other evidence, however, Borg excludes a category of possible justification for those background beliefs that are so vital for making correct judgments about the value and significance of religious experience.

The point is, our large-scale conceptual frameworks play a *regulative role* in our assessments of the religious significance of Jesus. Indeed, even our judgments about what is permissible to claim about the historical Jesus are governed by prior commitments we make about the reality of God, his nature, and his possible relation to the world and human experience. The naturalist will repudiate any feature of the biblical account of Jesus that requires a supernatural explanation. The very possibility of a virgin birth or a bodily resurrection from the dead will be excluded *a priori*. In contrast, the theist will be prepared to countenance these and other non-natural states of affairs, should there be adequate historical evidence for their occurrence. Given this regulative role of conceptual frameworks, we must exercise great care in our choice between conceptual frameworks. As truthseekers we should try first to believe what it is most reasonable to believe about logically prior issues like the existence of God.[37]

To his credit, Marcus Borg recognizes the logical priority of the God Question over the Jesus Question. Unfortunately, in his investigation of the God Question, he limits himself to the evidence of private religious experience and patterns of religious experience discernible across religious traditions. This approach is inadequate, for it results in a theology that is almost entirely conceptually empty. The term *God* is loose enough to range over incompatible conceptions of God found in alternative and competing religious traditions. It is difficult to see how this could yield any concrete claim about the nature of God, much less the religious significance of Jesus.[38]

Borg's strategy is also unduly pessimistic. He remarks that the so-called "proofs" for the existence of God are relatively uninteresting and unconvincing.[39] He refers, misleadingly, to the rich tradition of natural theology. *Natural theology* denotes the systematic formulation of reasons to believe, without relying upon any sacred texts, that God exists, that he has a particular nature, and that he stands in relation to the world in certain definite ways. It is unrealistic to hold natural theology to such high standards as those associated with rigorous, deductive proofs for the existence of God, as Borg seems to. The way to think about the pattern of natural theology is not in terms of "proof" for the existence of God but in terms of inference to the reality of God as the best explanation of a wide and diverse range of phenomena, including the origin of the universe, the innumerable instances of design in the universe, the presence of finite persons in the universe and their spiritual nature, the human capacity for language and self-determination, and so on.

Putative religious experience is only one type of phenomenon requiring explanation. A host of other phenomena of our experienced world also cry out for explanation. The natural theologian holds that these phenomena are best explained in terms of the activity and goals of a personal creator of the universe. Moreover, the degree of richness in detail of a proper conception of the Creator's being is proportionate to the range of data investigated in this way. That is, an increasingly precise account of God's nature is made possible as more and more phenomena are found to be best explained by assigning specific attributes and interests to him.[40]

It is impossible to lay too much stress upon the point I am making here. What one makes of Jesus depends fundamentally on what one makes of the existence and specific nature of God.

The Jesus Question and the Reality of God[41]

While Marcus Borg holds that Jesus' message "was not about believing in him," he does not deny that the Bible represents Jesus as one who expected people to believe in him. He simply asserts that there is a discrepancy between the message attributed to Jesus in the Gospels and Jesus' real message.[42] But anyone who believes that the Bible is a reliable source of religious knowledge naturally concludes that belief in Jesus Christ is the fundamental requirement for approval before God. (More about this in the next main section of this chapter.) Since an affirmative answer to the Jesus Question assumes a confidence that the Bible is a reliable source of knowledge about the world of the spirit, we must consider the rationality of believing that God has arranged for human salvation in the way described in the Bible.

In this section, we will consider the evidence for God's existence and for the general pattern of divine activity found in the entire sphere of created reality, including both the natural world of physical objects and the nonphysical realm of the spirit. I will argue that this evidence reveals a God of personal dimensions who arranged for the flourishing of human persons and who can therefore be expected to address in a concrete way the darkest features of the human condition where divine aid is most needed.[43]

Whether the claim that Jesus is the only way makes sense or not depends upon whether it is rational to believe that there is a personal, wise, and benevolent creator of the universe to whom we owe our existence as persons and who takes an active interest in the human condition. If a solution to the human predicament can be expected, it is because there are good reasons for thinking that there is a God of sufficient power and compassion to meet this expectation.

The Religious Quest

What is the evidence that there is a God, that he cares about his human creatures, and that he has a plan to meet the deepest needs and aspirations of their hearts? We begin by considering what prompts religious inquiry in the first place.

At a general level, the religious quest is driven by a natural desire to make sense of human existence within the larger framework of reality. This desire expresses itself in a variety of ways. At times we are simply curious about life's larger meaning. For example, what are our lives for? Is there an ideal goal of human striving? If so, how should we arrange our lives so that we might reach that goal? At other times we are hounded by unanswered questions and impatient to find the missing pieces to the puzzle of life. And sometimes we are nearly

We are moral creators. Why?
What is the gauge between right & wrong

R. Douglas Geivett

paralyzed by the paradoxes of our existence as we collide with the hard, angular features of our world.

Consider this small sample of perennial human concerns. We are moral creatures with moral duties to one another, but we seem confused about the source of morality's claim upon our lives, unsure of our judgments about what is right and wrong, and curiously impotent to consistently practice our morality. Though we are familiar with the brevity of life, and some of us even make a tolerably good show of accepting the finitude of our existence, we have an irresistible and uncanny hankering for permanence. We have no trouble relating to the ambivalence of Woody Allen's confession, "It's not that I'm afraid to die; I just don't want to be there when it happens." We ponder inconclusively the personal and cosmic significance of the many evils of human experience. And we are shocked to find the worst of human impulses lurking in that most unwelcome of places—the deep recesses of our own hearts. Even if we are fortunate enough to be spared life's greater tragedies (war, famine, plague, and the like), we fret about the monotony that accompanies a life of relative ease and comfort—and we come full circle to wonder again what life is about.

The Origin of the Universe

Under the pressure of this universal concern to make sense of our existence, we naturally turn our attention to the larger whole of which we are a part, that is, to the universe itself, and ask: What account is to be given of the staggering design (biological and otherwise) that we see all around us? Why, for that matter, is there anything at all, rather than nothing? And are there any clues to the ultimate origin of things?

The universe appears to have had a beginning.[4] Many scientists believe that the universe exploded abruptly into existence with a big bang and that it is likely to pass out of existence at some time in the remote future. Advances in astronomy in recent years have made it increasingly difficult to think of the universe as infinite in duration. Observation of the red shift of distant galaxies, indicating that the universe is expanding, together with the discovery of background radiation, has led many cosmologists to infer a primeval state of the universe that is infinitely dense. Moreover, since the rate of expansion of the universe continues to decelerate over time, it appears that the universe originated in the distant but finite past, approximately sixteen to twenty billion years ago.

Partly because of the religious implications of the hypothesis of a big bang and partly because of the fallibility of scientific theories, some have refused to accept the claim that the universe had a beginning. But there are other indications that the universe could not have always existed. Think of the universe as a series of events ordered in temporal sequence. And think of the publication of the book *Jesus Under Fire* as a recent event in a long chain of events that make up the total history of the universe. Now if the universe has always existed and if time has no beginning but stretches into the infinite past, then there is no first event in the chain that makes up the history of the universe. This means that an infinite number of events must have passed before the publication of *Jesus Under Fire*.

This is odd, for if an infinity of events had to occur before this book could be published, it never would have been published, and you would not be reading it right now. Since you are obviously reading this book, all events that must have occurred before you could begin reading have occurred. Thus, what can have no end—an infinite sequence of events making up the total history of the universe prior to the production of this book—has seemingly come to an end. The moment this book was released from the press, an absolute limit was set upon the sequence of events that had to occur before it could be released. But an infinity of events, arranged in temporal sequence, can have no limit.

It is difficult to avoid the conclusion that the number of events that make up the history of the universe is *not* infinite after all, but finite. *And if the complete temporal series is finite, then the universe had a beginning*—a beginning that marks the first in a finite series of events making up the total history of the universe, whether that event took the form of a big bang or not.[45]

Now if the universe had a beginning, it must have had a cause, for all events that consist in the coming into existence of an object have causes. It will not do to object that the first event of the universe might be an exception. An event without a cause is a brute fact that simply has no explanation. So we must choose between looking for a cause of the beginning of the universe or settling for no cause at all. But what good reason could one have for preferring no explanation over some available explanation?

Perhaps it will be argued that the first event in a causal sequence needs no cause because it can have no cause, since the only thing that could be the cause is some prior event and there can be no event prior to the first event. This will not do either, for the series of physical events in the universe is not the only causal series with a first term. Causal sequences are quite regularly and effortlessly initiated whenever a human agent performs a free act. We know ourselves to be agents with free will directly and introspectively, and together with the knowledge of our freedom comes the knowledge of the reality of first-cause causation, or "agent-causation."[46]

This is an important consideration for us, since we are now in a position to see what sort of cause is responsible for getting the universe going: it must be an agent on the order of personal being, yet surpassing human persons in greatness. And this agent must be a person of considerable power and resourcefulness because he will have created the awesome spectacle of our universe without using any physical materials! Whatever else is true of the Creator, surely this is enough to qualify him as God.

If our original query, the meaning of human existence, thus leads us to an awareness of God's existence, we will want to know whatever else we can about God. The fact that we owe our existence to a personal Creator of such astonishing power can be cause either for great concern or for great expectation. For our lives are set within a context whose initial conditions were established by the Creator of the universe. As the apostle Paul remarked to the Athenians at Mars Hill, " 'For in him we live and move and have our being.' As some of your own poets have said, 'We are his offspring' " (Acts 17:28). If we are not helpless, we surely are vulnerable. Since what we make of ourselves is conditioned by the arrangement and patterns of reality set up by our Creator, it can hardly matter that we might have a preference for a different arrangement. Surely it is best that we seek to know the actual arrangement of reality so that we can arrange our own lives in a realistic manner.

The Structure of Human Existence

It is instructive, then, to survey the structure of human existence with awareness of its dependence upon God in the background. Two dimensions of our existence deserve independent attention: its *physical* and its *nonphysical* parameters.

When we consider physical conditions set for our lives, we find a remarkable confluence of life-sustaining features in the universe. If the conditions in our universe were not what they are, within a very small margin of flexibility, no life of any kind would be found in this universe. Thus, while the present universe is a fit habitat for human and other forms of life, the initial probability of there being such a universe is quite small.[47] The confluence of so-called "cosmic constants" is improbable enough on the assumption that the universe is uncaused and undesigned; it is even more improbable on the supposition that we owe our existence to a Creator who has it in for us. If, on the other hand, our lives are special, and if what makes our lives special has anything to do with the physical conditions in which we come to have our lives, then the good of human life depends upon the Creator as well. This is cause for considerable comfort, for it offers an important clue concerning the Creator's good intentions for humans. Our bodies locate us in a physical world of astonishing complexity, *apparently ordered by its Creator to the goal of our physical well-being.*

But we are more than our bodies. We are also spiritual beings. We exercise free will, we deliberate, we have emotions, we act in ways that are worthy of praise or blame, and so on. Any attempt to reduce these sorts of mental events to physical processes that take place somewhere in our bodies (presumably between our ears) is implausible. We are directly aware of our own private mental states in a way that others cannot be. For example, even if my wife knows what I happen to be thinking at a particular moment, she does not know it in the same way that I do. She has to rely on my firsthand reports or make judgments about what I am thinking on the basis of her own observational evidence and past experience. But all *I* do is introspect, or "look within." Moreover, there is a greater chance that my wife is wrong about what I am thinking than that I am wrong about what I am thinking (though she has frighteningly accurate powers of perception in this regard).

The phenomenon of private access to our own mental states is really quite significant. We understand very little about the brain and its powers. But suppose now we had complete scientific knowledge of the brain and the central nervous system. If a cognitive scientist developed a description of the mental states of some other person, and if these conflicted with the firsthand reports of the person himself, which description of the person's mental states should be revised—the scientist's or the one provided by the person himself? Surely the latter is more authoritative. That person's own description functions as a test of the accuracy of the scientist's description. If a patient honestly reports having a visual sensation of the color blue, it would be ridiculous for a brain physiologist to insist that the patient is wrong simply because her report contradicts the conclusions the brain physiologist has reached on the basis of observing physical events going on inside the patient's head. So even if we had a complete or nearly complete science of the brain—and we are a long way from that—a person's private access to her own mental states would require a nonphysical explanation. In my view, this is evidence that, in addition to bodies, we have minds that are substantially nonmaterial.[48]

Now, among the phenomena of our mental life are various desires, some of which are spiritual. As C. S. Lewis observed, "If I find in myself a desire which no experience in this world can satisfy, the most probable explanation is that I was made for another world."[49] The trouble is, we have no direct awareness of the means to obtain a passport to that world. So we have a natural desire to flourish as persons, but we cannot reliably arrange to satisfy that desire on our own. Other desires include the desire to be good persons, the desire for immortality, the desire to be on good terms with all or most other persons, and the desire to know others on an intimate level. Among the persons many of us aspire to know well is the Person to whom we owe our existence. We are, however, estranged from our Creator.

The proliferation of religious options is ample testimony that humans everywhere desire meaningful contact with ultimate religious reality. But human religious diversity signals that something is amiss. It is impossible to discern a consistent pattern among the innumerable human strategies for seeking spiritual fulfillment. The sad track record of religious activity initiated by humans suggests that the conditions for genuine spiritual satisfaction must be set by our Creator and communicated in an accessible and compelling way to us his creatures.

But God need not remain a stranger to us, for both we and God are persons. As persons, we and God have the potential to enter into intersubjective relationship with one another. It even seems that human persons have capacities for intersubjective relationship that are far more expansive than those that are needed for even very intimate relationships with other human persons. There is more space in our souls than can be filled by anything other than God himself. That we and God are persons suggests that there might be certain conditions, characteristic of interpersonal relationships generally, for entering into relationship with God. When desirable interpersonal relationships occur between human persons, it is because the persons involved have opened themselves up to one another.

Now, the estrangement that many feel between themselves and God has a striking quality about it. They feel as if they are strangers in relation to God. The term *estrangement* seems apropos because it suggests a deterioration of some prior relationship, an interruption in fellowship between human persons and God. It is alienation experienced as a departure from something that was meant to be, and perhaps once was. Thus, the human desire to know God may well be ambivalent. But to the degree that it is sincere, the desire to know God also includes a desire to understand the cause of alienation from him and the conditions for reconciliation. This includes the conditions that can only be met by God as well as those that can only be met by humans. In this situation, God occupies a superior position both to know and to determine the necessary conditions for reconciliation. So our confidence concerning the conditions for reconciliation will depend upon God's initiative in revealing them to us.[50]

On the other hand, since we are persons ourselves, genuine interpersonal relationship with God cannot depend upon God alone. As William P. Alston has observed, divine-human dialogue, like all genuine dialogue, "requires two independent participants, neither of which wholly controls the responses of the other. . . . If there is to be genuine communication, each participant must be over against another participant that is responsible for one end of the exchange."[51] Thus, humans have a measure of responsibility.

This responsibility extends to the manner in which we seek or are prepared to be found by God. We cannot foreclose on the question of God's willingness to disclose himself and his purposes in some concrete, particularized way without first looking into the evidence for the authenticity of an alleged revelation from him—even if a quest for some *particular truth* of the matter is scandalous by today's ephemeral standards. It will hardly do to accuse God of hiding from us if we have not sincerely sought him in appropriate ways, or if we have insisted on prescribing for God the conditions under which we would approve a revelation of himself.[52]

We have thus been led to expect a particular revelation from God, a revelation answering the specific needs of the human condition. Any religious tradition withholding the hope of a revelation from God that announces a diagnosis of and remedy for the human predicament seems unduly pessimistic. In any case, the possibility of a particular revelation from God cannot be ruled out *a priori*. And before we begin the task of evaluating alternative religious perspectives, we already have rationally justified criteria for being responsible in executing this task.

A Word from God

There remains, then, the question of whether a particular revelation from God *has been* provided. Here the best policy seems to be to examine historically situated divine revelation claims and see how well each of them answers to the needs of the human predicament and what support each enjoys from relevant types of evidence.[53] Let me suggest three criteria that are useful for evaluating specific revelation claims. First, the revelation claim must be compatible with what is revealed about God apart from the source of that special revelation claim. That is, we should not accept the claim that Jesus is the only way if it contradicts evidence for a personal, transcendent Creator of the universe who cares enough for his human creatures to rescue them from spiritual ignorance and destruction. Second, the claim must embody a message suited to the human needs that prompted the expectation of divine revelation in the first place. It should represent a realistic appraisal of the human predicament and recommend a cure with a plausible prognosis. And third, a revelation claim must, when possible, be corroborated by external signs (such as miracles) to determine that it genuinely proceeds from God.[54]

In terms of these three criteria, *the Christian revelation claim enjoys the greatest support among the alternatives*. First, God is represented in the Christian Scriptures as the personal Creator of the universe, a being of great power and intelligence, who takes an active interest in the affairs of the universe and exhibits special concern for the finite persons who inhabit our part of the universe. Thus, the basic metaphysical presuppositions of the Bible dovetail with our inquiry into the origin of the universe and the contours of human existence.

Second, what about the hope that God has good news for human persons? If we take existing religious traditions to represent the possibilities, it is hard to imagine better news than what we find in the gospel of Jesus Christ.[55] First, the precise nature of our human predicament is diagnosed with unparalleled realism: we have rebelled against God. The particularity or exclusiveness of Christianity is, in this regard, a positive virtue rather than a liability. In view of the need for a precise diagnosis of the human condition, as well as a satisfactory remedy, we can explain the impetus behind currently fashionable forms of religious pluralism in terms of the human propensity to hide from the God whom we have offended. Second, our human predicament is met by God's merciful initiative, which takes the peerless form of the incarnation of God in Jesus Christ, his atoning death on behalf of human beings who have sinned against God, and his resurrection to new life as the guarantee of eternal blessedness for all who believe in Jesus Christ.

Third, the truth of this good news is confirmed by historically well-attested miracles, especially the resurrection of Jesus Christ.[56] According to the best historical evidence, we have no less than four reliable accounts (the Gospels of the New Testament) of the main events of Jesus' life and his self-understanding as God. As William Lane Craig argues in his chapter, the event of the resurrection of Jesus is confirmed by historical evidence that the tomb of Jesus was found empty just days after he was buried, and that, following his death and burial, Jesus appeared bodily alive to his disciples and others for a period of about forty days. The resurrection is further confirmed by the overwhelming improbability of the genesis of the Christian church within a few weeks of Jesus' ignominious death. Few other religious traditions can trace their history back to their inception with as much accuracy as Christianity, and Christianity has little value if it is only a religious myth—that is, if the events surrounding the life, death, and resurrection of Jesus are not historically accurate.

There is one further point to make about the Christian revelation claim. In the Bible, we have a permanent deposit of divine revelation in propositional form. Jesus Christ, who both claimed to be God and corroborated his claim by rising from the dead (see Rom. 1:4), also affirmed the divine authority of the Christian Scriptures.[57] On the strength of his authoritative witness to the divine origin of Scripture, Christians today can rely upon the Bible as a source of religious knowledge. We now turn to the witness of Scripture concerning God's provision of salvation, including its scope and conditions.

The Jesus Question and the Bible

In one of the earliest documents of the Christian church, the apostle Paul announced that "the message of the cross is foolishness to those who are perishing, but to us who are being saved it is the power of God" (1 Cor. 1:18). This passage indicates the nature and the objective of God's initiative in response to the human condition. "Salvation" is a matter of being reconciled to God, and the agent of reconciliation between God and his human creatures is Jesus Christ (2 Cor. 5:18–19; cf. 1 Tim. 2:3–6).

This was Jesus' own understanding as well: "I am the way and the truth and the life. No one comes to the Father except through me" (John 14:6). Here Jesus claims unequivocally to be the uniquely adequate means of access to filial relationship with God.[58] It is impossible to imagine a more intimate relationship with God than one in which he can be approached as Father. But one approaches God in this way only through Jesus Christ. The apostle John observed that the privilege of being a child of God accrues to those who believe in Jesus' name (John 1:12), which results in a new birth. This new birth leads to "eternal life."

Jesus was clear about the one condition necessary for receiving eternal life:

> For God so loved the world that he gave his one and only Son, that whoever believes in him shall not perish but have eternal life. . . . Whoever believes in him is not condemned, but whoever does not believe stands condemned already because he has not believed in the name of God's one and only Son. (John 3:16, 18)

In other words, refusal of God's prescribed condition for salvation forfeits the kind of relationship with God made possible through Jesus Christ alone.

On the same occasion when Jesus identified himself as the way, the truth, and the life, he linked his claim with the prior belief in God that his hearers already had: "You believe in God, believe also in Me" (John 14:1 NKJV). This suggests that Jesus himself appreciated the logical priority of the God Question over the Jesus Question. In effect, he was saying, "In order to appreciate who I am, you need to think properly about who God is; and if you believe in the right way in God, you will believe in me as well, for you will see the natural connection between us."

Jesus said on another occasion, "I and the Father are one" (John 10:30). He plainly expected that by his miraculous acts people would recognize the divine status of his message and work: "The works which the Father has given Me to accomplish, the very works that I do, bear witness of Me, that the Father has sent Me" (John 5:36 NASB; cf. Matt. 11:2–6). As a matter of fact, his miracles did have this effect on people. When the religious elite of Palestine questioned Jesus' authority to forgive the sins of a lame man—a uniquely divine prerogative— Jesus healed the man of his paralysis. In amazement, witnesses responded by praising God in obvious recognition of Jesus' relationship to God (Mark 2:1–12). This reaction was characteristic of firsthand observers. Later, on the day of Pentecost, Peter could rely on an ample stock of miracles performed by Jesus to remind his audience of God's authorization of Jesus' authority: "Men of Israel, listen to this: Jesus of Nazareth was a man accredited by God to you by miracles, wonders and signs, which God did among you through him, as you yourselves know" (Acts 2:22).[59]

From the very beginning, those closest to Jesus during his earthly life stressed the importance of believing in Jesus. Following a particularly successful day of evangelism and a night in jail for offending the religious intelligentsia with the Christian gospel, Peter boiled his message down to a concise statement for which Christianity has rightly become known: "Salvation is found in no one else, for there is no other name under heaven given to men by which we must be saved" (Acts 4:12). It is for this reason that members of the early church came to be called "Christians" (see 11:26).

In the early days, Christianity was also sometimes called "the Way" (see Acts 9:2; 19:9, 23). All other supposed ways were dead-end paths, and all other alleged gods imposters.

> We know that an idol is nothing at all in the world and that there is no God but one. For even if there are so-called gods, whether in heaven or on earth (as indeed there are many "gods" and many "lords"), yet for us there is but one God, the Father, from whom all things came and for whom we live; and there is but one Lord, Jesus Christ, through whom all things came and through whom we live.
>
> But not everyone knows this. Some people are still . . . accustomed to idols. (1 Cor. 8:4–7a)

The point of this section has been to illustrate the manner in which the religious significance of Jesus is presented in the Bible. From the words of Jesus himself, to the miraculous deeds he performed, to the effect of his actions on others, to the earliest Christian preaching after his departure, Jesus is presented as the only way to be saved. It is especially noteworthy that on one occasion Jesus even invited his listeners to reflect upon their belief in God as a way of making sense of his own claims (John 14:1). He believed that he could count on a right conception of God leading to a proper appraisal of his own significance.

Of course, there is also a sense in which the reference of the term *God* is brought into greater focus with the coming of Jesus Christ. God becomes better known to us in Jesus Christ, the Incarnation of God (see Col. 1:15–20; Heb. 1:1–3; 1 John 1:1–4). As the fulfillment of the human expectation of a divine remedy for the human condition, Jesus Christ far exceeds our expectations. God's interest in us is greater than we had even imagined. In the Incarnation, Jesus Christ as God invaded our "personal space" by taking on human flesh and subjecting himself to the vicissitudes of human life. In an act of radical transparency, God comes as close to us as is metaphysically possible. His concern for us knew no bounds, for his humility extended even to the manner of his departure: death on a cross. And in that death he traded places with us, receiving on himself the weight of our transgression so that we might become righteous before God (see 2 Cor. 5:21; Phil. 2:6–8; Heb. 2:10; 4:15).[60]

We might well hope that such a grand provision for relationship between God and humanity might be made. And well we might despair if we were unable to test this amazing story of salvation for historical accuracy. But because God's provision for the human race is tied to specific events in history and because these events are accompanied by miraculous confirmation of divine sponsorship, we can see that this story is not valuable merely for its power—it actually has happened! How, indeed, "shall we escape if we ignore such a great salvation" (Heb. 2:3)?

The Jesus Question and Personal Decision

Radical scholarly opinion about Jesus, abundantly manifested by the Jesus Seminar, assumes without justification a naturalistic view of the world. This view of the world effectively denies the reality of God by excluding the possibility of knowing that there is a God and, if there is a God, what he is like. To the degree that this worldview is at odds with the available evidence for the reality of God, a commitment to naturalism requires an irresponsible handling of the historical evidence about Jesus. When it is understood that distortion of the facts concerning Jesus is influenced at the most basic level by prior commitments concerning the reality of God and his possible relationship to us as persons, the discerning reader will recognize the need to be discriminating about which view of God he or she accepts, and on what grounds.

In this chapter I have argued that the religious quest, prompted by the desire to make ultimate sense of our lives, leads from a conception of God as the personal Creator of the universe to the expectation that our Creator is interested in the outcome of our quest. In the end, the project of religious inquiry is not simply a matter of arbitrarily choosing between a variety of human responses to "God" as vaguely perceived in diverse contexts of religious experience. Rather, it is a matter of recognizing God's own response to the specific contours of the human situation. In order to recognize God's provision of salvation, we must have some idea what to expect from God. And we will have no clear idea about what to expect from God without understanding something of his character. Thus we are led to consider the prospects for natural theology.

In doing natural theology, we are, of course, limited to the materials at our disposal. But as it happens, the materials are quite expansive and informative. We find that we owe our existence to a personal being of great power and intelligence. This means that the fundamental conditions for human existence were established by God. We also know that we ourselves are personal beings. Thus, we are more like our Creator than anything else we have experience of. This implies the possibility of an interpersonal relationship between ourselves and God. And, if we may take our own experience as personal selves to be an indication of what may be true of God, we may suppose that God also takes some interest or pride in what he has made.

All this suggests a God who is far from indifferent about the human situation. However, God's interest in us and his initiative toward us respects our capacity for self-determination as free creatures. Thus, we find members of the human community resisting God's attempts to establish lines of communication with himself. Some, in fact, are scandalized by the prospects of a precise diagnosis of the human condition with a specific remedy. This very tendency is symptomatic of human alienation from God. But while the propensity to dictate to God the conditions of divine-human relationship is pervasive, it is hardly rational. The religious pluralist's insistence that God cannot have arranged for our salvation in the exclusivist way of Christianity presupposes a greater knowledge of God than radical religious pluralists are in a position to have on their own assumptions.

So let us suppose that God does take an interest in the human condition. Would it not be puzzling if it turned out that the resurrection of Jesus Christ, a well-attested historical phenomenon, had nothing to do with God's interest in the human condition? When an event like the resurrection takes place in a world that owes its existence to the sort of God we have been describing, we should give some consideration to the possibility that God is up to something.

For those who are impressed by these considerations but still have trouble believing, there is something you can do. You can put the Christian view of the world to the test in the laboratory of your own life. You can do this by performing a kind of devotional experiment. If you think the Christian worldview is reasonable, but your heart has not caught up with your mind, you need to understand that this is a normal part of spiritual development in the Christian way. In countless ways, our passions prevent us from taking prudent action. But once we recognize this, we are in a better position to be led by rational considerations rather than impulse. For many, reluctance to embrace Jesus Christ is not an intellectual issue at all, though it is often confused for one. Even when all of your favorite intellectual questions have been answered and your most precious objections rebutted, it is still possible to withhold assent to something as momentous as Christianity.

But perhaps your explicit assent is not what is needed just now. Perhaps that will come in due time if you make appropriate advance arrangements for it. Doubtless you are presently accustomed to viewing the world in a certain way. For example, you might approach the world as if God does not exist, or as if God does not matter to your existence, or as if Jesus Christ were just a laconic sage whose disciples got carried way. Then you might try thinking about your life a different way. Imagine how you would organize your life if you actually did accept the Christian worldview, and then take specific steps to organize your life that way for an extended period of time. The idea is to find ways compatible with your personality to see what life would be like for you if you actually believed.

This invitation to conduct a devotional experiment presupposes that you have already been sufficiently impressed by independent evidence for the truth of Christianity to warrant risking further confirmation of Christianity in this more subjective manner. This sort of experiment makes sense in light of the fact that worldviews get mapped onto our identities in powerful ways. Put another way, we become habituated to viewing the world a particular way. Coming to view the world some other way requires us to break an entrenched habit, one that has been reinforced around the clock for a long period of time. And that requires studied attention to a new way of approaching our lives.

As an initial exercise of this kind, you might try rereading this book—this time with the eyes of faith. Do the same with the New Testament Gospels. Whenever you encounter a difficulty, have a question, or experience doubt, think about the potential resources within Christianity to handle these concerns. If there is a Christian theist whom you trust, an experienced traveler on the way, harness yourself to that person and seek his or her guidance along the way. Many a hardened intellectual has found Jesus Christ in this way.[61]

This is an invitation to approach God in a manner that he has promised to honor if you are sincere. As it says in the New Testament, "anyone who comes to [God] must believe that he exists and that he rewards those who earnestly seek him" (Heb. 11:6). Jesus himself promised that if you seek, you will find (Luke 11:9).[62]

Notes

1. There are, of course, numerous Jewish Christians, whereas there are no Muslim Christians.

2. I am not suggesting that all of the Fellows of the Jesus Seminar profess to be Christians, nor even that those who do profess to be Christians agree about what to make of Jesus either historically or religiously.

3. This impression is reinforced by the failure of widespread "belief in God" to produce the sort of large-scale improvement of society that might be expected if people really did *believe in* God.

4. Not only is the claim that Jesus is the only way compatible with the Apostles' Creed, but the sentiment that Jesus Christ is the uniquely complete revelation of God and the sole source of salvation is expressed in the Creed. A number of expositions of the Creed bring this out. See especially the evangelical discussions by J. I. Packer, *The Apostles' Creed* (Wheaton, Ill.: Tyndale, 1977), and R. C. Sproul, *Basic Training: Plain Talk on the Key Truths of the Faith* (Grand Rapids: Zondervan, 1982). Compare also Wolfhart Pannenberg, *The Apostles' Creed in the Light of Today's Questions* (Philadelphia: Westminster, 1972), and Hans Schwarz, *What Christians Believe* (Philadelphia: Fortress, 1987). For helpful comparisons between traditional and modern translations of the Apostles' Creed, see Gerald Bray, *Creeds, Councils and Christ* (Leicester: Inter-Varsity Press, 1984), 204–6.

5. N. T. Wright illustrates this possibility by comparing first-century Jewish and Christian beliefs in God (*The New Testament and the People of God* [Minneapolis: Fortress, 1992], 471–76).

6. Richard Lederer, *More Anguished English* (New York: Dell); excerpted in *Current Books* 2 (Spring 1994): 35.

7. Members of the Jesus Seminar do hold that someone named Jesus actually lived. But for them there is not a sufficient match between the historical Jesus and the biblical Jesus to permit the judgment that the biblical Jesus actually existed. This has the effect of driving a wedge between the Jesus of history and the Jesus of the Bible.

8. Robert W. Funk, Roy W. Hoover, and the Jesus Seminar, *The Five Gospels: What Did Jesus Really Say?* (New York: Polebridge, 1993), 7.

9. Ibid., 5.

10. See, for example, ibid., ix and 34.

11. See ibid., 35.

12. Richard B. Hays, in his critical review of *The Five Gospels*, identifies several elements of a portrait of Jesus that surfaces in this book (see "The Corrected Jesus," *First Things* [May 1994]: 47). But Hays also observes that "what the members of the Jesus Seminar have done, in effect, is merely to offer us an anthology of their favorite Jesus-sayings" (p. 46).

13. Marcus Borg, *Meeting Jesus Again for the First Time: The Historical Jesus and the Heart of Contemporary Faith* (San Francisco: HarperSanFrancisco, 1994), ch. 2. The details of his presentation here are elaborated in his earlier, pre-Seminar book *Jesus: A New Vision* (San Francisco: Harper & Row, 1987).

14. Borg, *Meeting Jesus Again*, 16.

15. Ibid., 17.

16. Ibid., 20.

17. The same point could be illustrated by noting how paleontologists have constructed dubious models of specific dinosaurs on the basis of selective attention to observa-

tional evidence. Philosopher of science Rom Harré uses this example to show that "statements that are accepted as expressions of well-attested beliefs may have to be abandoned or revised according to the theory one holds as much as with respect to the experiences one has" (*Varieties of Realism: A Rationale for the Natural Sciences* [London: Basil Blackwell, 1986], 36). The same point can be made about the "findings" of the Jesus Seminar.

18. See Borg, *Meeting Jesus Again*, 29–31.

19. Ibid., 6.

20. Ibid., 13.

21. Ibid., 14.

22. Ibid.

23. Ibid.

24. Ibid., 13.

25. Ibid., 15.

26. See ibid., 31–39.

27. Ibid., 37.

28. See ibid., 47–58.

29. Ibid., 59.

30. Ibid., 60.

31. See ibid., chs. 4 and 5.

32. Several decades ago, C. S. Lewis predicted that novel reconstructions of the "historical Jesus" would follow the familiar tendency to be patterned after extant ideologies. Since the ideologies themselves are ephemeral, so too are the reconstructions of the "historical Jesus," with the result that "each 'historical Jesus' is unhistorical." Lewis went on to describe the religiously deleterious effects of this tendency. See C. S. Lewis, *The Screwtape Letters*, rev. ed. [New York: Macmillan, 1961], 116–20, or Letter XXIII in any edition.

33. Borg, *Meeting Jesus Again*, 44–45, n. 42.

34. Ibid., 131.

35. Ibid., 38.

36. See Wayne Proudfoot, "Explaining Religious Experience," in *Contemporary Perspectives on Religious Epistemology*, ed. R. Douglas Geivett and Brendan Sweetman (New York: Oxford University Press, 1992), 336–52.

37. I do not hold that conceptual schemes themselves are incommensurable, or that the entire range of our cognitive lives is controlled by concepts operating in the background for us. I adopt a foundationalist view of perception, for example, according to which preconceptual contents of sensory experience, which are nonpropositional and therefore do not require justification, provide justification for perceptual judgments. For contemporary defenses of this type of position, see Reinhardt Grossmann, *The Fourth Way: A Theory of Knowledge* (Bloomington: Indiana University Press, 1990); Paul K. Moser, *Knowledge and Evidence* (Cambridge: Cambridge University Press, 1989); and Roderick M. Chisholm, *Theory of Knowledge*, 3d ed. (Englewood Cliffs, N.J.: Prentice Hall, 1989). The much-paraded contention that objectivity is impossible at all levels of inquiry is exaggerated and self-referentially defeating.

38. For a detailed critique of the type of religious pluralism reflected in Borg's writings, see my article "John Hick's Approach to Religious Pluralism," *Proceedings of the Wheaton College Theology Conference* 1 (Spring 1992): 39–55.

39. Borg, *Meeting Jesus Again*, 38.

40. Caroline Franks Davis describes one way to view the role of religious experience as part of a comprehensive or cumulative case for theism that includes a wide-ranging natural theology (*The Evidential Force of Religious Experience* [Oxford: Clarendon, 1989], 239–50). Even William P. Alston, a philosopher known for emphasizing the cognitive value of religious experience, acknowledges the value of natural theology in strengthening the justification for Christian belief: "The Christian may have recourse to natural theology to provide metaphysical reasons for the truth of theism as a general world-view; and then, within the field of theistic religions, he may argue that historical evidence gives much stronger support to the claims of Christianity than to those of its theistic rivals. . . . I believe that much can be done to support a theistic metaphysics, and that something can be done by way of recommending the 'evidences of Christianity' " (Alston, *Perceiving God: The Epistemology of Religious Experience* [Ithaca, N.Y.: Cornell University Press, 1991], 270). And William J. Wainwright, another advocate of the justificatory value of religious experience, writes that "if there is independent (of religious experience) evidence for claims about God or other supernatural realities, the argument for religious experience's cognitive validity is even stronger" (*Philosophy of Religion* [Belmont, Calif.: Wadsworth, 1988], 128). British philosopher Richard Swinburne, of course, is explicit about the importance of relating religious experience to the broader framework of natural theology (see *The Existence of God* [Oxford: Clarendon, 1979]).

41. The material in this section parallels material I have written for the volume *Religious Pluralism: Four Views*, ed. Timothy L. Phillips and Dennis R. Okholm (Grand Rapids: Zondervan, 1995).

42. Borg, *Meeting Jesus Again*, 29.

43. Because this evidence reveals much of the pattern of God's action on behalf of humans apart from what the Bible teaches, many theologians use the phrase "general revelation" to refer to this type of evidence.

44. By *universe* I mean the familiar array of galaxies, stars, and other entities that make up physical reality; I am not referring to it.

45. This type of argument has been called the *kalam* cosmological argument for the existence of God. For detailed expositions and defenses of the argument, see William Lane Craig, *The* Kalam *Cosmological Argument* (London: Macmillan, 1979); William Lane Craig and Quentin Smith, *Theism, Atheism, and Big Bang Cosmology* (Oxford: Clarendon, 1993); R. Douglas Geivett, *Evil and the Evidence for God* (Philadelphia: Temple University Press, 1993), ch. 6; and J. P. Moreland, *Scaling the Secular City* (Grand Rapids: Baker, 1987), ch. 1. See also Dallas Willard, "The Three-Stage Argument for the Existence of God," in *Contemporary Perspectives on Religious Epistemology*, ed. R. Douglas Geivett and Brendan Sweetman (New York: Oxford University Press, 1992), 212–24.

46. For developments of this idea, see Roderick Chisholm, "Human Freedom and the Self," in *Free Will*, ed. Gary Watson (Oxford: Oxford University Press, 1982); Roderick Chisholm, *On Metaphysics* (Minneapolis: University of Minnesota Press, 1989), 3–15; Geivett, *Evil and the Evidence for God*, 114–22; Stewart C. Goetz, "A Noncausal Theory of Agency," *Philosophy and Phenomenological Research* 44 (December 1988): 303–16; William L. Rowe, *Thomas Reid on Freedom and Morality* (Ithaca, N.Y.: Cornell University Press, 1991); and William L. Rowe, "Two Concepts of Freedom," *Proceedings of the American Philosophical Association* 61, supp. (September 1981): 43–64.

47. This claim constitutes an appeal to what philosophers call "the anthropic principle." For detailed discussions of this principle, see John D. Barrow and Frank J. Tipler, *The*

Anthropic Cosmological Principle (New York: Oxford University Press, 1986); M. A. Corey, *God and the New Cosmology: The Anthropic Design Argument* (Lanham, Md.: Rowman & Littlefield, 1993); John Leslie, *Universes* (London: Routledge, 1989); and Hugh Ross, "Astronomical Evidence for a Personal, Transcendent God," *The Creation Hypothesis: Scientific Evidence for an Intelligent Designer*, ed. J. P. Moreland (Downers Grove, Ill.: InterVarsity Press, 1994), 141–72.

48. For further discussion of these issues, see W. S. Anglin, *Free Will and the Christian Faith* (Oxford: Clarendon, 1990); Richard Swinburne, *The Evolution of the Soul* (Oxford: Clarendon, 1986); J. P. Moreland and David Ciocchi, eds., *Christian Perspectives on Being Human* (Grand Rapids: Baker, 1993); and J. P. Moreland and Gary R. Habermas, *Immortality: The Other Side of Death* (Nashville: Thomas Nelson, 1992). For a comparison between Christianity and Buddhism on the nature of the self, which illustrates the religious significance of differences in the metaphysics of personhood, see Paul J. Griffiths, *Apology for Apologetics: A Study in the Logic of Interreligious Dialogue* (Maryknoll, N.Y.: Orbis, 1991), 85–108.

49. C. S. Lewis, *Mere Christianity* (New York: Macmillan, 1952), 106.

50. For more on the religious implications of the structure of the soul and of the desires of the human heart, see Dallas Willard, *The Spirit of the Disciplines: Understanding How God Changes Lives* (San Francisco: Harper & Row, 1988); C. Stephen Evans, *Existentialism: The Philosophy of Despair and the Quest for Hope* (Grand Rapids: Zondervan, 1984); James Houston, *The Heart's Desire: A Guide to Personal Fulfillment* (Oxford: Lion, 1992); Peter Kreeft, *Heaven: The Heart's Deepest Longing* (San Francisco: Ignatius, 1989); Calvin Miller, *A Hunger for Meaning* (Downers Grove, Ill.: InterVarsity Press, 1984); and Rebecca Manley Pippert, *Hope Has Its Reasons: Surprised by Faith in a Broken World* (San Francisco: Harper & Row, 1989).

51. William P. Alston, *Divine Nature and Human Language: Essays in Philosophical Theology* (Ithaca, N.Y.: Cornell University Press, 1989), 148.

52. This, I think, provides an initial line of response to those who argue that if theism was true, then God's existence would be more evident than it is. See, e.g., Theodore M. Drange, "The Argument from Non-Belief," *Religious Studies* 29 (1993): 417–32, and J. L. Schellenberg, *Divine Hiddenness and Human Reason* (Ithaca, N.Y.: Cornell University Press, 1993).

53. It needs to be noticed that, on the whole, theists have distinguished themselves as "peoples of the Book." That is, they have embraced some form of propositional revelation. Orthodox Jews consider the Hebrew Scriptures to be uniquely inspired. According to the Islamic tradition, God or Allah in effect dictated his word to his prophet Mohammed, producing the Koran. And Christians acknowledge the unique divine authority of the Old and New Testaments of the Bible. It is rare for a theist to hold that no form of special revelation has been given.

54. As observed in the previous note, revelational theisms differ in their judgment concerning the precise locus of propositional revelation from God. The evidence of miracles is therefore useful for adjudicating between competing revelation claims. For more on the significance of miracles for corroborating revelation claims, see Richard Swinburne, *Revelation: From Metaphor to Analogy* (Oxford: Clarendon, 1992), chs. 5 and 6, and R. Douglas Geivett, "The Interface of Theism and Christianity in a Two-Step Apologetic," in *Ratio: Essays in Christian Thought* 1 (Autumn 1993): 211–30. See also Anglin, *Free Will and the Christian Faith*, 186–208.

55. The term *gospel* simply means "good news."

56. The miracles of Christianity serve at least two vital purposes: they attract attention to the Christian revelation claim, and they corroborate the Christian revelation claim.

57. See John W. Wenham, *Christ and the Bible* (Downers Grove, Ill.: InterVarsity Press, 1972), and Bernard Ramm, *Special Revelation and the Word of God* (Grand Rapids: Eerdmans, 1961), 110–11, 115–18. On the notion of "propositional revelation," see Paul Helm, *The Divine Revelation* (Westchester, Ill.: Crossway, 1982), 21–27; Leon Morris, *I Believe in Divine Revelation* (Grand Rapids: Eerdmans, 1976), 113–18; and Ronald H. Nash, *The Word of God and the Mind of Man* (Grand Rapids: Zondervan, 1982), 35–54.

58. See Craig Blomberg's discussion in chapter 1 on the reliability of the portrait of Jesus in the Gospel of John.

59. Subsequent messengers confirmed their firsthand witness concerning Jesus by performing miracles of their own. That is, the Christian message concerning Jesus was accompanied by miracles as a sign of divine sponsorship even when others besides Jesus conveyed the message. The chief difference is that they testified of Jesus, not of themselves (see Heb. 2:3–4).

60. For a more detailed discussion of the biblical data concerning the religious significance of Jesus, see R. Douglas Geivett and W. Gary Phillips, "Christian Particularism: An Evidentialist Approach," in *Religious Pluralism: Four Views*.

61. For development of the concept of a devotional experiment, see Caroline Franks Davis, "The Devotional Experiment," *Religious Studies* 22 (1986): 15–28. George N. Schlesinger's essay, "The Availability of Evidence in Support of Religious Belief," *Faith and Philosophy* 1 (October 1984): 42–56, is also helpful in this regard.

62. I wish to thank Dennis Monokroussos, Gary Phillips, and Ken Tang Quan, as well as the editors of this volume, for helpful comments on an earlier draft of this chapter.

Chapter 8

JESUS OUTSIDE THE NEW TESTAMENT: WHAT IS THE EVIDENCE?

EDWIN M. YAMAUCHI

Edwin M. Yamauchi (Ph.D., Brandeis University) is Professor of history at Miami University in Oxford, Ohio. He is the author of a number of books on archaeology, including *Persia and the Bible, Harper's World of the New Testament, The Stones and the Scriptures*, and *The Archaeology of the New Testament Cities in Western Asia Minor*.

Introduction

I have at times been asked by students at the university where I teach whether any ancient sources outside the New Testament mention Jesus.[1] In classes on Western civilization I discuss such sources, but point out that though such texts provide welcome confirmation of certain facts about Jesus, they are inferior to the information provided by the Gospels. In this chapter I will assess the historical value of the ancient sources of information about Jesus found outside the New Testament, and I will also discuss some of the more eccentric claims about Jesus that are based on these sources.

Only a few writers, such as Arthur Drews, have gone so far as to deny the existence of Jesus.[2] Craig Evans comments that "the belief that Jesus never existed was picked up by Marx and Engels and came to be the 'official' view of Marxism."[3] On the other hand, there are not a few who claim to have found references to Jesus where no one else can detect them. At times scholars have offered strange interpretations about the "true" nature of Jesus from sources outside the New Testament. Let me discuss some of these Jewish, Roman, and Christian sources.

Jewish Sources

The Dead Sea Scrolls

Almost everyone has heard about the Dead Sea Scrolls, manuscripts hidden in caves near Qumran, first discovered in 1947 by Bedouin. These sensational texts come from about 150 B.C. to A.D. 68, when the Romans destroyed the settlement of Qumran. Although still a matter of dispute, most scholars identify the community that wrote and copied the scrolls as the Essenes, a group more strict than the Pharisees.

I was introduced to the study of the Scrolls while in graduate school at Brandeis University by a most distinguished authority, Professor Shemaryahu Talmon of Hebrew University. The Scrolls continue to intrigue me for the light they shed on the Old Testament text, on the development of Judaism in the period between the Old and New Testaments, and on the Jewish background of Jesus.[4] Some scholars, however, have made bizarre claims about the significance of the Scrolls for our understanding of Jesus.

Dupont-Sommer

The earliest wave of claims appeared in the 1950s in the first flush of excitement over the Scrolls. André Dupont-Sommer was the first to suggest that the

Qumran community should be identified as Essenes. In his 1952 book, *The Dead Sea Scrolls*,[5] Dupont-Sommer, an ex-Catholic priest and an agnostic, claimed that the Teacher of Righteousness, the important early leader of the Qumran community, was an amazing anticipation of Jesus in that he also was tortured, put to death, and reappeared.[6] This last claim was based on his idiosyncratic translation of the verb *hophia'* ("appeared") in the *Habbakuk Commentary* 2.15. In his 1962 translation Dupont-Sommer conceded that the verb could be translated as "appear" with "no supernatural implication,"[7] but still insisted that the subject of the verb was the Teacher of Righteousness. But other scholars (e.g., T. H. Gaster[8] and G. Vermes[9]) have taken the subject of the verb to be the Wicked Priest, thus eliminating the support for Dupont-Sommer's interpretation of a supernatural manifestation of a martyred Teacher of Righteousness, who anticipated Jesus.

Wilson

It was the essayist Edmund Wilson (d. 1972) who first drew widespread attention to the Scrolls by his best-selling work, *The Scrolls from the Dead Seas*, published in 1955.[10] By publicizing the Scrolls Wilson felt that he had exposed "the myth of the origins of Christianity."[11] He suggested that Jesus may have spent some of his childhood years with the Essenes and alleged that New Testament scholars were avoiding the study of the Scrolls. Wilson based his popularization on the theories of Dupont-Sommer and John Marco Allegro.

Allegro theorised that Christianity started as fertility cult centered on Hallucanogenies

John Marco Allegro (d. 1988) was a British scholar who had the privilege of serving on the first international committee of scholars entrusted with the publication of the Dead Sea Scrolls. He had originally studied Hebrew to prepare for the Methodist ministry, but he abandoned any pretensions of faith and in numerous books did his best to overthrow Christianity. On the basis of his interpretation of the *Nahum Commentary*, Allegro asserted that the Teacher of Righteousness had been crucified, though the text does not say this at all. Allegro concluded that the Scrolls demonstrated that the Gospel story of Jesus was a fiction, based on the earlier example of the Teacher of Righteousness.

In an August 1966 article in *Harper's Magazine*[12] Allegro claimed that he knew the secret meaning of New Testament names, suggesting that the name "Jesus" meant "Essene" and that Peter's name concealed an Essene title.[13] In 1970 Allegro left the University of Manchester and published a most bizarre book, *The Sacred Mushroom and the Cross*.[14] He had come to discern that the name "Jesus" meant "Semen, which saves," and that "Peter" meant "Mushroom," thus revealing that Christianity was originally a disguised fertility cult centered on a hallucinogenic mushroom![15]

Thiering

If in reviewing the conclusions of Allegro we are tempted to suspect that we are hearing the ravings of someone influenced by a hallucinogenic drug, we now have the proposals of a scholar, Barbara Thiering, which may remind us of an Alice-in-Wonderland scenario. Thiering, who teaches at the University of Sydney in Australia, recently published a well-publicized book, *Jesus and the Riddle of the Dead Sea Scrolls*.[16] She has been featured on television programs as well. In her earlier works, Thiering had concluded that the Qumran literature and the New Testament came from different wings of a single community, so that the New Testament should be read as a coded commentary, and she carries out a mind-boggling program of reinterpreting the Scrolls and the New Testament on this basis. According to Thiering, Jesus was born not in Bethlehem but south of the Qumran plateau. The Magi were "Diaspora Essenes."[17] Places are not where one thinks they are: the Sea of Galilee is really the Dead Sea, Capernaum is a site called Mazin, and Jerusalem is Qumran.

She is convinced that the same person in the Gospels and in Josephus could have several names. Simon Magus (Acts 8), for example, was also the poor man Lazarus (Luke 16:19–31) = a.k.a. (also known as) Lazarus, the brother of Mary and Martha = Simon the Zealot = Simon the Leper. When Jesus raised Lazarus, he was releasing Simon Magus from Cave 4 at Qumran. Jesus was crucified along with Simon Magus and Judas at Qumran. After he recovered from his crucifixion by imbibing snake poison that rendered him unconscious, Jesus married Mary Magdalene and later Lydia of Philippi! Though there is not a shred of evidence for such a remarkable reconstruction, her outrageous scenario has attracted widespread media attention.

Eisenman and Wise

A more restrained but still idiosyncratic interpretation of the Dead Sea Scrolls has been offered by Robert H. Eisenman, chair of Religious Studies at California State University in Long Beach, California. During a visit to Jerusalem, Eisenman realized that the true significance of James, the brother of Jesus, had been edited from the collective memory of Christianity, just as his own Jewish background had been suppressed by his relatives. In a short study in 1986 Eisenman identifed the Qumran Teacher of Righteousness with James.[18] He maintains that Paul was the "archetypal self-hating Jew."

Eisenman, who was denied access to the Scrolls by the official committee, recently played a key role in acquiring and then publishing a set of photos of all of the Scrolls. He then collaborated with a scholar at the University of Chicago, Michael Wise, in publishing the translations of hitherto unreleased texts of Cave IV.[19] In a press release in November 1991, Eisenman called attention to a so-called "Pierced Messiah Text" from Qumran, which attracted widespread media attention. This fragment (4Q285) with five lines of Hebrew text has been identified as part of the *War Scroll*. Eisenman and Wise stressed that this text for the first time revealed a "pierced messiah" similar to Christianity's concept of a crucified Christ.

One of the ambiguities of ancient Hebrew texts is the fact that they are all written with consonants only; this means that scholars must supply the vowels. Eisenman and Wise based their interpretation on their vocalization of the key verb *WHMTW* as *w*ʿ*hamitu*—"*they will kill*" the Prince of the Congregation, i.e., the "Messiah." Eisenman felt that his earlier views that the Scrolls were written by Jews who were involved in Christianity had now been vindicated. A sensationalizing book by M. Baigent and R. Leigh[20] has followed Eisenman, claiming that the delay in the publication of all the Scrolls was the result of a conspiracy on the part of the Vatican (since many of the original Dead Sea Scrolls scholars were Catholic).[21]

The translation of Eisenman and Wise has aroused a chorus of objections from other scholars. For example, G. Vermes and his colleagues at Oxford are unanimous in vocalizing the key verb *w*ʿ*hemito*, that is, "the Prince of the Congregation *will kill him*"—most probably a wicked king.[22] Though either vocalization for the verb is possible, the entire context of the War Scroll is that of a triumphant and not a suffering Messiah.

O'Callaghan

In 1972 a distinguished Spanish expert on papyri, José O'Callaghan, created quite a stir when he identified some Greek fragments from Qumran Cave VII as the earliest New Testament manuscripts ever discovered, including a fragment of the Gospel of Mark, which he dated to A.D. 50. I must confess that I was one of a number of scholars who hailed this discovery. However, more careful study by other scholars has concluded that the manuscripts were too tiny and that O'Callaghan's theory required too much reconstruction to be persuasive.[23] Recently a German scholar, C. P. Thiede, has championed O'Callaghan's identifications,[24] but most scholars remain skeptical.[25]

Summary

In general one can say that the Dead Sea Scrolls, although they certainly do not mention Jesus or any of his disciples, do provide invaluable new information on one particular sect of Jews in his day. The dualism (i.e., the strong contrast between good and evil) found in the texts helps us to understand the Gospel of John not as a Greek document far removed from Jesus' Palestine, as some scholars have maintained, but as James H. Charlesworth has characterized it, "perhaps the most Jewish of the canonical gospels."[26] He notes that there are both striking similarities and sharp differences between Jesus and the Teacher of Righteousness.[27]

The Dead Sea Scrolls provide no clear evidence that would revise the New Testament picture of Jesus, nor do the Scrolls justify some of the eccentric claims about Jesus made on the basis of the Scrolls. What they have given us is a deeper understanding of the world in which Jesus lived and ministered.

Josephus

The most important witness to Jesus is the Jewish historian Josephus, who wrote four works in Greek: an autobiographical *Life*, a defense of Judaism in a rebuttal of an anti-Semite, *Contra Celsum*, a vivid eyewitness account of the revolt against Rome (A.D. 66–74), *The Jewish War*; and a history of the Jews from Adam to his era, *The Antiquities*.[28] After he surrendered the fortress of Jotapata to the Roman general, Vespasian, Josephus became an apologist for the Romans and denounced the Jews who had led the rebellion against Rome.

Josephus (*Ant.* 18.116–19) has an important passage about the imprisonment and execution of John the Baptist by Herod Antipas. No scholar has questioned the authenticity of this passage, though there are some differences between Josephus's account and that in the Gospels (Matt. 14:1–12; Mark 6:14–29; Luke 9:7–9). These differences, however, are easily explained.[29]

According to the Gospels Jesus had brothers and sisters (Matt. 13:55; Mark 3:21),[30] the most prominent of whom was James,[31] who was apparently converted by the appearance of the risen Christ (1 Cor. 15:7; cf. John 7:5) and became the head of the church in Jerusalem about A.D. 50 (Acts 15:19–23). Josephus (Ant. 20.200) describes how the high priest Ananus took advantage of the death of the Roman governor Festus in A.D. 62 to organize a mob to stone James, whom he identifies as "the brother of Jesus who was called the Christ." Few scholars have questioned the genuineness of this passage.[32]

The most celebrated passage in Josephus is the so-called "Testimonium Flavianum" (*Ant.* 18.63–64) about Jesus:

> About this time there lived Jesus, a wise man, if indeed one ought to call him a man. For he was one who wrought surprising feats and was a teacher of such people as accept the truth gladly. He won over many Jews and many of the Greeks. He was the Christ. When Pilate, upon hearing him accused by men of the highest standing amongst us, had condemned him to be crucified, those who had in the first place come to love him did not give up their affection for him. On the third day he appeared to them restored to life, for the prophets of God had prophesied these and countless other marvellous things about him. And the tribe of the Christians, so called after him, has still to this day not disappeared.

Scholarly opinion about this passage can be divided into three camps: (1) those who defend the essential authenticity of the passage; (2) those who reject the entire passage;[33] (3) those who believe that the passage has an authentic core but also includes Christian insertions. Most recent scholarship has favored the last option.[34]

This passage was cited by the great church historian Eusebius (fourth century) in three of his works. The witness of Origen (third century) is crucial. He was apparently familiar with the passage in Josephus about James but not with the Testimonium Flavianum as Eusebius knew it, for he wrote, "The wonder is that though he [Josephus] did not admit our Jesus to be Christ, he none the less gave his witness to so much righteousness in James." Elsewhere Origen says of Josephus that "he disbelieved in Jesus as Christ."[35]

Almost everyone agrees that a number of phrases in the passage are so patently Christian that a Jew like Josephus would not have penned them:

1. "If indeed one ought to call him a man" imples that Jesus was more than human.
2. "He was the Christ." Josephus elsewhere says very little about messianic expectations, because he wanted to downplay those beliefs.
3. "On the third day he appeared to them restored to life." This seems to be an unambiguous testimony to the resurrection of Christ.[36]

On the other hand, most of the passage is *not* typically Christian:

1. Jesus is called "a wise man." Though the phrase is complimentary, it is less than one would expect from Christians.
2. "For he was one who wrought surprising feats." This is not necessarily a statement that could only have come from a Christian.
3. "He won over many Jews and many of the Greeks" is simply an observation.
4. "Those who had in the first place come to love him did not give up their affection for him," conforms to Josephus' characteristic style.
5. "And the tribe of the Christians, so called after him, has still to this day not disappeared." Most scholars would agree that the word *phylon* "tribe," is not a typically Christian expression.

The Jewish scholar Paul Winter concludes:

Although Josephus certainly did not call Jesus the Messiah and did not assert that his resurrection on the third day had been announced by divine prophets, the impression gained from an intimate study of his report is that he was not on the whole unsympathetic toward Jesus.[37]

In 1971 an Israeli scholar, S. Pines, published a monograph on an Arabic version of Josephus done by Agapius, the tenth-century Melkite bishop of Hierapolis in Syria. A comparison between the Arabic and the Greek texts reveals the following differences: (1) Agapius' version of Josephus assumes the humanity of Jesus. (2) His text does not refer to Jesus' miracles but rather to his good conduct and virtue. (3) The appearance after three days is mentioned as a "report." (4) A disclaimer, "perhaps," is inserted before the statement that "he was the Messiah." All these differences lead Pines to conclude that the Arabic version may preserve a text that is close to the original, untampered text of Josephus.[38]

In summary, Josephus knew that Jesus was the brother of James, the martyred leader of the church in Jerusalem, and that he was a wise teacher who had established a wide and lasting following, despite the fact that he had been crucified under Pilate at the instigation of some of the Jewish leaders.

The Talmud

We have a number of polemical passages against Jesus in the Talmud (c. A.D. 400–500), an important collection of writings by Jewish rabbis.[39] In the *Babylonian Talmud* Sanhedrin 107b we read:

> One day he (Rabbi Joshua) was reciting the Shema (Deut. 6:4) when Jesus came before him. He intended to receive him and made a sign to him. He (Jesus) thinking that it was to repel him, went, put up a brick and worshipped it. . . . And a Master has said, "Jesus the Nazarene practiced magic and led Israel astray."

In the *Babylonian Talmud* Sanhedrin 43a we read:

> It was taught: On the eve of the Passover Yeshu (the Nazarene) was hanged. For forty days before the execution took place, a herald went forth and cried, "He is going forth to be stoned because he has practiced sorcery and enticed Israel to apostasy. Anyone who can say anything in his favor, let him come forward and plead on his behalf."

As indicated in these passages the *Talmud* does not deny the miracles of Jesus but attributes them to magic.[40] Jesus is identified in some sources as a student of Rabbi Joshua ben Parahya, who flourished around 100 B.C. and who was noted for his magic.[41]

The *Talmud* also contains a number of Ben Pandera[42] stories, according to which Jesus was the son of the Roman mercenary Pandera, "who begot a child with Joseph's adulterous wife, Mary, during her menstrual period."[43] These calumnies were expanded by the Middle Ages into the notorious anti-Christian traditions of a work called the *Toledoth Jeshu*.[44] This includes such fanciful stories as Jesus and Judas fighting in mid-air, Jesus crossing the Sea of Galilee on a millstone, and the hanging of Jesus on a cabbage stalk. In spite of their late and legendary nature, some of the roots of the *Toledoth* may go back to the early periods of antagonism between the Jews and the Christians.[45]

As all of these references are polemical and of uncertain and probably late date, their value is assessed negatively by G. H. Twelftree: "The Rabbinic literature is, then, of almost no value to the historian in his search for the historical Jesus. . . ."[46] M. Wilcox, on the other hand, believes that in spite of their hostility these texts do provide some corroborative evidence:

> The Jewish traditional literature, although it mentions Jesus only quite sparingly (and must in any case be used with caution), supports the Gospel claim that he was a healer and miracle-worker, even though it ascribes these activities to sorcery. In addition, it preserves the recollection that he was a

teacher, and that he had disciples (five of them!), and that at least in the earlier Rabbinic period not all of the sages had finally made up their minds that he was a "heretic" or a "deceiver."[47]

Roman Sources

When I begin a course on Roman history, I point out that the two most important historical sources for the first century of the Roman Empire are Tacitus and Suetonius, both of whom wrote at the beginning of the second century A.D. Both have important references to Christians, as does also Pliny the Younger.[48] If one wonders why there are not more Roman sources for Jesus, we need to realize that for the reign of Tiberius there are only four sources: Suetonius, Tacitus, Velleius Paterculus (a contemporary), and Dio Cassius (c. A.D. 230).[49]

Jesus was born during the reign of the emperor Augustus (27 B.C.–A.D. 14), probably before 4 B.C., the date when Herod the Great died.[50] Though the practice of an enrollment under Augustus mentioned in Luke 2:2 is in accordance with Roman practice, the specific association with the governor of Syria, Quirinius, presents some problems.[51]

Jesus was crucified under the Roman governor, Pontius Pilate[52] (A.D. 26–36), in the reign of Tiberius (A.D. 14–37), either in 30 or more probably in 33.[53] It is probable that records were sent by Pilate to Tiberius.[54] Justin Martyr in his *First Apology* (chs. 35, 48) refers to documents of the trial of Jesus. About A.D. 200 Tertullian of Carthage speaks in his *Apologeticus* (chs. 5, 21) of a dispatch from Pilate to Tiberius. The so-called *Acts of Pilate*, which have been preserved, however, are clearly nonhistorical. F. Scheidweiler has argued that they may have been known to Justin Martyr (mid-second century).[55]

Suetonius (c. A.D. 70 – c. 160)

In his life of the emperor Claudius (A.D. 41–54), Suetonius has an intriguing passage about disturbances in the Jewish community at Rome: "Since the Jews constantly made disturbances at the instigation of Chrestus, he expelled them from Rome." "Chrestus" is possibly a variant spelling of "Christus."[56] One of the problems with Suetonius's statement is that it seems to imply that "Chrestus" was a person who was present in Rome. Most scholars assume that Suetonius misunderstood his sources.[57] The majority of scholars have inferred that the disturbances among the Jewish community were caused by the preaching of the gospel by Jewish-Christian missionaries.[58] There are two possible dates for this expulsion, either 41 or 49, with most scholars favoring the latter.[59] The expulsion of the Jews is no doubt related to Acts 18:2, which speaks of the departure from Rome of Aquila and Priscilla, whom Paul met at Corinth about A.D. 50.[60]

A growing number of scholars, however, have accepted the argument that the "Chrestus" mentioned in Suetonius was simply a Jewish agitator with a common name, and that he had no association with Christianity.[61] Some also maintain that

Aquila and Priscilla were Jews, who may have become Christians only after they came into contact with Paul. An important argument against the view that the Chrestus incident in 49 involved Christians is the fact that about 60, when Paul was under house arrest in Rome, the Jewish leaders who came to Paul betray no knowledge of the Christian movement (Acts 28:21–22).[62]

In his *Vita Nero* 16.11–13 (Nero reigned A.D. 54–68), Suetonius relates the persecution of Christians without, however, explaining the reason for this treatment: "Punishment was inflicted on the Christians, a class of men given to a new and mischievous superstition." In a later passage he describes in great detail the fire that devastated ten of the fourteen districts of Rome.[63]

Tacitus (c. A.D. 55 – c. 117)

It is Tacitus who, in a celebrated passage written in 115, explicitly states that Nero persecuted the Christians as scapegoats to divert suspicion away from himself for the devastating fire of A.D. 64:

> But all human efforts, all the lavish gifts of the emperor, and the propitiations of the gods did not banish the sinister belief that the conflagration was the result of an order. Consequently, to get rid of the report, Nero fastened the guilt and inflicted the most exquisite tortures on a class hated for their abominations, called Christians by the populace. Christus, from whom the name had its origin, suffered the extreme penalty during the reign of Tiberius at the hands of one of our procurators, Pontius Pilatus, and a most mischievous superstition thus checked for the moment, again broke out not only in Judaea, the first source of the evil, but even in Rome, where all things hideous and shameful from every part of the world find their center and become popular. Accordingly, an arrest was first made of all who pleaded guilty: then, upon their information, an immense multitude was convicted, not so much of the crime of firing the city, as of hatred against mankind.[64]

Note that Tacitus, who despised Christians even more than he despised Jews, knew that they were called after Christ, who had been crucified ("suffered the extreme penalty") under Pontius Pilate in the reign of Tiberius. He was also aware that the movement, temporarily "checked" by Jesus' death, had spread from Judea to Rome, where an "immense multitude" professed its faith and were willing to die rather than recant.

Pliny the Younger (A.D. 61 or 62 – c. 113)

Pliny the Younger was the nephew of the famous encyclopedist, Pliny the Elder, who died during the eruption of Vesuvius in A.D. 79.[65] He became the governor of Bithynia in northwestern Turkey early in the second century. In a letter written about 111 to the emperor Trajan (A.D. 98–117), he refers to the burgeoning Christian movement:

I have never been present at an examination of Christians. Consequently, I do not know the nature of the extent of the punishments usually meted out to them, nor the grounds for starting an investigation and how far it should be pressed. . . . I have asked them if they are Christians, and if they admit it, I repeat the question a second and third time, with a warning of the punishment awaiting them. If they persist, I order them to be led away for execution; for, whatever the nature of their admission, I am convinced that their stubbornness and unshakeable obstinacy ought not to go unpunished . . . . They also declared that the sum total of their guilt or error amounted to no more than this: they had met regularly before dawn on a fixed day to chant verses alternately amongst themselves in honour of Christ as if to a god,[66] and also to bind themselves by oath, not for any criminal purpose, but to abstain from theft, robbery, and adultery, . . . This made me decide it was all the more necessary to extract the truth by torture from two slave-women, whom they call deaconesses. I found nothing but a degenerate sort of cult carried to extravagant lengths.[67]

These important Roman sources establish several facts quite independent of the New Testament: that Christ was crucified under Pilate in the reign of Tiberius, that despite this ignominious death his followers worshiped him as a god, and that they had become exceedingly numerous at Rome by the 60s (perhaps even in the 50s) and by the end of the first century were widespread in northwestern Asia Minor among both urban and rural areas (including both free and slave).

Christian Sources Outside the New Testament

Up to here in my examination of ancient sources of information about Jesus found outside the New Testament, my focus has centered on non-Christian sources, some of which support essential facts of the New Testament record. I now turn to look at Christian extrabiblical texts that have at times been used as sources for distorted portraits of Jesus.

Agrapha

The word *agrapha* (literally "unwritten") designates sayings of Jesus not found in the canonical Gospels (Matthew, Mark, Luke, and John).[68] Both the Apocryphal Gospels and the Church Fathers contain sayings and accounts of the acts of Jesus that are not found in the canonical Gospels.[69]

In 1896 B. P. Grenfell and A. S. Hunt found at Oxyrhynchus in Egypt a papryus with eight unknown sayings of Jesus.[70] This fragment, known as Oxy P1, dates from the second century A.D. In 1904 a second papyrus with five sayings of Jesus (c. 250) was also published. It was only much later with the discovery of the Coptic Gospel of *Thomas* that scholars realized that all these were Greek fragments of this same Gospel.[71] This Gospel, which contains 114 logia or sayings of

Jesus, is the most famous of about fifty some treatises found in about a dozen codices (i.e., books), written in Coptic about 400.[72]

The date and the value of the Gospel of *Thomas* is greatly disputed. Craig Blomberg has discussed these issues in more detail in chapter 1, "Where Do We Begin Studying Jesus?" but I raise here some important points for consideration. Many scholars believe that the original Greek Gospel of *Thomas* was written in Edessa in Syria c. 140.[73] There are two sharply divided attitudes toward this Gospel. Many believe this work is secondary in character, since "the bulk of the material seems to have its origin in the canonical Gospels."[74] On the other hand, an important group of scholars, influenced especially by the views of Helmut Koester of Harvard and James Robinson of Claremont,[75] view *Thomas* as early and independent.[76] The Jesus Seminar includes this work as a "fifth Gospel." But an examination of their analysis, which is exceedingly skeptical of the authenticity of the canonical Gospels, reveals that the Fellows of the Seminar were equally skeptical about the logia of *Thomas*. They consider only three of its sayings that have no canonical parallels worthy of serious consideration.

> *Thomas* 42: "Jesus said, 'Be passersby,' " which they color gray (Jesus did not say this, but the ideas contained in it are close to his own).[77]
> *Thomas* 97, "Jesus said, 'The (Father's) imperial rule is like a woman who was carrying a (jar) full of meal. While she was walking along (a) distant road, the handle of the jar broke and the meal spilled behind her (along) the road. She didn't know it; she hadn't noticed a problem. When she reached her house, she put the jar down and discovered that it was empty.' "[78] The Seminar codes this saying pink (Jesus probably said something like this).
> *Thomas* 98, "The Father's imperial rule is like a person who wanted to kill someone powerful. While still at home he drew his sword and thrust it into the wall to find out whether his hand would go in. Then he killed the powerful one." This is also coded pink. The average reader will wonder why the scholars chose these statements and not others; ultimately their judgments are highly subjective.

The first comprehensive study of agrapha by Alfred Resch (1889) collected 361 such sayings. Of these J. H. Ropes (1896) concluded that only fourteen were valuable and thirteen possibly valuable. The most important recent study of the agrapha is by Joachim Jeremias, *Unknown Sayings of Jesus*.[79] He selected eighteen sayings (including 1 Thess. 4:15ff.)[80] that he considered possibly authentic. A more critical evaluation has now been offered by O. Hofius, who regards only five agrapha as possibly authentic and four as probably authentic.[81] The possibly authentic agrapha include:

> From Oxyrhynchus Papyrus 840: "Woe to you blind who see not! You have washed yourself in water that is poured forth, in which dogs and swine lie night and day, and washed and scoured your outer skin, which harlots and flute girls also anoint, bathe, scour, and beautify to arouse desire in men, but

inwardly they are filled with scorpions and with [all manner of ev]il. But I and [my disciples], of whom you say that we have not [bathed, have bath]ed ourselves in the liv[ing and clean] water, which comes down from [the Father in heaven]."

Syriac *Liber Graduum*:: "As you were found so will you be taken away."

Gospel of *Thomas* 8: "The kingdom is like a wise fisherman who cast his net into the sea; he drew it up from the sea full of small fish; among them he found a large (and) good fish; that wise fisherman threw all the small fish down into the sea; he chose the large fish without regret."

Clement of Alexandria, Origen, and Eusebius: "Ask for the great things and God will add to you the little things."

Many Church Fathers: "Be approved money changers."

The four probably authentic agrapha are:

1. Codex Beza at Luke 6:5: "On the same day he saw a man working on the sabbath. Then said he unto him: 'Man, if thou knowest what you are doing, you are blessed. But if you do not know, you are cursed and a transgressor of the law."

2. Gospel of *Thomas* 82: "Whoever is near me is near the fire; whoever is far from me is far from the kingdom."

3. Gospel to the Hebrews: "And never be joyful save when you look upon your brother in love."

4. Oxyrhynchus Papyrus 1224: "[He that] stands far off [today] will tomorrow be [near you]."

Hofius agrees with the earlier study of Jeremias that there are few agrapha which can be placed on the level of those in the canonical Gospels. The vast majority of the agrapha are dependent on Gospel materials. Hofius concludes, "The palpable tie-in with the pre-existing tradition of dominical sayings [i.e., sayings of the Lord Jesus] makes it definitely doubtful, in my opinion, that the early Church freely, on a large scale, and without inhibitions, produced sayings of the earthly Jesus."[82] This is a direct criticism of the view of certain scholars, like those of the Jesus Seminar, who believe that many if not most of the sayings of Jesus in the Gospels were freely invented by the church.

Apocryphal Gospels

Irenaeus, the bishop of Lyons in France (c. 180), recognized only the four canonical Gospels.[83] He refers to "an unspeakable number of apocryphal and spurious writings, which they themselves [i.e., heretics] had forged, to bewilder the minds of the foolish." Origen (third century) notes, "The Church possesses four Gospels, heresy a great many."

Of the fifty some apocryphal Gospels, many are known simply by title or by a few scatterd quotations and allusions in the Church Fathers.[84] Most apocryphal

Gospels fall into two categories: (1) legendary, or (2) heretical. The former includes the so-called Infancy Gospels, which ascribe fanciful miracles to the child Jesus and which are important for the legendary background of the Virgin Mary.[85] The earliest Infancy Gospel, the Protevangelium of James (second century) describes Jesus' birth in a cave, a tradition also attested in Justin Martyr.

Many of the texts from Nag Hammadi betray a docetic view of Christ, which was common to the Gnostics; that is, they did not accept the idea that the Son of God was truly human but only seemed to be so and therefore could not really suffer.[86] Two texts from Nag Hammadi, *The Second Treatise (Logos) of the Great Seth* and the *Apocalypse of Peter*, for example, portray the Savior as laughing at the foolishness of the bystanders, who mistakenly believe that they have crucified him, when actually a substitute was on the cross.[87]

Until recently the Apocryphal Gospels were dated to the second century or later and were considered of almost no value for reconstructing the words and deeds of Jesus. The translation of the Gospel of *Thomas* in 1959 stimulated renewed interest in the study of these texts. Under the influence of Helmut Koester of Harvard, a radical revision has been undertaken by some scholars: (1) on the one hand, a devaluation of the canonical Gospels, and (2) on the other hand, a reevaluation of the apocryphal Gospels as at least worthy of equal consideration.[88] This has influenced scholars such as John Dominic Crossan to include among sources that he dates to A.D. 30–60 such works as *Thomas*, the *Egerton Gospel*, the *Gospel of the Hebrews*, and the *Gospel of Peter*.[89]

Koester believes that the *Egerton* [or Unknown] *Gospel*, which is preserved on a papyrus fragment dated c. 200,[90] provided some material for the Gospel of John.[91] But D. F. Wright points out in a detailed study that Koester's arguments regarding this "Unknown Gospel" (Pap. Egerton 2) are seriously flawed.[92]

Eusebius reports that Serapion, a bishop of Antioch about 200, had objected to the use of a *Gospel of Peter* because of its docetic view of Christ. This Gospel has been preserved on a substantial eighth-century parchment discovered at Akhmim in Upper Egypt in 1886.[93] Probably composed in Syria in the first half of the second century, it absolves Pilate of any blame and describes Jesus as coming out of the tomb with two angels, "and the heads of the two reaching to heaven, but that of him who was led of them by the hand overpassing the heavens."[94]

We have only quotations from the *Gospel of the Hebrews*, which may have been written in Egypt in the early second century. This Gospel, which was probably composed in Aramaic, was used by Jewish-Christians.[95] One of the verses quoted from this Gospel both by Origen and by Jerome has Jesus saying, "But now my mother the Holy Spirit took me by one of my hairs and carried me off to the great mountain Tabor." The word for *spirit* in Semitic languages, *ruha*, is feminine.

In 1958 professor Morton Smith of Columbia University discovered in the Mar Saba monastery southeast of Jerusalem an eighteenth-century Greek manuscript that claimed to be a letter from a famous church father, Clement of

Alexandria (160 –215). In a scholarly work that has persuaded most scholars, Smith defended the authenticity of the letter.[96]

In the letter Clement berates the Gnostic Carpocratians for their immorality.[97] He comments on the fact that they have perverted a copy of *Secret Mark*, which Mark allegedly wrote in addition to his Gospel. Clement quotes two fragments from this work, a longer section that resembles the raising of Lazarus (John 11) and a shorter section about an encounter with the young initiate's family in Jericho.

F. F. Bruce analyses the document as a patchwork "with its internal contradiction and confusion . . . a thoroughly artificial composition, quite out of keeping with Mark's quality as a story-teller."[98] But Smith himself believed that *Secret Mark*, though it was not written by Mark, was composed about 95 and was later used by the canonical Gospel of Mark. Helmut Koester, though differing in some details, has likewise accepted a similar dependence.[99] It is altogether astonishing that scholars who are so skeptical of the first-century Gospels should erect such a far-reaching theory on the basis of three paragraphs from an eighteenth-century manuscript![100]

Morton Smith, an ex-Episcopalian priest, proceeded on the basis of his manuscript discovery to expose the true nature of the Gospels and of Jesus in two popular books: *The Secret Gospel*[101] and *Jesus the Magician*.[102] In the former book Smith interpreted Jesus' encounter with a nude young man as an initiatory baptism that involved homosexuality.[103] In the latter work Smith, who took seriously the accusations of the *Talmud* and Celsus, characterized Jesus as a magician and the communion service as a magical ceremony.[104]

Conclusions

We have seen how otherwise sane scholars have sometimes irresponsibly treated texts outside of the New Testament in attempts to displace the Gospels' portrait of Jesus in accordance with their preconceptions. The theories of such scholars (e.g., Dupont-Sommer, Wilson, Allegro, Thiering, Eisenman, Smith) attract great media attention for a while, but cannot be taken seriously. More significant, but equally unconvincing, are attempts by important scholars as Koester and Crossan to displace the canonical Gospels with the apocryphal Gospels for the basis of rediscovering Jesus.

Even if we did not have the New Testament or Christian writings, we would be able to conclude from such non-Christian writings as Josephus, the *Talmud*, Tacitus, and Pliny the Younger that: (1) Jesus was a Jewish teacher; (2) many people believed that he performed healings and exorcisms; (3) he was rejected by the Jewish leaders; (4) he was crucified under Pontius Pilate in the reign of Tiberius; (5) despite this shameful death, his followers, who believed that he was still alive, spread beyond Palestine so that there were multitudes of them in Rome by A.D. 64; (6) all kinds of people from the cities and countryside—men and women, slave and free—worshiped him as God by the beginning of the second century.[105]

In spite of what some modern scholars claim, the extrabiblical evidence will not sustain their eccentric pictures of Jesus that attract such widespread media attention because of their novelty. In contrast to these idiosyncratic and ephemeral revisions, the orthodox view of Jesus still stands as the most credible portrait when all of the evidence is considered, including the corroboration offered by ancient sources outside the New Testament.

Notes

1. John P. Meier, "The Testimonium: Evidence for Jesus Outside the Bible," *Bible Review* 7 (June 1991): 20, reports, "Over the years, when editors and journalists have asked me to write about the historical Jesus, almost invariably the first question they raise is: Can you really prove he existed?"

2. A. Drews, *Die Christusmythe*, 3d ed. (1909; reprint, Jena: Diedrichs, 1924); English trans., *The Christ Myth* (London: Unwin, 1910). Other skeptics have included: P.-L. Couchoud, *The Creation of Christ*, trans. C. B. Bonner (London: Watts, 1939); G. A. Wells, *Did Jesus Exist?* (Buffalo: Prometheus, 1975); R. Augstein, *Jesus Son of Man*, trans. H. Young (New York: Urizen, 1977).

3. Craig A. Evans, "Life-of-Jesus Research and the Eclipse of Mythology," *TS* 54 (1993): 7, n. 22.

4. G. Vermes, *The Dead Sea Scrolls: Qumran in Perspective* (Philadelphia: Fortress, 1981); N. Fujita, *A Crack in the Jar* (Mahwah, N.J.: Paulist, 1986); J. A. Fitzmyer, *Responses to 101 Questions on the Dead Sea Scrolls* (New York: Paulist, 1992); H. Shanks, ed., *Understanding the Dead Sea Scrolls* (New York: Random House, 1992); Edward M. Cook, *Solving the Mysteries of the Dead Sea Scrolls* (Grand Rapids: Zondervan, 1994).

5. A. Dupont-Sommer, *The Dead Sea Scrolls* (New York: Macmillan, 1952).

6. Ibid., 99: "In every case where the resemblance compels or invites us to think of a borrowing, this was on the part of Christianity."

7. A. Dupont-Sommer, *The Essene Writings from Qumran* (Cleveland: World, 1962).

8. T. Gaster, *The Dead Sea Scriptures*, 3d ed. (Garden City, N.Y.: Doubleday, 1976), 324.

9. G. Vermes, *The Dead Sea Scrolls in English*, 3d ed. (Baltimore: Penguin, 1987), 288–89. See also J. G. Harris, *The Qumran Commentary on Habakkuk* (London: Mowbray, 1966), 41; W. H. Brownlee, *The Midrash Pesher of Habakkuk* (Missoula, Mont.: Scholars, 1979), 179.

10. E. Wilson, *The Scrolls from the Dead Sea* (New York: Oxford University Press, 1955).

11. E. Wilson, *Israel and the Dead Sea Scrolls* (New York: Farrar, Straus & Giroux, 1978), 386.

12. J. M. Allegro, "The Untold Story of the Dead Sea Scrolls," *Harper's Magazine* 232 (August 1966): 46–64.

13. For a response see, P. W. Skehan, "Capriccio Allegro or How Not to Learn in Ten Years," *Christian Century* (5 October 1966): 1201–13.

14. J. M. Allegro, *The Sacred Mushroom and the Cross* (Garden City, N.Y.: Doubleday, 1970).

15. Fifteen of Britain's leading Christian and Jewish scholars wrote a letter to the *London Times* (25 May, 1970), 9, denouncing Allegro's work as "an essay in fantasy rather than philology."

16. B. Thiering, *Jesus and the Riddle of the Dead Sea Scrolls* (San Francisco: Harper & Row, 1992). The publishers are said to have spent $30,000 to publicize this bizarre book.

17. The Magi were probably Babylonian astrologers. See my *Persia and the Bible* (Grand Rapids: Baker, 1990), ch. 13.

18. R. H. Eisenman, *James the Just in the Habakkuk Pesher* (Leiden: Brill, 1986).

19. R. Eisenman and M. Wise, *The Dead Sea Scrolls Uncovered* (Rockport, Mass.: Element, 1992).

20. M. Baigent and R. Leigh, *The Dead Sea Scrolls Deception* (New York: Summit, 1992).

21. See the effective refutation of their allegation by Hershel Shanks in *BAR* 17:6 (1991): 66–71.

22. G. Vermes, "The Oxford Forum for Qumran Research Seminar on the Rule of War from Cave 4 (4Q285)," *JJS* 43 (1992): 85–90. See also M. Bockmuehl, "A 'Slain Messiah' in 4Q Serekh Milhamah (4Q285)?" *TynBul* 43 (1992): 155–69; M. G. Abegg, Jr., "Messianic Hope and 4Q 285: A Reassessment," *JBL* 113 (1994): 81–91.

23. See my "Qumran New Testament Fragments," in *The New International Dictionary of Biblical Archaeology*, ed. E. M. Blaiklock and R. K. Harrison (Grand Rapids: Zondervan, 1983), 379–81.

24. C. P. Thiede, *The Earliest Gospel Manuscript? The Qumran Fragment 7Q5 and Its Significance for New Testament Studies* (London: Paternoster, 1992).

25. See D. B. Wallace, "7Q5: The Earliest NT Papyrus?" *WTJ* 56 (1994): 173–80.

26. J. H. Charlesworth, ed., *John and the Dead Sea Scrolls* (New York: Crossroad, 1990), xv.

27. J. H. Charlesworth, *Jesus and the Dead Sea Scrolls* (New York: Doubleday, 1993), 35–37.

28. See my "Josephus and the Scriptures," *Fides et Historia* 13 (1980): 42–63. See also: T. Rajak, *Josephus: The Historian and His Society* (Philadelphia: Fortress, 1984); L. H. Feldman and G. Hata, eds., *Josephus, Judaism and Christianity* (Detroit: Wayne State University Press, 1987); S. Mason, *Josephus and the New Testament* (Peabody, Mass.: Hendrickson, 1992); C. L. Rogers, Jr., *The Topical Josephus* (Grand Rapids: Zondervan, 1992).

29. L. H. Feldman, "Josephus," *The Anchor Bible Dictionary*, ed. D. N. Freedman (Nashville: Abingdon, 1992), 3:990. See C. H. H. Scobie, *John the Baptist* (Philadelphia: Fortress, 1964), 18; H. Hoehner, *Herod Antipas* (Cambridge: Cambridge University Press, 1972), 131–36.

30. See J. J. Gunther, "The Family of Jesus," *EvQ* 46 (1974): 25–41. The official Catholic position is that the Virgin Mary had no other children and that the "brothers" of Jesus were either half-brothers of Jesus through Joseph's earlier marriage (cf. Protevangelium of James) or that they were cousins (Jerome). The recent official catechism maintains that they are the sons of another Mary (see *Catechism of the Catholic Church* [Liguori: Liguori Publications, 1994], 126).

31. R. B. Ward, "James of Jerusalem in the First Two Centuries," *ANRW* 2, no. 26.1 (1992): 779–812.

32. See the article by Craig A. Evans in this book for more on this passage and on Josephus.

33. One of the few recent scholars to reject the passage on the basis of rather restrictive linguistic assumptions is J. N. Birdsall, "The Continuing Enigma of Josephus's Testimony About Jesus," *BJRL* 67 (1985): 608–22.

34. Meier, "Testimonium," 22. See also J. P. Meier, "Jesus in Josephus: A Modest Proposal," *CBQ* 52 (1990): 76–103; idem, *A Marginal Jew: Rethinking the Historical Jesus* (New York: Doubleday, 1991), ch. 3. For the extensive bibliography on this passage, see W. Bauer, "The Alleged Testimony of Josephus," in *New Testament Apocrypha*, ed. E. Hennecke and W. Schneemelcher (Philadelphia: Fortress, 1963), 1:436–37; P. Winter, "Josephus on Jesus and James . . . ," *The History of the Jewish People in the Age of Jesus Christ*, ed. G. Vermes and F. Millar (Edinburgh: Clark, 1973), 1:428–41; L. H. Feldman, *Josephus and Modern Scholarship: 1937–1980* (Berlin: de Gruyter, 1984), 679–703.

35. The first citation of Origen is from a comment on Matt. 10:17 in his *Commentary on Matthew*; the second is from *Contra Celsum* 1.47.

36. A Jewish scholar who has accepted the resurrection of Jesus without, however, accept-

ing him as the Messiah is P. Lapide, *The Resurrection of Jesus: A Jewish Perspective* (Minneapolis: Augsburg, 1983).

37. P. Winter, "Josephus on Jesus," *JHS* 1 (1968): 301. Another Jewish scholar, G. Vermes ("The Jesus Notice of Josephus Re-examined," *JJS* 38 [1987]: 10), similarly concludes: "All this seems to imply that Josephus deliberately chose words reflecting a not unsympathetic neutral stand." See also L. H. Feldman, "The *Testimonium Flavianum*: The State of the Question," *Christological Perspectives II*, ed. R. Berkey and S. Edwards (New York: Pilgrim, 1982), ch. 14.

38. S. Pines, *An Arabic Version of the Testimonium Flavianum and Its Implications* (Jerusalem: Israel Academy of Sciences and Humanities, 1971). On the other hand, a Slavonic or Old Russian version of Josephus, which is dated to between the seventh and eleventh centuries A.D., is regarded as a quite unreliable witness to Josephus. It was used by a Jewish scholar, R. Eisler, to portray Jesus as a political revolutionary. See F. F. Bruce, *Jesus & Christian Origins Outside the New Testament* (Grand Rapids: Eerdmans, 1974), ch. 3.

39. Cf. H. L. Strack and G. Stemberger, *Introduction to the Talmud and Midrash*, trans. M. Bockmuehl, (Minneapolis: Fortress, 1992). See Bruce, *Jesus & Christian Origins*, ch. 4; J. Klausner, *Jesus of Nazareth* (Boston: Beacon, 1925), 18–47.

40. According to Origen, the anti-Christian critic Celsus expressed similar views late in the second century: "It was by magic that he was able to perform the miracles which he appeared to have done" (*Contra Celsum* 1.6); H. Chadwick, *Origen, Contra Celsum* (Cambridge: Cambridge University Press, 1980), 10.

41. Joshua ben Perahya occurs prominently in the Jewish Aramaic magic-bowl texts of the sixth century A.D. See my "Aramaic Magic Bowls," *JAOS* 85 (1965): 511–23.

42. This name is probably a play on the Greek word *parthenos*, "virgin." Origen also reports a similar charge made by Celsus: "Let us return, however, to the words put into the mouth of the Jew, where the mother of Jesus is described as having been turned out by the carpenter who was betrothed to her, as she had been convicted of adultery and had a child by a certain soldier named Panthera." *Contra Celsum* 1.32; Chadwick, *Origen*, 31; cf. R. J. Hoffmann, *Celsus on the True Doctrine* (New York: Oxford University Press, 1987), 57.

43. Klausner, *Jesus of Nazareth*, 18–47.

44. Ibid., 47–54. The earliest witness to the *Toledoth* is by the Archbishop of Lyons in 826; scholars believe that the *Toledoth* was composed around the fifth or sixth century.

45. E. Bammel, "Christian Origins in Jewish Tradition," *NTS* 13 (1967): 317–35.

46. G. H. Twelftree, "Jesus in Jewish Tradition," *Gospel Perspectives V*, ed. D. Wenham (Sheffield: JSOT, 1985), 324.

47. M. Wilcox, "Jesus in the Light of His Jewish Environment," *ANRW* 2, no. 25.1 (1982): 133.

48. See J. E. A. Crake, "Early Christians and Roman Law," *Phoenix* 9 (1965): 61–70; T. D. Barnes, "Legislation Against the Christians," *JRS* 58 (1968): 34–43; L. Herrmann, *Chrestos* (Bruxelles: Latomus, 1970); P. Winter, "Tacitus and Pliny on Christianity," *Klio* 52 (1970): 497–502; D. L. Stockton, "Christianos ad Leonem," *The Ancient Historians and His Materials*, ed. B. Levick (Farnborough: Gregg Intl., 1975), ch. 14. Extensive bibliographies on these sources are provided by M. Stern, *Greek and Latin Authors on Jews and Judaism II: From Tacitus to Simplicius* (Jerusalem: The Israel Academy of Sciences and Humanities, 1980).

49. See M. L. W. Laistner, *The Greater Roman Historians* (Berkeley: University of California Press, 1963). Comparing the sources for Tiberius and the sources for Jesus,

the distinguished Roman historian, A. N. Sherwin-White, *Roman Society and Roman Law in the New Testament* (Oxford: Clarendon, 1965), 187, exclaims: "So, it is astonishing that while Graeco-Roman historians have been growing in confidence, the twentieth-century study of the Gospel narratives, starting from no less promising material, has taken so gloomy a turn in the development of form-criticism . . . that the historical Christ is unknowable and the history of his mission cannot be written." The Jewish scholar Joseph Klausner, *From Jesus to Paul* (Boston: Beacon, 1961), 260, declares: "If we had ancient sources like those in the Gospels for the history of Alexander the Great or Julius Ceasar for example, we should not cast any doubt upon them whatsoever."

50. The dating system we use, B.C. = Before Christ and A.D. = Anno Domini, that is, Year of the Lord, was devised by a monk, who miscalculated the reign of Augustus. See J. Finegan, *Handbook of Biblical Chronology* (Princeton: Princeton University Press, 1964); H. Hoehner, *Chronological Aspects of the Life of Christ* (Grand Rapids: Zondervan, 1977); J. Vardaman and E. Yamauchi, eds., *Chronos, Kairos, Christos* (Winona Lake, Ind.: Eisenbrauns, 1989); C. J. Humphreys, "The Star of Bethlehem, a Comet in 5 B.C. and the Date of Christ's Birth," *TynBul* 43 (1992): 31–56.

51. See J. M. Lawrence, "Publius Sulpicius Quirinius and the Syrian Census," *Restoration Quarterly* 34 (1992): 193–205.

52. Pontius Pilate is described in Josephus and in Philo. It is sometimes alleged that their portrait of an inflexible Pilate contradicts the Gospels' portrayal of a vacillating governor yielding to the pressures of a Jewish mob. See E. Yamauchi, "Historical Notes on the Trial and Crucifixion of Jesus Christ," *CT* 15 (9 April 1971): 6–11. Some scholars, such as P. Maier, "Sejanus, Pilate, and the Date of the Crucifixion," *Church History* 37 (1968): 1–11, have pointed out that Pilate's changed behavior can be attributed to the death of his patron, Sejanus, in A.D. 31. B .C. McGing, "Pontius Pilate and the Sources," *CBQ* 53 (1991): 416–38, argues that the sources are not contradictory.

53. C. J. Humphreys and G. Waddington, "The Jewish Calendar, a Lunar Eclipse, and the Date of Christ's Crucifixion," *TynBul* 43 (1992): 331–51.

54. M. Sordi, *The Christians and the Roman Empire* (Norman: University of Oklahoma Press, 1986), 16, speculates that Pilate must have sent a report to Tiberius not about the death of Jesus but about the spread of the Christian movement.

55. F. Scheidweiler, "The Gospel of Nicodemus, Acts of Pilate and Christ's Descent into Hell," in *New Testament Apocrypha*, ed. E. Hennecke and W. Schneemelcher, 1:444–45.

56. *Vita Claudius* 25.4. See L. H. Feldman, *Jew & Gentile in the Ancient World* (Princeton: Princeton University Press, 1993), 304; Stern, *Greek and Latin Authors*, 2:116.

57. A literal understanding of Suetonius was the basis for the novel view that Jesus wound up in Rome; see R. Graves and J. Podro, *Jesus in Rome: A Historical Conjecture* (London: Cassell, 1957).

58. Stern, *Greek and Latin Authors*, 2:116; A. Momigliano, *Claudius: The Emperor and His Achievement* (Cambridge: Heffer, 1961), 33; E. M. Smallwood, *The Jews Under Roman Rule from Pompey to Diocletian* (Leiden: Brill, 1981), 211; M. Harris, "References to Jesus in Early Classical Authors," in *Gospel Perspectives V*, 354–55; B. Levick, *Claudius* (New Haven: Yale University Press, 1990), 121.

59. F. J. Foakes Jackson and K. Lake, *The Beginnings of Christianity: The Acts of the Apostles* (1932; reprint, Grand Rapids: Baker, 1966), 5:459–60.

60. F. F. Bruce, "Christianity Under Claudius," *BJRL* 44 (1961): 316–17; C. J. Hemer, *The Book of Acts in the Setting of Hellenistic History* (Tübingen: Mohr, 1989), 167–68.

61. W. H. C. Frend, *Martyrdom and Persecution in the Early Church* (New York: New York University Press, 1967), 122; B. W. Winter, "The Imperial Cult," and A. D. Clarke, "Rome and Italy," *The Book of Acts in Its Graeco-Roman Setting*, ed. D. W. J. Gill and C. Gempf (Grand Rapids: Eerdmans, 1994), 99 and 469–71.

62. S. Benko, "The Edict of Claudius of A.D. 49 and the Instigator Chrestus," *TZ* 25 (1969): 406–18; idem, "Pagan Criticism of Christianity During the First Two Centuries A.D.," *ANRW* 2, no. 23.2 (1980): 1058–62. See also D. Slingerland, "Chrestus: Christus?" in *New Perspectives on Ancient Judaism*, vol. 4, ed. J. Neusner et al. (Lanham, Md.: University Press of America, 1989), ch. 10.

63. M. T. Griffin, *Nero, the End of a Dynasty* (New Haven: Yale University Press, 1985), 126–33.

64. Tacitus, *Annals* 15.44.

65. See R. L. Wilken, *The Christians as the Romans Saw Them* (New Haven: Yale University Press, 1984), chs. 1–2.; F. G. Downing, "Pliny's Prosecution of Christians: Revelation and 1 Peter," *JSNT* 34 (1988): 105–23.

66. The phrase *quasi deo* is interpreted by Harris, "References to Jesus," 347, as highlighting "the distinctiveness of Jesus in relation to other known gods. In what did that distinctiveness consist? In the fact that, unlike other gods who were worshipped, Christ was a person who had lived on earth."

67. Pliny the Younger, *Letters*, 10.96.

68. See my "Agrapha" in *ISBE*, ed. G. W. Bromiley (Grand Rapids: Eerdmans, 1979), 1:69–71.

69. An important edition of various agrapha, including citations in the original languages and translations, arranged according to different categories such as "Parables," "Prophetic and Apocalyptic Sayings," "Wisdom Sayings," etc., is W. Stroker, ed., *Extracanonical Sayings of Jesus* (Atlanta: Scholars, 1989).

70. See my "Logia" in *ISBE*, ed. G. W. Bromiley (Grand Rapids: Eerdmans, 1986), 3:152–54.

71. J. A. Fitzmyer, "The Oxyrhynchus Logoi of Jesus and the Coptic Gospel According to Thomas," *TS* 20 (1959): 505–60; reprinted in his *Essays on the Semitic Background of the New Testament* (Missoula, Mont.: Scholars, 1974), ch. 15.

72. This cache was discovered in 1945 at Nag Hammadi in Upper Egypt. See J. M. Robinson, "The Discovery of the Nag Hammadi Codices," *BA* 42 (1979): 206–24. All of these texts, including the Gospel of *Thomas*, have been translated into English in J. M. Robinson, ed., *The Nag Hammadi Library*, 3d ed. (San Francisco: HarperSan Francisco, 1990). Cf. my "The Nag Hammadi Library," *Journal of Library History* 22 (1987): 425–41.

73. See E. Yamauchi, *Pre-Christian Gnosticism*, 2d ed. (Grand Rapids: Baker, 1983), 89–91, 211–13. M. J. Desjardins, "Where Was the Gospel of Thomas Written?" *Toronto Journal of Theology* 8 (1992): 121–33, suggests that it was written in Antioch.

74. K. Snodgrass, "The Gospel of Thomas: A Secondary Gospel," *The Second Century* 7 (1989–90): 38. That this is also true of the sayings contained in the other Nag Hammadi tractates is the conclusion of C. Tuckett, *Nag Hammadi and the Gospel Tradition* (Edinburgh: Clark, 1986).

75. See especially J. M. Robinson and H. Koester, *Trajectories Through Early Christianity* (Philadelphia: Fortress, 1971).

76. For a critique of H. Koester's views, see C. M. Tuckett, "Q and Thomas, Evidence of a Primitive 'Wisdom Gospel'?" *Ephemerides Theologicae Lovanienses* 67 (1991): 346–60.

77. R. W. Funk, R. W. Hoover, and the Jesus Seminar, *The Five Gospels: What Did Jesus Really Say?* (New York: Macmillan, 1993), 496.

78. Ibid., 523–24. Items in parentheses are added to aid in the translation.

79. J. Jeremias, *Unknown Sayings of Jesus*, 2d ed. (1957; reprint, London: SPCK, 1964).

80. Jeremias made this conclusion from the phrase "the Lord's own word" in 1 Thess. 4:15. Other scholars interpret this not as an agraphon but as a revelation to the church through a prophet. See Robert L. Thomas, "1 Thessalonians," in F. Gaebelein, ed., *The Expositor's Bible Commentary*, vol. 11 (Grand Rapids: Zondervan, 1978), 276–77.

81. O. Hofius, "Unknown Sayings of Jesus," in *The Gospel and the Gospels*, ed. P. Stuhlmacher (Grand Rapids: Eerdmans, 1991), 336–60. Bracketed items are restorations in the fragmentary texts.

82. Ibid., 359.

83. See B. M. Metzger, *The Canon of the New Testament* (Oxford: Clarendon, 1987), 154–55; cf. W. R. Farmer and D. M. Farkasfalvy, *The Formation of the New Testament Canon* (New York: Paulist, 1983), 47.

84. See my "Apocryphal Gospels" in *ISBE*, 1:181–88.

85. The standard edition is the two-volume work of E. Hennecke and W. Schneemelcher, *New Testament Apocrypha*, trans. R. McL. Wilson (Philadelphia: Westminster, 1965).

86. See my "The Crucifixion and Docetic Christology," *CTQ* 46 (1982): 1–20. The idea that Jesus did not die on the cross was incorporated into the Qur'an (4:156–57) by Muhammad.

87. Hence the title of John Dart's book, *The Laughing Savior* (New York: Harper & Row, 1976).

88. H. Koester, "Apocryphal and Canonical Gospels," *HTR* 73 (1980): 105–30. This view has also been promoted by his former students, such as Ron Cameron, *The Other Gospels: Non-Canonical Gospel Texts* (Philadelphia: Westminster, 1982).

89. J. D. Crossan, *The Historical Jesus: The Life of a Mediterranean Jewish Peasant* (San Francisco: HarperSanFrancisco, 1991).

90. H. Koester, *Ancient Christian Gospels* (Philadelphia: Trinity Press, 1990), 206–16.

91. H. Koester, *Introduction to the New Testament II: History and Literature of Early Christianity* (Philadelphia: Fortress, 1982), 222.

92. D. F. Wright, "Apocryphal Gospels: The 'Unknown Gospel' (Pap. Egerton 2) and the Gospel of Peter," *Gospel Perspectives* V, 207–32; cf. also his, "Papyrus Egerton 2 (the *Unknown Gospel*)—Part of the *Gospel of Peter*?" *The Second Century* 5 (1985–86): 129–50. See J. Jeremias, "An Unknown Gospel with Johannine Elements," in *New Testament Apocrypha*, 1:95; Metzger, *The Canon of the New Testament*, 167–69.

93. Bruce, *Jesus & Christian Origins*, 88–93; Hennecke and Schneemelcher, *New Testament Apocrypha*, 1:179–87.

94. For a criticism of Koester's arguments for a positive evaluation of this Gospel, see the articles by D. F. Wright cited in n.90. John Dominic Crossan, *The Cross That Spoke: The Origins of the Passion Narrative* (San Francisco: Harper & Row, 1988), has extracted from the *Gospel of Peter* a so-called Cross Gospel, which he claims was the main source for the Passion narratives of the canonical Gospels. For a critique of this radical proposal, see R. E. Brown's Appendix I, "The Gospel of Peter—A Noncanonical Passion Narrative," in his *The Death of the Messiah* (New York: Doubleday, 1994), 2:1317–49. See also the criticisms of A. Kirk, "Examining Properties: Another Look at the *Gospel of Peter*'s Relationship to the New Testament Gospels," *NTS* 40 (1994): 572–95.

95. Bruce, *Jesus and Christian Origins*, 99–105; Metzger, *The Canon of the New Testament*,

169–70; P. Vielhauer, "Jewish-Christian Gospels," in *New Testament Apocrypha*, 1:117–65.

96. M. Smith, *Clement of Alexandria and a Secret Gospel of Mark* (Cambridge: Harvard University Press, 1973); see also his "Clement of Alexandria and Secret Mark: The Score at the End of the First Decade," *HTR* 75 (1982): 449–61. It is ironic that one of the skeptics was A. D. Nock of Harvard University, to whom Smith had dedicated the book. E. Osborn, a leading authority on this Church Father, in his "Clement of Alexandria: A Review of Research, 1957–1982," *The Second Century* 3 (1983): 222–23, views the letter as a pious forgery.

97. See my *Gnostic Ethics and Mandaean Origins* (Cambridge: Harvard University Press, 1970) for remarks on both licentious and ascetic groups of Gnostics.

98. F. F. Bruce, *The "Secret" Gospel of Mark* (London: Athlone, 1974), 12.

99. Koester, *Ancient Christian Gospels*, 273–303. Cf. also John D. Crossan, *Four Other Gospels* (Minneapolis: Winston, 1985); H.-M. Schenke, "The Mystery of the Gospel of Mark," *The Second Century* 4 (1984): 65–82.

100. For a clear exposition of the issues, see C. B. Smith II, "Mark the Evangelist and His Relationship to Alexandrian Christianity in Biblical, Historical, and Traditional Literature" (master's thesis, Miami University, 1992). For a technical review of these claims, see F. Neirynck, "The Apocryphal Gospels and the Gospel of Mark," *The New Testament in Early Christianity*, ed. J. -M. Sevrin (Leuven: Leuven University Press, 1989), 123–75.

101. M. Smith, *The Secret Gospel* (New York: Harper & Row, 1973).

102. M. Smith, *Jesus the Magician* (San Francisco: Harper & Row, 1978).

103. Smith, *The Secret Gospel*, 114. See my review, "A Secret Gospel of Jesus as 'Magus'?" *Christian Scholar's Review* 4 (1975): 238–51.

104. For a review of these claims, see my "Magic or Miracle? Demons, Diseases and Exorcisms," in *Gospel Perspectives VI: The Miracles of Jesus*, ed. D. Wenham and C. Blomberg, (Sheffield: JSOT, 1986), 89–183.

105. We have better historical documentation for Jesus than for the founder of any other religion. Although the *Gathas* of Zoroaster (c. 1000 B.C.) are believed to be authentic, most of the Zoroastrian scriptures were not put into writing until after the third century A.D. The most popular Parsi biography of Zoroaster was written in A.D. 1278. The scriptures of Buddha (sixth century B.C.) were not put into writing until after the Christian era, and the first biography of Buddha was written in the first century A.D. Although we have the undoubted sayings of Muhammad (A.D. 570–632) in the Qur'an, the first biography of the prophet was not written until 767, over a century after his death.

CONCLUSION:
WHAT DOES ALL OF THIS MEAN?

MICHAEL J. WILKINS AND J. P. MORELAND

In our view the arguments of the preceding chapters combine to answer suffi-ciently the salvos launched against Jesus of Nazareth by radical critics like those in the Jesus Seminar. They also provide a positive case for the integrity of the biblical witness. To put the matter in its simplest terms, the New Testament claims about Jesus of Nazareth are true, and it is reasonable to believe this is so. We hope that this book has whetted your appetite for the intellectual aspect of the quest for God. If you are to live a life of integrity before God, it is impera-tive that your beliefs be true and that your questions have intellectually satisfy-ing answers. Of course we cannot settle all of the important issues in one volume, even if we were able. Therefore, if you have further questions, please consult the select bibliography included at the end of the volume. The resources there will guide you into a further study of this most important topic.

What about the spiritual implications of this material? All of us come to this discussion with our own life story and history. Some of us have had the benefit of a stable family, a steady income, a solid education, and a fulfilling career. Others of us have had to undergo a life story that begs for fairness and an equal chance. Currently in the modern world there is untold suffering and a growing sense of hopelessness and fragmentation. At every turn assaults are being leveled at time-tested biblical principles for human flourishing. The upshot of such assaults is that many people are left without direction in life, without hope in the midst of suffering, or without a purpose for why we are here.

Jesus Christ provides the only truly satisfying solution to the dilemma of the modern person. This is why the ideas of the Jesus Seminar are so devastating. They are not only intellectually insufficient, but they leave people spiritually bankrupt and hopeless. If we adopt the portrait of Jesus that is offered in some of their works, we have simply a wise teacher, a religious sage, a pious spinner of tales and proverbs, a revolutionary figure, a Jewish peasant and Cynic preacher, or a spirit-person. This is the kind of Jesus who cannot offer eternal salvation or the power to live life as we know we should. Fortunately, as we have seen, the con-clusions of the Jesus Seminar do not stand up to careful scrutiny.

Jesus Christ came to offer a kingdom in which human life can be lived with such richness and sufficiency that genuine hope can be offered to anyone, irre-spective of his or her circumstances of life. He offers a purpose for life, to bring pleasure to the One who made us, to enjoy the richness of his fellowship, and to spread the good news about Jesus Christ to the ends of the earth. He offers us for-giveness for the darkness and failings that come from the depths of our hearts. And who among us does not need this forgiveness each day of our lives? It has been the testimony of millions throughout the centuries that through certain spiritual practices his reality, guidance, and companionship can be our daily source of nourishment. He has left us clear moral guidelines about the funda-mental issues of life. He formed a community of those who have gathered together in his name, in which we can find the type of human relationships we were made to experience. Make no mistake about it; the demands of following Jesus Christ are indeed taxing. But it needs to be said in this context that the price of not following him is higher still.

What does all of this have to do with you? Simply this. All that Jesus came to offer in the ancient world is available to you in the modern world. If you are not a follower of Jesus Christ, then you now have open to you a life of fellowship with the risen Christ in his kingdom. But you must begin this life by placing your personal trust in Jesus Christ and his gospel. If you are seeking for a relationship with the God of this universe, then we challenge you to consider the claim of Jesus Christ to be God who has entered history to offer you a relationship with him. Anyone of us authors or those of our persuasion would gladly interact with you personally about how you can enter into that relationship, or we would be eager to direct you to someone in your area who would be happy to tell you more. Seek out someone with whom you can interact. Don't let this rest. This is an issue of eternal significance.

If you are already a follower of Jesus Christ, we have tried to offer you an intellectual response to a set of difficulties that might hinder you, or challenge you, in your spiritual journey. It remains your privilege and responsibility to rededicate yourself to growing as Jesus' disciple. We as the authors of this book have already made our choice and embarked on our journeys. What will your choice be? The world we face at the beginning of the third millennium needs to hear the message of Jesus Christ. Our prayer is that you have had your faith strengthened as you wrestled with the issues of this book. We pray that you will now go forward better equipped to live life to the fullest in the way that God intended it to be lived. And we further pray that you will join us as we tell the world that Jesus is indeed the Christ, the Son of the Living God, the answer to the most basic needs of the modern person.

A Select Bibliography for Further Study

[B] = Basic [I] = Intermediate [A] = Advanced

I. The Historical Jesus

A. Studies in the Gospels

[I]   Anderson, Norman. *The Teaching of Jesus.* The Jesus Library. Michael Green, series editor. Downers Grove, Ill.: InterVarsity, 1983.

[B]   Barnett, Paul. *Is the New Testament History?* London: Hodder & Stoughton, 1986.

[B]   Black, David Alan, and David Dockery. *New Testament Criticism and Interpretation.* Grand Rapids: Zondervan, 1991.

[I]   Blomberg, Craig. *The Historical Reliability of the Gospels.* Downers Grove, Ill.: InterVarsity, 1987.

[B]   Bockmuehl, Markus. *This Jesus: Martyr, Lord, Messiah.* Edinburgh: T. & T. Clark, 1994.

[A]   Burridge, Richard A. *What Are the Gospels? A Comparison with Graeco-Roman Biography.* Cambridge: Cambridge Univ. Press, 1992.

[I]   Charlesworth, James H. *Jesus within Judaism.* New York: Doubleday, 1988.

[A]   Chilton, Bruce, and Craig A. Evans, eds. *Studying the Historical Jesus: Evaluations of the State of Current Research.* Leiden: Brill, 1994.

[A]   Ellis, E. Earle. "New Directions in Form Criticism." Pp. 25–52 in *Prophecy and Hermeneutic.* Tübingen: Mohr, 1978.

[A]   _____. "Gospels Criticism." Pp. 237–253 in *The Gospel and the Gospels,* ed. P. Stuhlmacher. Grand Rapids: Eerdmans, 1991.

[B]   France, R. T. *The Evidence for Jesus.* Downers Grove, Ill.: InterVarsity, 1986.

[A]   France, R. T., and David Wenham. *Gospel Perspectives I: Studies of History and Tradition in the Four Gospels.* Sheffield: JSOT, 1980.

[I]   Goetz, S. C., and Craig L. Blomberg. "The Burden of Proof," *JSNT* 11 (1981): 39–83.

[B, I, A] Green, Joel B., Scot McKnight, and I. Howard Marshall. *Dictionary of Jesus and the Gospels* (Downers Grove, Ill.: InterVarsity, 1992).

[I]   Habermas, Gary R. *Ancient Evidence for the Life of Jesus: Historical Records of His Death and Resurrection.* Nashville: Thomas Nelson, 1984.

[A]   _____. "Resurrection Claims in Non-Christian Religions." *Religious Studies* 25 (1989): 167–77.

[I]   Hagner, Donald A. *The Jewish Reclamation of Jesus.* Grand Rapids: Zondervan, 1984.

[I]   Harvey, A. E. *Jesus and the Constraints of History.* Philadelphia: Westminster, 1982.

[B]   Hays, Richard B. "The Corrected Jesus," *First Things* 43 (1994): 43–48.

[I]   Marshall, I. Howard. *Luke: Historian and Theologian.* Rev. ed. Grand Rapids: Zondervan, 1989.

[I]   _____. *The Origins of New Testament Christology.* Updated ed. Downers Grove, Ill.: InterVarsity, 1990.

[A]   Meier, John P. *A Marginal Jew: Rethinking the Historical Jesus.* Volume 1. New York: Doubleday, 1991.

[I]   Meyer, Ben F. *The Aims of Jesus.* London: SCM, 1979.

[I] Riesner, Rainer. "Jesus as Preacher and Teacher." Pp. 185–210 in *Jesus and the Oral Gospel Tradition*. JSNTMS 64. Ed. Henry Wansbrough. Sheffield: Sheffield Academic Press, 1991.

[I] Sanders, E. P. *The Historical Figure of Jesus*. London: Penguin, 1993.

[I] Witherington, Ben, III. *The Christology of Jesus*. Minneapolis: Fortress, 1990.

[B] Wright, N.T. *Who Was Jesus?* Grand Rapids: Eerdmans, 1992.

B. Miracles

[I] Brown, Colin. *Miracles and the Critical Mind*. Grand Rapids: Eerdmans, 1984.

[B] Geisler, Norman L. *Miracles and Modern Thought*. Grand Rapids: Zondervan, 1982.

[I] Geivett, Douglas, and Gary Habermas, eds. *Miracles: Has God Acted in History?* Downers Grove, Ill.: InterVarsity, forthcoming.

[B] Lewis, C. S. *Miracles: A Preliminary Study*. New York: Macmillan, 1947.

[A] Swinburne, Richard. *The Concept of Miracle*. New York: St. Martin's, 1970.

[A] Wenham, David, and Craig Blomberg, eds. *Gospel Perspectives VI: The Miracles of Jesus*. Sheffield: JSOT, 1986.

C. The Resurrection

[A] Alsup, John. *The Post-Resurrection Appearances of the Gospel Tradition*. Stuttgart: Calwer Verlag, 1975.

[A] Bode, Edward Lynn. *The First Easter Morning*. Analecta Biblica 45. Rome: Biblical Institute, 1970.

[B] Craig, William Lane. *The Son Arises*. Chicago: Moody, 1981.

[A] ____. *The Historical Argument for the Resurrection of Jesus*. Lewiston, N.Y.: Edwin Mellin, 1985.

[B] ____. *Knowing the Truth about the Resurrection*. Ann Arbor: Servant, 1988.

[A] ____. *Assessing the New Testament Evidence for the Historicity of the Resurrection of Jesus*. Lewiston, N.Y.: Edwin Mellin, 1989.

[A] Gundry, Robert H. *Soma in Biblical Theology*. Cambridge: Cambridge Univ. Press, 1976.

[I] Paley, William. *A View of the Evidences of Christianity*. 2 vols. 5th ed. Rep. ed.: Westmead, England: Gregg, 1970.

D. Jesus Outside the New Testament

[B] Bruce, F. F. *Jesus and Christian Origins Outside the New Testament*. Grand Rapids: Eerdmans, 1974.

[I] Cameron, Ron. *The Other Gospels: Non-Canonical Gospel Texts*. Philadelphia: Westminster, 1982.

[I] Charlesworth, J. H., ed. *Jesus and the Dead Sea Scrolls*. New York: Doubleday, 1992.

[I] Cook, E. M. *Solving the Mysteries of the Dead Sea Scrolls*. Grand Rapids: Zondervan, 1994.

[A] Hennecke, E., and W. Schneemelcher, eds. *New Testament Apocrypha*. 2 volumes. Philadelphia: Fortress, 1963 and 1965.

[I] Klausner, J. *Jesus of Nazareth*. Boston: Beacon, 1925.

[I] Rogers, C. L., Jr. *The Topical Josephus*. Grand Rapids: Zondervan, 1992.

[B] Maier, P. L. *Josephus: The Essential Writings*. Grand Rapids: Kregel, 1988.

[I] Robinson, J. M., ed. *The Nag Hammadi Library*. 3d ed. San Francisco: Harper & Row, 1990.

[B] Shanks, H., ed. *Understanding the Dead Sea Scrolls*. New York: Random House, 1992.

[I] Sordi, M. *The Christians and the Roman Empire*. Norman, Okla.: Univ. of Oklahoma Press, 1986.

Bibliography

[A]   Stroker, W., ed. *Extracanonical Sayings of Jesus*. Atlanta: Scholars, 1989.
[A]   Wenham, D., ed. *Gospel Perspectives V: The Jesus Tradition Outside the Gospels.* Sheffield: JSOT, 1985.
[I]   Wilken, R. L. *The Christians As the Romans Saw Them.* New Haven: Yale Univ. Press, 1984.
[B]   Yamauchi, E. "Agrapha" and "Apocrypahl Gospels." Pp. 69–71 and 181–88 in *International Standard Bible Encyclopedia.* Ed. G. W. Bromiley. Volume 1. Grand Rapids: Eerdmans, 1979.
[B]   Wright, N. T. *Who Was Jesus?* Grand Rapids: Eerdmans, 1992.

II. The Existence of God

A. The Case for God's Reality

[B]   Craig, William Lane. *The Existence of God and the Beginning of the Universe.* San Bernardino, Calif.: Here's Life, 1979.
[A]   Geivett, R. Douglas, and Brendan Sweetman, eds. *Contemporary Perspectives on Religious Epistemology.* New York: Oxford Univ. Press, 1992.
[B]   Lewis, C. S. *Mere Christianity.* New York: Macmillan, 1943; rev. ed., 1952.
[I]   Moreland, J. P., and Kai Nielsen. *Does God Exist?* Buffalo: Prometheus, 1993.
[I]   Moreland, J. P. *Scaling the Secular City.* Grand Rapids: Baker, 1987.
[B]   Nash, Ronald. *Faith and Reason.* Grand Rapids: Zondervan, 1988.
[A]   Swinburne, Richard. *The Existence of God.* Oxford: Clarendon, 1979.

B. Defenses of Christian Particularism

[I]   Craig, William Lane. " 'No Other Name': A Middle Knowledge Perspective on the Exclusivity of Salvation through Christ." *Faith and Philosophy* 6 (April 1989): 172–88.
[I]   ____. "Should Peter Go to the Mission Field?" *Faith and Philosophy* 10 (April 1993): 261–65.
[B]   Fernando, Ajith. *The Christian's Attitude Toward World Religions.* Wheaton, Ill.: Tyndale, 1987.
[I]   Geivett, R. Douglas. "John Hick's Approach to Religious Pluralism." *Proceedings of the Wheaton College Theology Conference* 1 (Spring 1992): 39–55.
[I]   Geivett, R. Douglas, and W. Gary Phillips. "Christian Particularism: A Particularist Approach." In *Religious Pluralism: Four Views.* Ed. Timothy L. Phillips and Dennis R. Okholm. Grand Rapids: Zondervan, 1995.
[I]   Nash, Ronald H. *Is Jesus the Only Savior?* Grand Rapids: Zondervan, 1994.
[A]   Plantinga, Alvin. "A Defense of Religious Exclusivism." Pp. 529–44 in *Philosophy of Religion: An Anthology.* 2d ed. Ed. Louis P. Pojman. Belmont, Calif.: Wadsworth, 1994.
[B]   Richard, Ramesh P. *The Population of Heaven.* Chicago: Moody, 1994.
[I]   Stetson, Brad. *Pluralism and Particularity in Religious Belief.* Westport, Conn.: Praeger, 1994.

C. The Expectation of Revelation

[I]   Anselm, Saint. *Cur Deus Homo?* In *St. Anselm: Basic Writings.* Trans. S. N. Deane. 2d ed. LaSalle, Ill.: Open Court, 1962.
[B]   Barnes, Albert. *The Atonement.* 1860. Reprint: Minneapolis: Bethany, 1980.
[B]   Gerstner, John H. *Reasons for Faith.* Grand Rapids: Baker, 1967.
[B]   Howe, Reuel L. *Man's Need and God's Action.* Greenwich, Conn.: Seabury, 1953.
[I]   Taylor, Nathaniel W. *Lectures on the Moral Government of God.* 2 vols. New York: Clark, Austin & Smith, 1859.

Bibliography

[I]   Pedraz, Juan L. *I Wish I Could Believe*. New York: Alba House, 1983.
[A]   Swinburne, Richard. *Revelation: From Metaphor to Analogy*. Oxford: Clarendon, 1992.
[A]   ____. *The Christian God*. Oxford: Clarendon, 1994.
[B]   Walker, James B. *The Philosophy of the Plan of Salvation*. 1887. Reprint: Minneapolis.: Bethany, n.d.

D. The Problem of Evil
[B]   Geisler, Norman L. *The Roots of Evil*. Grand Rapids, Michigan: 1978.
[I]   Geivett, Douglas. *Evil and the Evidence for God*. Philadelphia: Temple Univ. Press, 1993.
[B]   Lewis, C. S. *The Problem of Pain*. New York: Macmillan, 1962.
[A]   Plantinga, Alvin. *God, Freedom, and Evil*. New York: Harper & Row, 1974.

E. Christianity and Science
[A]   Denton, Michael. *Evolution: A Theory in Crisis*. London: Burnett Books, 1985.
[B]   Johnson, Phillip. *Darwin on Trial*. 2d ed. Downers Grove, Ill.: InterVarsity, 1993.
[A]   Moreland, J. P. *Christianity and the Nature of Science*. Grand Rapids: Baker, 1989.
[I]   ____, ed. *The Creation Hypothesis*. Downers Grove, Ill.: InterVarsity, 1993.
[I]   Pearcey, Nancy R., and Charles B. Thaxton. *The Soul of Science*. Wheaton, Ill.: Crossway Books, 1994.
[B]   Ratzsch, Del. *Philosophy of Science*. Downers Grove, Ill.: InterVarsity, 1986.

F. The Devotional Experiment and Religious Experience
[A]   Alston, William P. *Perceiving God: The Epistemology of Religious Experience*. Ithaca, N.Y.: Cornell Univ. Press, 1991.
[A]   Franks Davis, Caroline. "The Devotional Experiment." *Religious Studies* 22 (March 1986): 15–28.
[A]   ____. *The Evidential Force of Religious Experience*. Oxford: Clarendon, 1989.
[I]   Lycan, William G., and George N. Schlesinger. "You Bet Your Life: Pascal's Wager Defended." Pp. 270–82 in *Contemporary Perspectives on Religious Epistemology*. Ed. R. Douglas Geivett and Brendan Sweetman. New York: Oxford Univ. Press, 1992.
[I]   Morris, Thomas V. *Making Sense of It All: Pascal and the Meaning of Life*. Grand Rapids: Eerdmans, 1992.
[A]   ____. "Pascalian Wagering." Pp. 257–69 in *Contemporary Perspectives on Religious Epistemology*. Ed. R. Douglas Geivett and Brendan Sweetman. New York: Oxford Univ. Press, 1992.

III. Discipleship and the Spiritual Life with Jesus (Contemporary Works)
[B]   Foster, Richard J. *Celebration of Discipline*. Rev. ed. San Francisco: HarperSanFrancisco, 1988.
[I]   Foster, Richard J., and James Bryan Smith, eds. *Devotional Classics*. San Francisco: HarperSanFrancisco, 1994.
[I]   Issler, Klaus, and Ronald Habermas. *How We Learn*. Grand Rapids: Baker, 1994.
[I]   Willard, Dallas. *The Spirit of the Disciplines*. San Francisco: Harper & Row, 1988.
[I]   ____. *In Search of Guidance*. San Francisco: HarperSanFrancisco, 1993.
[I]   Wilkins, Michael J. *Following the Master: Discipleship in the Steps of Jesus*. Grand Rapids: Zondervan, 1992.
[A]   ____. *Discipleship in the Ancient World and Matthew's Gospel*. 2d ed. Grand

SUBJECT INDEX

Author Index

Scripture Index

The Jesus question cannot simple be answered
by leaving the answer ultamiately up to God.
This would be like atheism — either one
believes or one choses not to believe, to
just say you don't know is an answer
in the negitive ^(like sitting on) with the option to believe
at a latter date. The Jesus question
needs to be answered, not for the
believer but for the non-believer, or
those on the fense.

1) Light & Dark

2) Sky & earth

3) Sea & Land/vegitation

4) Planets

5) Sea creatures & birds

6) Land creatures & man

7) Rest

1) explosion creating light & dark

2) Gases vaporize condenss
   to become planet

3) Seas & Land separat/veg.

4) Veg. gives off con which
   creates oxygen which turns
   opaque atmosphere to
   translucent (plants &
   sun can be seen)

5) Sea creatures form
   the bird

6) Land creature form
   & man form..

1 No other God